Domain-Specific Languages (DSLs): Custom Languages Tailored for Specific Application Domains to Enhance Productivity

By Theophilus Edet

Theophilus Edet

 theo.edet@comprequestseries.com

 facebook.com/theoedet

 twitter.com/TheophilusEdet

 Instagram.com/edettheophilus

Table of Contents

Preface

Software development is a vast and evolving discipline, with programmers constantly seeking ways to optimize efficiency, improve maintainability, and enhance productivity. Among the most effective strategies for achieving these goals is the use of domain-specific languages (DSLs), which are custom-built languages tailored for specific problem domains. Unlike general-purpose programming languages designed to be broadly applicable, DSLs offer precise abstractions that streamline workflows, enforce domain constraints, and reduce the complexity of software systems. This book, *Domain-Specific Languages (DSLs): Custom Languages Tailored for Specific Application Domains to Enhance Productivity*, explores the principles, design patterns, and real-world applications of DSLs, providing a structured approach to understanding how they revolutionize software engineering across multiple industries.

Why This Book?

The increasing complexity of modern software systems demands tools that simplify development and reduce cognitive overhead. DSLs provide a way to express domain logic with clarity and precision, enabling experts in fields such as finance, healthcare, artificial intelligence, and embedded systems to interact with software using concepts familiar to them. However, the effective design, implementation, and optimization of DSLs require specialized knowledge that is often scattered across various academic papers and industry documentation. This book consolidates these concepts into a coherent guide, making it accessible to software architects, developers, and researchers alike.

The book is structured to guide readers from fundamental concepts to advanced techniques. It begins with an introduction to the theoretical underpinnings of DSLs, covering essential concepts such as internal vs. external DSLs, declarative vs. imperative DSLs, and text-based vs. graphical DSLs. As the chapters progress, readers will delve into the practical aspects of DSL design, including parsing, code generation, and embedding DSLs into existing programming ecosystems. The later sections explore specialized topics such as algorithmic and data structure support for DSLs, the role of DSLs in various programming languages, and real-world case studies demonstrating their effectiveness in domains such as financial modeling, web development, and machine learning.

Who Should Read This Book?

This book is intended for a wide range of readers, from software engineers looking to implement custom languages in their projects to researchers exploring the theoretical aspects of DSL design. It serves as a valuable resource for programmers interested in leveraging DSLs to improve productivity and enforce domain constraints within their applications. Business professionals and domain experts with minimal programming experience can also benefit from the book's insights into how DSLs can be used to automate workflows, reduce errors, and streamline complex processes. Educators and students in software engineering, programming languages, and computer science will find the structured approach useful for understanding DSLs as a field of study.

A Practical and Research-Oriented Approach

While this book provides a theoretical foundation, it is not limited to academic discussions. Each chapter includes real-world examples and case studies that demonstrate how DSLs are used in industry to solve domain-specific problems efficiently. The book also incorporates practical implementation techniques, including best practices for designing DSLs, leveraging metaprogramming, and optimizing performance. Research directions are discussed in detail, offering insights into the future of DSL development, emerging trends, and ongoing challenges in DSL evolution.

The Journey Ahead

By the end of this book, readers will have a deep understanding of how DSLs can be designed, implemented, and applied to real-world problems. Whether you are a seasoned developer or a newcomer to the field, this book will equip you with the knowledge and tools to harness the power of domain-specific languages effectively.

Theophilus Edet

Domain-Specific Languages (DSLs): Custom Languages Tailored for Specific Application Domains to Enhance Productivity

In the ever-evolving landscape of software development, efficiency and precision are paramount. As applications become more complex and specialized, the need for tools that streamline workflows and enforce domain-specific constraints has grown significantly. This is where domain-specific languages (DSLs) come into play. Unlike general-purpose languages, which are designed for broad applicability, DSLs are tailored to specific domains, allowing for greater expressiveness, improved maintainability, and increased productivity. *Domain-Specific Languages (DSLs): Custom Languages Tailored for Specific Application Domains to Enhance Productivity* is a comprehensive guide that explores the principles, design patterns, and real-world applications of DSLs.

This book is structured into six parts, each focusing on a crucial aspect of DSL development, from foundational concepts to practical implementations and advanced research directions. Through a combination of theoretical insights, practical case studies, and programming examples, this book serves as a valuable resource for software engineers, researchers, and domain experts looking to leverage DSLs in their fields.

Understanding the Foundations of DSLs

The first part of this book lays the groundwork for understanding DSLs, beginning with a thorough examination of their core principles and classifications. It introduces the key distinctions between internal and external DSLs, declarative and imperative DSLs, as well as text-based and graphical DSLs. Readers will gain insight into how DSLs differ from general-purpose languages and why they are particularly effective in solving domain-specific problems. Additionally, the first part delves into the history of DSL development, tracing their evolution from early implementations to modern-day applications.

Examples and Applications of DSLs

The second part of the book explores the real-world applications of DSLs across various industries. It covers how DSLs are utilized in software engineering, including web development and database query languages, providing concrete case studies to illustrate best practices. The book then transitions into scientific computing, demonstrating how DSLs aid in mathematical modeling, simulations, and high-performance computing. Other domains covered in this section include game development, finance and business, networking and security, and artificial intelligence. Each module within this part highlights specific DSLs used in these fields, showing how they optimize workflows and enhance productivity.

Programming Language Support for DSLs

The third part examines the programming languages that offer robust support for DSL development. It begins with an introduction to selecting the right language for building DSLs, discussing the benefits and trade-offs of various options. Subsequent chapters explore how DSLs are implemented in 8 significant programming languages of Ada, C#, C++, Java, Python, Ruby, Scala, and XSLT. Each module provides an in-depth analysis of language-specific features, demonstrating how they can be leveraged to design and embed DSLs effectively. Readers will also find practical examples of DSL implementations within these 8 languages, helping them understand the nuances of DSL development in different programming environments.

Algorithm and Data Structure Support for DSLs

Designing and optimizing DSLs require a deep understanding of algorithms and data structures. The fourth part of this book delves into the computational foundations necessary for building efficient DSLs. It starts with parsing algorithms, covering lexical analysis, tokenization techniques, and syntax trees. The discussion then moves to code generation algorithms, highlighting techniques for generating executable code from DSLs. Template metaprogramming, abstract syntax trees (ASTs), and grammar trees are also explored, providing insights into how DSLs process and transform data. The final module in this part focuses on advanced data structures, demonstrating how DSLs handle large-scale data efficiently while maintaining performance.

Design Patterns and Real-World Case Studies

The fifth part of the book focuses on best practices in DSL design and real-world case studies. It begins by introducing key design patterns used in DSL development, including the Interpreter, Factory, and Visitor patterns. These patterns enhance DSL usability and maintainability, ensuring that they remain scalable and adaptable over time. The following modules provide case studies of DSL applications in various industries, including financial modeling, web development, network configuration, game development, and machine learning. These case studies offer valuable lessons on DSL implementation, highlighting both the benefits and challenges encountered in real-world scenarios.

Research Directions in DSLs

The final part of the book looks ahead to the future of DSLs, exploring emerging trends, challenges, and research opportunities. The discussion begins with an overview of new directions in DSL design, such as the rise of visual programming languages, AI-driven DSLs, and cloud-based DSL solutions. The book then examines the evolution of DSL tools and frameworks, addressing improvements in development environments and open-source contributions. A crucial module in this section covers the long-term maintenance of DSLs, tackling issues such as versioning, backward compatibility, and sustainability. The book concludes by analyzing the role of DSLs in future software development, their impact on agile methodologies, and their increasing adoption across industries.

A Holistic Approach to DSL Development

By organizing this book into these six structured parts, readers will develop a holistic understanding of DSLs—from their fundamental concepts to their implementation, optimization, and future prospects. Whether you are a software engineer aiming to design custom languages, a researcher exploring the theoretical aspects of DSLs, or a domain expert seeking to automate workflows, this book provides the insights and tools necessary to harness the power of domain-specific languages effectively.

Part 1:

Fundamentals of Domain Specific Languages

Domain-Specific Languages (DSLs) are specialized programming languages tailored for specific problem domains, enabling increased productivity, readability, and maintainability compared to general-purpose languages. This part explores DSL fundamentals, covering their types, design principles, implementation, and challenges. Understanding these concepts provides a strong foundation for developers to create and integrate DSLs effectively in real-world applications, ensuring they meet domain-specific needs while maintaining software robustness and flexibility.

Introduction to Domain-Specific Languages

Domain-Specific Languages (DSLs) are designed for specific areas of application, differentiating them from general-purpose languages like Python or Java. They optimize expressiveness and efficiency by focusing on particular domains such as network configuration, data analysis, or game development. Key characteristics of DSLs include restricted syntax tailored to their domain, higher abstraction, and improved productivity. The benefits of DSLs in software development include improved maintainability, domain expert involvement, and automation of complex processes. Unlike general-purpose languages, which provide broad capabilities across multiple domains, DSLs are narrowly focused, making them more intuitive for specific tasks while reducing unnecessary complexity.

Types of Domain-Specific Languages

DSLs come in multiple forms, each with distinct characteristics and use cases. Internal DSLs operate within the syntax and runtime of an existing general-purpose language, enhancing expressiveness without requiring separate tooling. External DSLs, on the other hand, have their own syntax and require dedicated parsers and interpreters. Another distinction exists between declarative DSLs, which specify what should be achieved (e.g., SQL), and imperative DSLs, which detail how to achieve it (e.g., Makefiles). DSLs can also be text-based, focusing on structured scripts, or graphical, using visual interfaces to simplify complex workflows. These categorizations highlight the versatility of DSLs in software development.

DSL Design Principles

Effective DSL design prioritizes domain knowledge, ensuring that the language aligns with the specific needs of its target users. Simplicity and expressiveness are crucial, allowing domain experts to interact with the DSL without extensive programming expertise. Syntax and semantics should be carefully designed to be intuitive, ensuring ease of learning while maximizing functionality. A well-designed DSL strikes a balance between flexibility and specificity—too much flexibility risks losing domain alignment, while excessive constraints limit its adaptability. These principles ensure that DSLs remain accessible, powerful, and maintainable, facilitating better software design within specialized domains.

Development and Implementation of DSLs

Building a DSL involves defining its syntax, semantics, and execution model. Various tools assist in DSL development, including parser generators like ANTLR, meta-programming frameworks, and domain-specific libraries. Integration into existing systems is a critical consideration, ensuring compatibility with existing software ecosystems. Successful DSL implementations provide improved automation, enhanced developer productivity, and reduced error rates. Real-world case studies demonstrate how DSLs streamline processes in areas such as financial modeling, network configuration, and machine learning pipelines, highlighting the practical impact of well-designed domain-specific languages in real-world applications.

DSL Compiler Design and Parsing

DSLs require efficient parsing and compilation mechanisms to transform high-level domain-specific commands into executable instructions. The distinction between interpreters and compilers is crucial, as DSLs may be compiled for efficiency or interpreted for flexibility. Lexical analysis and syntax analysis are foundational to DSL processing, ensuring valid program structures. Parsing techniques such as recursive descent and LL/LR parsing help process DSL code efficiently. The final stage, code generation, translates DSL expressions into lower-level code, enabling execution. These techniques form the backbone of DSL implementation, ensuring that domain-specific scripts can be executed reliably and efficiently.

Challenges and Limitations of DSLs

Despite their advantages, DSLs face challenges such as scalability and maintainability. A narrowly focused DSL may struggle to evolve alongside changing industry requirements. Additionally, tool support and ecosystem limitations can hinder adoption, as developers may require specialized tools to develop and maintain DSLs. Ensuring backward compatibility while accommodating domain evolution is a key challenge. Common pitfalls in DSL design include overly complex syntax, insufficient documentation, and inadequate user training. Addressing these challenges requires careful planning, iterative refinement, and strong community support to ensure the long-term success of a DSL.

This part establishes a strong foundation in DSLs, covering their fundamentals, design principles, and implementation strategies. Readers gain insights into DSL development, enabling them to design efficient, maintainable domain-specific languages that enhance productivity and streamline specialized tasks.

Module 1:
Introduction to Domain-Specific Languages

Domain-Specific Languages (DSLs) are specialized languages designed to solve problems within a particular domain, improving efficiency and expressiveness. Unlike general-purpose languages (GPLs), DSLs offer domain-specific abstractions that enhance productivity, maintainability, and collaboration. This module introduces DSLs, differentiates them from GPLs, explores their key characteristics, and highlights their benefits in software development. Understanding these aspects will provide a solid foundation for designing and implementing DSLs effectively.

Definition and Purpose of DSLs

A **Domain-Specific Language (DSL)** is a programming or specification language created for a particular application domain. Unlike general-purpose languages, which aim to be versatile, DSLs are narrowly focused, offering constructs and syntax tailored to a specific problem space. Examples include **SQL for database querying**, **HTML for web markup**, and **Makefile for build automation**. The primary purpose of DSLs is to **increase productivity, reduce complexity, and improve communication between domain experts and developers**. By providing a higher-level abstraction suited to a particular domain, DSLs minimize boilerplate code, reduce errors, and streamline problem-solving in specialized fields.

Differences Between General-Purpose and Domain-Specific Languages

General-purpose languages (GPLs) such as Python, Java, and C++ are designed to handle a wide range of computational problems. They include control structures, data manipulation features, and extensive standard libraries, making them highly flexible. However, this flexibility often results in verbose code when solving domain-specific problems. In contrast, DSLs provide **concise, expressive, and domain-optimized syntax**. For example, SQL enables complex database operations with minimal syntax compared to imperative implementations in a GPL. Another key difference is that **DSLs are often declarative**, specifying *what* should be done rather than *how* to do it, whereas GPLs are typically imperative, requiring step-by-step instructions.

Key Characteristics of DSLs

DSLs exhibit several defining characteristics that differentiate them from general-purpose languages. **Specialization** is a core feature—DSLs focus on solving specific domain problems efficiently. **Abstraction and simplicity** make them easier for domain experts to use, as they eliminate unnecessary complexities inherent in general-purpose programming. Another essential characteristic is **domain expressiveness**, where DSLs use terminology and structures familiar to the field they target. DSLs can be **external (standalone languages)**, such as Regex or SQL, or **internal (embedded within a host language)**, like LINQ in C# or Rake in Ruby. Their **limited scope and optimization** ensure better performance and maintainability within their intended use cases.

Benefits of Using DSLs in Software Development

DSLs offer multiple advantages in software development. They **improve developer productivity** by reducing the need for boilerplate code and enabling domain-specific optimizations. **Code readability and maintainability** are enhanced because DSLs use domain-relevant terminology, making them accessible to both developers and non-programmers. DSLs **reduce the likelihood of errors** by enforcing constraints specific to the domain. Furthermore, they **enable better collaboration** between technical and non-technical stakeholders, as DSLs act as a bridge between business logic and software implementation. Additionally, **DSLs enhance performance** since they can be optimized for specific tasks, unlike general-purpose languages that must accommodate a broad range of use cases.

This module has introduced the concept of **Domain-Specific Languages**, distinguishing them from general-purpose languages, outlining their characteristics, and discussing their benefits. DSLs empower developers by **simplifying complex problems**, **enhancing productivity**, and **bridging the gap between domain experts and programmers**. With this foundation, the next modules will explore how to design, implement, and leverage DSLs effectively in Python.

Definition and Purpose of DSLs

A **Domain-Specific Language (DSL)** is a specialized programming or specification language designed to solve problems within a particular domain. Unlike **General-Purpose Languages (GPLs)** such as Python, Java, or C++, which are versatile and applicable to multiple domains, DSLs focus on providing concise, expressive, and optimized syntax for a specific area of application. They enhance productivity by eliminating unnecessary complexity and offering **domain-specific abstractions** that make problem-solving more efficient.

Types of DSLs

DSLs can be classified into two broad categories:

- **External DSLs** – These are standalone languages with their own syntax and processing tools. Examples include **SQL (database querying)**, **Regular Expressions (text pattern matching)**, and **GraphQL (API querying)**.

- **Internal DSLs (Embedded DSLs)** – These are built within an existing general-purpose language, leveraging its syntax and constructs. Examples include **Flask routing in Python**, **LINQ in C#**, and **RSpec in Ruby**.

Why Use DSLs?

The primary **purpose** of a DSL is to **streamline development in a specialized field** by introducing domain-specific concepts that abstract away irrelevant details. Instead of writing verbose and repetitive code in a GPL, developers can express solutions **concisely** using DSL constructs. DSLs also facilitate collaboration between **technical and non-technical stakeholders**, as they use terminology that domain experts understand.

Example: DSL for Arithmetic Expressions in Python

To illustrate the need for DSLs, consider an arithmetic expression evaluator. Using a general-purpose approach in Python, we might write:

```
def evaluate(expression):
    return eval(expression)

print(evaluate("3 + 5 * 2"))
```

This approach works, but it is unsafe because eval() executes arbitrary code. Instead, we can define a small **DSL for arithmetic expressions**, ensuring only valid operations are allowed:

```
import ast
import operator

class ArithmeticDSL(ast.NodeVisitor):
    operators = {
        ast.Add: operator.add,
        ast.Sub: operator.sub,
        ast.Mult: operator.mul,
        ast.Div: operator.truediv
    }

    def visit_BinOp(self, node):
        left = self.visit(node.left)
        right = self.visit(node.right)
        return self.operators[type(node.op)](left, right)

    def visit_Num(self, node):
        return node.n

def evaluate_expression(expression):
    tree = ast.parse(expression, mode='eval')
    return ArithmeticDSL().visit(tree.body)

print(evaluate_expression("3 + 5 * 2"))
```

This **DSL approach** provides a **safe, controlled environment** to evaluate arithmetic expressions without exposing security risks like eval().

DSLs serve a **critical role** in modern software development by offering **expressiveness, abstraction, and security** tailored to specific domains. Whether used for database queries, configuration management, or mathematical computation, DSLs enable **more efficient**

problem-solving than general-purpose programming alone. In the next sections, we'll explore how DSLs differ from GPLs and their core characteristics.

Differences between General-Purpose and Domain-Specific Languages

General-Purpose Languages (GPLs) and Domain-Specific Languages (DSLs) serve different roles in software development. **GPLs** are designed for flexibility, allowing developers to build a wide range of applications. Examples include **Python, Java, C++, and JavaScript**. **DSLs**, on the other hand, are optimized for solving specific types of problems efficiently. Examples include **SQL (database queries), HTML (web structure), and Regex (pattern matching)**. Understanding their differences helps developers choose the right tool for the job and design effective DSLs.

Key Differences

Feature	General-Purpose Languages (GPLs)	Domain-Specific Languages (DSLs)
Scope	Broad, can be used for various applications	Narrow, designed for a specific domain
Syntax & Semantics	Complex, many constructs	Simple, optimized for domain tasks
Learning Curve	Steeper, requires understanding of programming concepts	Easier for domain experts
Performance	Generalized, may include unnecessary overhead	Optimized for specific tasks
Examples	Python, Java, C++, JavaScript	SQL, Regex, HTML, GraphQL

Declarative vs. Imperative Nature

Another significant distinction is that **many DSLs are declarative**, meaning they describe *what* should be done rather than *how* to do it. For example, **SQL** lets users specify the data they want without detailing how to retrieve it:

```
SELECT name, age FROM users WHERE age > 25;
```

In contrast, a GPL like Python requires explicit instructions to achieve the same result:

```
users = [{"name": "Alice", "age": 30}, {"name": "Bob", "age": 22}]
filtered_users = [user for user in users if user["age"] > 25]
```

DSLs abstract away procedural logic, making them **simpler** for domain experts to use.

Example: DSL for Mathematical Expressions in Python

18

To demonstrate the difference, let's compare a DSL approach with a traditional GPL approach for evaluating expressions.

GPL Approach (Verbose and Flexible)

```
def evaluate(expression):
    return eval(expression)

print(evaluate("3 + 5 * 2"))
```

This works but **poses security risks** if untrusted input is used.

DSL Approach (Safer and More Domain-Specific)

A **mathematical DSL** can be created using **Python's ast module** to safely parse expressions:

```
import ast
import operator

class MathDSL(ast.NodeVisitor):
    ops = {ast.Add: operator.add, ast.Sub: operator.sub, ast.Mult: operator.mul}

    def visit_BinOp(self, node):
        return self.ops[type(node.op)](self.visit(node.left),
            self.visit(node.right))

    def visit_Num(self, node):
        return node.n

def evaluate_dsl(expression):
    tree = ast.parse(expression, mode='eval')
    return MathDSL().visit(tree.body)

print(evaluate_dsl("3 + 5 * 2"))  # Output: 13
```

This **DSL approach** ensures that only valid mathematical operations are executed, making it safer and more controlled.

General-purpose languages offer **flexibility** but can be **verbose** and **prone to security risks** when used for domain-specific problems. DSLs, by contrast, provide **simplicity, safety, and efficiency**, making them valuable tools in modern software development. The next section will explore the key characteristics that define a well-designed DSL.

Key Characteristics of DSLs

Domain-Specific Languages (DSLs) are designed to solve problems within a specific domain by providing concise, expressive, and optimized syntax. Unlike General-Purpose Languages (GPLs), which support a broad range of applications, DSLs introduce **abstractions** that make domain-specific tasks **easier, safer, and more efficient**. A well-designed DSL exhibits several key characteristics that distinguish it from a general-purpose programming language.

1. Specialization and Narrow Focus

A **DSL is built for a specific domain**, offering features that simplify tasks within that domain. For instance, **SQL** specializes in database queries, allowing developers to retrieve and manipulate data without worrying about **low-level implementation details**. Similarly, **HTML** is specialized for structuring web pages, making it simple for developers to define content and layout.

Example: DSL for Configuration Files

Instead of using **Python code** to store configuration settings:

```
config = {
    "host": "localhost",
    "port": 5432,
    "debug": True
}
```

A **configuration DSL** like **YAML** simplifies this:

```
host: localhost
port: 5432
debug: true
```

This **domain-specific syntax** makes it easier for non-programmers to edit configuration files.

2. High-Level Abstraction

DSLs **hide unnecessary complexity** by providing high-level constructs suited to the domain. This abstraction **reduces boilerplate code** and improves **developer productivity**.

For example, consider **Regex**, a DSL for pattern matching. Instead of writing multiple loops and conditions in a GPL, a **single concise expression** suffices:

```
import re
match = re.search(r"\d{3}-\d{2}-\d{4}", "My SSN is 123-45-6789")
print(match.group())  # Output: 123-45-6789
```

Here, **Regex abstracts** the logic of searching for a pattern, making it **far more efficient** than writing equivalent logic in Python manually.

3. Expressiveness and Readability

DSLs use **natural and intuitive syntax** that aligns with domain terminology, making them **easier to read and understand**. For instance, the **Flask DSL for defining web routes** in Python allows a **clean, expressive syntax**:

```
from flask import Flask

app = Flask(__name__)
```

```
@app.route('/hello')
def hello():
    return "Hello, World!"
```

The @app.route('/hello') syntax makes it **clear and readable**, encapsulating the complexity of handling HTTP routes within Flask's **embedded DSL**.

4. Declarative vs. Imperative Approach

Many DSLs follow a **declarative paradigm**, specifying *what* should be done rather than *how* to do it. **SQL**, **HTML**, and **Makefile** are examples of **declarative DSLs**, where users define **outcomes** rather than writing step-by-step execution logic.

For example, in **Makefile**, a DSL for automating builds, you declare dependencies rather than writing manual execution steps:

```
build: main.c utils.c
    gcc -o myprogram main.c utils.c
```

The system **determines how to execute it**, reducing manual work and complexity.

5. Extensibility and Integration

Many DSLs are **designed to integrate with GPLs** rather than operate in isolation. Internal DSLs, like **LINQ in C#**, extend a general-purpose language's functionality while remaining embedded in its ecosystem.

Example: Internal DSL for SQL in Python

Instead of manually constructing SQL queries as strings:

```
query = "SELECT * FROM users WHERE age > 25"
```

An **internal DSL like SQLAlchemy** provides a **Pythonic** way to express the same logic:

```
from sqlalchemy import select, users

query = select(users).where(users.c.age > 25)
```

This approach makes queries **safer** by preventing SQL injection and **more maintainable** by using structured syntax.

A well-designed **DSL is specialized, expressive, and abstract**, providing **high-level syntax** for solving domain-specific problems **efficiently**. Whether declarative or imperative, standalone or embedded, DSLs **streamline development** and **reduce complexity** in their target domains. The next section will explore the benefits of using DSLs in software development.

Benefits of Using DSLs in Software Development

Domain-Specific Languages (DSLs) provide numerous advantages in software development by enabling concise, expressive, and optimized solutions for specific domains. Unlike General-Purpose Languages (GPLs), which are designed for a broad range of applications, DSLs offer **targeted abstractions**, improving **productivity, maintainability, and collaboration**. The benefits of DSLs can be categorized into key areas, including increased efficiency, reduced complexity, improved domain alignment, enhanced security, and better collaboration between developers and domain experts.

1. Increased Productivity and Efficiency

One of the biggest advantages of DSLs is their ability to **streamline development** by reducing the amount of code required to perform complex tasks. Instead of writing verbose and repetitive code in a GPL, developers can use a **domain-optimized syntax** to express solutions **more concisely**.

Example: SQL vs. Python for Data Retrieval

A **SQL DSL** allows for simple and readable data queries:

```
SELECT name, age FROM users WHERE age > 25;
```

The same query in **Python (without a DSL)** would require significantly more code:

```
users = [{"name": "Alice", "age": 30}, {"name": "Bob", "age": 22}]
filtered_users = [user for user in users if user["age"] > 25]
```

The SQL DSL **abstracts away complexity**, making queries **easier to write, read, and optimize**.

2. Reduced Complexity and Improved Readability

DSLs eliminate unnecessary **boilerplate code**, making programs more **readable and maintainable**. Instead of dealing with **low-level implementation details**, developers can focus on solving domain-specific problems.

Example: Flask DSL for Web Routing

A Flask **DSL for web development** provides an expressive way to define routes:

```
@app.route('/dashboard')
def dashboard():
    return "Welcome to your dashboard!"
```

This syntax is **cleaner** and **more intuitive** compared to manually handling HTTP requests in a lower-level framework.

3. Better Alignment with Domain Experts

DSLs enable **non-programmers** (such as data analysts, financial experts, or system administrators) to interact with software **without deep programming knowledge**. This is particularly beneficial in industries like **finance, healthcare, and engineering**, where domain experts need to work with computational tools.

Example: DSL for Infrastructure as Code (Terraform)

A **DevOps engineer** can define infrastructure in a **readable DSL** like Terraform instead of writing complex scripts:

```
resource "aws_instance" "web" {
  ami           = "ami-123456"
  instance_type = "t2.micro"
}
```

This makes infrastructure management **accessible to IT teams** without requiring deep programming knowledge.

4. Enhanced Security and Error Reduction

DSLs can **reduce security risks** by **restricting operations** to **valid domain-specific actions**. For example, an arithmetic DSL can prevent execution of malicious code that might occur with functions like Python's eval().

Example: Safe Arithmetic DSL in Python

Instead of using eval(), which is unsafe:

```
eval("3 + 5 * 2")  # Dangerous if used with untrusted input
```

A **custom arithmetic DSL** safely evaluates expressions:

```
import ast, operator

class SafeEval(ast.NodeVisitor):
    operators = {ast.Add: operator.add, ast.Sub: operator.sub, ast.Mult:
        operator.mul}

    def visit_BinOp(self, node):
        return self.operators[type(node.op)](self.visit(node.left),
            self.visit(node.right))

    def visit_Num(self, node):
        return node.n

def evaluate(expression):
    tree = ast.parse(expression, mode='eval')
    return SafeEval().visit(tree.body)

print(evaluate("3 + 5 * 2"))  # Output: 13
```

This **limits operations to arithmetic calculations**, preventing execution of arbitrary code.

5. Easier Maintenance and Evolution

DSLs are **designed to be extensible**, allowing developers to **add new domain-specific features** without affecting existing codebases. Since DSLs are **closer to the problem domain**, changes in business rules or requirements are **easier to implement** than modifying complex GPL code.

Example: DSL for Business Rules

A **financial rules DSL** allows policy updates **without modifying core code**:

```
IF transaction_amount > 10000 THEN flag_as_suspicious
```

Instead of updating Python code manually, business analysts can **modify rules directly** in a DSL format.

DSLs provide **efficiency, simplicity, security, and better collaboration**, making them **valuable assets in software development**. They **reduce complexity, increase productivity**, and **improve domain-specific problem-solving**. In the next module, we will explore **different types of DSLs**, including **internal vs. external DSLs, declarative vs. imperative DSLs, and text-based vs. graphical DSLs**.

Module 2:
Types of Domain-Specific Languages

Domain-Specific Languages (DSLs) come in different forms, each suited to specific use cases and integration needs. Understanding the different types of DSLs is crucial for choosing the right approach when designing custom languages. This module explores the fundamental classifications of DSLs, including **internal vs. external DSLs, declarative vs. imperative DSLs, and text-based vs. graphical DSLs**. Additionally, it examines **real-world DSL implementations** to highlight how they enhance productivity and simplify domain-specific problem-solving. By the end of this module, readers will have a clear understanding of the diverse nature of DSLs and their practical applications.

Internal DSLs vs. External DSLs

DSLs can be categorized as **internal (embedded) DSLs** or **external DSLs**, depending on their relationship with general-purpose programming languages. **Internal DSLs** exist within a host language and leverage its syntax, making them easier to implement and maintain. These DSLs benefit from the **tooling and ecosystem** of the host language while offering a domain-specific syntax. **Fluent APIs, annotation-based DSLs, and embedded scripting frameworks** are common forms of internal DSLs.

External DSLs, on the other hand, are entirely separate languages with their own syntax and parsing mechanisms. These DSLs require custom **lexers, parsers, and interpreters** to process their instructions. While they demand more effort in development, they provide **greater flexibility** and **domain-specific optimizations**. External DSLs are often used when a clean separation from a host language is necessary, such as in **SQL for databases** or **GraphQL for APIs**. Understanding the trade-offs between internal and external DSLs helps developers determine the best approach for their domain needs.

Declarative vs. Imperative DSLs

Another way to classify DSLs is based on their execution model: **declarative** or **imperative**. **Declarative DSLs** focus on describing *what* should be achieved rather than *how* to achieve it. These languages abstract away implementation details and rely on an underlying system to determine execution. Common examples include **SQL, HTML**, and **Makefile**, where users specify outcomes rather than writing step-by-step instructions.

In contrast, **imperative DSLs** specify detailed instructions for how tasks should be performed. These languages offer fine-grained control over execution, making them more **flexible but potentially verbose**. Scripting DSLs, configuration management DSLs, and embedded automation DSLs often fall into this category. The choice between **declarative and imperative**

25

DSLs depends on the balance between **simplicity, expressiveness, and control** required in a given domain.

Text-Based vs. Graphical DSLs

DSLs can also be categorized as **text-based** or **graphical**, depending on how they are represented and interacted with. **Text-based DSLs** are the most common and are defined using structured text files, scripts, or configuration formats. These DSLs are **easier to version control, automate, and integrate into traditional software development workflows**. Examples include **JSON, YAML, and domain-specific scripting languages**.

Graphical DSLs (GDSLs), on the other hand, provide a **visual interface** for defining domain logic. They use **diagrams, flowcharts, or drag-and-drop components** instead of textual syntax. These DSLs are often used in **model-driven development, workflow automation, and simulation software**, making complex logic more accessible to **non-programmers**. Tools like **UML modeling languages, Simulink, and LabVIEW** are prominent examples of graphical DSLs. While graphical DSLs enhance **usability and visualization**, they may introduce **challenges in version control, scalability, and automation**.

Examples of Successful DSL Implementations

Several widely adopted DSLs demonstrate the power and effectiveness of domain-specific languages across industries. **SQL (Structured Query Language)** is one of the most prominent DSLs, providing a powerful way to query and manipulate relational databases. **Regex (Regular Expressions)** serves as a highly specialized DSL for pattern matching, widely used in data validation, search, and text processing. **Terraform** is a DSL for defining and managing cloud infrastructure, allowing engineers to declare infrastructure as code. **GraphQL** simplifies API queries by allowing clients to specify exactly what data they need, reducing over-fetching and under-fetching issues.

Other successful implementations include **Makefile**, which automates build processes, and **ANTLR**, which allows the creation of custom DSLs for parsing and interpreting structured input. These examples highlight the **efficiency, productivity, and domain-specific optimizations** made possible through DSLs. By studying these implementations, developers can gain insights into best practices for designing and deploying DSLs tailored to their needs.

DSLs come in various forms, each offering unique advantages and trade-offs. Whether internal or external, declarative or imperative, text-based or graphical, DSLs provide **domain-optimized solutions** that enhance software development productivity. This module lays the foundation for understanding different DSL types, preparing readers to explore their practical applications. The following sections will provide **detailed code implementations** and **practical use cases**, demonstrating how each type of DSL can be constructed and utilized effectively.

Internal DSLs vs. External DSLs

Domain-Specific Languages (DSLs) are classified as **internal (embedded) DSLs** or **external DSLs**, based on their relationship with general-purpose programming languages (GPLs). Internal DSLs exist within the syntax and semantics of a host language, while external DSLs function as standalone languages with their own parsers and execution engines. Each type offers unique advantages and trade-offs, influencing its adoption based on ease of implementation, maintainability, and expressiveness. This section explores the characteristics of **internal and external DSLs**, their differences, and their real-world applications, followed by practical implementations using **Python as the host language** for internal DSLs and a simple parser for an external DSL.

Internal DSLs: Embedded within a Host Language

Internal DSLs, also called **embedded DSLs**, leverage the syntax and features of an existing GPL to create **domain-specific abstractions**. These DSLs do not require a custom parser, as they are written using the constructs of the host language. Internal DSLs are often built using **fluent APIs, operator overloading, decorators, and metaprogramming techniques**, making them **easy to integrate and maintain**.

One key advantage of internal DSLs is that they **inherit the tooling, libraries, and performance optimizations** of the host language. This makes them an attractive choice for developers who need a **domain-specific abstraction** without building a full-fledged custom language. Examples include **Flask for web development, PySpark for distributed computing**, and **TensorFlow's computational graphs**.

Python Implementation of an Internal DSL (Task Scheduling)

The following example demonstrates an **internal DSL** in Python for task scheduling using **fluent API design**:

```python
class Task:
    def __init__(self, name):
        self.name = name
        self.steps = []

    def do(self, action):
        self.steps.append(action)
        return self

    def execute(self):
        print(f"Executing {self.name}...")
        for step in self.steps:
            print(f" -> {step}")

# Using the internal DSL
task = Task("Backup Data").do("Compress files").do("Upload to cloud").do("Send
        email notification")
task.execute()
```

This DSL allows users to **chain commands fluently**, improving readability and domain specificity.

External DSLs: Standalone Languages with Custom Syntax

External DSLs are separate from any existing GPL, meaning they require **a custom lexer, parser, and execution mechanism**. These DSLs offer **greater flexibility**, allowing developers to design **highly expressive syntax** tailored for a specific problem domain. Unlike internal DSLs, external DSLs do not inherit the syntax constraints of a host language, making them **more readable for non-programmers**.

However, external DSLs require additional **parsing infrastructure**, often built using tools like **ANTLR, Lark, or PLY (Python Lex-Yacc)**. Examples of external DSLs include **SQL (database queries)**, **GraphQL (API queries)**, and **Terraform (Infrastructure-as-Code)**.

Python Implementation of an External DSL (Simple Arithmetic Parser)

Below is a basic example of an **external DSL** that parses and evaluates arithmetic expressions using **Lark**, a parsing library in Python:

```python
from lark import Lark, Transformer

# Defining an external DSL for arithmetic expressions
grammar = """
    start: expr
    expr: expr "+" term    -> add
        | expr "-" term    -> sub
        | term
    term: /\d+/
    %import common.WS
    %ignore WS
"""

class EvalTransformer(Transformer):
    def add(self, values):
        return int(values[0]) + int(values[1])

    def sub(self, values):
        return int(values[0]) - int(values[1])

    def term(self, value):
        return int(value[0])

# Parse and evaluate expressions
parser = Lark(grammar, parser='lalr', transformer=EvalTransformer())
result = parser.parse("10 + 5 - 3")
print(result)  # Output: 12
```

This **external DSL** defines a **custom arithmetic syntax**, which is parsed and evaluated by a dedicated execution engine. Unlike an internal DSL, this approach allows full control over syntax design but **requires additional parsing infrastructure**.

Choosing Between Internal and External DSLs

The choice between an **internal or external DSL** depends on the domain requirements:

- **Internal DSLs** are ideal when leveraging an existing host language, benefiting from **existing libraries, syntax, and tooling**. They are **easier to implement** and maintain but may be constrained by the syntax of the host language.

- **External DSLs** provide **more expressive power and readability**, allowing **custom syntax tailored for a specific audience**. However, they require **lexers, parsers, and interpreters**, increasing development complexity.

Internal and external DSLs provide different approaches to solving domain-specific problems. **Internal DSLs** integrate seamlessly into a host language, leveraging its ecosystem, while **external DSLs** offer a clean separation with greater flexibility at the cost of added complexity. Understanding these trade-offs is crucial for choosing the right DSL approach.

Declarative vs. Imperative DSLs

Domain-Specific Languages (DSLs) can be categorized based on their programming paradigm: **declarative** or **imperative**. This classification determines how a DSL expresses logic and how users interact with it. **Declarative DSLs** focus on defining *what* needs to be done without specifying *how* to achieve it. In contrast, **imperative DSLs** describe step-by-step instructions to perform a task. Each paradigm has its strengths, and the choice depends on the **problem domain, expressiveness, and control requirements**. This section explores the differences between declarative and imperative DSLs and provides **Python implementations** for both paradigms.

Declarative DSLs: Focusing on "What" Rather Than "How"

Declarative DSLs express logic **at a high level**, allowing the underlying system to determine execution details. These DSLs **abstract implementation complexity**, making them **easier to read, write, and maintain**. Examples of declarative DSLs include **SQL (database queries), HTML (markup), Regex (pattern matching), and Terraform (infrastructure-as-code)**.

The primary advantage of declarative DSLs is that they allow users to focus on the **desired outcome**, rather than low-level execution details. They are well-suited for **configuration, query languages, and rule-based systems**. However, declarative DSLs **lack flexibility** when precise control over execution is required.

Python Implementation of a Declarative DSL (Task Automation)

Below is an example of a **declarative DSL** for automating tasks, where users define **what needs to be done**, and the system determines execution:

```python
class TaskConfig:
    def __init__(self):
        self.tasks = []
```

```python
    def add_task(self, name, action):
        self.tasks.append((name, action))

    def execute(self):
        for name, action in self.tasks:
            print(f"Executing: {name}")
            action()
# Define tasks using a declarative DSL
config = TaskConfig()
config.add_task("Backup Files", lambda: print("Backing up..."))
config.add_task("Send Email", lambda: print("Sending email..."))
config.execute()
```

Here, the **user only specifies tasks**, while the system determines how to execute them. This makes the DSL **concise, structured, and reusable**.

Imperative DSLs: Specifying Step-by-Step Instructions

Imperative DSLs require users to define **explicit instructions** for how a task should be performed. These DSLs offer **greater control** over execution but require more effort to write and maintain. Examples of imperative DSLs include **shell scripting (Bash), procedural query languages (PL/SQL), and scripting automation tools (Ansible Playbooks, Makefiles)**.

The advantage of imperative DSLs is their **fine-grained control**, making them ideal for **low-level automation, scripting, and iterative computations**. However, they can be **verbose and harder to maintain** compared to declarative approaches.

Python Implementation of an Imperative DSL (Task Execution Engine)

Below is an example of an **imperative DSL** where users specify the exact steps for executing tasks:

```python
class TaskExecutor:
    def __init__(self, name):
        self.name = name
        self.steps = []

    def step(self, action):
        self.steps.append(action)
        return self

    def run(self):
        print(f"Running task: {self.name}")
        for step in self.steps:
            print(f"  -> {step}")
            eval(step)

# Using the imperative DSL
task = TaskExecutor("Database Maintenance")
task.step("print('Stopping database...')").step("print('Cleaning
        logs...')").step("print('Restarting database...')")
task.run()
```

This approach gives users **full control over execution** by allowing them to define **each operation explicitly**.

Choosing Between Declarative and Imperative DSLs

The choice between **declarative and imperative DSLs** depends on the use case:

- **Declarative DSLs** are ideal for **configuration, rules, and query-based operations**, where execution details can be abstracted. They offer **simplicity, reusability, and easier maintenance**.

- **Imperative DSLs** provide **step-by-step execution control**, making them suitable for **scripting, automation, and procedural workflows**. However, they tend to be **more verbose and harder to manage** over time.

Declarative and imperative DSLs serve distinct purposes in software development. **Declarative DSLs** allow users to focus on outcomes, improving readability and maintainability, while **imperative DSLs** offer precise control over execution. Understanding these paradigms helps developers design **effective DSLs** tailored to specific application domains.

Text-Based vs. Graphical DSLs

Domain-Specific Languages (DSLs) can be categorized based on their mode of interaction: **text-based DSLs** and **graphical DSLs**. **Text-based DSLs** use textual syntax to define operations, while **graphical DSLs** represent domain concepts through **visual elements such as diagrams, flowcharts, and block-based representations**. The choice between these DSLs depends on the **intended audience, domain complexity, and ease of use**. While text-based DSLs are widely used in **software development and scripting**, graphical DSLs offer an **intuitive, visual approach**, making them ideal for **workflow automation, business process modeling, and visual programming environments**. This section explores both types, with **Python-based implementations** for each.

Text-Based DSLs: Readable and Scriptable

Text-based DSLs are **the most common type of DSLs**, designed with **human-readable syntax** that resembles **natural language or programming constructs**. These DSLs are often **line-based** or **structured using keywords, indentation, and symbols**, allowing developers and domain experts to define **rules, configurations, or logic** efficiently.

The key advantages of text-based DSLs include **easy version control**, **automated processing**, and **integration with existing development tools**. Examples of text-based DSLs include **SQL (query language), Regular Expressions (pattern matching), JSON/YAML (configuration), and Makefiles (build automation)**.

Python Implementation of a Text-Based DSL (Simple Workflow Definition)

Below is an example of a **text-based DSL** for defining workflows in a structured format:

```python
class WorkflowDSL:
    def __init__(self):
        self.steps = []

    def step(self, name):
        self.steps.append(name)
        return self

    def execute(self):
        print("Executing Workflow:")
        for step in self.steps:
            print(f" -> {step}")

# Define a workflow using the DSL
workflow = WorkflowDSL().step("Load Data").step("Clean Data").step("Train
        Model").step("Deploy Model")
workflow.execute()
```

This example demonstrates a **structured, human-readable format** that allows users to **define workflows textually**.

Graphical DSLs: Visual Representations for Domain Concepts

Graphical DSLs use **visual notations** to represent logic and operations, making them suitable for **non-programmers, engineers, and business analysts**. These DSLs are widely used in **model-driven development, visual programming, and automation tools**. Examples include **UML (Unified Modeling Language), Simulink (control systems), Scratch (visual programming), and BPMN (Business Process Model and Notation)**.

Graphical DSLs excel in domains where **intuitive visualization is more effective than textual descriptions**. However, they require **specialized tooling, drag-and-drop editors, and diagramming software**, making them **less portable and harder to manage** in traditional version control systems.

Python Implementation of a Graphical DSL (Flowchart Representation Using Graphviz)

Below is an example of a **graphical DSL** that generates a **flowchart representation of a process** using **Graphviz**:

```python
from graphviz import Digraph

class FlowchartDSL:
    def __init__(self, name):
        self.graph = Digraph(name)

    def add_step(self, name):
        self.graph.node(name)
        return self
```

```
    def add_transition(self, from_step, to_step):
        self.graph.edge(from_step, to_step)
        return self

    def render(self):
        return self.graph

# Define a graphical DSL for a process
flowchart = FlowchartDSL("Machine Learning Pipeline")\
    .add_step("Load Data").add_step("Preprocess Data")\
    .add_step("Train Model").add_step("Evaluate Model")\
    .add_transition("Load Data", "Preprocess Data")\
    .add_transition("Preprocess Data", "Train Model")\
    .add_transition("Train Model", "Evaluate Model")

flowchart.render().view()  # Opens the generated graph
```

This example represents a **machine learning pipeline** using a **graphical DSL**, where steps are visually linked to form a **flowchart representation**.

Choosing Between Text-Based and Graphical DSLs

- **Text-Based DSLs** are **easier to develop and maintain**, work well with **version control**, and offer **high flexibility**. They are ideal for **developers and scripting environments**.

- **Graphical DSLs** are **user-friendly**, making them accessible to **non-programmers**. They provide **better visualization** but require **specialized tools** for editing and rendering.

Both **text-based and graphical DSLs** offer unique advantages. **Text-based DSLs** provide flexibility and ease of automation, while **graphical DSLs** offer an **intuitive, visual approach** to complex workflows. Choosing the right DSL depends on the target audience and the domain-specific **needs for readability, automation, and maintainability**.

Examples of Successful DSL Implementations

Domain-Specific Languages (DSLs) have transformed software development by **enhancing productivity, abstraction, and domain-specific problem-solving**. Several DSLs have achieved widespread adoption across industries, enabling developers, analysts, and domain experts to express solutions efficiently. This section explores **successful DSL implementations** across various domains, including **query languages, configuration management, infrastructure automation, and data processing**. These examples illustrate how DSLs provide **concise, expressive, and maintainable solutions** to complex problems. Python-based implementations will be provided where applicable to demonstrate how similar DSLs can be designed.

SQL: The Most Ubiquitous DSL for Databases

Structured Query Language (SQL) is a **classic example of a declarative DSL** designed for **database querying and management**. SQL enables users to retrieve, manipulate, and manage relational data using **high-level queries** without specifying low-level execution details. SQL's **expressiveness and efficiency** have made it the **de facto standard** for relational database interaction.

Python-Based SQL-Like DSL Example

Below is an implementation of a **simple SQL-like DSL** for querying in-memory data structures:

```
class SimpleSQL:
    def __init__(self, data):
        self.data = data

    def select(self, column):
        return [row[column] for row in self.data]

# Example usage
data = [{"name": "Alice", "age": 30}, {"name": "Bob", "age": 25}]
query = SimpleSQL(data)
print(query.select("name"))  # Output: ['Alice', 'Bob']
```

This example demonstrates **how SQL-style querying** can be embedded in Python.

Makefile: A DSL for Build Automation

Makefiles define **build automation rules** for compiling and linking programs. It is an **imperative, text-based DSL** that specifies dependencies and commands for **automating complex build processes**. Its concise syntax and execution model have made it a staple in **software engineering, especially in C and C++ development**.

A Python equivalent of a **Makefile-inspired DSL** for automating tasks might look like this:

```
class BuildDSL:
    def __init__(self):
        self.tasks = {}

    def task(self, name, action):
        self.tasks[name] = action

    def run(self, name):
        if name in self.tasks:
            self.tasks[name]()

# Define a build process
build = BuildDSL()
build.task("compile", lambda: print("Compiling source code..."))
build.task("link", lambda: print("Linking binaries..."))
build.run("compile")
```

This Python-based DSL **mimics Makefile's dependency-driven execution**, allowing users to define tasks and execute them efficiently.

Regular Expressions (Regex): A DSL for Pattern Matching

Regular expressions (Regex) are a **powerful DSL** used for **pattern matching and text processing**. Regex provides a compact, declarative syntax for defining patterns, making it invaluable for **string manipulation, validation, and search operations**.

Python natively supports Regex through the re module:

```
import re

pattern = r"\bDSL\b"
text = "This book covers DSL concepts."
match = re.search(pattern, text)
print("Match found!" if match else "No match")
```

This **Regex-based DSL** efficiently finds **specific patterns in text**, demonstrating **how DSLs simplify repetitive tasks**.

Graphviz: A Graphical DSL for Visualization

Graphviz is a **graphical DSL** used for defining and rendering graphs and diagrams. Its **DOT language** provides a structured yet **declarative way to define node and edge relationships**, making it popular for **network diagrams, flowcharts, and dependency graphs**.

Python offers an interface to Graphviz:

```
from graphviz import Digraph

dot = Digraph()
dot.node("A", "Start")
dot.node("B", "Process")
dot.edge("A", "B")
dot.render("graph", format="png", view=True)
```

This example demonstrates **how a graphical DSL can define and visualize relationships** using a concise, structured syntax.

Infrastructure as Code (IaC): Terraform and Ansible

Terraform and **Ansible** are **DSL-powered infrastructure automation tools** used for **provisioning and managing cloud resources**.

- **Terraform** uses a declarative **HashiCorp Configuration Language (HCL)** to define infrastructure as code.

- **Ansible Playbooks** provide an **imperative YAML-based DSL** for **automating server configurations**.

These DSLs enable **scalable, automated infrastructure management**, significantly reducing manual configuration errors.

Successful DSL implementations such as **SQL, Makefile, Regex, Graphviz, Terraform, and Ansible** demonstrate the **power and efficiency** of DSLs in different domains. These languages simplify complex tasks, improve maintainability, and provide **domain-specific expressiveness**. By studying these implementations, developers can design their own **effective, problem-oriented DSLs** tailored to specific needs..

Module 3:
DSL Design Principles

Designing an effective Domain-Specific Language (DSL) requires a deep understanding of **the domain, its constraints, and the intended users**. This module explores the fundamental principles that guide DSL design, ensuring that it remains **intuitive, expressive, and practical**. By focusing on domain knowledge, simplifying syntax, and balancing flexibility with specificity, developers can create DSLs that enhance productivity without unnecessary complexity. The following sections cover **the importance of domain knowledge, simplicity and expressiveness, syntax and semantics design, and the balance between flexibility and specificity**, all of which contribute to a well-structured, efficient DSL.

Focus on Domain Knowledge

A DSL is effective only if it accurately represents the **concepts, operations, and constraints** of the domain it serves. The first step in DSL design is **analyzing the domain and identifying its core abstractions**. This requires collaboration with **domain experts** to ensure that the language captures the essential features needed for solving domain-specific problems efficiently.

A well-designed DSL must reflect **how domain practitioners think and work**, rather than imposing unnecessary programming complexity. By aligning with domain knowledge, a DSL becomes more intuitive for users who may not be traditional programmers. For example, a financial DSL should incorporate **terms, formulas, and workflows familiar to finance professionals**, making it easier for them to write and understand DSL-based scripts. The key goal is to ensure that the DSL **bridges the gap between technical implementation and domain expertise**, enabling smoother adoption and more effective problem-solving.

Simplicity and Expressiveness

An effective DSL must strike a **balance between simplicity and expressiveness**. Simplicity ensures that the language is easy to **learn, use, and maintain**, while expressiveness allows it to capture **complex operations in a concise manner**. Overcomplicating a DSL with excessive syntax rules or programming constructs can hinder its usability, defeating its purpose.

Simplicity can be achieved by using **natural, declarative syntax** that mirrors how domain experts already describe problems. For example, a configuration DSL should provide **straightforward, human-readable structures** rather than complex procedural logic. Expressiveness, on the other hand, is achieved by ensuring that the DSL can **efficiently represent domain-specific tasks without unnecessary verbosity**. A well-designed DSL should allow users to accomplish complex tasks in fewer lines of code, while still remaining clear and understandable.

Syntax and Semantics Design

A DSL's **syntax (structure) and semantics (meaning)** determine how users interact with it. The syntax must be **intuitive, unambiguous, and domain-relevant**, avoiding unnecessary complexity. The choice between **keyword-based syntax, indentation-based syntax, or symbolic notation** should be guided by **how users naturally express domain concepts**.

Semantics define **what the DSL statements mean and how they are executed**. A DSL can adopt **declarative semantics (describing what should be done) or imperative semantics (specifying how it should be done)**. Ensuring semantic clarity prevents ambiguity and makes the DSL more predictable. Consistent syntax and semantics allow users to **write valid DSL scripts without confusion**, ensuring that their intent is correctly interpreted by the DSL engine.

Balancing Flexibility and Specificity in DSLs

A DSL must be **specific enough to simplify domain tasks**, yet **flexible enough to handle variations** within that domain. Overly rigid DSLs may become too restrictive, preventing users from expressing uncommon yet valid scenarios. On the other hand, excessive flexibility can lead to **unpredictable behavior** or DSL misuse, making it harder to maintain and enforce domain constraints.

Balancing flexibility and specificity requires designing **a core set of well-defined rules and extension mechanisms**. A good DSL provides **defaults and constraints that guide users** while still allowing customization where necessary. For example, a web automation DSL may offer **predefined commands for common interactions** (clicking buttons, filling forms) but also provide **escape hatches** for more advanced operations when needed. Finding the right balance ensures that the DSL remains **powerful, user-friendly, and adaptable to real-world domain challenges**.

Effective DSL design requires a deep understanding of **the target domain, clear and expressive syntax, intuitive semantics, and a balanced approach to flexibility and specificity**. A well-designed DSL allows domain experts to express solutions naturally while maintaining **efficiency, clarity, and usability**. By following these principles, developers can create DSLs that provide **real value, making complex domain tasks easier to accomplish**.

Focus on Domain Knowledge

A Domain-Specific Language (DSL) is only as effective as its alignment with the **problem domain** it is designed to address. The foundation of DSL design lies in **deep domain understanding**, ensuring that the language captures the **concepts, workflows, and constraints** relevant to domain experts. Unlike general-purpose languages that aim for broad applicability, a DSL should reflect **how practitioners think and work within their specialized field**. This section explores **why domain knowledge is crucial, how to analyze a domain effectively, and how to translate domain concepts into a well-structured DSL**.

Understanding the Domain and Its Core Abstractions

To design a DSL that truly serves its users, developers must **immerse themselves in the domain** and **identify its key abstractions**. This requires engaging with domain experts—whether they are **financial analysts, network engineers, biologists, or software architects**—to extract the fundamental **concepts, relationships, and processes** that define their work. The goal is to ensure that the DSL mirrors **natural thought processes and workflows**, making it intuitive for users to express solutions in their field.

For example, in the **finance domain**, common abstractions include **transactions, interest rates, and risk models**. A financial DSL should provide constructs that match these concepts, enabling users to write **declarative expressions** such as:

```
transaction(amount=5000, type="deposit", account="savings")
```

Instead of requiring imperative logic, the DSL should **allow domain experts to describe what they need in familiar terms**.

Mapping Domain Concepts to DSL Constructs

Once the key **domain entities and processes** are identified, the next step is to design **DSL constructs** that model them effectively. This involves choosing appropriate **keywords, operators, and syntax** that make the DSL easy to read and write. A well-designed DSL should minimize the **gap between the problem space (domain concepts) and the solution space (DSL syntax)**.

For instance, a **network automation DSL** should reflect networking concepts like **devices, configurations, and protocols**. Instead of requiring users to write complex scripts, the DSL should provide **high-level primitives** such as:

```
configure_router(ip="192.168.1.1", protocol="OSPF")
```

This approach makes the DSL **more accessible to networking professionals**, allowing them to **focus on their expertise rather than low-level programming details**.

Ensuring Domain-Specific Constraints and Validations

A DSL should **enforce domain constraints** to prevent users from making errors that would be impossible in a real-world scenario. Unlike general-purpose languages, which allow unrestricted programming logic, a DSL should **embed rules that align with domain logic**.

For example, in a **medical DSL** used for prescribing medications, the system should **prevent invalid prescriptions** based on known medical interactions. Instead of allowing arbitrary instructions, the DSL could enforce constraints like:

```
prescribe(drug="Aspirin", patient="John", contraindications=["Bleeding
          Disorder"])
```

This ensures that only **valid, medically safe prescriptions** can be made, reducing errors and increasing trust in the system.

A DSL's effectiveness is directly tied to **how well it models the problem domain**. By focusing on domain knowledge, designers can create a language that is **intuitive, constraint-aware, and expressive**. A well-designed DSL **reduces complexity for domain experts**, allowing them to **interact with the system naturally** while ensuring accuracy and efficiency.

Simplicity and Expressiveness

A well-designed Domain-Specific Language (DSL) should strike a balance between **simplicity and expressiveness**, ensuring that users can easily **learn, use, and maintain** the language while still being able to express complex domain-specific operations concisely. Simplicity makes a DSL approachable, reducing cognitive load, while expressiveness allows it to effectively **capture the intricacies of the domain**. This section explores the principles behind **keeping a DSL simple yet powerful**, including **human-friendly syntax, eliminating unnecessary complexity, and ensuring conciseness without sacrificing clarity**.

Making DSLs Simple and Intuitive

The primary goal of a DSL is to enable users—often **domain experts with limited programming experience**—to write instructions in a way that closely mirrors how they naturally describe problems. To achieve this, a DSL's syntax should be **clear, minimalistic, and intuitive**, avoiding unnecessary technical complexity.

For example, a **task automation DSL** should allow users to specify workflows in a straightforward, readable format:

```
task("Backup Database") >> task("Send Report")
```

This notation is **declarative and human-readable**, making it clear that the **backup task must complete before the report is sent**. The simplicity of this syntax removes the need for boilerplate code, making it more accessible than a general-purpose programming approach.

Eliminating Unnecessary Complexity

A DSL should avoid unnecessary **programming constructs** such as complex loops, manual memory management, or excessive configuration parameters. Instead, it should provide **built-in high-level abstractions** that simplify domain tasks.

Consider a **data transformation DSL** for processing structured data. Instead of requiring users to write procedural code, the DSL should allow them to describe transformations succinctly:

```
transform(data).filter("age > 30").group_by("city").aggregate("average",
            "income")
```

This approach abstracts away the underlying implementation details while keeping the DSL **expressive enough to perform sophisticated operations**.

Ensuring Expressiveness Without Verbosity

Expressiveness in a DSL means that users should be able to **represent complex domain-specific operations in a concise manner**. A common pitfall is **verbosity**, where users must write excessive or repetitive code to accomplish simple tasks. A well-designed DSL provides **compact yet powerful constructs** that retain clarity.

For example, in a **home automation DSL**, a user should be able to express event-driven behavior in a simple, readable manner:

```
on_motion_detected("living_room") >> turn_on("lights")
```

Instead of requiring an explicit event listener and callback function, the DSL directly expresses the intent in **a single, clear statement**.

A successful DSL must be **simple enough for users to adopt easily yet expressive enough to handle real-world domain scenarios effectively**. By focusing on **human-readable syntax, removing unnecessary complexity, and ensuring conciseness without sacrificing clarity**, DSL designers can create languages that are **both powerful and easy to use**. The result is a DSL that enhances **productivity, readability, and maintainability** for domain experts.

Syntax and Semantics Design

The design of a Domain-Specific Language (DSL) hinges on two critical aspects: **syntax (how the language looks) and semantics (what the language means and how it behaves)**. A well-structured DSL must have **clear, consistent, and intuitive syntax** that aligns with domain concepts while ensuring **precise and predictable semantics**. The goal is to create a language that is **both readable and executable**, reducing ambiguity and improving usability. This section explores **syntax choices, semantic clarity, and strategies for designing a DSL that is both expressive and reliable**.

Designing Intuitive and Consistent Syntax

The syntax of a DSL should be **intuitive, minimalistic, and natural** to its target users. The choice of syntax—whether **text-based, symbolic, or graphical**—depends on how users **naturally describe domain concepts**. A DSL's syntax should **eliminate**

unnecessary programming constructs and mirror real-world terminology to enhance usability.

For example, a **policy configuration DSL** should allow users to define rules in a **human-readable** manner:

```
policy("Access Control") {

    allow("admin").to("modify").on("database")

}
```

This syntax closely aligns with how administrators **think about policies**, making the DSL more accessible to non-programmers. **Consistent syntax rules** prevent confusion and ensure that users can predict how expressions behave.

Choosing Between Declarative and Imperative Semantics

A DSL's semantics determine **how statements are interpreted and executed**. The two primary approaches are **declarative and imperative semantics**.

- **Declarative DSLs** focus on **what should be done** rather than how to do it. This approach is common in **query languages, configuration languages, and automation tools**. A SQL query, for instance, is a declarative DSL where users specify **what data they need**, and the system determines the execution plan.

- **Imperative DSLs** require users to **specify step-by-step instructions** to achieve a task. This is useful when fine-grained control over execution is necessary, such as in a **robotics DSL** where each movement must be explicitly defined:

```
move_forward(10)
turn_right(90)
pick_object("box")
```

Choosing between declarative and imperative semantics depends on **the domain requirements**. Many DSLs adopt a **hybrid approach**, combining declarative constructs with imperative extensions for greater flexibility.

Ensuring Semantic Clarity and Predictability

Semantic clarity ensures that **DSL expressions behave as expected**, preventing ambiguity and unexpected behavior. A well-designed DSL should have **strict but understandable rules** for how its syntax translates into execution.

For example, a **workflow automation DSL** should clearly define **dependencies and execution order**:

```
task("Extract Data") >> task("Transform Data") >> task("Load Data")
```

Here, the semantics ensure **tasks execute sequentially**, preventing misinterpretations. Without clear semantics, users might assume tasks execute **in parallel** or **in an undefined order**, leading to unpredictable results.

A well-designed DSL requires **clear syntax for readability and precise semantics for predictable behavior**. By aligning **syntax with domain conventions, choosing an appropriate execution model, and enforcing semantic clarity**, developers can create DSLs that are **user-friendly, efficient, and reliable**. This ensures that the language is **both intuitive for domain experts and powerful for software execution**.

Balancing Flexibility and Specificity in DSLs

Designing a Domain-Specific Language (DSL) requires careful consideration of **flexibility and specificity**. A DSL should be **specific enough** to efficiently capture domain concepts while being **flexible enough** to accommodate variations within the domain. If a DSL is too rigid, it may fail to address evolving requirements. Conversely, if it is too flexible, it may become indistinguishable from a general-purpose language, negating its primary advantage. This section explores **how to balance expressiveness with constraints**, ensuring that a DSL remains **usable, scalable, and effective** within its intended domain.

The Need for Specificity in DSL Design

The primary reason for creating a DSL is to provide **a tailored language that encapsulates domain rules and best practices**. Specificity ensures that users can express domain concepts **with minimal effort and maximum clarity**. A DSL should provide **domain-focused abstractions** that simplify problem-solving while enforcing **rules that prevent invalid or meaningless expressions**.

For example, a **financial trading DSL** should restrict transactions to **valid market operations**, ensuring compliance with trading regulations. Instead of allowing arbitrary function calls, it should offer **specific constructs** such as:

```
trade(stock="AAPL", action="buy", quantity=100, limit_price=150.00)
```

This level of specificity eliminates errors, ensures correctness, and makes the DSL **easier to learn and use**.

Incorporating Flexibility Without Compromising Domain Integrity

While specificity is crucial, a DSL must also allow for **variations and extensions** to accommodate changing needs. A rigid DSL may become obsolete if it cannot **adapt to evolving domain requirements**. To introduce flexibility, DSL designers can provide **extension mechanisms**, such as:

- **Parameterized Constructs:** Allowing users to **modify behavior** without altering the DSL's core syntax.

- **Custom Functions or Rules:** Enabling users to define domain-specific logic within a controlled framework.

- **Configuration Options:** Letting users tweak behaviors while maintaining domain integrity.

For instance, a **machine learning DSL** might allow users to specify models but also provide flexibility in **customizing parameters**:

```
train_model(type="neural_network", layers=3, optimizer="adam")
```

Here, the DSL remains domain-focused while allowing users to **adapt configurations** to different use cases.

Ensuring Maintainability and Scalability

A well-balanced DSL should be **maintainable and scalable**. This means avoiding **feature bloat**—adding unnecessary complexity that makes the language difficult to learn and use. Instead, DSL designers should focus on:

- **Providing clear documentation and intuitive syntax** to prevent confusion.

- **Enforcing constraints that guide users** without limiting legitimate use cases.

- **Modular design**, allowing features to evolve without breaking existing functionality.

A DSL that maintains a **careful balance between structure and adaptability** can evolve with its domain while remaining easy to use and understand.

Balancing **flexibility and specificity** is key to creating a **practical and effective DSL**. A well-designed DSL should offer **domain-specific constructs** that simplify problem-solving while allowing users to **extend or modify behavior when needed**. By enforcing **clear constraints, structured flexibility, and maintainability**, developers can build DSLs that remain **relevant, usable, and scalable** over time.

Module 4:
Development and Implementation of DSLs

The development of a Domain-Specific Language (DSL) involves a structured process that includes **designing, building, and integrating** the language within its target domain. A well-implemented DSL enhances productivity, simplifies complex tasks, and enforces domain rules effectively. This module explores the **DSL creation process, the tools available for building DSLs, strategies for integration into existing systems, and real-world case studies demonstrating the impact of DSL adoption**. By understanding these aspects, developers can create robust DSLs that improve software efficiency and maintainability.

Overview of DSL Creation Process

The process of developing a DSL follows a **systematic approach** that includes requirement analysis, design, implementation, and validation. The first step is **identifying the problem domain and defining the specific challenges that a DSL aims to solve**. By analyzing the domain, developers can determine whether an **internal or external DSL** is the best approach.

Once the purpose is defined, the next step is designing the **syntax and semantics** of the DSL. This involves choosing **human-readable constructs** and ensuring the language aligns with the **natural problem-solving approach of domain experts**. The implementation phase includes **parsing, interpreting, or compiling the DSL**, followed by thorough testing to validate correctness and usability. A well-structured development process ensures that the DSL effectively meets user needs while remaining maintainable and extensible.

Tools for Building DSLs

A variety of tools and frameworks exist to aid the creation of DSLs, ranging from **parser generators and interpreter frameworks to metaprogramming libraries**. These tools help **define, process, and execute DSL commands efficiently**, enabling developers to focus on domain-specific logic rather than low-level language mechanics.

For internal DSLs, **metaprogramming capabilities** of languages like Python, Ruby, and Scala allow seamless embedding of DSL constructs. For external DSLs, tools like **ANTLR, Lex/Yacc, and Xtext** assist in **lexical analysis, parsing, and language definition**. Additionally, **domain modeling frameworks** provide a structured way to implement DSLs without building a custom parser from scratch. Choosing the right tool depends on the complexity of the DSL, the target domain, and the desired level of control over the language's implementation.

Integrating DSLs into Existing Systems

A DSL should seamlessly integrate with existing **software architectures and workflows** to maximize its effectiveness. Successful integration involves designing the DSL to **interoperate with existing APIs, databases, and services**, ensuring that users can adopt it without disrupting their established processes.

A key challenge in integration is balancing **domain abstraction and execution efficiency**. Some DSLs act as **preprocessors**, translating high-level instructions into code that interacts with underlying general-purpose languages. Others work as **embedded scripting languages**, extending existing software functionality without requiring extensive modifications. Ensuring proper documentation and API compatibility is essential to encourage adoption and long-term maintainability.

Case Studies of DSL Development

The effectiveness of DSLs can be best understood through **real-world case studies** that demonstrate how they streamline domain-specific tasks. Examples include **SQL for database queries, HTML for web content structuring, and Gradle for build automation**. Each of these DSLs was designed to **simplify a complex problem domain, enhance productivity, and enforce best practices**.

Other case studies may include **custom-built DSLs for financial modeling, machine learning pipelines, and robotic automation**, each demonstrating how a well-designed DSL can transform software development. Examining these implementations provides valuable insights into best practices, common pitfalls, and strategies for developing successful DSLs.

Developing a DSL requires a structured approach that **balances domain specificity with implementation flexibility**. By leveraging the right tools, ensuring smooth integration, and learning from successful case studies, developers can create DSLs that significantly **enhance productivity and software maintainability**. This module provides the foundational knowledge necessary to design and implement effective DSLs tailored for specific application domains.

Overview of DSL Creation Process

The process of creating a Domain-Specific Language (DSL) follows a structured workflow that ensures the language effectively captures domain knowledge while remaining **usable, maintainable, and efficient**. This involves several key phases: **domain analysis, syntax and semantics design, implementation, testing, and integration**. The choice between an **internal DSL** (embedded within a host language) and an **external DSL** (with its own syntax and parser) plays a crucial role in how the DSL is developed.

A well-designed DSL enables domain experts to write **concise, expressive, and error-free** instructions specific to their field. For example, a DSL for financial trading should allow traders to describe transactions **without needing deep programming expertise**, improving efficiency and reducing errors.

Defining the Problem Domain

The first step in creating a DSL is understanding the **problem space and domain-specific requirements**. Developers must **consult domain experts**, analyze **common workflows**, and identify **repetitive patterns** that could benefit from automation. A **clear problem statement** ensures the DSL's features align with user needs.

For instance, in the field of **home automation**, users may want to define **rules for controlling smart devices**. Instead of writing complex Python code, a DSL can provide a **simplified, human-readable syntax**:

```
when motion_detected turn_on light for 10 minutes
```

By focusing on **natural expressions**, the DSL makes it easier for users to define automation rules **without learning complex programming concepts**.

Designing Syntax and Semantics

After defining the problem, the next step is **designing the DSL's syntax and semantics**. This involves choosing **keywords, operators, and constructs** that best represent the domain. The goal is to ensure the DSL is **intuitive and expressive** while **eliminating unnecessary complexity**.

For an **internal DSL**, developers can leverage an existing programming language's features. Python, with its **dynamic typing and metaprogramming capabilities**, is an excellent choice. Below is an example of a simple **internal DSL for task automation** using Python's fluent interface:

```python
class Task:
    def __init__(self, action):
        self.action = action
        self.condition = None

    def when(self, condition):
        self.condition = condition
        return self

    def execute(self):
        if eval(self.condition):
            print(f"Executing: {self.action}")

# Using the DSL
task = Task("Backup database").when("time.hour == 23")
task.execute()
```

This DSL allows users to define tasks **in a readable, declarative manner** without dealing with low-level code structures.

Implementation: Parsing and Execution

For **external DSLs**, developers need to implement a **parser and an interpreter** to process DSL scripts. Python offers tools like **ANTLR, PLY, or Lark** for parsing custom languages. Below is an example of a **simple parser using Lark** for a hypothetical **configuration DSL**:

```
from lark import Lark, Transformer

dsl_grammar = """
    start: command+
    command: "set" NAME "=" value
    value: NUMBER | STRING
    NAME: /[a-z_]+/
    STRING: /".*?"/
    NUMBER: /\d+/
    %import common.WS
    %ignore WS
"""

class ConfigTransformer(Transformer):
    def command(self, items):
        return {items[0]: items[1]}

parser = Lark(dsl_grammar, parser='lalr', transformer=ConfigTransformer())

# Parsing a simple DSL script
dsl_script = 'set max_retries = 5\nset message = "Hello, DSL!"'
parsed_output = parser.parse(dsl_script)
print(parsed_output)
```

This example demonstrates **how an external DSL can be implemented using a formal grammar and parsed into structured data**.

Testing and Validation

Once the DSL is implemented, **testing is essential** to ensure correctness and usability. Unit tests should cover:

- **Syntax validation** – Ensuring the DSL correctly parses valid expressions.

- **Execution correctness** – Ensuring DSL statements execute as expected.

- **Edge cases** – Handling invalid inputs gracefully.

For an internal DSL, Python's unittest module can be used to **validate functionality**:

```
import unittest

class TestDSL(unittest.TestCase):
    def test_task_execution(self):
        task = Task("Notify user").when("5 > 3")
        self.assertEqual(task.execute(), "Executing: Notify user")

if __name__ == "__main__":
    unittest.main()
```

48

Automated tests help maintain the DSL's reliability as it evolves over time.

Deploying and Iterating

The final step is **documenting, deploying, and refining the DSL**. Documentation should include:

- **Syntax rules and examples** to help users adopt the DSL easily.

- **Error handling mechanisms** to prevent incorrect usage.

- **Extension guidelines** for future enhancements.

By following a structured DSL creation process—from **domain analysis to implementation and testing**—developers can create **powerful, intuitive, and efficient** domain-specific languages that streamline complex workflows and improve software maintainability.

Tools for Building DSLs

Developing a Domain-Specific Language (DSL) requires specialized tools that facilitate **syntax definition, parsing, execution, and integration**. The choice of tools depends on whether the DSL is **internal or external**, as internal DSLs leverage existing programming languages, while external DSLs require custom parsers and interpreters. Python, being a **flexible and expressive language**, provides several frameworks for building both types of DSLs.

This section explores key tools such as **Python's metaprogramming features for internal DSLs** and **parser generators like ANTLR, Lark, and PLY for external DSLs**. By selecting the right tools, developers can streamline DSL creation and ensure robust functionality.

Tools for Internal DSLs

An internal DSL is embedded within a host language, using **existing syntax and features** to define domain-specific expressions. Python's **operator overloading, decorators, and fluent interfaces** make it an excellent choice for internal DSL development.

For instance, Python's **context managers** (with statements) can create a readable, declarative DSL for **configuring server settings**:

```
class ServerConfig:
    def __init__(self):
        self.settings = {}

    def __enter__(self):
        return self
```

```
        def __exit__(self, exc_type, exc_value, traceback):
            print(f"Config: {self.settings}")

        def set(self, key, value):
            self.settings[key] = value

# Using the DSL
with ServerConfig() as config:
    config.set("host", "localhost")
    config.set("port", 8080)
```

This approach leverages Python's built-in capabilities to create **readable, domain-specific syntax** without writing a separate parser.

Tools for External DSLs

External DSLs require tools for defining **syntax, parsing, and execution**. The most widely used tools in Python for this purpose include:

1. **ANTLR (Another Tool for Language Recognition)** – A powerful parser generator that supports multiple languages, including Python.

2. **Lark** – A lightweight and efficient parsing library for quickly building custom DSLs.

3. **PLY (Python Lex-Yacc)** – A Python implementation of the classic Lex and Yacc parsing tools.

A simple example using **Lark** to parse a basic arithmetic DSL:

```
from lark import Lark, Transformer

dsl_grammar = """
    ?start: expr
    ?expr: term
         | expr "+" term -> add
         | expr "-" term -> sub
    ?term: NUMBER
    NUMBER: /[0-9]+/
    %import common.WS
    %ignore WS
"""

class EvalTransformer(Transformer):
    def add(self, args):
        return args[0] + args[1]

    def sub(self, args):
        return args[0] - args[1]

parser = Lark(dsl_grammar, parser="lalr", transformer=EvalTransformer())
print(parser.parse("5 + 3 - 2"))  # Outputs: 6
```

This example demonstrates how **Lark parses DSL expressions and transforms them into executable Python code**, enabling the creation of domain-specific syntax.

Code Generation and Execution Tools

DSLs often need to **generate code or execute domain-specific instructions**. Python provides several tools for this:

- **AST (Abstract Syntax Trees)**: Python's ast module can generate and manipulate code dynamically.

- **exec() and eval()**: These functions execute dynamically generated code but should be used cautiously due to security risks.

- **Jinja2**: A template engine for generating code from DSL scripts.

Example of **dynamic code execution using AST**:

```
import ast

expr = "x + y"
parsed_expr = ast.parse(expr, mode='eval')
compiled_expr = compile(parsed_expr, "<string>", "eval")

x, y = 10, 5
print(eval(compiled_expr))  # Outputs: 15
```

This technique is useful for **interpreting and executing DSL scripts dynamically**.

Choosing the Right Tool

The selection of tools depends on the **complexity and requirements of the DSL**:

- **For internal DSLs**, Python's **metaprogramming and fluent interfaces** are sufficient.

- **For external DSLs, ANTLR, Lark, or PLY** provide structured parsing capabilities.

- **For execution and code generation**, Python's **AST module, eval(), and Jinja2** offer flexible runtime capabilities.

By leveraging these tools effectively, developers can build **robust, maintainable DSLs** that simplify domain-specific tasks and enhance productivity.

Integrating DSLs into Existing Systems

Integrating a Domain-Specific Language (DSL) into an existing system is a critical step in making the DSL **practical and useful** within a real-world software architecture. A DSL must be designed to interact **seamlessly with existing applications, databases, APIs, and business logic** to avoid creating isolated silos of functionality.

This section explores various **strategies for embedding and interfacing DSLs** within software systems. It covers **embedding internal DSLs in host applications, exposing**

external DSLs through APIs, and ensuring interoperability with existing tools and data formats. By following a structured integration approach, DSLs can enhance software efficiency and maintainability.

Embedding Internal DSLs in Applications

Internal DSLs, being **built within a host language**, can be **directly integrated into existing applications**. One common approach is embedding a DSL **within a framework or library** so that developers can write domain-specific logic using a concise and readable syntax.

For example, consider an **internal DSL for defining SQL-like queries** within a Python web application:

```
class Query:
    def __init__(self):
        self.filters = []

    def where(self, condition):
        self.filters.append(condition)
        return self

    def execute(self):
        return f"SELECT * FROM data WHERE {' AND '.join(self.filters)}"
# Using the DSL within an application
query = Query().where("age > 30").where("status = 'active'")
print(query.execute())  # Outputs: SELECT * FROM data WHERE age > 30 AND status
        = 'active'
```

This DSL allows developers to construct **complex queries in an intuitive and structured way**, making integration seamless.

Exposing External DSLs via APIs

For external DSLs, integration often involves **providing an interface that allows applications to send DSL scripts for processing**. This is commonly done by exposing a **REST or GraphQL API** that receives DSL commands, parses them, and returns the results.

A practical approach is using **Flask or FastAPI** in Python to create an API service that interprets a DSL and executes corresponding business logic. Below is an example of a **Flask-based API for executing commands from an external DSL**:

```
from flask import Flask, request, jsonify
from lark import Lark, Transformer

app = Flask(__name__)

dsl_grammar = """
    start: command+
    command: "notify" STRING
    STRING: /".*?"/
```

```
    %import common.WS
    %ignore WS
"""

class DSLInterpreter(Transformer):
    def command(self, items):
        return {"action": "notify", "message": items[0]}

parser = Lark(dsl_grammar, parser="lalr", transformer=DSLInterpreter())

@app.route("/execute", methods=["POST"])
def execute_dsl():
    script = request.json["dsl_script"]
    result = parser.parse(script)
    return jsonify(result)

if __name__ == "__main__":
    app.run(debug=True)
```

With this setup, applications can **send DSL commands via HTTP requests** and receive JSON responses, enabling easy **system-wide integration**.

Ensuring Interoperability with Existing Tools

For a DSL to be useful, it must **interoperate smoothly with databases, APIs, and external services**. This involves:

- **Connecting with Databases** – DSLs often need to **read and write structured data**. Integration with databases like **PostgreSQL, MySQL, or MongoDB** ensures that DSL scripts can retrieve or manipulate data dynamically.

- **Interfacing with APIs** – Many DSLs act as **configuration or automation tools** that interact with **cloud services, IoT devices, or third-party APIs**.

- **Supporting Standard Data Formats** – JSON, XML, or YAML-based DSLs can be easily parsed and integrated into existing systems.

An example of a **DSL-driven database query execution system**:

```
import sqlite3

class DBQueryDSL:
    def __init__(self, db_path):
        self.conn = sqlite3.connect(db_path)
        self.cursor = self.conn.cursor()

    def run(self, dsl_query):
        sql_query = f"SELECT * FROM users WHERE {dsl_query}"
        return self.cursor.execute(sql_query).fetchall()

# Executing a DSL query
db = DBQueryDSL("users.db")
print(db.run("age > 25 AND city = 'New York'"))
```

This allows the DSL to **translate user-friendly syntax into SQL statements** and execute them dynamically.

Error Handling and Security Considerations

When integrating a DSL into a production system, it is essential to consider **error handling and security**:

- **Input Validation** – Ensuring the DSL scripts do not introduce vulnerabilities like **SQL injection or code execution attacks**.

- **Sandbox Execution** – Running DSL commands in a **restricted environment** to prevent unauthorized system modifications.

- **Logging and Auditing** – Keeping track of DSL commands executed to ensure transparency and debugging capabilities.

For example, **sandboxing Python code execution** using exec() with restricted globals:

```
safe_globals = {"__builtins__": {}}
exec("print('Safe Execution')", safe_globals)  # Prevents access to system
            functions
```

By incorporating these safeguards, DSLs can be securely integrated into existing systems without introducing critical risks.

Integrating DSLs into existing systems involves **embedding internal DSLs within applications, exposing external DSLs via APIs, and ensuring compatibility with databases and services**. Choosing the right integration strategy depends on the **architecture and use case** of the DSL. By following best practices for **error handling, security, and data exchange**, developers can create powerful DSL-driven systems that are both **scalable and maintainable**.

Case Studies of DSL Development

Studying real-world implementations of Domain-Specific Languages (DSLs) provides insight into **how DSLs improve efficiency, simplify complex processes, and enhance maintainability**. This section explores three successful DSLs: **SQL (a declarative DSL for databases), TensorFlow (a DSL for machine learning), and Ansible (a configuration management DSL)**. These case studies illustrate how DSLs are designed, integrated, and optimized for specific domains.

By analyzing these examples, developers can learn valuable lessons in **syntax design, abstraction levels, and system integration**, guiding them toward creating their own effective DSLs.

Case Study 1: SQL – A Declarative DSL for Databases

Structured Query Language (SQL) is one of the most widely used DSLs, designed specifically for **interacting with relational databases**. SQL's declarative nature allows users to specify **what** data they need, rather than describing **how** to retrieve it.

Example SQL query to fetch data from a database:

```
SELECT name, age FROM users WHERE age > 30 ORDER BY name;
```

This simplicity makes SQL an excellent example of a **declarative DSL**. It abstracts away the complexity of database traversal, allowing developers to focus on **high-level data retrieval rather than low-level implementation details**.

Implementing an SQL-like DSL in Python using SQLite:

```
import sqlite3

conn = sqlite3.connect(":memory:")
cursor = conn.cursor()
cursor.execute("CREATE TABLE users (id INTEGER, name TEXT, age INTEGER)")
cursor.execute("INSERT INTO users VALUES (1, 'Alice', 35), (2, 'Bob', 28)")

def query_db(sql):
    cursor.execute(sql)
    return cursor.fetchall()

print(query_db("SELECT * FROM users WHERE age > 30"))
```

This example shows how an embedded DSL like SQL can **integrate seamlessly with existing systems**, making data manipulation straightforward.

Case Study 2: TensorFlow – A DSL for Machine Learning

TensorFlow is a **DSL for numerical computation and machine learning**, abstracting complex mathematical operations into **readable and efficient expressions**. It provides a structured way to define **neural networks and training models**.

Example of defining a simple computation graph in TensorFlow's DSL:

```
import tensorflow as tf

x = tf.constant(3.0)
y = tf.constant(4.0)
z = x * y
print(z.numpy())  # Outputs: 12.0
```

TensorFlow's DSL **hides low-level execution details** such as matrix operations and GPU optimizations, allowing machine learning engineers to **focus on high-level model building**.

Its **key DSL features** include:

- **Symbolic computation:** Defining computations as graphs rather than explicit step-by-step execution.

- **Automatic differentiation:** Enabling deep learning optimizations without requiring manual gradient calculations.

- **Hardware acceleration:** Leveraging GPUs and TPUs through optimized computation graphs.

This makes TensorFlow a prime example of a **DSL that abstracts complexity while maintaining high performance**.

Case Study 3: Ansible – A DSL for Configuration Management

Ansible is a **text-based declarative DSL** designed for **automating IT operations** such as server provisioning and software deployment. It simplifies configuration management using a **YAML-based DSL**.

Example of an Ansible playbook for installing and starting a web server:

```
- name: Install and Start Web Server
  hosts: web_servers
  tasks:
    - name: Install Apache
      apt:
        name: apache2
        state: present
    - name: Start Apache Service
      service:
        name: apache2
        state: started
```

This **DSL abstracts away system-level commands**, making server automation **more readable and maintainable**.

To execute such a playbook, a user only needs to run:

```
ansible-playbook setup.yml
```

Key benefits of Ansible's DSL include:

- **Human-readable syntax** using YAML, making it easy for system administrators to write configurations.

- **Declarative execution**, meaning users **describe the desired state** rather than scripting every step.

- **Scalability**, allowing large-scale infrastructure management with minimal effort.

Lessons Learned from These DSLs

From these case studies, we can extract valuable insights into **DSL development**:

- **Simplicity is key** – SQL, TensorFlow, and Ansible provide intuitive syntax that reduces cognitive load.

- **Abstract complexity while maintaining power** – Each DSL provides **high-level abstractions** without sacrificing **low-level optimizations**.

- **Domain relevance ensures adoption** – A DSL must **closely align with the needs of its target domain** to gain widespread acceptance.

- **Integration matters** – Each of these DSLs integrates well with existing tools and workflows, increasing their usability.

The success of SQL, TensorFlow, and Ansible demonstrates the power of **well-designed DSLs** in **simplifying domain-specific tasks, improving efficiency, and enhancing maintainability**. By understanding these real-world examples, developers can make **informed decisions** when designing their own DSLs. The key takeaway is that a DSL should provide **intuitive syntax, abstract complexity, and seamlessly integrate into existing workflows** to achieve maximum impact.

Module 5:
DSL Compiler Design and Parsing

Domain-Specific Languages (DSLs) rely on well-structured **compilation and parsing techniques** to transform high-level domain-specific instructions into executable code. This module explores the fundamental aspects of **DSL compilation**, focusing on the differences between **compilers and interpreters**, the role of **lexical and syntax analysis**, various **parsing techniques**, and the **process of generating executable code**. Understanding these concepts is crucial for developing **efficient, reliable, and optimized DSLs** tailored to specific application domains.

Compiler vs. Interpreter in DSLs

DSLs, like general-purpose languages, can either be **compiled or interpreted**. A **compiler** translates the entire DSL source code into machine code or an intermediate representation before execution, enhancing performance. Examples include SQL query optimizers that compile queries into efficient execution plans. On the other hand, an **interpreter** processes DSL commands line by line, making it more flexible but sometimes slower.

Choosing between a compiler and an interpreter depends on the **DSL's intended use**. For instance, a configuration management DSL like Ansible benefits from interpretation since configurations need frequent updates. Meanwhile, a DSL for hardware description, such as VHDL, leverages compilation for speed and efficiency. Hybrid approaches also exist, where DSLs use an intermediate representation (IR) before execution, balancing **flexibility and performance**.

Lexical Analysis and Syntax Analysis

Lexical analysis and syntax analysis are the **first two phases of compilation or interpretation**. Lexical analysis breaks the DSL's source code into **tokens**, which represent the smallest meaningful elements such as keywords, operators, and identifiers. A **lexer (tokenizer)** scans the input, removes unnecessary whitespace, and identifies the fundamental building blocks of the DSL.

Syntax analysis, also known as **parsing**, ensures that the sequence of tokens follows the correct **grammatical structure** of the DSL. This phase involves using **context-free grammars (CFGs)** or similar rules to validate the correctness of DSL expressions. Syntax errors detected at this stage help catch issues before execution. The parser typically generates an **Abstract Syntax Tree (AST)**, which represents the hierarchical structure of the program, making it easier to analyze and process.

58

Parsing Techniques for DSLs

Parsing is a crucial aspect of **DSL design**, determining how the language's syntax is structured and interpreted. Two primary parsing strategies exist: **top-down parsing** and **bottom-up parsing**.

Top-down parsing starts from the highest-level rule in the grammar and recursively breaks it down into smaller components. Recursive descent parsers and LL(k) parsers fall into this category, making them suitable for **simple and human-readable DSLs**.

Bottom-up parsing, such as LR parsing, builds the parse tree from the leaves (tokens) up to the root (high-level expressions). This approach is **more powerful but complex**, often used in DSLs that require sophisticated syntax handling.

Choosing a parsing technique depends on the **DSL's complexity, ease of implementation, and required processing efficiency**. Many modern DSLs rely on parser generators like **ANTLR, PLY (Python Lex-Yacc), or Lark** to automate the process, reducing the burden of manual parser development.

Generating Executable Code from DSLs

Once parsing is complete, the DSL must generate **executable code**. This step involves **translating the AST** into machine instructions, bytecode, or another form of execution. Depending on the DSL's purpose, this can take different approaches:

1. **Direct Execution** – The AST is traversed, and operations are executed on the fly (used in interpreted DSLs).

2. **Intermediate Representation (IR)** – The AST is converted into an IR, which is optimized and then executed (common in compiled DSLs).

3. **Code Generation** – The DSL outputs code in a general-purpose language (e.g., C, Python) that is then compiled.

Efficient **code generation** ensures that the DSL provides high performance while maintaining ease of use. Many DSLs also integrate **Just-In-Time (JIT) compilation** for optimized execution.

A well-designed DSL requires a **robust compilation and parsing process** to ensure efficiency and correctness. Choosing between a **compiler and an interpreter**, implementing **lexical and syntax analysis**, selecting the right **parsing technique**, and optimizing **code generation** are essential steps in developing an effective DSL. A deep understanding of these concepts helps developers build powerful, expressive, and performant DSLs that seamlessly integrate into software ecosystems.

Compiler vs Interpreter in DSLs

Domain-Specific Languages (DSLs) must be **translated into machine-executable instructions**, either through **compilation** or **interpretation**. The choice between the two depends on the DSL's intended use case, performance requirements, and execution environment. This section explores **the fundamental differences** between compiled and interpreted DSLs, their advantages, and practical implementation in Python.

A **compiler** translates an entire DSL program into machine code or an intermediate form before execution. This approach ensures faster runtime performance since execution happens after the translation phase. Examples include SQL query optimizers, which compile queries into optimized execution plans. A compiler-based DSL implementation is ideal for **performance-critical applications**, such as **hardware design** (e.g., VHDL).

An **interpreter**, on the other hand, processes DSL commands line by line, executing them immediately without converting the entire script beforehand. This approach provides flexibility, making it easier to **modify and execute DSL scripts dynamically**. DSLs used in **configuration management** (e.g., Ansible) and **interactive environments** (e.g., Python-based math DSLs) benefit from interpretation.

In many cases, **a hybrid approach** is used, where the DSL is first translated into an **intermediate representation (IR)** before execution. This balances **efficiency and flexibility**, commonly seen in modern scripting DSLs and **Just-In-Time (JIT) compiled DSLs**.

Implementing a Simple Interpreted DSL in Python

A straightforward example of an interpreted DSL in Python involves defining a **command-based** DSL for a hypothetical **arithmetic language**.

```python
class ArithmeticDSL:
    def __init__(self):
        self.variables = {}

    def evaluate(self, command):
        tokens = command.split()
        if tokens[0] == "set":  # Variable assignment
            self.variables[tokens[1]] = int(tokens[2])
        elif tokens[0] == "add":  # Addition operation
            return self.variables.get(tokens[1], 0) + int(tokens[2])
        elif tokens[0] == "mul":  # Multiplication operation
            return self.variables.get(tokens[1], 0) * int(tokens[2])
        else:
            raise ValueError(f"Unknown command: {tokens[0]}")

# Example usage:
dsl = ArithmeticDSL()
dsl.evaluate("set x 10")
print(dsl.evaluate("add x 5"))  # Output: 15
print(dsl.evaluate("mul x 2"))  # Output: 20
```

This simple **interpreter-based DSL** allows users to **define variables and perform basic arithmetic operations** without writing Python code directly.

Compiling a DSL to Python Bytecode

For a **compiled approach**, we can design a DSL that converts commands into **Python bytecode** for execution.

```
import dis

def compile_to_python(command):
    bytecode = compile(command, "<string>", "exec")
    return bytecode

dsl_code = "x = 10\ny = x * 2\nprint(y)"
compiled = compile_to_python(dsl_code)
exec(compiled)
```

Here, the DSL commands are **compiled into Python bytecode** before execution, making them more efficient than interpretation.

DSL designers must **carefully choose between an interpreter and a compiler** based on **execution speed, flexibility, and development complexity**. Interpreted DSLs allow quick iterations and dynamic execution, while compiled DSLs optimize performance. **Hybrid approaches** using **intermediate representations (IR) and JIT compilation** offer the best of both worlds, ensuring DSLs are both **efficient and adaptable** for real-world applications.

Lexical Analysis and Syntax Analysis

Lexical analysis and syntax analysis are **critical components** of DSL compilation and interpretation. They transform raw text input into structured data that a program can understand and process. **Lexical analysis** breaks source code into tokens, while **syntax analysis** ensures that the token sequence follows the DSL's grammatical structure. This section delves into the purpose of these phases and how they are implemented using Python.

Lexical analysis, also known as **tokenization**, is the first stage of processing a DSL. A **lexer** reads the input text, removes unnecessary whitespace, and categorizes words into meaningful components such as **keywords, identifiers, numbers, and operators**. Lexers typically use **regular expressions** or **finite state machines** to recognize patterns in the input text.

Syntax analysis, or **parsing**, is the second stage. It checks whether the tokenized input follows a valid syntax according to the **DSL's grammar rules**. A parser typically **builds an Abstract Syntax Tree (AST)**, a hierarchical representation of the source code, which is later processed to generate executable code or perform evaluations.

Lexical Analysis: Tokenizing a DSL in Python

61

A simple Python lexer can use the **re (regular expressions) module** to tokenize an arithmetic-based DSL.

```python
import re

TOKEN_SPECIFICATION = [
    ("NUMBER", r"\d+"),          # Integer numbers
    ("ADD", r"\+"),              # Addition operator
    ("MUL", r"\*"),              # Multiplication operator
    ("ASSIGN", r"="),            # Assignment operator
    ("IDENTIFIER", r"[a-zA-Z]+"),  # Variable names
    ("WHITESPACE", r"\s+"),      # Ignore whitespace
]

TOKEN_REGEX = "|".join(f"(?P<{name}>{pattern})" for name, pattern in
        TOKEN_SPECIFICATION)

def lexer(code):
    tokens = []
    for match in re.finditer(TOKEN_REGEX, code):
        kind = match.lastgroup
        value = match.group()
        if kind != "WHITESPACE":  # Ignore spaces
            tokens.append((kind, value))
    return tokens

# Example usage:
code = "x = 10 + 5"
print(lexer(code))
```

This lexer tokenizes the input string into **numbers, identifiers, and operators**, preparing it for syntax analysis.

Syntax Analysis: Building a Simple Parser in Python

After tokenization, we need to **validate and structure the tokens**. A **recursive descent parser** is a common method for parsing DSLs. Below is a simple **expression parser** that builds an AST from tokenized input.

```python
class Parser:
    def __init__(self, tokens):
        self.tokens = tokens
        self.position = 0

    def parse(self):
        return self.expression()

    def expression(self):
        left = self.term()
        while self.match("ADD"):
            operator = self.consume()
            right = self.term()
            left = (operator[0], left, right)
        return left

    def term(self):
        token = self.consume()
        return token

    def consume(self):
        token = self.tokens[self.position]
```

```
        self.position += 1
        return token

    def match(self, expected_type):
        return self.position < len(self.tokens) and
            self.tokens[self.position][0] == expected_type

# Example usage:
tokens = lexer("10 + 5")
parser = Parser(tokens)
ast = parser.parse()
print(ast)
```

This parser **constructs an AST** representing an arithmetic expression, which can then be used for further processing, such as evaluation or compilation.

Lexical and syntax analysis are **fundamental to DSL processing**, enabling raw text input to be transformed into structured, machine-readable representations. **Lexical analysis (tokenization) breaks input into components**, while **syntax analysis (parsing) ensures correct structure and builds an AST**. These techniques form the foundation of **compilers and interpreters**, allowing DSLs to execute structured commands effectively.

Parsing Techniques for DSLs

Parsing is a crucial step in processing DSLs, as it determines whether a program's structure adheres to the defined syntax. It takes tokenized input from the lexical analysis stage and organizes it into a hierarchical representation, usually an **Abstract Syntax Tree (AST)** or another structured form. The choice of parsing technique depends on the complexity of the DSL. Common approaches include **recursive descent parsing**, **operator precedence parsing**, and **LR parsing**. This section explores these techniques and demonstrates their implementation in Python.

Recursive Descent Parsing is a **top-down parsing technique** where each grammar rule is implemented as a function. It is straightforward to implement and works well for small DSLs with relatively simple grammar. However, it struggles with ambiguous or left-recursive grammars.

Operator Precedence Parsing is used when expressions involve **operators with different precedence levels** (e.g., multiplication before addition). This method ensures that expressions are evaluated in the correct order.

LR Parsing (Shift-Reduce Parsing) is a **bottom-up approach** widely used in modern compilers. It can handle complex grammars but typically requires specialized tools like **PLY (Python Lex-Yacc)** to implement efficiently.

Implementing Recursive Descent Parsing in Python

We can implement a simple recursive descent parser for arithmetic expressions in a DSL.

```
class Parser:
```

```python
    def __init__(self, tokens):
        self.tokens = tokens
        self.position = 0

    def parse(self):
        return self.expression()

    def expression(self):
        left = self.term()
        while self.match("ADD"):
            operator = self.consume()
            right = self.term()
            left = (operator[0], left, right)
        return left

    def term(self):
        token = self.consume()
        return token

    def consume(self):
        token = self.tokens[self.position]
        self.position += 1
        return token

    def match(self, expected_type):
        return self.position < len(self.tokens) and \
            self.tokens[self.position][0] == expected_type

# Example usage:
tokens = lexer("10 + 5")
parser = Parser(tokens)
ast = parser.parse()
print(ast)
```

This parser constructs an **AST** representing an arithmetic expression, which can be used for evaluation or compilation.

Operator Precedence Parsing

Operator precedence parsing ensures that **multiplication is evaluated before addition**.

```python
class PrecedenceParser:
    def __init__(self, tokens):
        self.tokens = tokens
        self.position = 0

    def parse(self):
        return self.expression()

    def expression(self, precedence=0):
        left = self.term()
        while self.match("ADD", "MUL"):
            operator = self.consume()
            right = self.term()
            left = (operator[0], left, right)
        return left

    def term(self):
        token = self.consume()
        return token

    def consume(self):
        token = self.tokens[self.position]
```

```
        self.position += 1
        return token

    def match(self, *expected_types):
        return self.position < len(self.tokens) and
            self.tokens[self.position][0] in expected_types

# Example usage:
tokens = lexer("10 + 5 * 2")  # Expected to evaluate as 10 + (5 * 2)
parser = PrecedenceParser(tokens)
ast = parser.parse()
print(ast)
```

This ensures **multiplication takes precedence over addition**, producing a correctly structured AST.

Parsing is the **core mechanism that transforms tokens into structured representations**, making execution possible. Recursive descent parsing is simple but limited, while operator precedence parsing ensures correct mathematical evaluation. More advanced DSLs may require **LR parsing** using Python tools like **PLY**. Selecting the right parsing technique ensures a DSL is both efficient and maintainable.

Generating Executable Code from DSLs

Once a DSL has been **tokenized and parsed**, the next step is to generate executable code. This involves converting the structured representation—usually an **Abstract Syntax Tree (AST)**—into machine-executable instructions. This step is essential for both **interpreted** and **compiled DSLs**, as it enables the DSL to execute meaningful operations. Depending on the DSL's purpose, code generation can take several forms, such as **direct interpretation, translation to another language, or compilation into machine code**.

For interpreted DSLs, the AST is directly traversed and evaluated without producing a separate executable file. This approach is **simpler and allows dynamic execution** but may be slower since the program is processed at runtime. For compiled DSLs, the AST is transformed into **another programming language or bytecode**, allowing optimized execution. Some DSLs also generate **virtual machine (VM) instructions**, which are then executed by a custom runtime.

Interpreting a DSL from AST Execution

A simple way to execute a DSL is through **AST traversal**, where each node in the AST is evaluated recursively. Here is a Python interpreter that executes arithmetic expressions from a DSL:

```
class Interpreter:
    def evaluate(self, node):
        if isinstance(node, tuple):
            operator, left, right = node
            left_val = self.evaluate(left)
            right_val = self.evaluate(right)
            if operator == "ADD":
                return left_val + right_val
            elif operator == "MUL":
```

```
                return left_val * right_val
        else:
            return int(node[1])  # Convert number token to integer

# Example usage:
tokens = lexer("10 + 5 * 2")
parser = PrecedenceParser(tokens)
ast = parser.parse()
interpreter = Interpreter()
result = interpreter.evaluate(ast)
print(result)  # Output: 20
```

This interpreter walks the AST, evaluates operations in the correct order, and returns the final result.

Translating DSL Code to Python

Another common approach is **translating DSL code into a general-purpose language like Python** for execution. This method is useful when a DSL needs to **leverage an existing language runtime** while maintaining domain-specific syntax.

```
class CodeGenerator:
    def generate(self, node):
        if isinstance(node, tuple):
            operator, left, right = node
            left_expr = self.generate(left)
            right_expr = self.generate(right)
            if operator == "ADD":
                return f"({left_expr} + {right_expr})"
            elif operator == "MUL":
                return f"({left_expr} * {right_expr})"
        else:
            return node[1]  # Return number token

# Example usage:
tokens = lexer("10 + 5 * 2")
parser = PrecedenceParser(tokens)
ast = parser.parse()
generator = CodeGenerator()
python_code = generator.generate(ast)
exec_result = eval(python_code)
print(exec_result)  # Output: 20
```

This method **converts DSL expressions into Python code**, allowing them to be evaluated using Python's execution environment.

Compiling DSL Code to Bytecode

For more performance-driven DSLs, the AST can be compiled into **bytecode for execution on a virtual machine**. This is commonly used in languages like Python, where code is compiled into **Python bytecode (.pyc files)** before execution.

Using Python's built-in compile() function, we can convert a string into executable bytecode:

```
dsl_code = "10 + 5 * 2"
python_code = generator.generate(parser.parse())
```

```
bytecode = compile(python_code, "<string>", "eval")
print(eval(bytecode))   # Output: 20
```

This approach improves performance by **avoiding repeated parsing** and allowing precompiled DSL programs to be executed efficiently.

Code generation is the **final step in the DSL processing pipeline**, transforming parsed structures into executable operations. Interpretation provides flexibility but can be slower, while translation to a general-purpose language enables integration with existing platforms. Compilation to bytecode improves execution speed and enables advanced optimizations, making DSLs **powerful tools for specialized domains**.

Module 6:
Challenges and Limitations of DSLs

Domain-Specific Languages (DSLs) offer powerful advantages, but they also come with challenges that developers must address. This module examines the primary limitations of DSLs, including scalability and maintainability issues, the difficulty of adapting to evolving domains, limitations in tool support and ecosystem development, and common pitfalls in DSL design. Understanding these challenges ensures that DSLs remain effective and sustainable in real-world applications. This module explores each challenge in detail, providing insights into how DSLs can be designed and maintained to overcome inherent limitations while still delivering their intended benefits.

Scalability and Maintainability Concerns

DSLs are often designed for **specific, well-defined problem domains**, which can make them difficult to scale beyond their initial scope. Unlike general-purpose languages, which have broad applicability, DSLs may require constant revisions and extensions as the domain evolves. This can lead to **technical debt** if the language design does not anticipate future changes. Additionally, DSLs may lack robust refactoring tools, making long-term maintenance challenging. Organizations adopting DSLs must ensure that their architecture is **modular, extensible, and well-documented**, allowing for gradual improvements without compromising stability. Without careful planning, DSLs risk becoming obsolete as requirements change.

Handling Evolving Domains

Many DSLs are designed based on **current domain knowledge**, but industries and technologies continuously evolve. A DSL that works well today may become inadequate as new requirements emerge. Unlike general-purpose languages that have extensive ecosystems supporting backward compatibility, DSLs may struggle with **versioning and migration issues**. If a DSL lacks a clear upgrade path, existing codebases may become **locked into an outdated version**, making transitions costly and complex. A well-designed DSL must incorporate **mechanisms for extensibility**, such as modular grammar definitions or flexible syntax rules, to ensure that it can adapt as the domain expands and evolves over time.

Tool Support and Ecosystem Limitations

One of the biggest barriers to DSL adoption is the lack of **mature tooling and ecosystem support**. Unlike established programming languages, which benefit from **IDEs, debuggers, linters, and performance profilers**, DSLs often have limited toolchains. Developers may struggle with debugging, testing, or integrating DSLs into **existing software development workflows**. This lack of support can discourage adoption, as organizations prefer technologies with **strong community backing and established best practices**. To mitigate this challenge, DSL developers should consider leveraging existing language infrastructure, such as **embedding DSLs within host languages or generating code that integrates with mainstream development tools**.

Overcoming Common Pitfalls in DSL Design

Designing an effective DSL is a complex task that requires balancing **expressiveness, usability, and performance**. Common mistakes include **overcomplicating the syntax**, making the DSL too rigid, or failing to align with user expectations. If a DSL is too verbose, it may be **cumbersome to use**, reducing developer productivity. Conversely, if it is too abstract, it may **lack clarity and become difficult to debug**. Additionally, performance considerations must be addressed, as some DSL implementations introduce **significant overhead**. To overcome these pitfalls, DSL designers should focus on **usability testing, clear documentation, and iterative refinement** based on user feedback.

While DSLs provide specialized solutions for domain-specific problems, they also introduce unique challenges. Scalability and maintainability require careful planning, while evolving domains necessitate **flexible language structures**. Tool support and ecosystem limitations can hinder adoption, and poor design choices can impact usability. By addressing these concerns proactively, developers can ensure that DSLs remain practical, adaptable, and efficient for long-term use.

Scalability and Maintainability Concerns

Scalability and maintainability are critical challenges in the design and evolution of Domain-Specific Languages (DSLs). Since DSLs are created to address highly specialized problems, they often lack the **generalized structures** that enable traditional programming languages to scale across multiple domains. As the complexity of a domain grows, a poorly designed DSL can become **unmanageable**, requiring constant modifications to accommodate new features. Additionally, maintaining a DSL involves more than just **syntax and parsing updates**; it requires ensuring compatibility with evolving **software architectures, toolchains, and performance expectations**.

One major issue with DSL scalability is **code complexity growth**. As more features are added, the DSL may require increasingly complex **parsing rules, execution logic, and integration mechanisms**. Without a well-structured design, a DSL may become **bloated and difficult to optimize**. For instance, a DSL initially designed for basic financial calculations may need to expand into risk assessment or compliance monitoring, leading to exponential growth in syntax rules. If not managed carefully, this growth can render the DSL too complex to use effectively.

To mitigate scalability issues, DSLs should incorporate **modular design principles**, allowing different components of the language to evolve independently. For example, instead of **embedding all features into the core language**, designers can use **extensible**

69

grammars or plugins that enable additional functionality **without disrupting existing syntax**. Below is an example of how modular DSL commands can be handled in Python using **function dispatching**:

```python
class DSLInterpreter:
    def __init__(self):
        self.commands = {
            "ADD": self.add,
            "MUL": self.multiply,
        }

    def add(self, a, b):
        return a + b

    def multiply(self, a, b):
        return a * b

    def execute(self, command, *args):
        if command in self.commands:
            return self.commands[command](*args)
        else:
            raise ValueError(f"Unknown command: {command}")

# Example usage
dsl = DSLInterpreter()
print(dsl.execute("ADD", 10, 5))   # Output: 15
print(dsl.execute("MUL", 3, 4))    # Output: 12
```

This approach ensures **new commands can be added dynamically** without modifying existing code, improving both scalability and maintainability.

Another key factor affecting DSL maintainability is **documentation and versioning**. As DSLs evolve, maintaining **backward compatibility** is essential to prevent breaking existing implementations. This can be achieved through **versioned syntax parsers** that support multiple iterations of a DSL, allowing developers to transition gradually rather than facing sudden incompatibilities.

Maintaining a DSL also involves **robust testing strategies**, as even minor syntax changes can introduce unexpected behaviors. Developers should implement **automated unit tests** for DSL constructs to ensure correctness across different versions. The following example shows a simple **unit test** for a DSL function:

```python
import unittest

class TestDSL(unittest.TestCase):
    def test_addition(self):
        dsl = DSLInterpreter()
        self.assertEqual(dsl.execute("ADD", 2, 3), 5)

if __name__ == "__main__":
    unittest.main()
```

This ensures that fundamental DSL functions remain intact, reducing maintenance overhead.

The **scalability and maintainability** of DSLs depend on modular design, clear versioning strategies, and robust testing frameworks. Without these safeguards, a DSL can become difficult to manage, ultimately limiting its long-term viability.

Handling Evolving Domains

One of the most significant challenges in Domain-Specific Language (DSL) development is handling evolving domains. Unlike general-purpose languages, which have broad applicability, DSLs are designed to address **specific problems within a particular domain**. However, domains do not remain static—industries change, regulations shift, and new methodologies emerge. A DSL that does not adapt to these changes risks becoming obsolete. Ensuring that a DSL remains relevant requires careful **design, extensibility, and maintainability** strategies.

A major challenge in evolving domains is **future-proofing the language**. If a DSL is designed with rigid syntax and semantics, it may not accommodate new concepts or evolving best practices. For example, a DSL for **data pipeline automation** may initially support only batch processing but later need to incorporate **real-time streaming capabilities**. If the DSL was not designed with extensibility in mind, it could require a complete rewrite. One way to avoid this issue is by adopting **modular language components** that allow for incremental expansion.

A practical approach is to implement a **dynamic command registration system** in Python, allowing new features to be added **without modifying core DSL logic**. Below is an example of how a DSL interpreter can dynamically **register new functions** as domain requirements evolve:

```python
class DSLInterpreter:
    def __init__(self):
        self.commands = {}

    def register_command(self, name, function):
        self.commands[name] = function

    def execute(self, command, *args):
        if command in self.commands:
            return self.commands[command](*args)
        else:
            raise ValueError(f"Unknown command: {command}")

# Example usage: dynamically adding new functions
dsl = DSLInterpreter()
dsl.register_command("SQUARE", lambda x: x * x)
dsl.register_command("CUBE", lambda x: x * x * x)

print(dsl.execute("SQUARE", 4))  # Output: 16
print(dsl.execute("CUBE", 3))    # Output: 27
```

This design enables **seamless expansion of the DSL** as new domain requirements arise. Developers can introduce **new commands without modifying existing code**, reducing maintenance overhead.

Another approach to handling evolving domains is **ensuring backward compatibility**. A common mistake in DSL development is breaking existing syntax when adding new features. To prevent this, versioned parsing techniques should be adopted. For instance, a DSL could support multiple versions by detecting which syntax rules apply to a given input:

```python
class VersionedDSL:
    def __init__(self):
        self.versions = {
            "1.0": self.parse_v1,
            "2.0": self.parse_v2
        }

    def parse_v1(self, command):
        return f"Processing V1 command: {command}"

    def parse_v2(self, command):
        return f"Processing V2 command: {command} with new syntax"

    def execute(self, version, command):
        if version in self.versions:
            return self.versions[version](command)
        else:
            raise ValueError(f"Unsupported DSL version: {version}")

# Example usage
dsl = VersionedDSL()
print(dsl.execute("1.0", "LOAD DATA"))  # Output: Processing V1 command: LOAD
        DATA
print(dsl.execute("2.0", "LOAD DATA"))  # Output: Processing V2 command: LOAD
        DATA with new syntax
```

This technique ensures that older programs written in previous DSL versions continue to function correctly while allowing **newer features to be integrated smoothly**.

Moreover, **maintaining extensibility through modular design** allows DSLs to remain adaptable. One way to achieve this is through **plugin-based architectures**, where new capabilities can be added as separate modules rather than modifying the DSL core. In Python, this can be implemented by **loading external scripts dynamically**:

```python
import importlib

class DSLWithPlugins:
    def load_plugin(self, module_name):
        module = importlib.import_module(module_name)
        return module.process()

# Example usage (assuming 'plugin.py' contains a 'process' function)
dsl = DSLWithPlugins()
result = dsl.load_plugin("plugin")  # Dynamically loads new functionality
print(result)
```

By supporting external plugins, a DSL can be extended **without requiring internal code changes**, making it **future-proof and adaptable** to an evolving domain.

Handling evolving domains in DSL design requires **flexibility, extensibility, and backward compatibility**. A rigid DSL will quickly become outdated, forcing costly rewrites. By using **dynamic command registration, versioned parsing, and plugin-based architectures**, DSL developers can ensure that their languages remain **adaptable, scalable, and relevant** even as industries and technologies continue to evolve.

Tool Support and Ecosystem Limitations

A critical factor in the success of any Domain-Specific Language (DSL) is the availability of **tools and ecosystem support**. Unlike general-purpose programming languages, which have well-established development environments, compilers, and debugging tools, many DSLs suffer from **limited tooling and fragmented ecosystems**. This limitation can hinder adoption, reduce productivity, and make maintenance difficult for developers working with the language.

One of the major challenges in DSL development is the **lack of robust integrated development environments (IDEs)**. Most general-purpose languages like Python, Java, and C++ benefit from advanced IDEs with **syntax highlighting, code completion, and debugging capabilities**. However, a custom DSL often lacks such support, forcing developers to rely on **text editors with minimal syntax awareness**. To mitigate this, DSL creators can **integrate with existing IDEs** using language plugins. For example, in Python, DSL syntax highlighting can be added to **Visual Studio Code (VS Code) or JetBrains IntelliJ** using TextMate grammar definitions.

Another major ecosystem limitation is **the absence of standard debugging tools**. Developers working with DSLs often face challenges when diagnosing issues, as many DSLs do not have **error messages or stack traces** similar to traditional programming languages. A potential solution is implementing a **custom error-handling system** that provides **meaningful error messages**. Below is a Python-based DSL error handler:

```
class DSLError(Exception):
    pass

class DSLInterpreter:
    def execute(self, command):
        try:
            if command == "INVALID":
                raise DSLError("Syntax Error: Unrecognized command")
            return f"Executing: {command}"
        except DSLError as e:
            return f"DSL Error: {str(e)}"

# Example usage
dsl = DSLInterpreter()
print(dsl.execute("VALID_COMMAND"))  # Output: Executing: VALID_COMMAND
print(dsl.execute("INVALID"))  # Output: DSL Error: Syntax Error: Unrecognized
        command
```

By incorporating **custom error handling**, DSLs can provide **developer-friendly debugging**, making it easier to identify mistakes and enhance usability.

Additionally, **performance monitoring and profiling tools** are often lacking in DSL ecosystems. While general-purpose languages have profiling tools such as **cProfile in**

Python, DSLs rarely come with built-in performance analysis features. A DSL can integrate profiling tools by **embedding a timing function within the execution process**, as shown below:

```python
import time

class DSLProfiler:
    def execute(self, command):
        start_time = time.time()
        result = f"Executing: {command}"
        end_time = time.time()
        return result, f"Execution Time: {end_time - start_time:.5f} seconds"

# Example usage
dsl = DSLProfiler()
print(dsl.execute("PROCESS DATA"))
```

This simple profiling approach provides insights into execution time, helping developers **identify bottlenecks** in their DSL implementations.

Another key ecosystem limitation is the **lack of standard libraries and frameworks**. General-purpose languages provide **rich ecosystems** of reusable libraries for tasks like data processing, networking, and UI development. In contrast, many DSLs lack **pre-built functionality**, forcing developers to **reinvent basic features**. One solution is to design DSLs with **interoperability** in mind, allowing them to leverage existing libraries from **Python or other host languages**.

For example, a DSL designed for **financial modeling** can integrate Python's **NumPy library** for mathematical computations:

```python
import numpy as np

class FinancialDSL:
    def calculate_interest(self, principal, rate, time):
        return principal * np.power((1 + rate), time)

# Example usage
dsl = FinancialDSL()
print(dsl.calculate_interest(1000, 0.05, 5))  # Output: 1276.28
```

By embedding general-purpose language features, DSLs can benefit from **existing tools and ecosystems**, making them more practical and appealing to developers.

Tool support and ecosystem limitations are among the biggest hurdles DSLs face in gaining widespread adoption. The lack of **IDEs, debugging tools, performance monitoring, and standard libraries** can significantly hinder productivity. However, by integrating with **existing development environments, implementing custom debugging tools, and supporting interoperability**, DSL creators can enhance usability and ensure long-term viability.

Overcoming Common Pitfalls in DSL Design

74

Designing a Domain-Specific Language (DSL) comes with several challenges that can lead to poor adoption, difficult maintenance, and inefficiency if not addressed properly. Many DSL projects fail due to **unclear scope, poor usability, lack of extensibility, and inefficient execution models**. Overcoming these pitfalls requires careful planning, balancing simplicity with power, and ensuring the DSL integrates well with existing ecosystems.

One of the most common pitfalls is **overcomplicating the language**. DSLs should be **concise and intuitive**, providing a natural way for users in a specific domain to express solutions. Overloading the language with **excessive syntax rules** can make it as complex as a general-purpose language, defeating its purpose. A good approach is to design the DSL **closely to the domain's natural expressions**. Consider a configuration DSL for a web server:

```
server {
    port 8080
    root "/var/www"
}
```

This structure is simple and easy to read, resembling **Nginx configuration syntax**. However, if we introduce complex syntax, it defeats the purpose:

```
server {
    define_port(8080);
    set_root_directory("/var/www");
}
```

To avoid this mistake, DSL designers must **strike a balance between expressiveness and simplicity**.

Another major pitfall is **lack of extensibility**. A DSL that is too rigid can quickly become obsolete when new requirements arise. For example, if a reporting DSL only supports CSV output, but users later need JSON, they may abandon the DSL entirely. A better approach is **providing extensibility hooks** so new features can be added without modifying the core language. Consider this Python-based reporting DSL:

```
class ReportDSL:
    def __init__(self):
        self.data = []

    def add_entry(self, entry):
        self.data.append(entry)

    def generate(self, format="csv"):
        if format == "csv":
            return ",".join(self.data)
        elif format == "json":
            import json
            return json.dumps(self.data)
        else:
            raise ValueError("Unsupported format")

# Usage
report = ReportDSL()
```

```
report.add_entry("Item 1")
report.add_entry("Item 2")
print(report.generate("json"))  # Output: ["Item 1", "Item 2"]
```

By allowing new formats like **JSON, XML, or even database storage**, the DSL remains **relevant and adaptable**.

Another frequent issue is **poor performance optimization**. Many DSLs are built as interpreters, which can be slow for complex tasks. Without **optimization techniques** such as **caching, just-in-time (JIT) compilation, or precompilation**, execution times can be prohibitively high. Suppose a DSL for image processing must **apply filters** to a large dataset. Instead of interpreting commands one by one, precompiling them can **significantly boost performance**.

```
import numba

@numba.jit(nopython=True)
def apply_filter(image):
    return image * 0.5  # Example: Darkening an image

# Optimized execution
```

Using **Numba's JIT compilation**, DSL execution can be accelerated by **compiling functions at runtime**, making them nearly as fast as natively compiled code.

Another pitfall is **poor error handling**. Many DSLs provide **vague error messages** that make debugging difficult. Users may encounter messages like:

```
Syntax Error
```

Without context, this error does not help users understand what went wrong. A better approach is to provide **detailed feedback**:

```
class DSLParser:
    def parse(self, command):
        if not command.startswith("CMD"):
            raise SyntaxError(f"Invalid command: {command}")

# Usage
parser = DSLParser()
try:
    parser.parse("INVALID_CMD")
except SyntaxError as e:
    print(f"Error: {e}")  # Output: Error: Invalid command: INVALID_CMD
```

By offering **descriptive error messages**, DSL users can **quickly diagnose issues** and avoid frustration.

Finally, **failing to integrate with existing tools and workflows** can limit a DSL's usability. Many DSLs operate in isolation, making it difficult for users to **combine them with existing software ecosystems**. A solution is to design DSLs that can **interact with general-purpose languages** like Python. For example, a DSL for **scientific computation** can expose a Python API:

76

```
from my_dsl import compute

result = compute("integrate x^2 from 0 to 10")
print(result)
```

This integration allows developers to use the DSL **without abandoning familiar environments**.

Avoiding common pitfalls in DSL design requires careful planning in **simplicity, extensibility, performance, error handling, and interoperability**. By ensuring a DSL is **easy to use, adaptable to new requirements, optimized for speed, and compatible with existing tools**, developers can create **sustainable, high-value DSLs** that remain useful over time.

Part 2:

Examples and Applications of Domain Specific Languages

Domain-Specific Languages (DSLs) have gained widespread adoption across multiple fields, enhancing efficiency and domain-driven problem-solving. This part explores various applications of DSLs, showcasing how they improve productivity and streamline development. From software engineering and scientific computing to game development, finance, networking, and artificial intelligence, this section presents real-world examples and case studies of DSLs in action. By understanding these applications, readers will develop insight into how DSLs are tailored for different industries, their impact on workflow automation, and the specialized tools that have emerged to optimize domain-specific tasks effectively.

DSLs in Software Engineering

DSLs play a crucial role in software engineering by simplifying complex tasks through targeted abstractions. Web development frameworks often include internal DSLs that enhance productivity, such as Ruby on Rails' ActiveRecord for database interactions. Similarly, DSLs for database query languages, like SQL, provide a structured way to manipulate and retrieve data efficiently. Several case studies highlight how DSLs improve maintainability and reduce boilerplate code in engineering projects. Best practices in DSL design focus on balancing expressiveness with simplicity, ensuring the language remains accessible while fulfilling software development needs without unnecessary complexity or performance trade-offs.

DSLs for Scientific Computing

Scientific computing relies on DSLs to handle mathematical modeling, simulations, and high-performance computing tasks. These DSLs optimize complex calculations, improving accuracy and reducing development time. Languages like MATLAB and Mathematica are prime examples of DSLs used for numerical analysis and symbolic computation. In high-performance computing, DSLs help researchers implement domain-specific algorithms that leverage parallelization. Integration with research workflows is a key advantage, allowing scientists to automate simulations, conduct large-scale experiments, and generate reproducible results with minimal manual intervention. This module demonstrates how DSLs accelerate scientific discovery while ensuring computational efficiency.

DSLs in Game Development

Game development benefits from DSLs that facilitate scripting, game logic, and interactive content creation. Game engines incorporate custom DSLs like UnrealScript and UnityScript to streamline development. These DSLs provide an intuitive way to define gameplay mechanics, character behaviors, and event-driven interactions. Handling game logic with DSLs improves maintainability, as non-programmers such as game designers can contribute to scripting without extensive coding knowledge. Performance considerations play a significant role, as poorly optimized DSLs may introduce latency. This module examines how DSLs contribute to game development workflows while maintaining performance efficiency.

DSLs in Finance and Business

Financial modeling and business process automation heavily rely on DSLs to simplify complex calculations and regulatory compliance. Algorithmic trading platforms use DSLs to specify trading strategies, reducing execution latency. In quantitative finance, DSLs enable risk analysis and portfolio management. Business process modeling tools utilize DSLs to define workflows, increasing automation and operational efficiency. These custom languages enhance decision-making in corporate environments, improving accuracy and transparency in financial and business applications. Case studies illustrate how financial institutions leverage DSLs to achieve greater scalability and data-driven insights.

DSLs in Networking and Security

Network administrators and security professionals utilize DSLs to manage configurations and enforce security policies. Languages like Cisco's IOS command syntax and OpenFlow DSLs streamline network automation, reducing manual errors. Custom languages in cybersecurity enhance threat detection and mitigation strategies, allowing organizations to implement real-time security policies efficiently. Automation plays a critical role in network management, with DSLs defining rule-based policies for access control and traffic monitoring. Secure software development benefits from DSLs that enforce coding standards, minimizing vulnerabilities. This module explores real-world case studies of DSLs in network administration and cybersecurity.

DSLs in Artificial Intelligence and Machine Learning

DSLs are increasingly used in artificial intelligence (AI) and machine learning (ML) to define models, preprocess data, and optimize algorithms. Languages such as TensorFlow and Keras act as DSLs for neural network specification, simplifying the design of complex AI architectures. In natural language processing (NLP), DSLs facilitate linguistic rule definitions and text analysis. Custom DSLs for AI problem-solving enable domain experts to configure machine learning pipelines efficiently. Integrating DSLs with AI frameworks enhances accessibility, allowing researchers and engineers to develop sophisticated models without deep programming expertise. This module examines the growing influence of DSLs in AI and ML.

This part provides a comprehensive exploration of DSL applications across diverse industries. Readers will gain valuable insights into how DSLs enhance productivity, simplify problem-solving, and automate workflows in specialized domains.

Module 7:

DSLs in Software Engineering

Domain-Specific Languages (DSLs) play a crucial role in software engineering, enabling developers to work with higher levels of abstraction tailored to specific tasks. This module explores the practical application of DSLs in web development, database query languages, and engineering fields. It also examines real-world case studies that highlight the success of DSLs in software engineering and outlines best practices for designing effective engineering-focused DSLs. By understanding how DSLs contribute to software development efficiency, maintainability, and expressiveness, developers can leverage these specialized languages to improve productivity and enhance software quality.

Using DSLs in Web Development

The web development landscape benefits significantly from DSLs, as they simplify tasks such as **templating, styling, and routing**. Many frameworks and technologies incorporate DSLs to streamline web development. For example, templating engines allow developers to define HTML structures dynamically with **domain-specific syntax** that improves code readability and maintainability. Similarly, **CSS preprocessors like Sass** introduce DSL-like capabilities for managing styles efficiently. Web frameworks such as **Ruby on Rails** leverage DSLs for defining **routes, database models, and application configurations** in a declarative manner, reducing boilerplate code and improving productivity. This section discusses how DSLs contribute to **rapid web application development** by providing intuitive and specialized syntax for handling web-related concerns.

DSLs for Database Query Languages

Database query languages are among the most widespread and impactful DSLs in software engineering. Structured Query Language (SQL) is a classic example of a DSL designed for **data retrieval, manipulation, and management**. While SQL itself is widely used, modern database systems introduce **embedded DSLs** within programming languages to improve query expressiveness and integration. Object-Relational Mapping (ORM) frameworks, such as **SQLAlchemy in Python** and **ActiveRecord in Ruby**, provide DSL-like interfaces to abstract database interactions. These DSLs allow developers to work with database records using **intuitive, high-level constructs** instead of writing raw SQL queries. This section explores how DSLs facilitate **seamless database interactions**, enhancing data management capabilities in software engineering.

Case Studies of Engineering DSLs

Successful DSLs in software engineering demonstrate the power of specialized languages in solving complex problems efficiently. Case studies such as **Gradle for build automation, Terraform for infrastructure as code (IaC), and MATLAB for scientific computing** highlight the effectiveness of DSLs in their respective domains. Gradle provides a DSL for configuring software builds declaratively, offering flexibility and automation. Terraform, a widely used DSL in DevOps, allows developers to define infrastructure through code, enabling reproducibility and scalability. MATLAB's DSL-like capabilities simplify numerical computing and algorithm development. This section presents case studies that illustrate **real-world DSL applications and their impact on software engineering workflows**.

Best Practices in Software Engineering DSL Design

Designing effective DSLs in software engineering requires adhering to **best practices that ensure usability, maintainability, and extensibility**. A well-designed DSL should be **intuitive, domain-relevant, and capable of reducing complexity** while enhancing developer productivity. Important considerations include choosing between **internal and external DSLs**, balancing **expressiveness with simplicity**, and ensuring **seamless integration** with existing tools and workflows. Moreover, robust **error handling, clear documentation, and comprehensive tooling support** are critical for DSL adoption. This section outlines best practices that guide **software engineers and language designers** in creating DSLs that effectively serve their intended purpose and stand the test of time.

DSLs are integral to modern software engineering, providing targeted solutions that enhance development efficiency. Whether in **web development, database management, or specialized engineering fields**, DSLs simplify complex processes and improve maintainability. By studying real-world examples and following **best practices in DSL design**, developers can harness the power of domain-specific languages to build more efficient and scalable software solutions.

Using DSLs in Web Development

Domain-Specific Languages (DSLs) have revolutionized web development by enabling concise, readable, and maintainable abstractions. Web applications often require structured data representation, templating, styling, and routing—all areas where DSLs excel. Many popular web frameworks incorporate DSLs to simplify these tasks. This section explores how DSLs enhance web development by reducing boilerplate code, improving readability, and making web applications more maintainable. By leveraging the power of DSLs, developers can build **dynamic web applications** with minimal effort while ensuring better structure and maintainability.

One of the most well-known DSLs in web development is **HTML**, which defines a structured way to describe web content. Although often considered a markup language, HTML is a **text-based DSL** specifically designed for the web. Similarly, **CSS** is a declarative DSL that dictates the styling of web pages. However, modern web development has introduced more powerful DSLs, such as **Sass and LESS**, which extend CSS with features like variables, nesting, and mixins. These tools allow for more expressive and maintainable styling definitions, making it easier to manage complex stylesheets.

Another example of a DSL in web development is **templating engines**, which provide a simplified syntax for generating dynamic HTML content. **Jinja2**, used in Python web frameworks like Flask and Django, is an internal DSL that allows developers to write cleaner, more modular templates. Below is an example of a Jinja2 template used in a Flask application:

```python
from flask import Flask, render_template

app = Flask(__name__)

@app.route("/")
def home():
    return render_template("index.html", title="Welcome", message="Hello from
            DSL-powered templating!")

if __name__ == "__main__":
    app.run(debug=True)
```

With a corresponding Jinja2 template (index.html):

```html
<!DOCTYPE html>
<html>
<head>
    <title>{{ title }}</title>
</head>
<body>
    <h1>{{ message }}</h1>
</body>
</html>
```

This demonstrates how a DSL simplifies the separation of logic from presentation in web applications. Instead of embedding Python code directly in HTML, Jinja2 allows for clean, readable templates that dynamically render content.

Routing is another area where DSLs play a crucial role. Web frameworks such as **Ruby on Rails** and **Flask** use DSLs to define routes concisely. In Flask, routes are specified using Python decorators, which function as an internal DSL:

```python
@app.route('/user/<name>')
def user_profile(name):
    return f"Welcome, {name}!"
```

This internal DSL abstracts the complexity of URL handling, making web application routing intuitive. Similarly, Ruby on Rails employs a declarative DSL for defining application routes:

```ruby
Rails.application.routes.draw do
  get 'users/:id', to: 'users#show'
end
```

Such DSLs improve code readability and reduce development time by eliminating boilerplate code.

Web development also benefits from DSLs in **GraphQL**, which provides a declarative query language for APIs. Unlike REST, GraphQL allows developers to specify exactly the data they need, leading to efficient data fetching and reduced over-fetching. A simple GraphQL query looks like this:

```
query {
  user(id: "123") {
    name
    email
    posts {
      title
      content
    }
  }
}
```

GraphQL's **text-based DSL** makes API interactions more expressive and efficient compared to traditional RESTful approaches.

DSLs enhance web development by providing **structured, expressive, and maintainable** solutions for templating, styling, routing, and API querying. From **HTML, CSS preprocessors, Jinja2, Flask routing, GraphQL,** to **Ruby on Rails DSLs**, these domain-specific languages streamline web development, making code more readable and reducing complexity. Understanding and leveraging DSLs in web applications leads to more efficient and scalable software solutions.

DSLs for Database Query Languages

Database query languages are among the most widely used domain-specific languages (DSLs), designed specifically for interacting with databases efficiently. Structured Query Language (SQL) is the most prominent DSL for relational databases, providing a declarative way to define, manipulate, and query data. Unlike general-purpose programming languages, SQL focuses solely on data retrieval and management, making it an essential tool for database-driven applications. Many modern programming languages integrate DSLs for database interaction, allowing developers to write database queries in a more idiomatic and expressive way within their codebases.

SQL operates as a **declarative DSL**, meaning developers specify *what* they want rather than *how* the database should execute the query. For example, retrieving user information from a table is expressed concisely in SQL:

```
SELECT name, email FROM users WHERE age > 25 ORDER BY name ASC;
```

This query efficiently retrieves names and emails of users older than 25, sorting them alphabetically. However, writing raw SQL queries directly in applications can lead to security risks like SQL injection and maintenance challenges. To address this, many

83

programming languages incorporate **internal DSLs** for database interactions, allowing developers to construct queries safely using built-in abstractions.

Python DSLs for Database Queries

Python supports various internal DSLs for database interactions, such as **SQLAlchemy**, an object-relational mapper (ORM) that abstracts SQL queries while maintaining expressiveness. Instead of writing raw SQL, developers use Python's DSL syntax to construct queries programmatically:

```
from sqlalchemy import create_engine, Column, Integer, String
from sqlalchemy.orm import sessionmaker, declarative_base

Base = declarative_base()

class User(Base):
    __tablename__ = 'users'
    id = Column(Integer, primary_key=True)
    name = Column(String)
    email = Column(String)

engine = create_engine("sqlite:///users.db")
Session = sessionmaker(bind=engine)
session = Session()

# Query using SQLAlchemy's DSL
users = session.query(User).filter(User.age > 25).order_by(User.name).all()
```

This example demonstrates how SQLAlchemy provides a **fluent, expressive API** that abstracts SQL's complexity while maintaining performance and safety. By using an internal DSL, developers gain **type safety, composability, and security** when interacting with databases.

NoSQL and Graph-Based DSLs

While SQL is a dominant DSL for relational databases, NoSQL databases introduce their own DSLs tailored to specific data models. **MongoDB**, for instance, uses a JSON-based query DSL rather than SQL. Instead of writing SELECT statements, queries are structured using JSON-like objects in Python:

```
from pymongo import MongoClient

client = MongoClient("mongodb://localhost:27017/")
db = client["mydatabase"]
collection = db["users"]

# Querying users older than 25
users = collection.find({"age": {"$gt": 25}}).sort("name", 1)
```

This MongoDB DSL provides a structured way to interact with document-oriented databases, enabling flexible schema designs and efficient querying for hierarchical or unstructured data.

Another important DSL in the database world is **GraphQL**, which allows querying graph-based data structures efficiently. Unlike SQL, GraphQL enables clients to specify precisely the data they need, avoiding over-fetching or under-fetching:

```
query = """
{
  user(id: "123") {
    name
    email
    posts {
      title
      content
    }
  }
}
"""
```

GraphQL acts as a **text-based DSL** that allows complex, nested data retrieval in a concise manner, making it highly useful for APIs that interact with multiple data sources.

DSLs for database query languages enhance data management by offering **structured, expressive, and safe** ways to interact with databases. SQL remains the gold standard for relational databases, while Python DSLs like SQLAlchemy and NoSQL query languages like MongoDB's JSON-based syntax offer powerful alternatives. GraphQL further extends the DSL paradigm by providing efficient and flexible data retrieval for modern applications. Understanding these DSLs helps developers build robust, scalable, and maintainable database-driven systems.

Case Studies of Engineering DSLs

Domain-Specific Languages (DSLs) are widely used in engineering disciplines to simplify complex computations, enhance productivity, and ensure correctness. Many industries, including embedded systems, robotics, and scientific computing, rely on DSLs to express domain-specific concerns efficiently. In this section, we examine real-world case studies of engineering DSLs that have significantly impacted software development and automation.

MATLAB as an Engineering DSL

MATLAB is a well-known DSL used in engineering, particularly in signal processing, numerical computing, and control systems. It provides a high-level, expressive syntax tailored for matrix operations and algorithm development. MATLAB's built-in functions and toolboxes allow engineers to perform complex calculations with minimal effort. For instance, solving a system of linear equations in MATLAB is straightforward:

```
A = [2, -1; 3, 4];
B = [1; 6];
X = A\B;
disp(X);
```

This example demonstrates MATLAB's DSL capabilities by providing concise syntax for matrix computations. Unlike general-purpose languages, MATLAB abstracts low-level numerical operations, making it easier for engineers to focus on problem-solving rather than implementation details.

Verilog and VHDL for Hardware Description

Hardware design requires precise control over digital circuits, which is where hardware description languages (HDLs) like **Verilog** and **VHDL** come into play. These DSLs allow engineers to describe circuit behavior, simulate hardware execution, and generate gate-level implementations. A simple Verilog module for an AND gate is as follows:

```
module and_gate (input A, input B, output Y);
   assign Y = A & B;
endmodule
```

Unlike procedural programming languages, Verilog provides a **declarative way to describe circuits**, making it indispensable for hardware engineers. By using HDLs, engineers can **simulate, test, and synthesize hardware components** before actual fabrication, reducing errors and design costs.

OpenSCAD for 3D Modeling

Another notable engineering DSL is **OpenSCAD**, which is used for parametric 3D modeling. Unlike traditional CAD software that relies on GUI-based modeling, OpenSCAD provides a script-based DSL to define 3D objects programmatically. A simple cube in OpenSCAD is defined as:

```
cube([10, 10, 10]);
```

This DSL allows engineers and designers to **precisely control model parameters**, making it ideal for procedural generation of 3D parts. OpenSCAD is commonly used in **mechanical engineering, 3D printing, and prototyping**, enabling repeatable and parameterized design workflows.

Engineering DSLs in Python: SymPy for Symbolic Computing

Python provides several DSLs for engineering applications, one of the most prominent being **SymPy**, a symbolic mathematics library. It enables algebraic manipulation, differentiation, and equation solving using an expressive API. For instance, solving an equation symbolically in SymPy looks like this:

```
from sympy import symbols, Eq, solve

x = symbols('x')
equation = Eq(2*x + 3, 7)
solution = solve(equation, x)
print(solution)
```

This DSL allows engineers to **define and manipulate mathematical expressions symbolically**, making it useful for computational mathematics, physics, and engineering simulations. Unlike numerical solvers, SymPy retains algebraic structures, enabling deeper mathematical insights.

DSLs have transformed engineering fields by providing domain-specific abstractions that enhance productivity and accuracy. MATLAB simplifies numerical computing, Verilog and VHDL enable hardware design, OpenSCAD streamlines 3D modeling, and SymPy enhances symbolic computation in Python. These DSLs empower engineers to focus on **domain problems rather than low-level implementation details**, making them essential tools in modern engineering workflows.

Case Studies of Engineering DSLs

Engineering-specific DSLs have revolutionized software development by providing tailored abstractions for complex domains. These DSLs simplify intricate workflows, enhance maintainability, and boost productivity. Examining practical implementations of DSLs in engineering disciplines highlights their benefits. Below are case studies of DSLs applied to software engineering tasks, all demonstrated using Python.

Case Study 1: SymPy – A DSL for Symbolic Mathematics

SymPy is a Python-based DSL for **symbolic mathematics**. Unlike general-purpose numerical libraries, SymPy allows for algebraic manipulations, differentiation, and equation solving symbolically, making it valuable for engineering applications.

A simple example of symbolic differentiation:

```
from sympy import symbols, diff

x = symbols('x')
expr = x**3 + 2*x**2 + x
derivative = diff(expr, x)

print(derivative)  # Output: 3*x**2 + 4*x + 1
```

Instead of numerical approximations, SymPy provides **exact algebraic solutions**, making it ideal for **engineering calculations and simulations**.

Case Study 2: Pint – A DSL for Unit Conversions

Pint is a **DSL for unit-aware computations**. Engineering applications frequently involve unit conversions and dimensional analysis, and Pint ensures correctness in unit-based calculations.

Example of unit conversion and validation:

```
from pint import UnitRegistry

ureg = UnitRegistry()
distance = 5 * ureg.meters
```

87

```
time = 2 * ureg.seconds
speed = distance / time

print(speed)  # Output: 2.5 meter / second
```

Using Pint prevents errors due to **inconsistent units**, which are common in **physics, engineering, and data analysis**.

Case Study 3: PyOpenSCAD – A DSL for Parametric 3D Modeling

OpenSCAD is a well-known **DSL for parametric 3D modeling**, and its Python counterpart, PyOpenSCAD, brings the power of **programmatic design** to Python users.

Generating a simple 3D cube using PyOpenSCAD:

```
from solid import cube
from solid.utils import scad_render

model = cube(10)
print(scad_render(model))
```

This DSL is particularly useful for **mechanical engineering, CAD design, and 3D printing**, offering **precise, scriptable modeling capabilities**.

Case Study 4: PyParsing – A DSL for Parsing Engineering Data

Parsing is essential in engineering applications where structured text data, logs, or reports need to be processed. PyParsing, a **DSL for parsing text-based data**, simplifies this process.

Example: Parsing a custom engineering data format:

```
from pyparsing import Word, alphas, nums, Combine

integer = Word(nums)
variable = Word(alphas)
assignment = variable + "=" + integer

result = assignment.parseString("force=500")
print(result)  # Output: ['force', '=', '500']
```

This DSL enables **flexible text-processing solutions** for engineering simulations, automation, and reporting.

These case studies illustrate how DSLs like **SymPy, Pint, PyOpenSCAD, and PyParsing** enhance productivity in **engineering applications**. By offering **domain-specific abstractions**, these DSLs reduce complexity, prevent errors, and streamline workflows, making them indispensable for engineering software development.

Best Practices in Software Engineering DSL Design

Designing a Domain-Specific Language (DSL) for software engineering requires careful consideration of expressiveness, usability, and integration. A well-structured DSL enhances developer productivity by encapsulating domain knowledge in a readable and maintainable syntax. Effective DSL design follows key principles such as clarity, minimalism, error handling, and extensibility. Below, we discuss best practices for creating a robust DSL, illustrated with Python-based examples.

1. Define a Clear and Expressive Syntax

A DSL should have an intuitive syntax that closely aligns with the problem domain. This makes the language more accessible to domain experts without requiring extensive programming knowledge. Consider a **configuration DSL** for defining application settings:

```python
class ConfigDSL:
    def __init__(self):
        self.settings = {}

    def set(self, key, value):
        self.settings[key] = value

    def get(self, key):
        return self.settings.get(key, None)

config = ConfigDSL()
config.set("database", "PostgreSQL")
config.set("timeout", 30)

print(config.get("database"))  # Output: PostgreSQL
```

This DSL provides a clean, readable API for defining configurations, avoiding the complexity of traditional configuration formats like XML or JSON.

2. Balance Simplicity with Functionality

A common pitfall in DSL design is making the language either too limited or too complex. The key is to strike a balance between minimal syntax and sufficient expressiveness. Consider a **task automation DSL**:

```python
class Task:
    def __init__(self, name):
        self.name = name

    def run(self):
        print(f"Running task: {self.name}")

task1 = Task("Data Backup")
task1.run()  # Output: Running task: Data Backup
```

This DSL is minimal but allows easy extension, such as adding scheduling features or dependencies.

3. Ensure Robust Error Handling

A well-designed DSL should include meaningful error messages and safeguards against incorrect usage. Using Python's exception handling, we can ensure that our DSL provides clear feedback:

```python
class SafeConfig:
    def __init__(self):
        self.settings = {}

    def set(self, key, value):
        if not isinstance(key, str):
            raise ValueError("Key must be a string")
        self.settings[key] = value

try:
    config = SafeConfig()
    config.set(123, "Invalid")  # Raises error
except ValueError as e:
    print(e)  # Output: Key must be a string
```

Good error handling improves the DSL's usability, helping developers identify and resolve issues quickly.

4. Design for Extensibility and Integration

A DSL should be **flexible enough to integrate with existing systems**. Using Python decorators, we can extend a simple logging DSL to support multiple backends:

```python
def log_message(func):
    def wrapper(*args, **kwargs):
        print(f"LOG: Executing {func.__name__}")
        return func(*args, **kwargs)
    return wrapper

@log_message
def process_data():
    print("Processing data...")

process_data()
```

By designing DSLs with extension points, developers can integrate additional functionality **without modifying core logic**.

Following best practices—such as **clear syntax, simplicity, robust error handling, and extensibility**—ensures a **maintainable and efficient DSL**. Well-designed DSLs improve productivity, enforce best practices, and **empower domain experts** to work with software more effectively.

Module 8:
DSLs for Scientific Computing

Scientific computing often requires specialized tools that optimize performance, enable precise mathematical modeling, and simplify complex simulations. Domain-Specific Languages (DSLs) play a crucial role in scientific computing by providing tailored abstractions that enhance productivity and accuracy. This module explores the role of DSLs in mathematical modeling, high-performance computing, and research workflows. It also examines existing scientific DSLs such as MATLAB and Mathematica, emphasizing their significance in data-driven fields like physics, engineering, and bioinformatics. Understanding DSLs in this context allows researchers and engineers to develop more efficient, scalable, and user-friendly computational solutions.

DSLs for Mathematical Modeling

Mathematical modeling is fundamental in scientific research, enabling professionals to represent real-world phenomena using equations and computational algorithms. DSLs designed for mathematical modeling provide an expressive and concise syntax that simplifies complex mathematical expressions while ensuring computational efficiency. These languages often include built-in support for symbolic computation, numerical analysis, and automated theorem proving. Scientists and engineers leverage DSLs to construct and analyze models with greater precision than general-purpose programming languages allow. By abstracting mathematical operations into a domain-specific syntax, DSLs minimize errors and streamline the process of developing models for physics, engineering, and economics.

Application in Simulations and High-Performance Computing

Simulations and high-performance computing (HPC) demand optimized computational tools that handle vast amounts of data and complex algorithms efficiently. DSLs tailored for HPC leverage domain knowledge to optimize execution speed, memory management, and parallel processing. Unlike general-purpose programming languages, which require extensive boilerplate code for such tasks, DSLs offer high-level constructs that simplify the development of parallel and distributed simulations. Researchers in computational physics, climate modeling, and molecular biology benefit from DSLs that enable them to write efficient simulation code while taking advantage of hardware acceleration, such as GPU and multi-core CPU processing, without deep knowledge of low-level optimizations.

Popular Scientific DSLs (e.g., MATLAB, Mathematica)

Several well-known DSLs have been widely adopted in the scientific community due to their ease of use, powerful built-in functions, and optimization capabilities. MATLAB, for instance, is extensively used in engineering and applied mathematics for numerical computing, signal processing, and system modeling. Mathematica, on the other hand, excels in symbolic computation, providing an environment for algebraic manipulations, calculus, and equation solving. Other DSLs, such as R for statistical computing and Julia for high-performance numerical analysis, have gained popularity due to their efficiency and expressiveness. Understanding these DSLs helps researchers choose the best tools for their computational needs.

Integrating DSLs into Research Workflows

Scientific research often involves multiple stages, from data acquisition and preprocessing to modeling, simulation, and visualization. DSLs facilitate seamless integration across these stages by offering domain-specific constructs tailored to each aspect of the research workflow. A well-integrated DSL reduces the complexity of working with heterogeneous data sources, enables reproducible computations, and enhances collaboration among researchers. By leveraging DSLs in their workflows, scientists can focus more on theoretical development and analysis rather than on low-level implementation details. Effective DSL integration also ensures that research findings are transparent, verifiable, and easily extendable.

DSLs play a crucial role in scientific computing by providing tailored tools for mathematical modeling, simulations, and research workflows. Their efficiency, expressiveness, and optimization capabilities make them indispensable in high-performance computing and various scientific disciplines. Understanding and utilizing DSLs in research environments empower scientists and engineers to achieve more accurate, scalable, and reproducible results.

DSLs for Mathematical Modeling

Mathematical modeling is a fundamental aspect of scientific computing, enabling researchers to represent and analyze complex real-world systems using mathematical structures. Domain-Specific Languages (DSLs) designed for mathematical modeling provide an expressive and concise syntax that simplifies the formulation of equations, transformations, and computations. These DSLs eliminate the verbosity associated with general-purpose programming languages by offering specialized constructs tailored for symbolic computation, differential equations, and numerical analysis. By abstracting complex mathematical operations, they reduce errors, improve productivity, and make computational models more accessible to scientists and engineers who may not have extensive programming experience.

One of the primary advantages of DSLs in mathematical modeling is their ability to facilitate symbolic computation. Unlike numerical computing, symbolic computation involves algebraic manipulations of mathematical expressions before numerical evaluation. Languages such as SymPy, a Python-based DSL, enable researchers to perform calculus operations, simplify equations, and manipulate matrices symbolically. This approach enhances model clarity and allows users to derive analytical solutions before resorting to numerical methods.

Example: Symbolic Computation with SymPy

The following Python example demonstrates how a DSL like SymPy can be used for symbolic differentiation and equation solving:

```python
from sympy import symbols, Eq, diff, solve

# Define symbolic variables
x = symbols('x')

# Define a mathematical function
f = x**3 + 2*x**2 - 5*x + 1

# Compute the derivative
df_dx = diff(f, x)
print("Derivative:", df_dx)

# Solve f(x) = 0
solutions = solve(f, x)
print("Roots of equation:", solutions)
```

This example highlights how a DSL eliminates the need for manual differentiation and equation solving, streamlining mathematical modeling tasks.

Another essential feature of mathematical modeling DSLs is their capability to handle differential equations, which are widely used in physics, engineering, and biology. Languages such as Modelica provide a domain-specific approach for defining continuous and discrete systems, enabling researchers to describe complex dynamical models using intuitive syntax.

Example: Solving a Differential Equation

```python
from sympy import Function, dsolve

# Define a function y dependent on x
y = Function('y')

# Define the differential equation dy/dx = y - x
differential_eq = Eq(diff(y(x), x), y(x) - x)

# Solve the equation
solution = dsolve(differential_eq, y(x))
print("Solution:", solution)
```

This demonstrates how a DSL abstracts the complexities of solving differential equations, allowing scientists to focus on modeling rather than implementation details.

Mathematical modeling DSLs also integrate numerical solvers that allow users to approximate solutions for systems of equations, optimization problems, and computational simulations. These capabilities make DSLs essential in fields such as economics, physics, and engineering, where mathematical modeling underpins critical decision-making processes. By leveraging DSLs, researchers can design robust models, automate computations, and derive meaningful insights with greater efficiency and accuracy.

Application in Simulations and High-Performance Computing

Simulations and high-performance computing (HPC) play a crucial role in scientific research, engineering, and real-world problem-solving. Domain-Specific Languages (DSLs) tailored for these areas provide optimized syntax and computational models that enable researchers to build complex simulations efficiently. These DSLs abstract away low-level implementation details, allowing scientists and engineers to focus on modeling rather than programming intricacies. By leveraging parallelism, distributed computing, and numerical optimization, DSLs for simulations and HPC significantly enhance computational efficiency.

One of the core advantages of using DSLs in simulations is their ability to define domain-specific abstractions that improve code clarity and maintainability. Unlike general-purpose programming languages, simulation-focused DSLs allow researchers to describe real-world systems using high-level constructs that closely resemble mathematical formulations. This makes it easier to translate theoretical models into computational frameworks. Languages like Stan, OpenModelica, and Simulink offer simulation environments that integrate well with scientific computing.

In high-performance computing, DSLs enable optimizations such as vectorization, automatic differentiation, and parallel execution on GPUs and multi-core processors. These features allow scientific applications to scale effectively, reducing computation time and enabling the simulation of highly complex systems. For example, Julia, a language designed for high-performance numerical computing, provides a rich ecosystem for simulations, including differential equation solvers and GPU acceleration.

Example: Running a Simulation with NumPy

Python-based DSLs like NumPy allow users to perform numerical simulations efficiently. Consider the following example of a simple Monte Carlo simulation to estimate the value of π:

```python
import numpy as np

# Number of random points
num_samples = 1000000

# Generate random points in a unit square
x = np.random.rand(num_samples)
y = np.random.rand(num_samples)

# Count points inside the unit circle
inside_circle = np.sum(x**2 + y**2 <= 1)

# Estimate the value of pi
pi_estimate = (inside_circle / num_samples) * 4
print("Estimated π:", pi_estimate)
```

This simulation illustrates how DSLs can simplify numerical experiments. NumPy provides optimized vectorized operations that execute efficiently, making it ideal for large-scale computations.

In HPC applications, DSLs also support parallelism, allowing simulations to be executed across multiple processors or GPUs. Libraries such as TensorFlow and JAX provide automatic differentiation and parallel computation capabilities, which are essential in fields like physics-based simulations, climate modeling, and computational biology.

Example: Parallel Computation with Numba

```
from numba import jit
import numpy as np

@jit(nopython=True)
def compute_pi(n_samples):
    count = 0
    for _ in range(n_samples):
        x, y = np.random.rand(), np.random.rand()
        if x**2 + y**2 <= 1:
            count += 1
    return (count / n_samples) * 4

# Run the simulation with JIT acceleration
print("Estimated π:", compute_pi(1000000))
```

This demonstrates how Just-In-Time (JIT) compilation using Numba enhances computational performance in simulations, making DSLs invaluable for HPC.

By incorporating DSLs into simulations and HPC, researchers gain the ability to efficiently model, analyze, and predict real-world phenomena at unprecedented scales. These DSLs streamline the implementation of complex numerical methods, optimize performance, and enable scalable computing solutions that drive innovation across scientific domains.

Popular Scientific DSLs (e.g., MATLAB, Mathematica)

Domain-Specific Languages (DSLs) play a significant role in scientific computing by providing tailored syntax and optimized libraries for mathematical modeling, simulations, and high-performance computing. Some of the most widely used scientific DSLs include MATLAB, Mathematica, R, Julia, and Maple. These languages offer built-in numerical computing functions, symbolic algebra capabilities, and domain-specific optimizations, making them essential for researchers and engineers. Unlike general-purpose programming languages, these DSLs focus on mathematical expressiveness, allowing users to write concise, readable code while leveraging advanced computational techniques.

MATLAB, for example, is a high-level language designed for numerical computing, offering powerful built-in functions for matrix operations, signal processing, and control systems. It excels in rapid prototyping and algorithm development, making it widely adopted in academia and industry. Mathematica, on the other hand, specializes in symbolic computation and offers a rule-based approach to mathematical modeling, allowing users to manipulate algebraic expressions and perform complex calculations interactively. Similarly, Julia is a newer DSL designed for high-performance numerical computing, combining the ease of use of Python with the speed of C.

These DSLs provide domain-specific abstractions that simplify scientific computations. Researchers can focus on problem-solving rather than low-level implementation details, significantly improving productivity. Additionally, these DSLs integrate seamlessly with visualization tools, allowing for effective data analysis and interpretation. Their extensive built-in libraries also make them particularly well-suited for machine learning, statistical analysis, and computational physics.

Example: Numerical Computation in MATLAB (Equivalent Python Code)

A simple example of solving a system of linear equations in MATLAB might look like this:

```
A = [3, 2; 1, 4];
b = [5; 6];
x = A \ b;
disp(x);
```

The equivalent Python implementation using NumPy, a popular numerical computing DSL, is as follows:

```
import numpy as np

A = np.array([[3, 2], [1, 4]])
b = np.array([5, 6])

# Solve Ax = b
x = np.linalg.solve(A, b)
print(x)
```

NumPy provides efficient matrix operations similar to MATLAB while offering better integration with general-purpose Python programming.

Example: Symbolic Computation in Mathematica (Equivalent Python Code with SymPy)

A symbolic differentiation example in Mathematica:

```
D[x^3 + 2*x^2 + x, x]
```

The equivalent Python implementation using SymPy is:

```
import sympy as sp

x = sp.symbols('x')
expr = x**3 + 2*x**2 + x
derivative = sp.diff(expr, x)
print(derivative)
```

SymPy, a DSL for symbolic mathematics, provides capabilities similar to Mathematica while being fully integrated with Python, making it ideal for automated algebraic computations.

Scientific DSLs like MATLAB, Mathematica, and Julia provide domain-specific advantages for numerical computing and symbolic mathematics. Python-based alternatives such as NumPy and SymPy offer similar functionality while maintaining flexibility. By using these DSLs, researchers can focus on high-level problem-solving, making complex computations more accessible, efficient, and scalable.

Integrating DSLs Into Research Workflows

Domain-Specific Languages (DSLs) for scientific computing are most effective when seamlessly integrated into research workflows. Scientists, engineers, and analysts rely on these DSLs to model complex systems, analyze large datasets, and conduct simulations efficiently. However, integrating these tools into broader workflows requires careful consideration of interoperability, reproducibility, and performance. Researchers must ensure that the DSL fits within the ecosystem of tools they use, including general-purpose programming languages, visualization frameworks, and data storage solutions.

A well-integrated DSL enhances productivity by automating repetitive tasks and abstracting complex computations into concise expressions. For example, a researcher using MATLAB for data analysis might integrate it with Python for machine learning or R for statistical modeling. Similarly, Julia, known for its high-performance numerical computing, can be used alongside Python's SciPy and NumPy libraries to extend functionality. Many scientific DSLs also support integration with databases, cloud computing platforms, and parallel processing frameworks, allowing researchers to scale their computations efficiently.

Version control and reproducibility are crucial when incorporating DSLs into research workflows. Tools such as Jupyter Notebooks enable researchers to document their work, combining code, visualizations, and explanatory text in a single environment. This ensures that experiments can be reproduced and verified by others. In addition, many DSLs support scripting and automation, allowing researchers to run large-scale simulations and batch-process datasets without manual intervention.

Example: Integrating MATLAB with Python for Data Analysis

A common workflow involves using MATLAB for numerical computations while leveraging Python for data visualization and machine learning. MATLAB can generate data, which is then analyzed further in Python:

```
% Save data from MATLAB
A = rand(10,10);
save('data.mat', 'A');
```

In Python, the data can be loaded and processed using NumPy:

```
import scipy.io
import numpy as np

# Load MATLAB-generated data
```

```
data = scipy.io.loadmat('data.mat')
A = data['A']

# Perform further analysis in Python
mean_value = np.mean(A)
print(mean_value)
```

This integration allows researchers to combine MATLAB's efficient numerical solvers with Python's advanced machine learning capabilities.

Example: Using Jupyter Notebooks for Reproducibility

Jupyter Notebooks provide an ideal environment for integrating multiple DSLs in research workflows. A single notebook can contain MATLAB, Python, and R code, making it easier to share results and collaborate.

```
# Example of symbolic differentiation using SymPy in Jupyter
import sympy as sp

x = sp.symbols('x')
expr = x**4 + 3*x**2 + 7
derivative = sp.diff(expr, x)

print(derivative)
```

By leveraging DSLs within Jupyter, researchers can maintain a clear record of their computations, ensuring that experiments are transparent and reproducible.

Integrating DSLs into research workflows streamlines data analysis, simulation, and modeling. Researchers benefit from combining multiple DSLs, leveraging strengths from each to improve efficiency. Version control, scripting, and Jupyter Notebooks help maintain reproducibility and collaboration. With proper integration, DSLs enhance scientific discovery by making complex computations more manageable and scalable.

Module 9:
DSLs in Game Development

Domain-Specific Languages (DSLs) have become a crucial part of game development, enabling developers to design and implement game mechanics with greater efficiency. By abstracting complex logic, game-specific DSLs empower designers, artists, and programmers to define behaviors without deep knowledge of general-purpose programming languages. This module explores how DSLs contribute to game development, covering game design and scripting, handling game logic, notable DSLs in the industry, and performance considerations. Understanding these aspects allows developers to leverage DSLs to create dynamic, interactive, and optimized gaming experiences.

DSLs for Game Design and Scripting

Game development involves intricate logic, event handling, and interactions between characters, environments, and physics engines. DSLs simplify this complexity by providing scripting tools tailored to game mechanics. Many modern game engines incorporate DSLs to allow designers and developers to define behaviors without modifying core engine code. For example, Unreal Engine introduced UnrealScript as an internal DSL to help define game behavior. Similarly, UnityScript (inspired by JavaScript) was an early scripting language for Unity before C# became the standard. These DSLs enable non-programmers to create game mechanics, control animations, and configure AI behaviors intuitively.

Custom scripting DSLs allow developers to define in-game events and rules efficiently. A well-designed game DSL enables modularity, meaning that developers can modify behavior without recompiling the entire game engine. For instance, Lua, a widely adopted embedded DSL, is used in games like *World of Warcraft* and *Angry Birds* for scripting game mechanics. Its lightweight and embeddable nature makes it an excellent choice for game studios looking to add flexibility to their development pipeline.

Handling Game Logic with DSLs

Game logic governs how a game responds to player inputs, AI decisions, and environmental changes. Implementing this logic using DSLs ensures consistency, readability, and maintainability. Game DSLs often provide declarative syntax to define rules and state transitions efficiently. For example, a DSL can be used to script interactions where a player picks up an object, triggers an event, or engages in combat.

Finite State Machines (FSMs) are commonly implemented using DSLs in game development. They help manage states such as "idle," "walking," "attacking," or "dead" for game characters. Instead of hardcoding these transitions in C++ or C#, developers can use a DSL that simplifies

99

the process, making it more intuitive and flexible. DSL-based logic can be used to define AI behavior patterns, level progression, or cutscene triggers without modifying the underlying engine code.

Examples of Game-Specific DSLs (e.g., UnrealScript, UnityScript)

Several domain-specific languages have been developed exclusively for game development. UnrealScript, introduced by Epic Games for Unreal Engine, allowed developers to script game mechanics efficiently before being replaced by Blueprints and C++. UnityScript, a JavaScript-inspired scripting language, was used in Unity before being phased out in favor of C#.

Another widely used DSL is GDScript, the primary scripting language for the Godot engine. Unlike general-purpose languages, GDScript is optimized for game development, providing seamless integration with Godot's scene system and high-level game features. Similarly, Ink, a DSL for interactive narrative scripting, is used in games to create branching dialogues and story-driven experiences. These DSLs demonstrate how domain-specific tools enhance productivity by catering to the unique requirements of game design and scripting.

Performance Considerations in Game DSLs

While DSLs simplify game development, they introduce performance considerations that must be addressed to ensure smooth gameplay. Game DSLs are often interpreted rather than compiled, which can lead to slower execution times. To mitigate this, many engines use Just-In-Time (JIT) compilation or caching mechanisms to optimize runtime performance.

Memory management is another crucial aspect. Since DSLs abstract underlying complexity, inefficient scripts can lead to memory leaks or increased CPU usage. Developers must ensure that their DSL-based scripts are optimized and do not create unnecessary overhead. Additionally, DSLs must integrate seamlessly with low-level game engine components to avoid bottlenecks in rendering, physics calculations, and AI processing.

Domain-Specific Languages play a vital role in game development by enabling efficient scripting, intuitive game logic implementation, and seamless designer-developer collaboration. From UnrealScript and Lua to GDScript and Ink, game-specific DSLs have transformed how game mechanics are scripted and executed. However, performance considerations, such as execution speed and memory management, must be carefully handled. With the right DSL design, developers can enhance productivity while maintaining high-performance standards in modern game development.

DSLs for Game Design and Scripting

Game development is an intricate process that requires scripting languages tailored to specific game mechanics. Domain-Specific Languages (DSLs) in game design streamline content creation, allowing designers, animators, and level designers to implement mechanics without deep programming expertise. Game scripting DSLs enable the definition of interactions, AI behavior, animations, and event triggers in a structured, readable manner. They serve as an abstraction layer over complex game engine APIs, ensuring that modifications can be made without altering low-level engine code.

A well-designed DSL for game scripting should be intuitive, expressive, and tightly integrated with the game engine. It should support high-level abstractions such as entity behavior, state transitions, and event-based interactions. Unlike general-purpose languages, game scripting DSLs prioritize real-time execution efficiency and ease of integration with rendering, physics, and AI systems. Many modern game engines, such as Unreal Engine and Unity, have incorporated DSLs to empower designers and programmers to define behaviors without writing low-level engine code.

One of the most widely used DSLs in game development is **Lua**, an embeddable scripting language that is lightweight, fast, and easy to integrate into game engines. Lua is used in popular games such as *World of Warcraft*, *Far Cry*, and *Angry Birds* to define AI behaviors, game rules, and UI interactions. Below is an example of a Lua-based game scripting DSL that controls character movement:

```lua
function moveCharacter(character, direction)
    if direction == "left" then
        character.x = character.x - 5
    elseif direction == "right" then
        character.x = character.x + 5
    elseif direction == "jump" then
        character.y = character.y - 10
    end
end
```

The example demonstrates how a DSL simplifies character movement, allowing designers to define actions without modifying engine internals. A well-structured DSL abstracts game logic, making it accessible to both programmers and non-programmers.

Building a Simple DSL for Game Scripting in Python

Python is an excellent choice for developing a DSL for game scripting due to its readability and ease of integration. Below is a simple internal DSL implemented in Python that allows designers to define game interactions declaratively:

```python
class GameObject:
    def __init__(self, name):
        self.name = name
        self.actions = []

    def do(self, action):
        self.actions.append(action)

    def execute(self):
        for action in self.actions:
            print(f"{self.name} {action}")

# Example usage
player = GameObject("Player")
player.do("moves forward")
```

```
player.do("jumps")
player.execute()
```

In this example, designers can define a sequence of actions for a game object without needing to write imperative game logic. The DSL abstracts complex game logic, making it more expressive and readable.

DSLs in game design and scripting significantly enhance the game development process by providing a structured, high-level approach to defining behaviors and interactions. Whether using embedded scripting languages like Lua or designing a custom DSL in Python, these languages empower developers and designers to create immersive experiences efficiently. A well-designed DSL ensures modularity, flexibility, and ease of iteration, making game development more accessible and efficient.

Handling Game Logic with DSLs

Game logic governs the rules and behaviors that dictate interactions within a game world. From character movement and AI decision-making to event triggers and combat systems, game logic must be efficiently implemented and managed. Domain-Specific Languages (DSLs) provide a structured approach to handling game logic by abstracting complex engine interactions into high-level commands that are readable and maintainable. Unlike general-purpose programming languages, DSLs allow game designers to define game mechanics without modifying low-level engine components, reducing development time and improving collaboration between developers and designers.

A well-designed game logic DSL should support event-driven programming, conditional logic, and state management. Many modern game engines, such as Unreal Engine and Unity, leverage DSLs to define gameplay mechanics. These DSLs simplify AI decision-making, dialogue systems, and animation sequences by using structured, human-readable commands. For example, Unreal Engine's Blueprints visual scripting system enables designers to define game logic without writing traditional code, making it easier to experiment with new mechanics and refine gameplay elements.

Implementing a Simple Game Logic DSL in Python

Python provides an excellent foundation for designing a DSL to handle game logic. Below is an example of an internal DSL that defines rules for an enemy AI in a turn-based game:

```
class EnemyAI:
    def __init__(self, name):
        self.name = name
        self.behaviors = {}

    def when(self, condition):
        def decorator(action):
            self.behaviors[condition] = action
            return action
        return decorator

    def execute(self, game_state):
```

```
        for condition, action in self.behaviors.items():
            if condition(game_state):
                action()
                break

# Example usage
enemy = EnemyAI("Goblin")

@enemy.when(lambda state: state["player_health"] < 20)
def attack():
    print("Goblin attacks!")

@enemy.when(lambda state: state["player_distance"] > 10)
def move_closer():
    print("Goblin moves closer!")

# Simulating game state
game_state = {"player_health": 15, "player_distance": 5}
enemy.execute(game_state)
```

In this example, the DSL allows designers to define AI behavior using high-level conditions and actions. The when function associates conditions with specific actions, making AI logic declarative and easy to modify.

State-Based Game Logic DSL

Many games rely on finite state machines (FSMs) to manage transitions between different game states. A DSL can abstract this process, making state-based logic more readable. Below is a simple FSM-based DSL for handling game character states:

```
class StateMachine:
    def __init__(self):
        self.states = {}
        self.current_state = None

    def state(self, name):
        def decorator(func):
            self.states[name] = func
            return func
        return decorator

    def set_state(self, name):
        self.current_state = name

    def execute(self):
        if self.current_state in self.states:
            self.states[self.current_state]()

# Example usage
game_state = StateMachine()

@game_state.state("idle")
def idle():
    print("Character is idle.")

@game_state.state("running")
def running():
    print("Character is running.")

@game_state.state("jumping")
def jumping():
    print("Character is jumping.")
```

```
game_state.set_state("running")
game_state.execute()
```

This approach allows game logic to be defined in a structured, declarative manner. Developers can easily modify game states without rewriting complex conditional statements.

Handling game logic with DSLs enhances the clarity and maintainability of game mechanics. By structuring AI behaviors, state transitions, and event handling in a declarative fashion, DSLs reduce the complexity of implementing game rules. Whether through condition-based AI logic or state machines, a well-designed DSL streamlines development, improves collaboration, and makes game logic easier to modify and scale.

Examples of Game-Specific DSLs

Game-specific DSLs have played a crucial role in shaping modern game development by providing structured ways to define gameplay mechanics, AI behaviors, and world interactions. DSLs like UnrealScript (formerly used in Unreal Engine), Unity's C#-based scripting, and other specialized languages offer a way to simplify game development. This section explores DSL-like implementations in Python, showing how a custom game scripting language can be built and used to define gameplay behavior dynamically.

Implementing a Simple Game-Specific DSL

One way to create a game-specific DSL is by designing a scripting language that allows designers to specify game mechanics in a structured way. Below is an example of a simple internal DSL in Python for defining game actions:

```
class GameScript:
    def __init__(self):
        self.commands = []

    def move(self, entity, direction):
        self.commands.append(f"{entity} moves {direction}")

    def attack(self, attacker, target):
        self.commands.append(f"{attacker} attacks {target}")

    def execute(self):
        for command in self.commands:
            print(command)

# Using the DSL
script = GameScript()
script.move("Player", "north")
script.attack("Player", "Goblin")
script.execute()
```

This internal DSL allows developers to define sequences of game actions in a structured manner. Designers can use this to create game behaviors without directly modifying engine logic.

Using a Configuration-Based DSL for Game AI

Another approach to DSLs in game development is using configuration files to define behaviors. Below is an example of a simple game AI behavior DSL using JSON:

```
import json

ai_behavior_json = """
{
    "enemy": {
        "type": "Goblin",
        "health": 50,
        "attack_pattern": ["melee", "retreat", "ranged"]
    }
}"""

ai_behavior = json.loads(ai_behavior_json)

def execute_ai_behavior(ai):
    print(f"Enemy {ai['type']} with {ai['health']} HP follows pattern: {',
        '.join(ai['attack_pattern'])}")

execute_ai_behavior(ai_behavior["enemy"])
```

This method allows game designers to tweak enemy behaviors without modifying the game engine. By loading the DSL from a JSON configuration file, AI behavior can be easily changed without writing additional code.

External DSL for Game Dialogue

A custom DSL can also be designed for handling game dialogue. Below is an example of a simple dialogue DSL parser:

```
class Dialogue:
    def __init__(self, script):
        self.lines = script.split("\n")

    def execute(self):
        for line in self.lines:
            speaker, text = line.split(":")
            print(f"{speaker.strip()}: \"{text.strip()}\"")

# Example DSL script
dialogue_script = """
NPC: Welcome, traveler.
Player: Who are you?
NPC: I am the guardian of this realm.
"""

dialogue = Dialogue(dialogue_script)
dialogue.execute()
```

This DSL allows dialogue to be written in a readable format, parsed, and displayed in the game dynamically.

Game-specific DSLs improve flexibility and maintainability in game development. By leveraging internal and external DSLs for scripting game logic, AI behavior, and dialogue, developers can create more interactive and scalable game systems.

Performance Considerations in Game DSLs

When integrating a domain-specific language into game development, performance is a critical factor. Poorly designed DSLs can introduce overhead that slows down real-time execution, impacting gameplay and responsiveness. This section explores performance considerations when designing and using DSLs in games, focusing on script execution speed, memory usage, and optimization strategies. Using Python, we demonstrate techniques for improving DSL efficiency, such as precompilation, caching, and lightweight parsing.

Reducing Execution Overhead with Precompilation

One of the main performance challenges in game DSLs is the cost of interpreting scripts at runtime. Precompiling DSL scripts into an optimized format can reduce this overhead. Below is an example of a simple DSL that compiles game actions into Python functions for faster execution:

```
import compileall

class GameScriptCompiler:
    def __init__(self, script):
        self.script = script
        self.compiled_code = None

    def compile(self):
        self.compiled_code = compile(self.script, "<game_script>", "exec")

    def execute(self):
        if self.compiled_code:
            exec(self.compiled_code)

# Example script in DSL format
game_script = """
player_position = [0, 0]

def move(direction):
    if direction == 'north':
        player_position[1] += 1
    elif direction == 'south':
        player_position[1] -= 1
move('north')
print(f'Player position: {player_position}')
"""

compiler = GameScriptCompiler(game_script)
compiler.compile()
compiler.execute()
```

By compiling the script before execution, this approach reduces the runtime cost of repeatedly parsing and interpreting game logic.

Optimizing Memory Usage with Lightweight Parsing

Another performance bottleneck arises from inefficient parsing techniques. Many DSLs parse text-based scripts dynamically, which can lead to high memory usage. Instead, tokenizing and caching parsed results can improve performance. Here is an optimized approach using a lightweight tokenizer:

```python
import re

class LightweightParser:
    def __init__(self):
        self.token_cache = {}

    def tokenize(self, script):
        if script in self.token_cache:
            return self.token_cache[script]

        tokens = re.findall(r"\w+", script)
        self.token_cache[script] = tokens
        return tokens

# Example DSL script
dsl_script = "move player north"

parser = LightweightParser()
tokens = parser.tokenize(dsl_script)
print("Parsed Tokens:", tokens)
```

By caching tokenized results, repeated executions of the same script avoid redundant processing, improving efficiency.

Using Just-in-Time (JIT) Compilation for Performance Gains

For computationally expensive operations, just-in-time (JIT) compilation can significantly boost DSL performance. The numba library in Python provides an example of how game logic written in a DSL can be optimized:

```python
from numba import jit

@jit(nopython=True)
def calculate_damage(attack, defense):
    return max(attack - defense, 0)

damage = calculate_damage(50, 30)
print(f"Damage dealt: {damage}")
```

JIT compilation converts the function into machine code at runtime, ensuring high-speed execution comparable to compiled languages like C++.

Performance considerations in game DSLs impact execution speed, memory consumption, and system responsiveness. By using precompilation, lightweight parsing, and JIT techniques, developers can optimize DSL execution to meet the real-time demands of game development.

Module 10:
DSLs in Finance and Business

Domain-Specific Languages (DSLs) play a crucial role in finance and business applications, enabling precise modeling, efficient automation, and streamlined data analysis. Financial modeling, quantitative trading, business process modeling, and workflow automation all benefit from DSLs designed for domain-specific operations. This module explores the role of DSLs in these areas, emphasizing their advantages in handling complexity, improving efficiency, and reducing errors in critical financial and business operations.

DSLs for Financial Modeling and Analysis

Financial modeling requires accuracy, repeatability, and ease of interpretation. Traditional programming languages, such as Python or C++, provide flexibility but can introduce unnecessary complexity when dealing with domain-specific financial calculations. DSLs in financial modeling simplify tasks like risk analysis, portfolio optimization, and cash flow forecasting by offering an expressive and constrained syntax tailored for financial computations.

Many financial DSLs, such as QuantLib and Modelica, are designed to abstract mathematical operations and provide a structured approach to financial modeling. These DSLs support rapid prototyping, ensuring analysts and financial engineers can focus on financial logic rather than low-level programming details. By using DSLs, businesses achieve improved efficiency in developing and maintaining financial models.

Custom DSLs in Algorithmic Trading and Quantitative Finance

Algorithmic trading and quantitative finance involve processing vast amounts of data and executing trades with minimal latency. Custom DSLs in these fields help traders and financial analysts define strategies without the complexities of general-purpose programming. Trading strategies must be expressed in a manner that is both human-readable and machine-executable, ensuring faster backtesting and optimization.

DSLs such as EasyLanguage (used in TradeStation) and QuantConnect's Lean framework enable traders to express rules in a structured way, reducing the potential for implementation errors. Additionally, DSLs allow financial institutions to enforce compliance rules and risk management constraints while giving quants and traders flexibility in defining strategies. The ability to create domain-specific abstractions ensures that trading logic remains consistent, traceable, and easy to modify based on market conditions.

Business Process Modeling DSLs

Business process modeling involves defining workflows, decision logic, and operational rules in a structured manner. General-purpose programming languages often introduce unnecessary complexity when modeling business logic, leading to inefficiencies in business application development. DSLs designed for business process modeling, such as BPMN (Business Process Model and Notation) and DMN (Decision Model and Notation), provide a standardized way to define and execute workflows.

By using DSLs in business process modeling, organizations can create executable models that integrate with enterprise systems, reducing the reliance on manual coding. These models ensure consistency across different departments and facilitate collaboration between technical and non-technical stakeholders. The structured nature of DSLs helps businesses quickly adapt to changing requirements while maintaining operational efficiency.

Automating Workflows in Business Applications

Workflow automation is essential for improving operational efficiency in modern enterprises. Traditional workflow automation tools often require complex configurations that may not be intuitive for business users. DSLs in workflow automation simplify the definition of tasks, approval processes, and event-driven actions, making them more accessible to business analysts and non-technical users.

Custom DSLs for workflow automation enable organizations to create rule-based automation logic that integrates with databases, APIs, and third-party services. Whether automating invoice approvals, order processing, or customer support workflows, DSLs help streamline operations by reducing manual intervention and minimizing errors. The use of DSLs in business automation enhances scalability, maintainability, and agility, allowing organizations to respond quickly to evolving business needs.

The application of DSLs in finance and business provides significant advantages in modeling, automation, and operational efficiency. Whether used for financial modeling, algorithmic trading, business process modeling, or workflow automation, DSLs enhance precision and reduce complexity in domain-specific applications. By leveraging DSLs, organizations can optimize their processes, improve accuracy, and achieve better decision-making capabilities while ensuring maintainability and adaptability.

DSLs for Financial Modeling and Analysis

Financial modeling involves constructing mathematical representations of financial assets, risk assessments, and investment strategies. Traditional programming languages like Python and R provide extensive numerical computing libraries, but they require domain expertise in both finance and programming. Domain-Specific Languages (DSLs) streamline financial modeling by providing tailored syntax, built-in abstractions, and optimized execution models that focus on financial computations while reducing unnecessary complexity.

A well-designed DSL for financial modeling enables analysts to express models in a concise and readable format. For instance, a DSL can provide specialized constructs for defining cash flow projections, portfolio optimization, and risk assessments without dealing with low-level implementation details. Python-based DSLs, such as Pyomo for mathematical optimization and QuantLib for financial derivatives pricing, showcase how DSLs simplify complex computations while maintaining flexibility and extensibility.

A simple Python-based DSL for financial modeling can provide a structured way to define financial instruments and perform calculations. Consider the following example, which defines a DSL for modeling financial assets and computing net present value (NPV):

```python
class FinancialInstrument:
    def __init__(self, name, cash_flows, discount_rate):
        self.name = name
        self.cash_flows = cash_flows
        self.discount_rate = discount_rate

    def compute_npv(self):
        return sum(cf / (1 + self.discount_rate) ** t for t, cf in
            enumerate(self.cash_flows, start=1))

# Define a bond with cash flows over 5 years
bond = FinancialInstrument("Corporate Bond", [100, 100, 100, 100, 1100], 0.05)
print(f"NPV of {bond.name}: ${bond.compute_npv():.2f}")
```

In this example, the DSL encapsulates financial computations such as discounting future cash flows to compute NPV. This abstraction enables financial analysts to focus on business logic rather than programming details.

Another advantage of DSLs in financial modeling is their ability to define domain-specific constraints and validation rules. For example, a DSL can enforce risk management constraints, ensuring that financial models adhere to regulatory requirements. Consider a simple rule-checking function integrated into the DSL:

```python
class RiskValidator:
    @staticmethod
    def check_discount_rate(rate):
        if not (0 <= rate <= 1):
            raise ValueError("Discount rate must be between 0 and 1")

# Example usage
try:
    RiskValidator.check_discount_rate(1.2)  # Invalid discount rate
except ValueError as e:
    print(f"Error: {e}")
```

This demonstrates how DSLs can enforce domain-specific rules, reducing errors and improving the reliability of financial models.

In practice, financial DSLs extend beyond simple calculations by integrating with databases, external APIs, and visualization tools. They can provide declarative ways to define financial contracts, perform Monte Carlo simulations, and optimize portfolios.

Financial institutions increasingly rely on DSLs to enhance modeling accuracy, automate analysis workflows, and ensure compliance with industry standards.

By incorporating DSLs into financial modeling, businesses achieve increased efficiency, improved readability, and reduced risk of computational errors. A well-structured DSL ensures that financial professionals can express models clearly while leveraging powerful computational capabilities behind the scenes.

Custom DSLs in Algorithmic Trading and Quantitative Finance

Algorithmic trading and quantitative finance rely on high-speed, automated decision-making to execute trades based on mathematical models and real-time market data. Traditional programming languages like Python, C++, and Java provide extensive libraries for numerical analysis and execution, but they require detailed implementation of strategies. A Domain-Specific Language (DSL) simplifies this process by offering a structured way to express trading rules, risk constraints, and portfolio strategies while abstracting low-level complexity.

A well-designed DSL for algorithmic trading allows traders and quantitative analysts to define strategies using a declarative approach rather than imperative programming. These DSLs provide built-in constructs for order execution, risk management, and market data processing. Examples of such DSLs include QuantConnect's Lean framework and TradeStation's EasyLanguage, which allow users to define trading logic in a human-readable format while leveraging high-performance execution.

Consider a simple Python-based DSL for defining trading strategies. The DSL should allow traders to express rules concisely while handling market data processing and order execution internally. Here's an example of a minimal trading DSL that enables users to define a strategy using domain-specific constructs:

```
class TradingStrategy:
    def __init__(self, name):
        self.name = name
        self.rules = []

    def add_rule(self, condition, action):
        self.rules.append((condition, action))

    def execute(self, market_data):
        for condition, action in self.rules:
            if condition(market_data):
                action()

# Example: Buy when price drops below a threshold
def buy_action():
    print("Executing BUY order")

def price_below_threshold(data, threshold=100):
    return data["price"] < threshold

# Define strategy
strategy = TradingStrategy("Mean Reversion")
strategy.add_rule(lambda data: price_below_threshold(data, 100), buy_action)
```

```
# Simulate market data
market_data = {"price": 95}
strategy.execute(market_data)
```

In this example, the DSL allows traders to define rules declaratively, separating strategy logic from execution details. The rule-based approach ensures flexibility and readability, enabling traders to focus on financial logic rather than programming intricacies.

A DSL for algorithmic trading must also integrate risk management and order constraints. For example, traders may want to ensure that their strategy does not place orders exceeding a certain risk threshold. A DSL can incorporate risk management as a built-in feature:

```
class RiskManager:
    @staticmethod
    def enforce_risk_limit(order_size, max_limit=1000):
        if order_size > max_limit:
            raise ValueError("Order size exceeds risk limit")

try:
    RiskManager.enforce_risk_limit(1200)
except ValueError as e:
    print(f"Risk Violation: {e}")
```

By embedding risk constraints, DSLs help prevent unintended high-risk trades and ensure compliance with financial regulations.

In quantitative finance, DSLs extend beyond execution to modeling and backtesting. They allow analysts to specify mathematical models for portfolio optimization, volatility modeling, and derivatives pricing in a structured format. Python-based DSLs such as Zipline (for backtesting) and SymPy (for symbolic computation) demonstrate how DSLs enhance financial analysis.

A well-designed DSL for algorithmic trading increases efficiency by allowing traders to focus on strategy definition rather than implementation details. It enhances readability, enforces risk management, and ensures rapid execution while integrating seamlessly with financial data sources.

Business Process Modeling DSLs

Business Process Modeling (BPM) involves designing, analyzing, and optimizing workflows within an organization. Traditional BPM solutions often rely on graphical tools like BPMN (Business Process Model and Notation), but DSLs provide a more flexible and automatable approach. A Domain-Specific Language (DSL) tailored for BPM allows business analysts and developers to define processes in a structured, human-readable format while ensuring correctness and automation.

A BPM DSL abstracts complex workflows into declarative rules that describe sequences of activities, decision points, and execution constraints. These DSLs facilitate business rule enforcement, compliance tracking, and system integration while minimizing errors. By leveraging a DSL, businesses can define workflows programmatically and adapt them dynamically to changing requirements without rewriting core logic. Examples of BPM DSLs include Camunda Modeler and Activiti, which provide textual and graphical representations of business processes.

A well-structured BPM DSL should allow users to define workflows using a clear syntax that captures tasks, transitions, and conditions. Consider a simple Python-based DSL for defining business processes:

```python
class Task:
    def __init__(self, name, action):
        self.name = name
        self.action = action
        self.next_task = None

    def set_next(self, next_task):
        self.next_task = next_task

    def execute(self):
        print(f"Executing: {self.name}")
        self.action()
        if self.next_task:
            self.next_task.execute()

# Example tasks
def approve_invoice():
    print("Invoice approved")

def send_notification():
    print("Notification sent to finance department")

# Define workflow
approve = Task("Approve Invoice", approve_invoice)
notify = Task("Send Notification", send_notification)
approve.set_next(notify)

# Execute business process
approve.execute()
```

In this example, tasks are represented as objects, and execution follows a sequential workflow. By structuring workflows in this manner, businesses can easily modify task sequences, integrate new steps, and ensure smooth process automation.

A more advanced BPM DSL could include conditional branching, event triggers, and parallel execution. For instance, a DSL could introduce decision points that alter the process flow based on conditions:

```python
class DecisionNode:
    def __init__(self, condition, true_task, false_task):
        self.condition = condition
        self.true_task = true_task
        self.false_task = false_task

    def execute(self, data):
        if self.condition(data):
            self.true_task.execute()
        else:
            self.false_task.execute()
```

```
# Example decision logic
def invoice_above_threshold(data):
    return data["amount"] > 5000

# Define tasks
high_value_approval = Task("High-Value Approval", lambda: print("Escalated to
            senior management"))
regular_approval = Task("Regular Approval", approve_invoice)

decision = DecisionNode(invoice_above_threshold, high_value_approval,
            regular_approval)

# Execute workflow
invoice_data = {"amount": 6000}
decision.execute(invoice_data)
```

This example introduces conditional logic, allowing invoices above a certain threshold to be escalated. Such features make BPM DSLs highly adaptable for business process automation.

In addition to defining processes, BPM DSLs can integrate with external systems such as databases, messaging queues, and APIs. For example, a DSL can trigger automated email notifications or update CRM records when a process step is completed.

By encapsulating business logic in a structured DSL, organizations can achieve greater process transparency, reduce manual intervention, and ensure consistency across operations. A well-designed BPM DSL improves efficiency by providing an expressive, maintainable, and scalable approach to defining and executing workflows.

Automating Workflows in Business Applications

Automation in business applications streamlines repetitive tasks, reduces errors, and enhances productivity. Domain-Specific Languages (DSLs) provide a structured way to define workflows, making it easier for businesses to manage process automation efficiently. A well-designed DSL allows organizations to model, execute, and monitor workflows dynamically, reducing the need for manual intervention.

A workflow automation DSL abstracts the complexities of process management, defining task sequences, decision points, and event triggers in a concise syntax. Businesses use DSLs to automate customer onboarding, invoicing, compliance checks, and reporting. Instead of relying on rigid, predefined workflows, a DSL provides flexibility by allowing business users and developers to modify processes without altering underlying application code.

Consider a simple DSL designed to automate a document approval process. The DSL defines tasks, conditions, and transitions in a structured way:

```
class Workflow:
    def __init__(self, name):
        self.name = name
        self.tasks = []
```

```python
    def add_task(self, task):
        self.tasks.append(task)

    def run(self):
        for task in self.tasks:
            task.execute()

class Task:
    def __init__(self, name, action):
        self.name = name
        self.action = action

    def execute(self):
        print(f"Executing task: {self.name}")
        self.action()

# Example business process
def review_document():
    print("Document reviewed")

def approve_document():
    print("Document approved")

workflow = Workflow("Document Approval Process")
workflow.add_task(Task("Review", review_document))
workflow.add_task(Task("Approve", approve_document))

workflow.run()
```

This DSL-based automation defines sequential task execution, ensuring that business processes run efficiently. Each task is encapsulated in a reusable structure, making it easy to modify or extend workflows without disrupting existing automation.

A more advanced DSL can integrate with external services such as databases, APIs, and messaging queues to enable real-time automation. For example, a DSL could trigger an email notification when a process step is completed:

```python
import smtplib

class EmailNotification:
    def __init__(self, recipient, subject, message):
        self.recipient = recipient
        self.subject = subject
        self.message = message

    def send(self):
        print(f"Sending email to {self.recipient}: {self.subject}")
        # Simulated email sending logic
        # server = smtplib.SMTP("smtp.example.com", 587)
        # server.sendmail("noreply@example.com", self.recipient, self.message)
        # server.quit()

# Example integration in workflow
def notify_manager():
    email = EmailNotification("manager@example.com", "Approval Required",
        "Please review the document.")
    email.send()

workflow.add_task(Task("Notify Manager", notify_manager))
workflow.run()
```

This example demonstrates how a DSL-based workflow automation system can interact with external components, such as sending notifications, updating records, or triggering system events.

To handle complex workflows, DSLs can introduce decision logic and parallel execution. A rule-based system enables different execution paths based on conditions:

```python
class ConditionalTask:
    def __init__(self, condition, true_task, false_task):
        self.condition = condition
        self.true_task = true_task
        self.false_task = false_task

    def execute(self, data):
        if self.condition(data):
            self.true_task.execute()
        else:
            self.false_task.execute()

# Example condition
def is_high_priority(data):
    return data["priority"] == "high"

high_priority = Task("Escalate to Manager", lambda: print("Escalation
        initiated"))
regular_review = Task("Regular Review", review_document)

decision_task = ConditionalTask(is_high_priority, high_priority, regular_review)
decision_task.execute({"priority": "high"})
```

This example introduces conditional branching, allowing workflows to dynamically adjust based on business rules.

By leveraging DSLs for workflow automation, businesses can achieve greater efficiency, enforce compliance, and reduce manual workload. A well-structured DSL provides a scalable and maintainable approach to business process automation, ensuring that workflows remain adaptable and responsive to evolving business needs.

Module 11:
DSLs in Networking and Security

Domain-Specific Languages (DSLs) play a significant role in networking and security by simplifying configuration management, monitoring, and policy enforcement. These specialized languages offer declarative and structured ways to define networking rules, automate security policies, and enhance threat detection. By reducing human errors and enforcing consistency, DSLs help manage complex infrastructures efficiently while improving security and compliance. This module explores the application of DSLs in networking and security, focusing on network configuration, cybersecurity automation, policy management, and case studies demonstrating their effectiveness in securing software systems.

DSLs for Network Configuration and Monitoring

Networking environments require precise configuration to ensure connectivity, performance, and security. Traditionally, administrators configure routers, firewalls, and switches using command-line interfaces, leading to inconsistencies and misconfigurations. DSLs simplify this process by providing structured and reusable language constructs for defining network rules. These languages abstract complex configuration settings, making them easier to read, modify, and enforce. For instance, Software-Defined Networking (SDN) relies on DSLs to define traffic flows and automate routing policies. In network monitoring, DSLs facilitate real-time analysis of traffic patterns, anomaly detection, and event-driven responses. This ensures rapid identification and mitigation of issues in dynamic network environments.

Custom Languages in Cybersecurity

Cybersecurity requires a proactive approach to threat detection, access control, and system hardening. Custom DSLs enable security teams to define attack patterns, specify firewall rules, and automate penetration testing. Security Information and Event Management (SIEM) systems often include query DSLs to filter and analyze logs efficiently. These languages allow security analysts to detect suspicious activities and craft responses to potential threats. Intrusion Detection Systems (IDS) and Web Application Firewalls (WAF) leverage DSLs to define rules that identify malicious traffic. By using declarative security policies, organizations can enforce access restrictions, detect anomalies, and respond to cyber threats systematically.

Automating Network Policies with DSLs

Network policies define how data flows between devices, ensuring secure communication and access control. Implementing these policies manually across diverse environments is error-prone and time-consuming. DSLs provide a structured approach to automating network policies, defining access control lists, traffic shaping rules, and encryption protocols. A policy enforcement DSL ensures that configurations remain compliant with security guidelines. For example, cloud platforms use Infrastructure as Code (IaC) DSLs to enforce security policies across virtualized networks. This automation reduces human intervention while ensuring that policies are applied consistently, reducing misconfigurations and security vulnerabilities.

Case Studies in Secure Software Development Using DSLs

The effectiveness of DSLs in security and networking is evident in real-world applications. Organizations developing secure software integrate DSLs to enforce security constraints during development. Secure coding DSLs help developers adhere to best practices by defining rules that prevent vulnerabilities such as SQL injection and cross-site scripting. Additionally, regulatory frameworks like GDPR and HIPAA require organizations to implement stringent security controls. DSLs enable automated compliance checking by translating regulatory requirements into enforceable rules. Case studies demonstrate how DSLs improve security posture by automating security audits, enforcing best practices, and reducing exposure to threats.

DSLs enhance security and networking by providing structured ways to define configurations, automate security policies, and enforce compliance. Their role in networking and cybersecurity helps organizations maintain secure infrastructures while reducing manual workload. The increasing reliance on automation and software-defined policies underscores the growing importance of DSLs in securing modern IT environments.

DSLs for Network Configuration and Monitoring

Network configuration and monitoring are critical components of modern IT infrastructure. Misconfigurations can lead to performance degradation, security vulnerabilities, and downtime. Domain-Specific Languages (DSLs) simplify network configuration and monitoring by providing a structured, human-readable format for defining rules, policies, and automation workflows. These languages eliminate the need for manually inputting complex commands across different devices, reducing errors and ensuring consistency. DSLs also enable real-time monitoring by defining triggers for alerts and automated responses to network anomalies. Software-Defined Networking (SDN), cloud infrastructure, and large-scale data centers benefit significantly from DSL-based automation, making network management more reliable and scalable.

In network configuration, DSLs provide abstractions for defining routing, firewall rules, VLAN assignments, and load balancing policies. Instead of configuring each network device manually using vendor-specific command-line interfaces, administrators can write high-level DSL scripts that apply changes uniformly across multiple devices. These scripts ensure compliance with predefined security policies and minimize human errors. For instance, a DSL for SDN can define traffic rules declaratively, which the controller then enforces across the network. Similarly, Infrastructure as Code (IaC) tools like Terraform and Ansible use DSLs to manage cloud networking, allowing teams to deploy scalable and secure architectures programmatically.

A simple DSL for defining network rules in Python might use a declarative approach to specify firewall policies. Consider the following example of a basic DSL for configuring firewall rules:

```
class FirewallRule:
    def __init__(self, action, protocol, port, source="any", destination="any"):
        self.action = action
        self.protocol = protocol
        self.port = port
        self.source = source
        self.destination = destination

    def __str__(self):
        return f"{self.action.upper()} {self.protocol.upper()} {self.port} FROM
            {self.source} TO {self.destination}"
class FirewallConfig:
    def __init__(self):
        self.rules = []

    def add_rule(self, action, protocol, port, source="any", destination="any"):
        self.rules.append(FirewallRule(action, protocol, port, source,
            destination))

    def apply(self):
        for rule in self.rules:
            print(rule)

# Example usage
fw = FirewallConfig()
fw.add_rule("allow", "tcp", 80, source="192.168.1.0/24", destination="10.0.0.1")
fw.add_rule("deny", "udp", 53, source="any", destination="any")
fw.apply()
```

This DSL simplifies firewall configuration by allowing administrators to define rules in a structured format without manually interacting with complex command-line tools. Each rule specifies an action (allow/deny), protocol (TCP/UDP), port, source, and destination, ensuring clarity and consistency.

Beyond configuration, DSLs enable real-time monitoring of network traffic. Many monitoring solutions, such as SNMP-based tools, use specialized DSLs to define alert thresholds and automated remediation workflows. For example, a monitoring DSL might specify conditions under which an alert should be triggered, such as high latency, packet loss, or unexpected traffic spikes. These policies help network administrators respond proactively to issues before they impact users.

DSLs enhance network configuration and monitoring by reducing complexity, ensuring policy compliance, and enabling automation. They provide structured ways to define networking rules, reducing manual effort and improving security. As networks become more dynamic and cloud-centric, DSL-based automation will continue to play a vital role in ensuring efficient and reliable network management.

Custom Languages in Cybersecurity

Cybersecurity is a complex field requiring precise control over security policies, threat detection, and incident response. Domain-Specific Languages (DSLs) play a crucial role in automating these tasks, enabling security professionals to define and enforce security measures in a structured, efficient manner. By leveraging DSLs, organizations can create rule-based security systems, automate vulnerability scans, and define custom intrusion detection policies. These languages reduce human error, enforce consistency, and improve response times by providing a high-level abstraction over raw security configurations, making them indispensable for modern cybersecurity infrastructure.

One of the most common applications of DSLs in cybersecurity is in rule-based intrusion detection systems (IDS) and firewalls. Security administrators use DSLs to define policies that dictate which traffic should be allowed or blocked. A well-known example is the Snort rules language, which allows defining network traffic signatures for detecting threats. Similarly, security-oriented DSLs are used in malware analysis, log parsing, and security policy enforcement. These DSLs enable rapid adaptation to evolving security threats by allowing administrators to update security policies without rewriting low-level system code.

To illustrate a simple custom DSL for defining security policies, consider a Python-based DSL that allows security teams to define access control rules in a structured manner. The following example defines a basic security policy language that restricts access based on user roles and resource permissions:

```python
class SecurityPolicy:
    def __init__(self):
        self.rules = []

    def allow(self, role, resource):
        self.rules.append((role, resource, "ALLOW"))

    def deny(self, role, resource):
        self.rules.append((role, resource, "DENY"))

    def evaluate(self, role, resource):
        for rule in self.rules:
            if rule[0] == role and rule[1] == resource:
                return rule[2]
        return "DENY"  # Default deny policy

# Example usage
policy = SecurityPolicy()
policy.allow("admin", "/secure_data")
policy.deny("guest", "/secure_data")

print(policy.evaluate("admin", "/secure_data"))  # Outputs: ALLOW
print(policy.evaluate("guest", "/secure_data"))  # Outputs: DENY
```

This DSL provides a structured way to define access control rules without hardcoding them into the application. Security teams can update the rules dynamically, ensuring compliance with evolving security policies.

Another important use of DSLs in cybersecurity is automating security incident response. Security Orchestration, Automation, and Response (SOAR) platforms often integrate custom scripting DSLs to define automated workflows for handling security events. For example, an organization may define a DSL-based policy that automatically quarantines a compromised endpoint when a security breach is detected.

Moreover, DSLs are valuable in log analysis and security event correlation. Custom languages allow security teams to specify patterns in logs that indicate suspicious activity. For instance, a DSL could define rules for identifying brute-force login attempts by monitoring repeated failed login attempts from the same IP address within a short time frame.

DSLs in cybersecurity provide structured, automated, and adaptable methods for defining security policies, intrusion detection rules, and automated responses. By abstracting low-level security configurations into human-readable policies, these languages enhance security operations, reduce misconfigurations, and improve threat detection efficiency. As cyber threats continue to evolve, DSLs will remain a key tool for improving security posture and response capabilities.

Automating Network Policies with DSLs

Managing network policies manually can be complex and error-prone, especially in large-scale enterprise environments. Domain-Specific Languages (DSLs) provide a structured approach to defining, enforcing, and automating network policies, reducing the risk of misconfigurations while improving security and performance. DSLs allow network administrators to define routing rules, firewall policies, and access control configurations in a human-readable yet machine-executable format, making network management more efficient and scalable.

A key advantage of using DSLs for network policy automation is their ability to abstract low-level configurations into high-level declarative rules. Instead of manually configuring individual network devices, administrators can specify policies using a DSL, which can then be translated into device-specific configurations. For example, software-defined networking (SDN) controllers use DSLs to define network behaviors dynamically, ensuring centralized policy enforcement across distributed environments.

A practical example of a network policy DSL can be seen in firewall rule management. Traditionally, firewalls require rules to be manually defined in complex configuration files. With a custom DSL, network security policies can be expressed in a structured and intuitive way, ensuring consistency and reducing errors. Consider the following Python-based DSL for defining network firewall rules:

```python
class FirewallPolicy:
    def __init__(self):
        self.rules = []

    def allow(self, source, destination, port):
```

```
        self.rules.append((source, destination, port, "ALLOW"))

    def deny(self, source, destination, port):
        self.rules.append((source, destination, port, "DENY"))

    def evaluate(self, source, destination, port):
        for rule in self.rules:
            if rule[0] == source and rule[1] == destination and rule[2] == port:
                return rule[3]
        return "DENY"  # Default deny policy

# Example usage
firewall = FirewallPolicy()
firewall.allow("192.168.1.10", "192.168.1.20", 80)
firewall.deny("192.168.1.100", "192.168.1.20", 22)

print(firewall.evaluate("192.168.1.10", "192.168.1.20", 80))  # Outputs: ALLOW
print(firewall.evaluate("192.168.1.100", "192.168.1.20", 22))  # Outputs: DENY
```

This DSL allows administrators to define network access policies in a structured way, reducing the complexity of configuring individual firewall rules. By using such a DSL, organizations can integrate automated policy enforcement with their network management workflows, ensuring compliance with security standards while minimizing human error.

Another use case of DSLs in network policy automation is traffic shaping and Quality of Service (QoS) management. Network operators can define policies that allocate bandwidth dynamically based on traffic type and priority. For instance, a DSL could be used to prioritize video conferencing traffic over general web browsing, ensuring optimal performance for critical applications.

DSLs are also widely used in cloud-based networking environments, where infrastructure-as-code (IaC) approaches rely on policy definition languages to automate network provisioning. Tools like HashiCorp's Terraform allow administrators to define network configurations declaratively, enabling repeatable and version-controlled network policy management.

DSLs play a crucial role in automating network policies by simplifying policy definition, reducing misconfigurations, and ensuring consistent enforcement. Whether applied to firewall management, traffic shaping, or cloud networking, DSLs provide a powerful mechanism for improving network security and performance while reducing administrative overhead.

Case Studies in Secure Software Development Using DSLs

Secure software development is a critical concern in modern computing, and Domain-Specific Languages (DSLs) have emerged as a valuable tool for enforcing security best practices, automating vulnerability detection, and enhancing compliance with security policies. By embedding security rules into DSLs, developers can reduce human error and improve code security while maintaining productivity. This section explores real-world case studies that demonstrate the effectiveness of DSLs in secure software development.

One prominent example is **SELinux Policy Language**, a DSL designed to define and enforce security policies at the operating system level. Security-Enhanced Linux (SELinux) provides mandatory access control (MAC) by allowing administrators to write fine-grained security policies using a declarative language. These policies restrict how applications access system resources, preventing privilege escalation and unauthorized data access. SELinux's DSL ensures that only explicitly permitted actions are executed, reducing the attack surface of critical systems.

Another case study is **Puppet DSL for Infrastructure Security**, which is widely used for automating security configurations in IT environments. Puppet, an infrastructure-as-code tool, enables administrators to define security policies in a high-level DSL that ensures compliance with security best practices. Consider the following example of a Puppet DSL snippet that enforces secure SSH configurations:

```
class ssh_security {
  file { '/etc/ssh/sshd_config':
    ensure  => 'file',
    content => template('ssh/sshd_config.erb'),
    mode    => '0600',
    owner   => 'root',
    group   => 'root',
  }

  service { 'sshd':
    ensure => running,
    enable => true,
  }
}
```

This policy ensures that the SSH configuration file follows security guidelines and that the SSH daemon remains running with secure settings. Using this DSL, organizations can standardize security policies across all managed servers, reducing misconfigurations and security vulnerabilities.

In the domain of **web security**, the **OWASP ZAP scripting language (ZEST)** provides another example of a DSL used for security testing. ZEST is a high-level scripting language that allows security professionals to automate penetration testing tasks, such as scanning web applications for vulnerabilities. By leveraging a DSL like ZEST, security testers can define reusable security test scripts that detect cross-site scripting (XSS), SQL injection, and other common vulnerabilities.

For application-level security, **CodeQL**, a DSL developed by GitHub, enables security researchers to analyze source code for vulnerabilities. CodeQL allows users to write security rules in a declarative syntax, identifying potential security flaws across large codebases. The following Python-based CodeQL query detects SQL injection vulnerabilities:

```
from CodeQL import *

class SQLInjection(Query):
    def execute(self):
```

```
return self.match("SELECT * FROM users WHERE name = '" + user_input +
    "'")
```

By using CodeQL, developers and security teams can proactively scan repositories for security weaknesses before deployment, improving software security.

DSLs are instrumental in secure software development across various domains, including system security, infrastructure automation, web application security, and static analysis. By integrating DSLs into security workflows, organizations can enhance protection against cyber threats, enforce security policies consistently, and reduce the risks associated with human error in software development.

Module 12:
DSLs in Artificial Intelligence and Machine Learning

Domain-Specific Languages (DSLs) have become an essential tool in artificial intelligence (AI) and machine learning (ML) by providing intuitive abstractions for model specification, training workflows, and data processing. By simplifying the complex processes involved in AI development, DSLs enhance productivity, improve code maintainability, and enable domain experts without deep programming expertise to define models and workflows effectively. This module explores the role of DSLs in AI, covering their application in ML model specification, their use in natural language processing (NLP), problem-solving techniques, and their integration with existing AI frameworks.

DSLs for Machine Learning Model Specification

Defining machine learning models requires managing complex hyperparameters, data transformations, and optimization algorithms. DSLs streamline this process by providing domain-specific syntax that abstracts low-level implementation details. DSLs such as Keras and TensorFlow's computation graphs allow developers to describe models in a more readable and structured format. By using a DSL for model specification, AI researchers and engineers can focus on designing better architectures instead of handling implementation details. The ability to declaratively define ML models also improves reproducibility and facilitates automated tuning and optimization in large-scale AI projects.

Custom DSLs in Natural Language Processing

Natural Language Processing (NLP) involves parsing, tokenization, entity recognition, and sentiment analysis, often requiring complex pipelines with various linguistic transformations. Custom DSLs simplify NLP tasks by providing higher-level constructs that abstract away low-level text processing. Examples include Stanford NLP's CoreNLP DSL and spaCy's rule-based matching language. These DSLs enable developers to define linguistic rules efficiently, making it easier to create robust NLP applications. By leveraging DSLs in NLP, businesses and researchers can rapidly prototype and deploy text-based AI applications while maintaining consistency in language processing logic across multiple projects.

DSLs for AI Problem Solving

Many AI applications require defining constraints, rules, or optimization strategies, which can be expressed efficiently through DSLs. In areas like constraint programming, expert systems, and reinforcement learning, DSLs help formalize problem-solving techniques by offering specialized syntax for defining rules and heuristics. Examples include Prolog for logic-based reasoning and Gurobi's mathematical programming DSL for optimization tasks. These domain-specific languages allow AI practitioners to express complex problem-solving logic in a structured manner, reducing errors and improving efficiency. The declarative nature of these DSLs makes AI models more interpretable, an essential factor in areas such as explainable AI.

Integration with Existing AI Frameworks

To be practical, DSLs in AI must integrate seamlessly with existing frameworks like TensorFlow, PyTorch, and Scikit-learn. Many DSLs are designed as embedded languages within Python or other general-purpose languages, ensuring interoperability with established AI tools. Integration allows developers to define AI models declaratively while leveraging the computational efficiency and scalability of mainstream frameworks. By embedding DSLs within AI toolchains, organizations can standardize workflows, enforce best practices, and facilitate collaboration between AI researchers, data scientists, and software engineers.

DSLs in artificial intelligence and machine learning provide structured ways to define models, process natural language, solve optimization problems, and integrate with existing frameworks. By abstracting complexity and offering high-level declarative syntax, these languages enhance productivity and ensure consistency in AI development. As AI systems continue to evolve, DSLs will play an increasingly vital role in making AI more accessible, efficient, and maintainable.

DSLs for Machine Learning Model Specification

Machine learning (ML) involves defining models, specifying training procedures, and optimizing hyperparameters, all of which can be complex and error-prone. Domain-Specific Languages (DSLs) simplify this process by providing high-level abstractions that allow users to focus on model design rather than low-level implementation details. DSLs help structure model definitions, enhance readability, and ensure consistency across experiments. Many modern ML frameworks embed DSL-like features to support model specification, enabling practitioners to define architectures declaratively.

One example of a widely used DSL for ML model specification is **Keras**, which provides a user-friendly way to define deep learning models. Instead of manually defining computation graphs and managing complex dependencies, Keras allows users to specify layers in a sequential or functional manner.

Defining an ML Model Using a DSL Approach

Consider an example where we use a simple DSL to define a deep learning model. This DSL abstracts away boilerplate code and allows users to focus on architecture specification. Below is a DSL-like approach using **Python** with Keras:

```
from tensorflow import keras
from tensorflow.keras.layers import Dense, Dropout

# Defining the model using a high-level DSL-like approach
```

```
model = keras.Sequential([
    Dense(128, activation='relu', input_shape=(784,)),  # Input Layer
    Dropout(0.2),  # Regularization
    Dense(64, activation='relu'),  # Hidden Layer
    Dense(10, activation='softmax')  # Output Layer for classification
])

# Compile the model with loss function, optimizer, and evaluation metric
model.compile(optimizer='adam',
              loss='sparse_categorical_crossentropy',
              metrics=['accuracy'])

# Summary of the model
model.summary()
```

This structured, declarative model definition removes the need for low-level tensor operations, making it easier to read and modify.

Benefits of Using a DSL for ML Model Specification

1. **Readability and Maintainability** – A DSL-based approach makes model definitions intuitive and reduces the risk of implementation errors.

2. **Rapid Prototyping** – Abstracting the model definition allows data scientists to experiment with different architectures quickly.

3. **Consistency and Reproducibility** – DSLs enforce standardization, making it easier to reproduce and share ML models across teams.

Custom DSLs for Model Specification

In some cases, organizations develop their own DSLs tailored to specific ML needs. For example, TensorFlow has **TensorFlow Probability** for probabilistic models, and ML pipelines often use **configuration-based DSLs** such as YAML or JSON to define training workflows declaratively.

```
model:
  layers:
    - type: Dense
      units: 128
      activation: relu
    - type: Dropout
      rate: 0.2
    - type: Dense
      units: 10
      activation: softmax
optimizer: adam
loss: sparse_categorical_crossentropy
metrics: accuracy
```

This YAML-based DSL allows defining ML models in a structured manner, which can be easily parsed and executed using a backend system.

DSLs in machine learning model specification streamline the development process, improve maintainability, and ensure consistency across projects. By abstracting away implementation complexities, they allow data scientists and engineers to focus on designing better models rather than dealing with low-level programming details. As AI continues to evolve, DSLs will play a crucial role in enhancing ML productivity.

Custom DSLs in Natural Language Processing

Natural Language Processing (NLP) involves complex tasks such as tokenization, parsing, sentiment analysis, and text generation. Developing robust NLP applications requires handling vast amounts of text data, implementing sophisticated algorithms, and managing linguistic nuances. Domain-Specific Languages (DSLs) simplify these challenges by providing high-level abstractions that allow developers to focus on language processing rather than low-level implementation details.

Custom DSLs for NLP streamline workflows by offering declarative syntax for text processing, making them ideal for applications in machine translation, chatbot development, and text summarization. Many modern NLP frameworks integrate DSL-like features to define linguistic rules, automate data preprocessing, and simplify model deployment.

Building a Simple DSL for NLP

A custom DSL for NLP can provide a structured way to define text-processing pipelines. Consider a DSL that allows users to specify NLP operations declaratively, which we will implement in Python using a simple interpreter.

```python
import re
from collections import Counter

class SimpleNLPDSL:
    def __init__(self, text):
        self.text = text

    def tokenize(self):
        self.text = self.text.split()
        return self

    def remove_punctuation(self):
        self.text = [re.sub(r'[^\w\s]', '', word) for word in self.text]
        return self

    def to_lowercase(self):
        self.text = [word.lower() for word in self.text]
        return self

    def word_frequency(self):
        return Counter(self.text)

# Example usage
dsl = SimpleNLPDSL("Hello, world! NLP with DSLs is powerful. Hello, AI!")
word_counts = (dsl.tokenize()
               .remove_punctuation()
               .to_lowercase()
```

```
                    .word_frequency())
 print(word_counts)
```

In this example, the **SimpleNLPDSL** class provides a high-level, chainable API for text processing. Instead of manually writing separate functions for tokenization, punctuation removal, and case normalization, users can compose operations declaratively.

DSLs for Defining Grammar Rules

DSLs are also useful for defining linguistic rules in NLP applications such as grammar checkers and chatbots. Many NLP frameworks, such as **SpaCy and NLTK**, provide DSL-like features for text parsing and rule-based analysis. A custom DSL for grammar checking might allow defining rules as follows:

```
 import spacy

 nlp = spacy.load("en_core_web_sm")

 def check_grammar(text):
     doc = nlp(text)
     for token in doc:
         if token.pos_ == "VERB" and token.dep_ == "aux":
             print(f"Possible grammar issue with: {token.text}")

 text = "She do not like it."
 check_grammar(text)
```

This implementation leverages **SpaCy's NLP pipeline**, which behaves like a DSL by allowing declarative text analysis.

Advantages of NLP DSLs

1. **Simplified Text Processing** – DSLs abstract complex NLP operations, reducing the need for verbose, low-level code.

2. **Rule-Based Language Processing** – Custom DSLs enable defining domain-specific linguistic rules, making them ideal for grammar checking and chatbot design.

3. **Integration with Machine Learning** – DSLs can be combined with ML models to preprocess text and extract features efficiently.

Custom DSLs enhance NLP workflows by offering structured, high-level abstractions for text processing and linguistic rule definition. Whether used for simple text transformations or sophisticated language analysis, DSLs improve efficiency, readability, and maintainability in NLP applications. As NLP continues to evolve, DSLs will play a critical role in defining linguistic processing pipelines.

DSLs for AI Problem Solving

Artificial Intelligence (AI) requires sophisticated problem-solving techniques, including search algorithms, optimization, and reasoning. While general-purpose programming languages provide flexibility, they often lead to verbose and complex implementations of AI models. Domain-Specific Languages (DSLs) address this by offering specialized constructs for defining AI problems declaratively, making it easier to express logic, constraints, and heuristics.

DSLs for AI problem solving streamline tasks such as rule-based inference, constraint satisfaction, and decision automation. Languages like **Prolog** exemplify AI-specific DSLs, providing a logic-based approach to knowledge representation and automated reasoning. Python-based DSLs can also simplify AI tasks through expressive domain-specific constructs.

Building a Simple DSL for AI Rule-Based Systems

A common approach in AI problem solving is rule-based reasoning, where logical rules define relationships between entities. A simple DSL can help define rules declaratively while leveraging an inference engine for decision-making. Consider the following Python-based DSL for defining AI rules:

```python
class RuleEngine:
    def __init__(self):
        self.rules = []
        self.facts = set()

    def add_rule(self, condition, action):
        self.rules.append((condition, action))

    def add_fact(self, fact):
        self.facts.add(fact)

    def infer(self):
        new_facts = set()
        for condition, action in self.rules:
            if condition(self.facts):
                new_facts.add(action)
        self.facts.update(new_facts)

# Define conditions
def has_symptom(facts):
    return "fever" in facts and "cough" in facts

# Create AI rule engine
engine = RuleEngine()
engine.add_fact("fever")
engine.add_fact("cough")
engine.add_rule(has_symptom, "possible_flu")
engine.infer()

print(engine.facts)  # Output: {'fever', 'cough', 'possible_flu'}
```

This DSL allows users to define conditions and rules declaratively. The **RuleEngine** processes facts and applies inference, automatically deducing new knowledge based on predefined logic.

DSLs for Constraint Satisfaction Problems

Another AI application is **Constraint Satisfaction Problems (CSPs)**, where DSLs provide an intuitive way to define constraints and search for solutions. Consider a simple DSL-like approach to solve a Sudoku puzzle:

```python
from ortools.sat.python import cp_model

def solve_sudoku():
    model = cp_model.CpModel()
    grid = [[model.NewIntVar(1, 9, f"x{i}{j}") for j in range(9)] for i in
            range(9)]

    # Example constraints
    for i in range(9):
        model.AddAllDifferent(grid[i])  # Rows must have unique numbers
        model.AddAllDifferent([grid[j][i] for j in range(9)])  # Columns must be
            unique

    solver = cp_model.CpSolver()
    solver.Solve(model)

solve_sudoku()
```

Here, **Google OR-Tools** provides a DSL-like API for defining constraints, ensuring concise and readable AI problem representations.

Benefits of DSLs in AI Problem Solving

1. **Declarative Problem Representation** – DSLs allow users to define AI rules, logic, and constraints without focusing on low-level implementation.

2. **Automated Inference and Search** – AI-specific DSLs streamline rule-based reasoning and constraint satisfaction, making complex problems easier to solve.

3. **Integration with AI Frameworks** – DSLs work alongside libraries like TensorFlow and OR-Tools to optimize AI workflows.

DSLs play a crucial role in AI problem solving by offering high-level abstractions for logic inference, constraint modeling, and decision automation. Whether used for rule-based reasoning, search algorithms, or optimization tasks, DSLs improve expressiveness, maintainability, and efficiency in AI-driven applications.

Integration with Existing AI Frameworks

Domain-Specific Languages (DSLs) for Artificial Intelligence (AI) are most effective when they integrate seamlessly with existing AI frameworks. While DSLs simplify AI model specification, problem-solving, and constraint management, they must work alongside powerful machine learning (ML) and AI libraries such as **TensorFlow**, **PyTorch**, **Scikit-learn**, and **Google OR-Tools**. By leveraging these frameworks, DSLs can act as high-level declarative layers, enabling researchers and engineers to focus on AI problem formulation rather than implementation details.

Integration involves bridging DSLs with these frameworks through custom parsers, transpilers, or embedded DSLs within general-purpose languages. The key advantage of such integration is **workflow automation**, allowing AI models to be defined in a concise domain-specific syntax while utilizing optimized computational backends for execution.

Embedding a DSL in Python for AI Integration

An effective approach to integrating DSLs into AI workflows is embedding them within an existing language. Consider a DSL that provides a declarative syntax for defining neural network layers while leveraging **TensorFlow** under the hood.

```python
import tensorflow as tf

class SimpleDSL:
    def __init__(self):
        self.model = tf.keras.Sequential()

    def add_layer(self, layer_type, units, activation=None):
        if layer_type == "dense":
            self.model.add(tf.keras.layers.Dense(units, activation=activation))

    def compile_model(self, optimizer, loss):
        self.model.compile(optimizer=optimizer, loss=loss)

    def summary(self):
        self.model.summary()

# Using the DSL
dsl = SimpleDSL()
dsl.add_layer("dense", 128, "relu")
dsl.add_layer("dense", 10, "softmax")
dsl.compile_model(optimizer="adam", loss="sparse_categorical_crossentropy")
dsl.summary()
```

This embedded DSL provides an abstraction over **TensorFlow**, enabling users to specify layers in a high-level format. Instead of using TensorFlow's verbose API, users interact with a concise DSL that maps directly to optimized deep-learning functions.

Integrating DSLs for Natural Language Processing (NLP)

DSLs are also beneficial in **Natural Language Processing (NLP)**, where they simplify text preprocessing, tokenization, and model definition. By integrating with **spaCy** or **NLTK**, a DSL can define linguistic rules declaratively.

```python
import spacy

class NLPDSL:
    def __init__(self, language="en_core_web_sm"):
        self.nlp = spacy.load(language)

    def extract_entities(self, text):
        doc = self.nlp(text)
```

```
        return [(ent.text, ent.label_) for ent in doc.ents]
# Using the DSL for NLP tasks
dsl = NLPDSL()
print(dsl.extract_entities("Google was founded by Larry Page and Sergey Brin in
        1998."))
```

This DSL integrates with **spaCy**, allowing users to define and execute NLP tasks efficiently. By abstracting away implementation details, it simplifies entity recognition and text processing while utilizing spaCy's optimized engine.

DSLs for AI Workflow Automation

AI frameworks require structured workflows involving data preprocessing, model training, evaluation, and deployment. A DSL can provide a high-level workflow definition that integrates with ML frameworks. Consider a simple DSL to automate an ML pipeline:

```
class MLWorkflowDSL:
    def __init__(self):
        self.steps = []

    def add_step(self, description, function, *args):
        self.steps.append((description, function, args))

    def execute(self):
        for desc, func, args in self.steps:
            print(f"Executing: {desc}")
            func(*args)

# Defining a simple ML workflow
from sklearn.datasets import load_iris
from sklearn.model_selection import train_test_split
from sklearn.ensemble import RandomForestClassifier

def load_data():
    data = load_iris()
    return train_test_split(data.data, data.target, test_size=0.2)

def train_model(X_train, y_train):
    model = RandomForestClassifier()
    model.fit(X_train, y_train)
    return model

# Using the DSL to automate workflow
dsl = MLWorkflowDSL()
dsl.add_step("Loading Data", load_data)
X_train, X_test, y_train, y_test = load_data()
dsl.add_step("Training Model", train_model, X_train, y_train)
dsl.execute()
```

This simple DSL abstracts ML pipeline execution, reducing boilerplate code while allowing seamless integration with **Scikit-learn**.

Benefits of DSL Integration with AI Frameworks

1. **Higher-Level Abstractions** – DSLs provide a declarative interface, reducing verbosity in AI model definitions.

133

2. **Performance Optimization** – Integration with TensorFlow, PyTorch, and Scikit-learn allows DSLs to leverage hardware acceleration and efficient algorithms.

3. **Simplified Workflow Automation** – DSLs enable streamlined model training, evaluation, and deployment with minimal boilerplate code.

4. **Improved Readability & Maintainability** – By using intuitive syntax, DSLs make AI workflows more accessible to domain experts.

Integrating DSLs with AI frameworks enhances productivity by simplifying model definitions, workflow automation, and text processing. Whether embedded within general-purpose languages or as standalone DSLs interfacing with TensorFlow, PyTorch, or NLP libraries, these tools improve efficiency in AI development. By leveraging existing AI frameworks, DSLs bridge the gap between domain expertise and technical implementation, making AI more accessible and scalable.

Part 3:

Programming Language Support for Domain Specific Languages

Programming languages play a crucial role in the design, implementation, and optimization of domain-specific languages (DSLs). Each language offers unique features that influence how DSLs are embedded, interpreted, or compiled. This part explores how various programming languages support DSL development, beginning with general language selection strategies before examining specific implementations in Ada, C#, C++, Java, Python, Ruby, Scala, and XSLT. By understanding how different languages facilitate DSL creation, developers can make informed choices that balance performance, expressiveness, and ease of integration, ensuring efficient and maintainable DSL implementations.

Introduction to Programming Languages for DSLs

Selecting the right programming language for DSL development is a foundational step in designing efficient domain-specific tools. Various languages provide features that influence whether a DSL should be embedded within an existing language or built as an external tool. Host languages such as Python, Ruby, and Scala support internal DSLs through metaprogramming and operator overloading, while lower-level languages like C++ facilitate external DSL creation through advanced parsing techniques. Leveraging existing libraries and frameworks can accelerate DSL development by providing robust parsing, code generation, and execution capabilities. This module establishes the fundamental principles of choosing a suitable language for DSL design.

DSLs in Ada

Ada is well-known for its reliability and safety features, making it a strong candidate for DSL development, particularly in system-level and embedded applications. Its strict type system and compile-time checks ensure DSLs built in Ada are both robust and secure. Ada's extensive support for domain modeling enables DSLs to represent high-integrity systems accurately. Real-world examples illustrate how Ada has been employed in defense, avionics, and critical infrastructure through DSLs tailored for secure, high-assurance computing. While Ada's advantages lie in its rigor, this module also examines challenges such as its verbosity and smaller ecosystem compared to more widely adopted languages.

DSLs in C#

C# offers powerful features for DSL development, particularly for internal DSLs. The Language Integrated Query (LINQ) framework is a prime example of a domain-specific language that seamlessly integrates with the C# ecosystem. Its strong typing, reflection, and extension methods make it ideal for embedding DSLs into existing applications. This module presents case studies demonstrating how C# DSLs simplify data manipulation, business logic execution, and domain modeling. Best practices emphasize optimizing performance through efficient memory management and leveraging C#'s dynamic capabilities while avoiding excessive abstraction that could reduce maintainability.

DSLs in C++

C++ serves as a foundation for many external DSLs due to its efficiency and fine-grained control over system resources. Its template metaprogramming capabilities and the Standard Template Library (STL) facilitate powerful DSL implementations that optimize performance. Many high-performance computing and simulation applications leverage C++ for DSL development. This module explores how DSLs in C++ benefit from strong type safety, performance optimizations, and extensive compiler support. However, it also highlights challenges such as the complexity of syntax and the need for careful memory management in DSL implementations.

DSLs in Java

Java provides a balance between flexibility and structure in DSL development. Embedded DSLs in Java often use method chaining, fluent interfaces, and annotations to create readable and expressive syntax. Java's extensive ecosystem includes libraries designed to support DSL creation, such as ANTLR for parsing and Groovy for scripting. This module demonstrates how Java DSLs streamline enterprise application development by facilitating rule-based engines, configuration management, and workflow automation. Java's cross-platform nature and integration capabilities make it an appealing choice for DSL development, despite its verbosity compared to more dynamically typed languages.

DSLs in Python, Ruby, Scala, and XSLT

Python, Ruby, Scala, and XSLT each offer distinct advantages for DSL development. Python's dynamic typing, metaprogramming, and concise syntax make it one of the most popular choices for internal DSLs. Ruby's metaprogramming capabilities allow for highly readable DSLs that resemble natural language. Scala leverages functional programming and a strong type system to create expressive and scalable DSLs. Meanwhile, XSLT, a declarative language designed for XML transformation, enables DSLs in data processing and document generation. This module explores how each of these languages facilitates DSL implementation in specialized domains.

By examining programming language support for DSLs, this part equips developers with the knowledge to select the best language for their needs. Understanding language-specific features ensures efficient, scalable, and maintainable DSLs.

Module 13:
Introduction to Programming Languages for DSLs

Domain-Specific Languages (DSLs) require a strong foundation in programming languages to be effectively designed, implemented, and maintained. The choice of language influences DSL expressiveness, usability, and integration potential. This module explores the programming languages suitable for DSL creation, strategies for embedding DSLs into host languages, and how leveraging existing libraries and frameworks can accelerate DSL development. By understanding the fundamental principles of programming languages in DSL construction, developers can make informed decisions on how to best design and implement domain-specific solutions efficiently.

Overview of Language Support for DSL Creation

The development of a DSL depends significantly on the programming language in which it is implemented. Some languages offer extensive features for defining internal and external DSLs, making them preferable for certain domains. For example, Lisp's macro system facilitates DSL creation, while Python's metaprogramming capabilities make it a flexible choice. Haskell's strong typing and functional paradigms support declarative DSLs, whereas Java and C# provide robust frameworks for embedding DSLs within enterprise applications. Each language's features determine how DSLs handle syntax, semantics, and execution. Understanding these capabilities helps in selecting the right language for specific DSL needs.

Choosing the Right Programming Language for DSL Development

Selecting the right language for DSL development depends on several factors, including ease of parsing, extensibility, and integration with existing software ecosystems. Languages with built-in parsing tools like ANTLR (for Java) or PEG.js (for JavaScript) simplify external DSL design. Functional languages like Haskell and Scala encourage declarative DSLs, which suit mathematical modeling and domain-specific optimizations. Meanwhile, scripting languages such as Python and Ruby allow rapid prototyping and embedding of DSLs in broader software solutions. The decision should align with the intended DSL use case, its target audience, and the ecosystem in which it will be deployed.

Embedding DSLs into Host Languages

An embedded DSL operates within a host language, taking advantage of its syntax and runtime while providing a more specialized interface for domain-specific tasks. Python, Ruby, and Scala excel in hosting DSLs due to their flexible syntax and metaprogramming capabilities.

Embedding allows a DSL to leverage existing host language libraries while maintaining tight integration with broader application logic. The challenge lies in balancing the DSL's expressiveness with readability and maintainability. Using language features like operator overloading, function chaining, and domain-specific abstractions, developers can create embedded DSLs that blend seamlessly into their host environments.

Leveraging Existing Libraries and Frameworks

Instead of building DSLs from scratch, developers can take advantage of existing libraries and frameworks to accelerate development. Tools like ANTLR, Lark (for Python), and JetBrains MPS provide powerful parsing capabilities for external DSLs. Similarly, metaprogramming libraries in Lisp, Ruby, and JavaScript allow dynamic DSL construction. Frameworks such as Xtext (for Java) and Roslyn (for .NET) help with code analysis, transformation, and execution in DSL-based applications. By leveraging these resources, developers can focus on refining their DSL's semantics and usability rather than implementing low-level parsing and execution mechanics.

Programming language choice and implementation strategies greatly impact DSL effectiveness. Whether using a standalone language or embedding a DSL within an existing host language, developers must consider syntax flexibility, parsing capabilities, and integration potential. Leveraging libraries and frameworks can further streamline DSL development. Understanding these principles ensures the creation of robust and scalable domain-specific solutions.

Overview of Language Support for DSL Creation

Programming languages play a fundamental role in the development of Domain-Specific Languages (DSLs), influencing syntax, expressiveness, and implementation complexity. Certain languages offer extensive features for both internal and external DSLs, making them more suitable for specific applications. Internal DSLs are embedded within a general-purpose language, leveraging its syntax and capabilities, while external DSLs require independent parsing and execution. Python, Lisp, Haskell, and Scala excel in supporting internal DSLs, while Java, Rust, and C++ are commonly used for building external DSLs with parsing tools. Understanding language-specific strengths helps in selecting the best platform for DSL development.

Languages like **Python** allow DSL creation through operator overloading, metaprogramming, and dynamic typing. Python's flexibility makes it a prime choice for internal DSLs, especially in automation, machine learning, and configuration management. Below is an example of an internal DSL using Python's expressive syntax for defining a query language:

```
class Query:
    def __init__(self, table):
        self.table = table
        self.filters = []

    def where(self, condition):
```

```
        self.filters.append(condition)
        return self

    def __str__(self):
        conditions = " AND ".join(self.filters)
        return f"SELECT * FROM {self.table} WHERE {conditions};"

query = Query("employees").where("age > 30").where("department = 'IT'")
print(query)  # Outputs: SELECT * FROM employees WHERE age > 30 AND department =
        'IT';
```

For external DSLs, **Java** is a popular choice due to its robust parsing frameworks like **ANTLR**. Below is an example of defining a simple arithmetic grammar using ANTLR:

```
grammar Arithmetic;

expr: term (('+'|'-') term)*;
term: factor (('*'|'/') factor)*;
factor: NUMBER | '(' expr ')';

NUMBER: [0-9]+;
WS: [ \t\r\n]+ -> skip;
```

This grammar enables parsing mathematical expressions, which can then be evaluated in a Java application.

Lisp provides unparalleled support for DSL creation through macros, enabling developers to manipulate code as data. Below is an example of a simple Lisp macro for defining a conditional operator:

```
(defmacro when (condition &body body)
  `(if ,condition
       (progn ,@body)))
```

This allows for concise DSL-style expressions like:

```
(when (> x 10)
  (print "X is greater than 10"))
```

Haskell is favored for functional DSLs due to its strong type system and parser combinators. Below is an example of a basic DSL for defining mathematical expressions:

```
data Expr = Add Expr Expr | Mul Expr Expr | Num Int

eval :: Expr -> Int
eval (Num n) = n
eval (Add a b) = eval a + eval b
eval (Mul a b) = eval a * eval b
```

With this, one can define and evaluate expressions like:

```
eval (Add (Num 5) (Mul (Num 2) (Num 3)))  -- Outputs: 11
```

Different programming languages bring unique strengths to DSL creation. Python excels in internal DSLs with dynamic typing, Java provides robust parsing frameworks for external DSLs, Lisp's macros allow deep syntax customization, and Haskell enforces correctness in functional DSLs. Choosing the right language and tools ensures that the DSL remains expressive, maintainable, and efficient within its domain.

Choosing the Right Programming Language for DSL Development

Selecting the appropriate programming language for DSL development depends on several factors, including the type of DSL (internal or external), the domain's requirements, and the level of control needed over parsing and execution. Internal DSLs are typically implemented within an existing general-purpose language, leveraging its syntax and runtime capabilities, while external DSLs require a separate parsing and execution engine. Languages like Python, Lisp, Scala, and Ruby excel in internal DSL development due to their flexible syntax and metaprogramming features. Meanwhile, languages like Java, Rust, and C++ are often used for external DSLs, where robust parsing and performance optimization are crucial.

Python is a popular choice for internal DSLs due to its readable syntax, operator overloading, and support for dynamic execution. Below is an example of a simple DSL for defining workflows in Python:

```python
class Task:
    def __init__(self, name):
        self.name = name

    def then(self, next_task):
        print(f"{self.name} → {next_task.name}")
        return next_task

# Example of an internal DSL usage
task1 = Task("Data Cleaning")
task2 = Task("Feature Engineering")
task3 = Task("Model Training")

task1.then(task2).then(task3)
```

This allows defining workflows in a readable, domain-specific way without needing complex syntax.

Lisp is another powerful language for DSL development due to its macro system, enabling deep syntax customization. A DSL for defining configuration settings can be created using macros:

```lisp
(defmacro define-setting (name value)
  `(defparameter ,name ,value))

(define-setting max-connections 100)
(define-setting timeout 30)
```

This allows users to define settings in a declarative DSL-like syntax while still leveraging Lisp's execution model.

For external DSLs, Java combined with ANTLR is a strong choice. The following example defines a simple grammar for mathematical expressions using ANTLR:

```
grammar MathExpr;
expr: expr ('+'|'-') expr
    | expr ('*'|'/') expr
    | NUMBER
    ;
NUMBER: [0-9]+;
WS: [ \t\r\n]+ -> skip;
```

This grammar enables parsing of arithmetic expressions, allowing a custom DSL for mathematical computations.

Scala is another excellent choice for DSLs, particularly internal ones, due to its concise syntax and strong type inference. Below is an example of a simple domain-specific rule engine:

```
case class Rule(condition: Boolean, action: () => Unit) {
  def apply(): Unit = if (condition) action()
}

val rule1 = Rule(5 > 3, () => println("Condition met"))
rule1()
```

This enables readable and expressive rule definitions, making it suitable for business logic modeling.

When choosing a language for DSL development, it is important to balance expressiveness, ease of parsing, execution performance, and ecosystem support. Python and Lisp are excellent for embedded DSLs due to their flexible syntax and metaprogramming capabilities, while Java and Rust offer robust tools for parsing and compiling external DSLs. Scala provides a balance between functional and object-oriented approaches, making it ideal for rule-based and reactive DSLs.

Embedding DSLs into Host Languages

Embedding a DSL into a host language involves designing the DSL in a way that it integrates seamlessly within an existing general-purpose programming language. This approach allows developers to leverage the features of the host language while providing domain-specific constructs that improve expressiveness and productivity. Internal DSLs are a common example of embedded DSLs, as they rely on the syntactic flexibility and runtime capabilities of their host language. Python, Ruby, and Scala are particularly well-suited for this due to their dynamic features, operator overloading, and metaprogramming capabilities.

One common technique for embedding a DSL is using function chaining or fluent interfaces. In Python, this can be achieved through method chaining, which allows DSL expressions to be written in a natural, readable manner. The following example demonstrates an embedded DSL for constructing SQL-like queries:

141

```python
class Query:
    def __init__(self, table):
        self.table = table
        self.fields = "*"
        self.conditions = ""

    def select(self, *fields):
        self.fields = ", ".join(fields)
        return self

    def where(self, condition):
        self.conditions = f"WHERE {condition}"
        return self

    def build(self):
        return f"SELECT {self.fields} FROM {self.table} {self.conditions};"

# Example usage
query = Query("employees").select("name", "age").where("age > 30").build()
print(query)
# Output: SELECT name, age FROM employees WHERE age > 30;
```

This approach makes query construction more intuitive, mimicking the structure of actual SQL statements.

Another way to embed DSLs is through decorators, which provide a natural way to define rules or behaviors in a domain-specific way. The following Python example illustrates how decorators can be used to create an embedded DSL for event-driven programming:

```python
event_handlers = {}

def on_event(event_name):
    def wrapper(func):
        event_handlers[event_name] = func
        return func
    return wrapper

@on_event("user_login")
def greet_user():
    print("Welcome back!")

# Simulating an event trigger
event_handlers["user_login"]()
# Output: Welcome back!
```

This DSL enables users to register event handlers in a declarative way, improving code readability and maintainability.

In Scala, DSLs can be embedded using implicit conversions and operator overloading, making the syntax highly expressive. The following example demonstrates an embedded DSL for defining access control rules:

```scala
case class User(role: String)

class PermissionChecker(user: User) {
  def can(action: String): Boolean = user.role match {
    case "admin" => true
    case "editor" if action == "edit" => true
    case _ => false
  }
}
```

```
}
implicit def userToPermissionChecker(user: User): PermissionChecker = new
        PermissionChecker(user)

// Example usage
val user = User("editor")
println(user can "edit")   // Output: true
println(user can "delete")  // Output: false
```

This allows for natural language-like expressions, improving the DSL's usability.

Embedded DSLs take advantage of the syntactic and runtime features of their host language, allowing developers to build domain-specific solutions without implementing a full parser or compiler. By leveraging method chaining, decorators, operator overloading, and implicit conversions, internal DSLs can offer a seamless and intuitive way to interact with domain logic while maintaining the power of the underlying host language.

Leveraging Existing Libraries and Frameworks

Building a DSL from scratch can be complex and time-consuming. However, leveraging existing libraries and frameworks can significantly accelerate development, improve reliability, and reduce maintenance costs. Many programming languages offer powerful tools that assist in DSL creation, such as parsing libraries, domain-specific frameworks, and embedded scripting environments. Python, with its extensive ecosystem, provides numerous options for building and integrating DSLs efficiently.

One of the most useful libraries for DSL development in Python is **Lark**, a parsing toolkit that simplifies the creation of both internal and external DSLs. The following example demonstrates how Lark can be used to create a DSL for defining mathematical expressions:

```
from lark import Lark, Transformer

grammar = """
    start: expr
    expr: expr "+" term  -> add
        | expr "-" term  -> sub
        | term
    term: /\d+/
"""

class EvalTransformer(Transformer):
    def add(self, values):
        return values[0] + values[1]

    def sub(self, values):
        return values[0] - values[1]

    def term(self, values):
        return int(values[0])

parser = Lark(grammar, parser="lalr", transformer=EvalTransformer())
result = parser.parse("10 + 5 - 3")
print(result)  # Output: 12
```

Here, Lark provides a simple way to define and parse a DSL for mathematical expressions. The grammar defines how expressions should be parsed, and the transformer interprets them into concrete operations.

Another useful tool is **PLY (Python Lex-Yacc)**, which allows for defining token-based DSLs similar to traditional compiler design. The following example demonstrates a simple DSL for basic command execution:

```python
import ply.lex as lex
import ply.yacc as yacc

tokens = ("PRINT", "STRING")
t_PRINT = r'PRINT'
t_STRING = r'"[^"]*"'
t_ignore = ' \t\n'

def t_error(t):
    print("Illegal character!")
    t.lexer.skip(1)

lexer = lex.lex()

def p_statement_print(p):
    'statement : PRINT STRING'
    print(p[2][1:-1])  # Remove quotes

def p_error(p):
    print("Syntax error!")

parser = yacc.yacc()
parser.parse('PRINT "Hello, DSL!"')  # Output: Hello, DSL!
```

PLY allows developers to define a fully functional DSL using tokenization and grammar rules. This method is beneficial when a structured, formal syntax is needed.

Frameworks like **ANTLR** provide cross-language support for DSL development, allowing DSLs to be designed in Python, Java, or C++. Similarly, **Scala's parser combinators** simplify DSL creation in the JVM ecosystem. In web applications, **Flask-RESTful** can be used to define API-based DSLs, while **SQLAlchemy** offers an embedded DSL for database querying.

By leveraging existing libraries and frameworks, developers can reduce the complexity of DSL development while maintaining high performance and flexibility. These tools provide essential parsing, interpretation, and execution capabilities that make DSL implementation more efficient and maintainable.

Module 14:
DSLs in Ada

Ada is a high-level, strongly typed programming language designed for reliability and maintainability, making it an excellent choice for Domain-Specific Languages (DSLs), particularly in safety-critical and real-time systems. This module explores Ada's suitability for DSL development, its application in system-level and embedded DSLs, real-world case studies, and the advantages and challenges of using Ada for DSLs. Given Ada's focus on safety, concurrency, and robustness, it presents unique opportunities and constraints when designing DSLs tailored to specific domains such as avionics, automotive, and defense systems.

Ada's Suitability for DSL Development

Ada's design prioritizes safety and correctness, making it an ideal choice for DSLs where reliability is paramount. The language enforces strong typing, preventing many common programming errors that can arise in dynamically typed languages. Additionally, Ada's built-in concurrency model facilitates DSLs in domains that require parallel execution, such as real-time control systems. The language's support for modular programming ensures DSLs remain scalable and maintainable. Ada's ability to create custom types and strong compile-time checking also allows developers to build DSLs with domain-specific constraints, ensuring that errors are caught early in the development process.

Using Ada for System-Level and Embedded DSLs

Ada's suitability for system-level and embedded DSLs is evident in its use within aerospace, defense, and industrial automation. Its deterministic execution model and real-time capabilities make it ideal for embedded systems requiring precise timing and reliability. DSLs written in Ada can define system configurations, automate hardware interactions, and enforce safety policies. Additionally, Ada's ability to interface with lower-level assembly code allows it to create high-performance DSLs while maintaining strong abstraction and type safety. The language's support for Ravenscar tasking profiles and its certified safety standards make it a preferred choice for DSLs in mission-critical environments.

Case Studies and Examples

Several real-world applications demonstrate Ada's effectiveness in DSL development. For example, SPARK, a formally verified subset of Ada, is widely used in high-assurance systems where correctness proofs are required. The avionics industry leverages Ada-based DSLs for flight control systems, ensuring that complex algorithms remain verifiable and maintainable. Additionally, Ada is used in safety-critical automotive software, where custom DSLs enforce compliance with standards such as ISO 26262. These case studies illustrate how Ada's robust

145

type system, modularity, and verification capabilities contribute to reliable and maintainable DSL implementations in complex domains.

Ada's Advantages and Challenges for DSLs

Ada offers several advantages for DSL development, including safety, strong typing, and modularity. Its ability to define precise type constraints and ensure correctness through compile-time checks reduces runtime errors. Additionally, Ada's support for concurrency and real-time execution makes it ideal for DSLs in embedded and safety-critical domains. However, Ada's learning curve can be steep, and its ecosystem is smaller compared to languages like Python or C++. The limited availability of modern tooling and libraries may also pose challenges for DSL development. Nonetheless, for applications demanding reliability and correctness, Ada remains a powerful choice for DSLs.

Ada's strong typing, reliability, and real-time capabilities make it a compelling language for DSL development, particularly in embedded and safety-critical domains. While its ecosystem may not be as extensive as other languages, its advantages in correctness and maintainability outweigh these limitations for specialized applications. Understanding Ada's strengths and challenges enables developers to leverage its features effectively when designing DSLs.

Ada's Suitability for DSL Development

Ada's design philosophy revolves around safety, reliability, and maintainability, making it particularly well-suited for Domain-Specific Language (DSL) development in high-assurance systems. Ada enforces strong typing, modular programming, and concurrency control, reducing the risks of runtime errors and increasing system correctness. These features make Ada an attractive option for DSLs in domains such as aerospace, automotive, medical, and defense applications, where precision and reliability are paramount.

One of the primary advantages of Ada for DSL development is its ability to define strict type constraints. This ensures that DSLs built using Ada can enforce domain-specific rules at compile time rather than runtime, preventing subtle logic errors that might otherwise go undetected. Ada's type system allows for the creation of user-defined types with strong constraints, making it possible to develop DSLs that embed domain-specific safety checks directly into the language itself.

Ada's support for modular programming also plays a crucial role in DSL design. Developers can create reusable, well-structured modules that encapsulate domain logic, reducing code duplication and improving maintainability. This modular approach ensures that DSLs remain scalable, even in complex systems with multiple interacting components.

Another key aspect of Ada's suitability for DSLs is its built-in concurrency model. Ada provides high-level constructs such as tasks, protected objects, and rendezvous-based synchronization, making it particularly useful for developing DSLs that model concurrent processes. This is essential for domains such as real-time systems, where multiple processes must execute in parallel while ensuring safety and determinism.

To illustrate Ada's capabilities in DSL development, consider a simple example of a DSL for configuring an industrial automation system. Ada's package system allows developers to define domain-specific abstractions with strict type enforcement.

```
package Automation_DSL is
   type Sensor_ID is range 1 .. 100;
   type Actuator_ID is range 1 .. 50;
   type State is (On, Off);

   procedure Set_Sensor(Sensor : Sensor_ID; State : State);
   procedure Set_Actuator(Actuator : Actuator_ID; State : State);
end Automation_DSL;
```

This DSL enforces type safety at compile time, preventing invalid sensor or actuator identifiers from being used. The procedures Set_Sensor and Set_Actuator encapsulate domain-specific logic, ensuring that the automation system operates within defined constraints.

Despite its advantages, Ada is not without its challenges in DSL development. The language's syntax and design choices may present a steep learning curve for developers unfamiliar with its paradigms. Additionally, while Ada's ecosystem is stable, it lacks the extensive third-party libraries available in more mainstream languages like Python or Java, which could limit its applicability for some DSL implementations.

However, for applications requiring strict correctness, safety, and reliability, Ada remains one of the best choices for DSL development. By leveraging its strong typing, concurrency model, and modular design, developers can create highly dependable DSLs tailored to specific application domains.

Using Ada for System-Level and Embedded DSLs

Ada's robust type system, concurrency support, and real-time capabilities make it particularly suitable for developing Domain-Specific Languages (DSLs) targeting system-level and embedded applications. Many embedded systems, such as avionics, automotive control units, and industrial automation, demand highly reliable and deterministic software. Ada's design aligns well with these requirements, enabling DSLs that facilitate system configuration, state management, and real-time execution constraints.

One key feature that makes Ada suitable for system-level DSLs is its support for real-time programming. The language includes built-in tasking mechanisms, protected types for synchronization, and a well-defined real-time scheduling model. These features enable developers to create DSLs that handle real-time constraints without the need for external concurrency libraries or operating system-dependent features.

Ada's package system and strong type safety also contribute to its viability for embedded DSLs. Developers can define domain-specific abstractions with strict type enforcement, ensuring that invalid configurations are caught at compile time. This is particularly useful in safety-critical applications where runtime errors must be minimized. Additionally, Ada's support for low-level memory manipulation makes it possible to build efficient DSLs for interacting directly with hardware while maintaining type safety.

A practical example of an Ada-based DSL for an embedded system could be a language that specifies configuration settings for a real-time control system. The following example defines a DSL for setting execution priorities and task scheduling in an embedded system:

```
package RTOS_Config is
    type Priority_Level is range 1 .. 10;
    type Task_ID is range 1 .. 50;

    procedure Set_Task_Priority(Task : Task_ID; Priority : Priority_Level);
    procedure Configure_Scheduler(Mode : String);
end RTOS_Config;
```

This DSL ensures that only valid priority levels and task identifiers are used, reducing configuration errors in real-time operating system (RTOS) setups. By encapsulating domain-specific logic in Ada's package system, developers can create a declarative DSL that simplifies system configuration while maintaining safety and correctness.

Another strength of Ada in embedded DSLs is its deterministic memory management. Unlike garbage-collected languages, Ada provides fine-grained control over memory allocation, making it ideal for environments with limited resources. Embedded DSLs in Ada can leverage stack-based memory allocation and avoid unpredictable pauses associated with garbage collection, ensuring consistent performance in real-time applications.

Despite its advantages, Ada does present some challenges for embedded DSL development. The language's strict safety mechanisms can sometimes make low-level optimizations more complex, requiring careful balancing between performance and reliability. Additionally, Ada's ecosystem, while mature, is not as widely adopted as C or Rust in embedded systems, which may limit the availability of third-party tools and libraries.

Overall, Ada's combination of real-time capabilities, type safety, and deterministic execution makes it an excellent choice for developing DSLs in system-level and embedded domains. By leveraging Ada's features, developers can create expressive, domain-specific abstractions that enhance the reliability and maintainability of embedded software.

Case Studies and Examples

Ada has been used in several real-world applications as the foundation for Domain-Specific Languages (DSLs) in critical system domains. Due to its strong type safety, concurrency model, and real-time support, Ada enables the development of DSLs that enforce strict correctness guarantees, making it particularly suited for aviation, defense, and industrial automation.

One notable example is the **SPARK Ada subset**, which acts as a formal verification DSL for high-integrity systems. SPARK is used in safety-critical applications such as aerospace and railway signaling, where system correctness is paramount. The SPARK subset of Ada removes features that introduce ambiguity, ensuring that programs can be formally verified using mathematical proofs. For instance, SPARK is used in the software controlling Airbus A380 flight systems, ensuring reliability through static analysis techniques.

A simple example of SPARK as a DSL for safety-critical development is shown below:

```
package Safe_Calculations with SPARK_Mode is
   function Safe_Divide (A, B : Integer) return Integer
      with Pre => B /= 0,   -- Ensures no division by zero
           Post => Safe_Divide'Result * B = A;
end Safe_Calculations;
```

This DSL ensures that division by zero cannot occur, leveraging Ada's contract-based programming features to prevent runtime errors.

Another successful Ada-based DSL is **Real-Time Systems Modeling (RTSM)**, which simplifies scheduling and task allocation for embedded control systems. RTSM provides a high-level abstraction over Ada's real-time tasking model, allowing engineers to define system constraints declaratively.

A simplified Ada-based RTSM DSL example could look like this:

```
task type Control_Task (Priority : Integer) with
   Priority => Priority;
```

This snippet enables engineers to specify task priorities explicitly, ensuring deterministic execution without requiring low-level thread management.

Ada has also been leveraged for **mission-critical automation in industrial systems**. A case study from the European Space Agency (ESA) demonstrated the use of an Ada-based DSL for spacecraft system configuration. By defining domain-specific abstractions for spacecraft telemetry and control, ESA engineers improved software reliability and maintainability.

While Ada-based DSLs provide strong guarantees of correctness, their adoption is often limited by the language's niche ecosystem. However, for industries that require high-assurance software, Ada remains a top choice for designing DSLs that enforce safety, correctness, and efficiency.

Ada's Advantages and Challenges for DSLs

Ada provides several advantages for developing Domain-Specific Languages (DSLs), particularly in safety-critical, embedded, and real-time systems. However, despite its strengths, it also faces challenges that limit its broader adoption. Understanding these advantages and limitations helps developers make informed decisions when choosing Ada as the foundation for a DSL.

One of Ada's primary advantages is its **strong type system**, which enforces strict compile-time checks, reducing runtime errors. This is particularly useful for DSLs designed for mission-critical applications. For example, in a DSL for flight control systems, Ada's type system can prevent invalid state transitions:

```
subtype Altitude is Integer range 0 .. 40000;
Current_Altitude : Altitude := 10000;
```

By restricting values at compile time, Ada ensures that the DSL prevents erroneous altitude assignments, improving reliability.

Ada also excels in **concurrency and real-time execution**, making it an excellent choice for DSLs targeting embedded and real-time applications. Its tasking model simplifies parallel processing and ensures predictable behavior, which is critical in domains like avionics and industrial automation. For instance, a DSL for real-time control might define tasks as follows:

```
task type Sensor_Task is
    entry Start;
    entry Stop;
end Sensor_Task;
```

This abstraction allows DSL users to focus on high-level behavior rather than low-level thread management.

Another advantage is Ada's **contract-based programming model**, which allows DSL designers to define preconditions, postconditions, and invariants for functions. This ensures that domain-specific rules are enforced at the language level. For example, a financial modeling DSL could enforce transaction integrity:

```
function Transfer (Amount : Money) return Boolean
    with Pre => Amount > 0,
         Post => Balance'Result = Balance'Old - Amount;
```

This prevents invalid transactions while keeping DSL users focused on business logic rather than implementation details.

Despite these advantages, Ada faces challenges that impact its use in DSL development. One major challenge is its **limited ecosystem and tooling**. Compared to mainstream languages like Python or Java, Ada has fewer third-party libraries, IDE integrations, and community-driven resources. This can slow down DSL adoption and development.

Additionally, Ada has a **steep learning curve**, requiring developers to become proficient in its strict syntax and design principles. This makes it harder for teams unfamiliar with Ada to adopt it for DSL development, especially when alternatives like Python offer more accessible DSL creation frameworks.

Finally, Ada's **niche usage in industry** limits its application beyond safety-critical domains. While it excels in defense, aerospace, and industrial automation, it is rarely chosen for web development, general business applications, or modern AI-driven systems.

Ada's strengths in type safety, concurrency, and contract-based programming make it a powerful choice for designing high-assurance DSLs. However, its limited ecosystem, complexity, and niche industry focus present adoption challenges. For mission-critical DSLs, Ada remains a top contender, but for general-purpose DSLs, more widely supported languages may offer greater flexibility.

Module 15:
DSLs in C#

Domain-Specific Languages (DSLs) in C# leverage the language's rich feature set to enable expressive, domain-focused solutions. C# is particularly suited for internal DSLs, allowing developers to embed custom domain syntax seamlessly into applications. This module explores how C# facilitates DSL development, emphasizing LINQ, real-world use cases, and best practices for performance and maintainability.

C# for Creating Powerful Internal DSLs

C# provides extensive support for internal DSLs, making it an excellent choice for developers looking to integrate domain-specific logic directly within their applications. Internal DSLs in C# take advantage of features such as extension methods, fluent interfaces, and lambda expressions to create intuitive, readable code structures that resemble natural language.

The power of internal DSLs in C# is evident in frameworks like Entity Framework, where query expressions are seamlessly embedded within C# code to define database interactions declaratively. Fluent APIs, commonly seen in unit testing frameworks like NUnit or FluentAssertions, also exemplify how C# enables expressive domain-specific syntax. These techniques allow developers to create custom abstractions tailored to specific problem domains without requiring a separate language parser or interpreter.

The Role of LINQ and Other C# Features in DSL Design

Language Integrated Query (LINQ) is one of C#'s most powerful features for DSL development. LINQ provides a declarative way to work with collections, databases, XML, and other data sources, making it a foundational tool for DSL design. LINQ's composability allows developers to build expressive and efficient DSLs without departing from C#'s syntax.

Additionally, C# features such as expression trees, reflection, and the Roslyn compiler API empower developers to construct sophisticated DSLs. Expression trees allow DSLs to analyze and transform code at runtime, while Roslyn enables deep code analysis and generation. These capabilities support the development of dynamic and efficient DSLs that integrate seamlessly with the .NET ecosystem.

Real-World Examples of C# DSLs

C# DSLs are widely used in various domains, including web development, financial modeling, and automation. Fluent API-based DSLs like AutoMapper simplify object mapping, while SpecFlow provides a C# DSL for behavior-driven development (BDD). Another example is the

Dapper micro-ORM, which utilizes a lightweight DSL for database access, optimizing performance while maintaining simplicity.

Game development engines such as Unity also employ C# DSLs to manage in-game logic. Unity's C# scripting environment allows developers to create domain-specific abstractions that simplify game mechanics, physics interactions, and UI components. These real-world applications demonstrate how DSLs in C# enhance productivity by streamlining domain-specific tasks.

Best Practices and Performance Tips in C# DSLs

Creating an efficient DSL in C# requires adhering to best practices that ensure maintainability, performance, and usability. One key consideration is balancing abstraction and flexibility—while DSLs should simplify domain-specific operations, they must also allow for extensibility when needed. Developers should leverage C#'s strong typing system to enforce constraints and prevent misuse of DSL constructs.

Performance optimization is another critical aspect. LINQ-based DSLs should be carefully designed to avoid unnecessary memory allocations and deferred execution pitfalls. Expression trees and Roslyn-based DSLs should be optimized to minimize runtime overhead. Ensuring clear documentation and intuitive DSL syntax further enhances usability and adoption among developers.

C# offers a robust platform for developing internal DSLs, thanks to features like LINQ, fluent APIs, and expression trees. From database querying to game development and automation, C# DSLs streamline domain-specific tasks while maintaining performance and readability. By following best practices, developers can create powerful DSLs that integrate seamlessly within the .NET ecosystem, enhancing productivity and maintainability.

C# for Creating Powerful Internal DSLs

C# is a strong candidate for developing internal DSLs, offering a range of features that enable expressive, readable, and domain-focused solutions. Internal DSLs in C# are designed to be embedded within applications, allowing developers to write declarative, domain-specific logic without the need for external tools or custom parsers. This section explores key techniques for constructing internal DSLs in C# using fluent interfaces, extension methods, and lambda expressions.

A common approach to building DSLs in C# is through **fluent interfaces**, where method chaining improves readability and usability. Consider a simple DSL for defining financial transactions:

```
public class Transaction
{
    public string From { get; private set; }
    public string To { get; private set; }
    public decimal Amount { get; private set; }
```

```csharp
public Transaction FromAccount(string from)
{
    From = from;
    return this;
}

public Transaction ToAccount(string to)
{
    To = to;
    return this;
}

public Transaction WithAmount(decimal amount)
{
    Amount = amount;
    return this;
}

public void Execute()
{
    Console.WriteLine($"Transferring {Amount:C} from {From} to {To}.");
}
}
```

Using this DSL, a financial transaction can be written in an intuitive, human-readable way:

```csharp
new Transaction()
    .FromAccount("Alice")
    .ToAccount("Bob")
    .WithAmount(1000)
    .Execute();
```

Another powerful technique for internal DSLs in C# is **extension methods**, which allow custom behavior to be added to existing types. For instance, a DSL for validating user input might look like this:

```csharp
public static class ValidationExtensions
{
    public static bool IsEmail(this string input) =>
        Regex.IsMatch(input, @"^[^@\s]+@[^@\s]+\.[^@\s]+$");
}

string email = "test@example.com";
Console.WriteLine(email.IsEmail() ? "Valid email" : "Invalid email");
```

Lambda expressions and **expression trees** further enhance DSL capabilities by enabling dynamic execution and transformation of code. This is particularly useful in scenarios like query building, where expressions need to be parsed at runtime.

C# also supports **operator overloading**, which allows DSLs to introduce custom syntax. For example, a simple math DSL could redefine operators for vector addition:

```csharp
public class Vector
{
    public int X { get; }
    public int Y { get; }

    public Vector(int x, int y)
    {
```

```
        X = x;
        Y = y;
    }

    public static Vector operator +(Vector a, Vector b) =>
        new Vector(a.X + b.X, a.Y + b.Y);
}
```

These techniques make C# an excellent platform for DSL development, allowing developers to create domain-specific abstractions without leaving the language. By leveraging fluent interfaces, extension methods, lambda expressions, and operator overloading, developers can design DSLs that are both expressive and maintainable.

The Role of LINQ and other C# Features in DSL Design

Language Integrated Query (LINQ) is one of the most powerful features in C# and plays a crucial role in DSL design. LINQ provides a declarative syntax for working with collections, databases, XML, and other data sources, making it an excellent foundation for internal DSLs. The ability to write expressive, chainable, and readable queries makes LINQ a model for designing DSLs that simplify complex data manipulations.

Consider a simple example of LINQ's declarative style:

```
var results = people
    .Where(p => p.Age > 18)
    .OrderBy(p => p.Name)
    .Select(p => p.Name);
```

This code exemplifies the advantages of a well-structured DSL: it is **readable, expressive, and declarative**. The same principles can be applied when designing DSLs in C#.

Building Custom DSLs with LINQ

Developers can extend LINQ's query capabilities to create domain-specific query languages. This is done using **custom extension methods** that mimic the syntax and functionality of LINQ but are tailored to specific domains. Consider a simple example of a DSL for querying employee records:

```
public static class EmployeeExtensions
{
    public static IEnumerable<Employee> OlderThan(this IEnumerable<Employee>
        employees, int age)
    {
        return employees.Where(e => e.Age > age);
    }
}

var seniorEmployees = employees.OlderThan(40);
```

Here, the OlderThan method integrates seamlessly into LINQ-style queries, creating a domain-specific query language for filtering employees based on age.

Expression Trees in DSLs

155

C# supports **expression trees**, a feature that allows DSLs to dynamically construct and manipulate code. LINQ uses expression trees to translate queries into SQL when working with databases, making it an essential tool for designing query-based DSLs. Consider a DSL that converts queries into a structured format for analysis:

```
Expression<Func<Employee, bool>> expr = e => e.Age > 30;
Console.WriteLine(expr.Body); // Outputs: (e.Age > 30)
```

This capability enables DSLs that transform user-defined expressions into SQL, JSON, or other representations dynamically.

Fluent Interfaces and Method Chaining

LINQ's method-chaining approach is ideal for internal DSLs, as it promotes a **human-readable** and **composable** syntax. This technique can be used for designing DSLs in various domains, such as financial calculations, workflow automation, and event processing.

Consider a financial DSL that allows composing tax calculations fluently:

```
public class TaxCalculation
{
    private decimal amount;

    public TaxCalculation(decimal baseAmount)
    {
        amount = baseAmount;
    }

    public TaxCalculation ApplyTax(decimal percentage)
    {
        amount += amount * (percentage / 100);
        return this;
    }

    public decimal GetAmount() => amount;
}

var total = new TaxCalculation(1000).ApplyTax(5).ApplyTax(10).GetAmount();
```

This approach ensures the DSL remains intuitive and readable while still leveraging the full power of C#.

C# provides a robust foundation for DSL development, with LINQ serving as an exemplary model for designing expressive query DSLs. By leveraging extension methods, expression trees, and fluent interfaces, developers can craft powerful, readable, and domain-specific abstractions. These techniques enable seamless integration of DSLs into real-world applications, making C# a preferred language for DSL development.

Real-World Examples of C# DSLs

C# has been used extensively in real-world applications to develop Domain-Specific Languages (DSLs) that improve productivity, simplify complex problems, and enhance maintainability. From data processing frameworks to configuration management and workflow automation, C# DSLs have found their way into various domains. This section explores real-world examples that highlight the power and versatility of C# in DSL development.

FluentValidation: A DSL for Data Validation

One of the most widely used C# DSLs is FluentValidation, a library that provides a fluent interface for defining validation rules. Instead of writing cumbersome if-else conditions to validate user input, FluentValidation allows developers to define constraints in an expressive and readable manner.

Consider the following example of a DSL for validating user input:

```
using FluentValidation;

public class User
{
    public string Name { get; set; }
    public int Age { get; set; }
}

public class UserValidator : AbstractValidator<User>
{
    public UserValidator()
    {
        RuleFor(user => user.Name).NotEmpty().WithMessage("Name is required.");
        RuleFor(user => user.Age).GreaterThan(18).WithMessage("User must be at
            least 18 years old.");
    }
}

var user = new User { Name = "", Age = 16 };
var validator = new UserValidator();
var results = validator.Validate(user);

foreach (var failure in results.Errors)
{
    Console.WriteLine(failure.ErrorMessage);
}
```

This DSL provides a declarative, human-readable way to enforce business rules, making validation logic **more maintainable and reusable**.

SpecFlow: A DSL for Behavior-Driven Development (BDD)

SpecFlow is another example of a real-world C# DSL, used for Behavior-Driven Development (BDD). It allows developers to write executable specifications using a DSL based on Gherkin syntax.

A typical feature file using SpecFlow's DSL looks like this:

```
Feature: User Login

Scenario: Valid login
```

```
Given the user enters a valid username and password
When they submit the login form
Then they should be redirected to the dashboard
```

The corresponding C# implementation would map these steps to code:

```
[Given(@"the user enters a valid username and password")]
public void GivenTheUserEntersValidCredentials()
{
    // Simulate user entering credentials
}

[When(@"they submit the login form")]
public void WhenTheySubmitTheLoginForm()
{
    // Simulate form submission
}

[Then(@"they should be redirected to the dashboard")]
public void ThenTheyShouldBeRedirected()
{
    // Validate redirection
}
```

This DSL allows business analysts and developers to collaborate effectively, bridging the gap between requirements and implementation.

Entity Framework (EF) Core: A DSL for Database Interactions

Entity Framework Core (EF Core) is an internal DSL in C# that simplifies database interactions. It abstracts SQL queries and provides a LINQ-based API for working with relational databases.

For example, querying a database using EF Core's DSL looks like this:

```
var customers = dbContext.Customers
    .Where(c => c.IsActive)
    .OrderBy(c => c.LastName)
    .ToList();
```

Instead of writing raw SQL, developers can use EF Core's DSL to interact with databases in a **type-safe, expressive, and maintainable** manner.

Real-world examples such as FluentValidation, SpecFlow, and EF Core demonstrate the power of C# DSLs in simplifying complex tasks. These DSLs enhance code readability, improve maintainability, and boost productivity. By leveraging fluent interfaces, declarative syntax, and language features like LINQ, C# developers can create expressive DSLs tailored to specific problem domains.

Best Practices and Performance Tips in C# DSLs

Developing Domain-Specific Languages (DSLs) in C# requires careful planning to balance expressiveness, performance, and maintainability. A well-designed DSL should be intuitive, efficient, and integrate seamlessly into existing workflows. This section explores

158

best practices and performance optimization techniques when building C# DSLs, ensuring they remain scalable, performant, and easy to use.

Designing Intuitive and Expressive DSLs

A good DSL should be **readable and intuitive**. Users of the DSL should be able to express complex logic in a way that feels natural and reduces boilerplate code. Fluent interfaces, operator overloading, and method chaining are common techniques for improving readability.

Consider the design of a fluent API for configuring a logging system:

```
public class Logger
{
    public Logger SetLevel(string level) { /* Implementation */ return this; }
    public Logger SetOutput(string output) { /* Implementation */ return this; }
    public Logger EnableTimestamps() { /* Implementation */ return this; }
    public void Log(string message) { /* Implementation */ }
}

var logger = new Logger()
    .SetLevel("Info")
    .SetOutput("Console")
    .EnableTimestamps();

logger.Log("System started");
```

This fluent approach makes the DSL readable and easy to use while ensuring a **clean API design**.

Performance Considerations in C# DSLs

Performance is a critical aspect of DSL design. Poorly implemented DSLs can introduce unnecessary memory allocations, slow execution times, and inefficient processing. Consider the following performance-related techniques:

1. **Minimizing Object Allocations**
   Avoid unnecessary object instantiations. Using **structs instead of classes** for immutable, small-sized objects can reduce memory overhead and improve performance.

   ```
   public readonly struct QueryCondition
   {
       public string Field { get; }
       public string Operator { get; }
       public string Value { get; }

       public QueryCondition(string field, string op, string value)
       {
           Field = field;
           Operator = op;
           Value = value;
       }
   }
   ```

159

2. **Leveraging Expression Trees for Optimization**
   Expression trees allow for **compile-time evaluation** of queries, improving performance in DSLs that involve filtering, searching, or computations.

   ```
   Expression<Func<User, bool>> filter = u => u.Age > 18 && u.IsActive;
   var compiledFilter = filter.Compile();
   bool isAllowed = compiledFilter(new User { Age = 20, IsActive = true });
   ```

   Using expression trees ensures that the filtering logic is **compiled and optimized** before execution, reducing unnecessary processing.

3. **Lazy Evaluation for Improved Efficiency**
   Instead of executing operations immediately, **lazy evaluation** defers execution until results are required. This technique is particularly useful in query DSLs.

   ```
   var activeUsers = dbContext.Users
       .Where(u => u.IsActive)
       .OrderBy(u => u.LastName)
       .AsQueryable();
   ```

   The query isn't executed until iteration begins, reducing unnecessary computations and improving efficiency.

Testing and Debugging C# DSLs

DSLs should be **thoroughly tested** to ensure they behave correctly in different scenarios. Unit testing, integration testing, and property-based testing can validate DSL behavior.

Consider testing a query DSL using xUnit:

```
public class QueryDslTests
{
    [Fact]
    public void ShouldGenerateCorrectSqlQuery()
    {
        var query = new Query().From("Users").Where("Age > 18").ToSql();
        Assert.Equal("SELECT * FROM Users WHERE Age > 18;", query);
    }
}
```

Providing **detailed error messages and debugging tools** for DSL users ensures a smoother development experience.

Building a high-quality DSL in C# requires balancing **readability, performance, and maintainability**. By using fluent interfaces, minimizing memory allocations, leveraging expression trees, and employing lazy evaluation, developers can create DSLs that are both efficient and user-friendly. Proper testing and debugging further ensure reliability, making DSLs robust tools for domain-specific problem-solving.

Module 16:
DSLs in C++

Domain-Specific Languages (DSLs) built using C++ offer exceptional performance and flexibility. C++ is well-suited for DSL development due to its powerful metaprogramming capabilities, static typing, and direct hardware interaction. This module explores how C++ can serve as a foundation for both external and internal DSLs, leveraging features like templates, the Standard Template Library (STL), and custom parsers. By examining domain-specific applications and performance considerations, this module highlights best practices in creating efficient and expressive DSLs using C++.

C++ as a Base for External DSLs

C++ is commonly used as the foundation for external DSLs due to its robust ecosystem of parsing libraries and its ability to generate highly optimized machine code. External DSLs—languages that operate independently of the host language—are often implemented using tools like Lex and Yacc, ANTLR, or Boost.Spirit. These tools enable developers to define a custom syntax for a DSL while leveraging C++ for efficient execution.

One of the key advantages of using C++ for external DSLs is its **low-level control and high-performance execution**. Many game engines, simulation systems, and financial modeling frameworks implement their DSLs using C++ to benefit from fast execution speeds. Additionally, C++ can interact directly with system resources, making it ideal for embedded systems where **custom scripting languages** are necessary. However, designing an external DSL in C++ requires handling **parsing, lexing, and compilation**, which can introduce complexity in implementation and maintenance.

Using C++ Features Like Templates and STL in DSLs

C++ offers powerful language constructs, such as **templates, STL, and operator overloading**, that can be leveraged to create internal DSLs—DSLs embedded within C++ itself. Templates allow for the creation of **generic, compile-time evaluated DSL components**, making them highly efficient and type-safe. The STL provides data structures and algorithms that can be repurposed for **expressive DSL syntax**, reducing development effort.

Operator overloading enhances DSL readability by allowing custom syntax that closely resembles natural language expressions. Additionally, **expression templates** enable C++ DSLs to transform abstract syntax trees (ASTs) at compile time, significantly improving performance. Using these techniques, developers can implement **domain-specific computation models** in fields like scientific computing, finance, and graphics processing.

Examples of Domain-Specific Applications

C++ DSLs are widely used in various industries due to their performance and flexibility. Examples include:

- **Game Development**: Many game engines, such as Unreal Engine, incorporate custom scripting DSLs that interface with a C++ core.

- **Embedded Systems**: C++ DSLs are commonly used for hardware description and real-time control applications.

- **Financial Computing**: Quantitative trading platforms implement DSLs for modeling financial instruments, risk analysis, and algorithmic trading.

- **Graphics Processing**: Shading languages, such as GLSL and HLSL, serve as DSLs for high-performance rendering, often interfacing with C++ graphics engines.

These applications highlight the **efficiency and expressiveness** of C++ DSLs, showcasing their real-world impact across various domains.

Performance Considerations in C++ DSLs

Performance is a crucial factor in designing C++ DSLs. One of C++'s major strengths is its **ability to generate highly optimized machine code**, making it ideal for high-performance DSLs. To ensure efficiency, developers must carefully manage **memory usage, inline functions, and template metaprogramming**. Avoiding unnecessary heap allocations and leveraging **move semantics** can further optimize DSL performance.

Compile-time evaluation using **constexpr functions and expression templates** allows certain computations to be resolved before runtime, significantly reducing execution overhead. Additionally, **just-in-time (JIT) compilation** can be integrated into C++ DSLs to improve performance for dynamic applications, balancing flexibility with execution speed.

C++ provides a powerful foundation for DSL development, offering **low-level control, performance optimization, and metaprogramming capabilities**. Whether designing an external DSL with parsing tools or an internal DSL using templates and operator overloading, C++ enables developers to create efficient and expressive domain-specific solutions. By understanding best practices and optimizing for performance, developers can harness the full potential of C++ DSLs for a wide range of applications.

C++ as a Base for External DSLs

C++ is widely used for building external DSLs due to its powerful parsing capabilities, high-performance execution, and seamless integration with system-level programming. External DSLs, which function independently of the host language, require a well-defined syntax, parsing logic, and a robust execution model. C++ provides a rich ecosystem of tools such as **Lex & Yacc, ANTLR, Boost.Spirit, and LLVM** that facilitate the creation of external DSLs. These tools enable developers to define custom grammars and efficiently transform user-defined instructions into executable code.

A primary reason for using C++ as a foundation for external DSLs is its **ability to generate optimized machine code**. Many high-performance applications—such as **game engines, financial modeling software, and simulation frameworks**—rely on C++ to define specialized scripting languages. These DSLs allow users to define complex behaviors without directly modifying C++ source code. Additionally, C++-based DSLs can efficiently interact with **hardware, operating system resources, and real-time processing requirements**, making them ideal for domains requiring low-level control and deterministic execution.

Building an External DSL in C++

To construct an external DSL using C++, we must follow these core steps:

1. **Define the Language Syntax**: Specify the grammar using **BNF (Backus-Naur Form)** or other formal grammar notation.

2. **Implement a Lexer**: Use a tool like **Lex/Flex or ANTLR** to tokenize the input.

3. **Build a Parser**: Generate an Abstract Syntax Tree (AST) using **Yacc/Bison, Boost.Spirit, or ANTLR**.

4. **Interpret or Compile the DSL Code**: Translate parsed instructions into C++ function calls, bytecode, or optimized machine code.

Below is an example of using **Boost.Spirit** to create a simple external DSL for arithmetic expressions:

```cpp
#include <boost/spirit/include/qi.hpp>
#include <iostream>
#include <string>

namespace qi = boost::spirit::qi;

bool parseExpression(const std::string& input) {
    auto it = input.begin();
    bool success = qi::phrase_parse(it, input.end(), qi::double_ >>
        *(qi::char_('+') >> qi::double_), qi::space);
    return success && (it == input.end());
}

int main() {
    std::string expression = "3.14 + 2.71 + 1.41";
    if (parseExpression(expression)) {
        std::cout << "Valid DSL expression!" << std::endl;
    } else {
        std::cout << "Invalid syntax." << std::endl;
    }
    return 0;
```

}

This example defines a **DSL for arithmetic expressions** and validates its syntax using Boost.Spirit. The **parser ensures correct tokenization** of floating-point numbers and operators while allowing whitespace flexibility.

Challenges and Considerations

While external DSLs offer **expressiveness and reusability**, their implementation in C++ presents certain challenges:

- **Parsing Complexity**: Designing a custom parser requires expertise in formal grammars and compiler theory.

- **Performance Trade-offs**: Although external DSLs provide flexibility, parsing overhead can impact performance. **JIT compilation** (e.g., LLVM) can mitigate this issue.

- **Security Concerns**: Allowing user-defined code execution introduces risks. Implementing **sandboxing, static analysis, and runtime validation** is essential.

C++ serves as an excellent base for external DSLs due to its **performance, parsing libraries, and extensibility**. By leveraging tools like **Boost.Spirit, ANTLR, and LLVM**, developers can define expressive DSLs optimized for specific domains. However, designing an external DSL requires balancing **ease of use, security, and runtime efficiency** to ensure a robust implementation.

Using C++ Features like Templates and STL in DSLs

C++ provides powerful features such as **templates and the Standard Template Library (STL)** that can significantly enhance the development of **internal DSLs**. Internal DSLs are embedded within a host language, leveraging its syntax and structures to create domain-specific functionality without requiring a separate parser. With C++'s **template metaprogramming, operator overloading, and type traits**, DSLs can achieve a high level of expressiveness while maintaining compile-time efficiency.

One of the most prominent advantages of using **templates** in DSLs is their ability to enable **compile-time computation**. This is particularly useful in **scientific computing, graphics processing, and embedded systems**, where performance is crucial. The **STL** further provides a robust set of algorithms and data structures that DSLs can utilize for efficient memory management and computational tasks. By integrating templates and STL containers, developers can build **highly expressive, type-safe, and performant DSLs** for specialized applications.

Leveraging C++ Templates in DSLs

Templates are fundamental to building **fluent interfaces and DSL constructs** in C++. The **expression templates** technique allows the creation of custom mathematical expressions in a manner that **avoids unnecessary temporary objects and improves performance**. Consider the following **simple DSL for symbolic algebra** using templates:

```
#include <iostream>

// Base template for expressions
template<typename T>
struct Expression {
    T value;
    Expression(T v) : value(v) {}
};

// Operator overloading to enable DSL-like syntax
template<typename L, typename R>
struct Add : Expression<L> {
    R right;
    Add(L l, R r) : Expression<L>(l), right(r) {}

    auto evaluate() const { return this->value + right.value; }
};

// Overloaded + operator to enable DSL expression style
template<typename L, typename R>
auto operator+(const Expression<L>& lhs, const Expression<R>& rhs) {
    return Add<L, R>(lhs.value, rhs.value);
}

int main() {
    Expression<int> x(5);
    Expression<int> y(3);
    auto result = x + y;   // Using the DSL expression

    std::cout << "Result: " << result.evaluate() << std::endl;
    return 0;
}
```

In this example, we define an **internal DSL for symbolic expressions**. Using **operator overloading and templates**, we allow users to write expressions in a **human-readable form** while optimizing execution via **expression templates**. The operator+ function enables a DSL-style syntax for algebraic expressions.

Using STL for Efficient DSL Constructs

The **Standard Template Library (STL)** plays a crucial role in DSLs by providing **efficient, reusable, and optimized data structures**. **Vectors, maps, and functional utilities** allow developers to create powerful DSL constructs without manually managing low-level memory allocation.

Consider an **internal DSL for configuration management** using std::map and lambda functions:

```
#include <iostream>
#include <map>
#include <functional>
```

```cpp
class ConfigDSL {
    std::map<std::string, std::function<void()>> commands;
public:
    void addCommand(const std::string& name, std::function<void()> action) {
        commands[name] = action;
    }

    void runCommand(const std::string& name) {
        if (commands.find(name) != commands.end()) {
            commands[name]();
        } else {
            std::cout << "Command not found!" << std::endl;
        }
    }
};

int main() {
    ConfigDSL config;
    config.addCommand("start", [] { std::cout << "System starting...\n"; });
    config.addCommand("stop", [] { std::cout << "System stopping...\n"; });

    config.runCommand("start");
    config.runCommand("stop");

    return 0;
}
```

This example demonstrates a **DSL for configuration management**. Users can define commands using a **declarative style**, and the system executes corresponding actions dynamically. The use of std::map and std::function allows for **flexible and extensible command registration**, making it easier to manage configurations dynamically.

C++ templates and STL provide **powerful mechanisms for designing internal DSLs**, enabling **expressiveness, performance optimization, and reusability**. **Expression templates, operator overloading, and lambda functions** allow DSLs to define **natural syntax**, while STL containers help manage **efficient memory allocation and runtime execution**. By combining these features, developers can build **highly performant, flexible, and user-friendly** DSLs tailored to specific domains.

Examples of Domain-Specific Applications

C++ is widely used in **high-performance computing, finance, embedded systems, game engines, and scientific simulations**, making it a powerful choice for developing DSLs tailored to these domains. By leveraging **compile-time optimizations, expression templates, and metaprogramming**, C++ DSLs can **express complex domain logic in a readable and performant manner**. In this section, we will explore **three real-world examples** of C++ DSLs: **a mathematical computation DSL, a game engine scripting DSL, and a network packet filtering DSL**.

Mathematical Computation DSL

Many scientific and engineering applications require **symbolic algebra and numerical computing**. Creating a **DSL for symbolic differentiation** allows users to define

166

mathematical expressions in a **declarative manner** while automatically computing derivatives. Below is an example of a **C++ DSL for automatic differentiation** using templates:

```cpp
#include <iostream>

// Base expression template
template<typename T>
struct Expression {
    T value;
    Expression(T v) : value(v) {}
};

// Differentiable expression: x^2
template<typename T>
struct Square : Expression<T> {
    Square(T v) : Expression<T>(v) {}

    auto evaluate() const { return this->value * this->value; }
    auto differentiate() const { return 2 * this->value; }
};

int main() {
    Square<int> x(3);
    std::cout << "Function: x^2, Value: " << x.evaluate() << ", Derivative: " <<
        x.differentiate() << std::endl;
    return 0;
}
```

This **internal DSL** enables users to **define symbolic functions and compute derivatives automatically**, eliminating the need for manual differentiation. **Expression templates ensure high performance by evaluating expressions at compile time**.

Game Engine Scripting DSL

Game engines often require **embedded scripting DSLs** to **control animations, character behavior, and AI logic**. While C++ is the backbone of many engines, scripting languages like **Lua** are often used for flexibility. However, C++ **can implement an internal DSL** using **operator overloading and method chaining** for a **fluent interface**.

```cpp
#include <iostream>
#include <string>

// Simple DSL for character actions
class Character {
    std::string name;
public:
    Character(std::string n) : name(n) {}

    Character& move(std::string direction) {
        std::cout << name << " moves " << direction << "." << std::endl;
        return *this;
    }

    Character& attack(std::string target) {
        std::cout << name << " attacks " << target << "." << std::endl;
        return *this;
    }
};
```

```cpp
int main() {
    Character hero("Knight");
    hero.move("forward").attack("Dragon");
    return 0;
}
```

This **fluent interface DSL** allows for **chaining of commands** (hero.move("forward").attack("Dragon")), making scripting **intuitive and readable** for game developers.

Network Packet Filtering DSL

C++ is commonly used in **network security and filtering applications**. A **DSL for packet filtering** can provide a declarative way to specify **firewall rules or traffic monitoring conditions**. The following example demonstrates a **simple internal DSL** for defining packet filter rules:

```cpp
#include <iostream>
#include <string>

// Packet filtering DSL
class PacketFilter {
    std::string rule;
public:
    PacketFilter& allow(std::string protocol) {
        rule = "ALLOW " + protocol;
        return *this;
    }

    PacketFilter& deny(std::string protocol) {
        rule = "DENY " + protocol;
        return *this;
    }

    void apply() const {
        std::cout << "Applying Rule: " << rule << std::endl;
    }
};

int main() {
    PacketFilter firewall;
    firewall.allow("TCP").apply();
    firewall.deny("UDP").apply();
    return 0;
}
```

This example **provides a human-readable syntax for defining firewall rules**, allowing users to specify conditions like firewall.allow("TCP").deny("UDP"). The result is a **clear and expressive network security policy definition**.

C++ DSLs can **simplify domain-specific applications** while **optimizing performance** using **templates, operator overloading, and fluent interfaces**. The examples presented demonstrate how C++ DSLs can be effectively used in **mathematical computation, game scripting, and network security**. These implementations showcase **how expressive and**

performant DSLs can be built directly within C++, enhancing productivity across specialized domains.

Performance Considerations in C++ DSLs

Developing a Domain-Specific Language (DSL) in C++ requires balancing expressiveness and performance. Since C++ is widely used for **high-performance computing, real-time systems, and embedded applications**, DSLs built in C++ must **avoid unnecessary overhead** while ensuring **maintainability and usability**. Key performance factors include **compile-time optimizations, memory management, runtime efficiency, and multi-threading capabilities**. This section explores **performance considerations in C++ DSLs**, covering **expression templates, lazy evaluation, efficient memory usage, and parallel execution**.

Compile-Time Optimizations with Expression Templates

C++'s **template metaprogramming** enables **compile-time computations** that eliminate runtime overhead. **Expression templates** are a powerful technique for optimizing DSLs that involve **mathematical computations or symbolic processing**. By leveraging **operator overloading and template instantiation**, expressions can be **evaluated at compile time**, reducing redundant operations.

The example below demonstrates a **C++ expression template for vector addition**:

```cpp
#include <iostream>
#include <vector>

// Expression template for vector operations
template<typename T>
class Vector {
    std::vector<T> data;
public:
    Vector(std::initializer_list<T> values) : data(values) {}

    template<typename F>
    Vector operator+(const Vector<F>& other) const {
        Vector<T> result({});
        for (size_t i = 0; i < data.size(); ++i)
            result.data.push_back(data[i] + other.data[i]);
        return result;
    }

    void print() const {
        for (const auto& v : data) std::cout << v << " ";
        std::cout << std::endl;
    }
};

int main() {
    Vector<int> v1 = {1, 2, 3};
    Vector<int> v2 = {4, 5, 6};
    Vector<int> v3 = v1 + v2;  // Optimized vector addition

    v3.print();  // Output: 5 7 9
    return 0;
}
```

This **eliminates intermediate temporary objects**, reducing memory usage and improving **runtime performance**. Expression templates are particularly useful for **scientific computing DSLs and graphics programming**, where performance is critical.

Lazy Evaluation for Improved Runtime Efficiency

Lazy evaluation delays computation **until the result is needed**, reducing unnecessary calculations. This is particularly useful for **functional DSLs, symbolic processing, and mathematical computations** in C++. The following **lazy evaluation technique** avoids redundant operations:

```cpp
#include <iostream>
// Lazy evaluation class
class LazyMultiply {
    int a, b;
public:
    LazyMultiply(int x, int y) : a(x), b(y) {}

    int evaluate() { return a * b; }  // Computed only when needed
};

int main() {
    LazyMultiply computation(5, 6);
    std::cout << "Result: " << computation.evaluate() << std::endl;  // Output:
        30
    return 0;
}
```

This method ensures that **multiplication is only computed when explicitly requested**, reducing unnecessary computations in complex expressions.

Module 17:
DSLs in Java

Java is a versatile and widely used programming language that provides a strong foundation for developing Domain-Specific Languages (DSLs). With its rich standard library, object-oriented features, and extensive ecosystem, Java enables developers to create both **internal and external DSLs** for various domains. The use of **fluent interfaces, annotation processing, and reflection** makes Java well-suited for embedded DSLs that seamlessly integrate with existing applications. This module explores Java's flexibility in DSL design, methods for embedding DSLs, popular Java DSL libraries, and how Java-based DSLs can be integrated into enterprise applications for enhanced productivity.

Java's Flexibility in DSL Design

Java's **static typing, garbage collection, and extensive API support** make it a flexible choice for DSL development. While Java is not traditionally associated with scripting or language extensibility, developers can create **internal DSLs** using **method chaining, lambda expressions, and annotation-based configurations**. Unlike dynamically typed languages like Python or Ruby, Java enforces **strict type safety**, which benefits large-scale DSL development.

For external DSLs, Java-based tools like **ANTLR** provide **parser generators** that enable developers to define and process custom language syntax. Java's ecosystem also includes libraries such as **Xtext** and **JavaCC**, which simplify DSL parsing and interpretation. This flexibility allows Java to support DSLs for diverse fields such as **business rule processing, data querying, and UI automation**.

Using Java for Embedded DSLs

Embedded DSLs in Java leverage **fluent interfaces** and **builder patterns** to create readable, expressive APIs within the language itself. **Fluent APIs** allow developers to construct DSL expressions that mimic natural language, improving code clarity and maintainability.

Java's support for **annotations and reflection** further enhances embedded DSLs by enabling declarative programming styles. For example, Java frameworks like **Spring and Hibernate** use annotation-based DSLs for dependency injection and database query definitions. These techniques make Java-based DSLs highly effective for **enterprise application development, test automation, and configuration management**.

Another advantage of embedded DSLs in Java is their ability to **interoperate with existing Java libraries and frameworks**. Since the DSL exists within Java itself, developers can utilize Java's robust tooling, including IDE support, debugging tools, and static analysis features, ensuring that DSLs remain maintainable and scalable.

Examples of Java DSL Libraries

Several Java-based libraries facilitate DSL development by providing domain-specific syntax and constructs. **JUnit**, a popular testing framework, incorporates a DSL-style API that simplifies writing unit tests. Similarly, **Spring Expression Language (SpEL)** provides a concise way to define dynamic expressions within Java applications.

Xtext, a framework for developing external DSLs, enables Java developers to create **custom languages with syntax highlighting, parsing, and code generation support**. **MPS (Meta Programming System)** is another tool that supports Java-based DSL development, allowing users to define language constructs with graphical and textual representations.

These libraries illustrate how Java enables **DSL development across multiple domains**, from test automation to complex rule engines. With the availability of these tools, developers can create domain-specific solutions without reinventing the wheel, making Java-based DSLs a practical choice for modern software development.

Integrating Java DSLs with Existing Applications

One of Java's strengths is its **ability to integrate DSLs seamlessly into enterprise applications**. Since Java runs on the **Java Virtual Machine (JVM)**, DSLs built with Java can interact with other JVM-based languages like **Kotlin, Groovy, and Scala**. This allows developers to mix DSLs with existing Java codebases while taking advantage of Java's performance optimizations.

For example, **business rule engines** like **Drools** allow organizations to define **business logic as an external DSL** while integrating it with Java-based applications. Similarly, **Gradle**, a build automation tool, provides a **Groovy-based DSL** that integrates seamlessly with Java projects.

By leveraging Java's modular architecture and API design, DSLs can be embedded into web applications, microservices, and enterprise systems, providing domain-specific functionalities while maintaining Java's robust ecosystem.

Java offers a powerful platform for developing **internal and external DSLs**, providing a balance between **readability, maintainability, and performance**. The use of **fluent interfaces, annotation processing, and Java-based DSL libraries** allows developers to create expressive, domain-specific solutions tailored to business needs. With its strong integration capabilities, Java-based DSLs can be seamlessly incorporated into enterprise applications, making them a valuable tool for software development and automation.

Java's Flexibility in DSL Design

Java provides a structured yet flexible approach to designing **Domain-Specific Languages (DSLs)**, offering both **internal DSLs** that integrate seamlessly with Java code and **external DSLs** that function independently. While Java is not as naturally expressive as dynamic languages like Python or Ruby, developers can still leverage **fluent interfaces, annotation processing, reflection, and parser generators** to build effective DSLs. These features enable Java to support DSLs in domains such as **business logic automation, data querying, and network configuration**.

Internal DSLs with Fluent Interfaces

Internal DSLs in Java rely on **fluent interfaces**, a technique where method chaining creates a readable, domain-specific syntax. Consider an example of a **simple rule-based DSL** for defining validation rules:

```
public class RuleBuilder {
    private String field;
    private String condition;
    private String value;

    public RuleBuilder field(String field) {
        this.field = field;
        return this;
    }

    public RuleBuilder condition(String condition) {
        this.condition = condition;
        return this;
    }

    public RuleBuilder value(String value) {
        this.value = value;
        return this;
    }

    public String build() {
        return "Rule: " + field + " " + condition + " " + value;
    }

    public static void main(String[] args) {
        String rule = new RuleBuilder()
            .field("Age")
            .condition(">")
            .value("18")
            .build();

        System.out.println(rule);
    }
}
```

This **fluent API** allows users to write validation rules in a **clear, readable format**, mimicking natural language. Java's method chaining technique makes it possible to develop expressive internal DSLs that integrate seamlessly with existing applications.

External DSLs with Parser Generators

173

For external DSLs, Java provides **parser generators** like **ANTLR** and **JavaCC**, which allow developers to define **custom syntax** and convert it into executable Java code.

A simple **ANTLR grammar** for a custom **mathematical DSL** might look like this:

```
grammar MathDSL;

expr : term (('+'|'-') term)*;
term : factor (('*'|'/') factor)*;
factor : INT | '(' expr ')';

INT : [0-9]+ ;
WS : [ \t\r\n]+ -> skip ;
```

Once this grammar is compiled using ANTLR, it generates a **Java parser** that can evaluate mathematical expressions written in this DSL. External DSLs built using **ANTLR** or **JavaCC** are particularly useful for domains such as **financial modeling, configuration languages, and business rule engines**.

Annotation Processing for DSL-like Behavior

Java's **annotation processing** provides another powerful way to create **declarative DSLs**. Java frameworks like **Spring and Hibernate** use annotations to define **configuration-based DSLs**.

A simple example is using **custom annotations** for a DSL that marks fields as required:

```
@Retention(RetentionPolicy.RUNTIME)
@Target(ElementType.FIELD)
@interface Required {}

class User {
    @Required
    private String name;
}
```

Reflection can be used to **enforce constraints dynamically**, making it possible to develop lightweight DSLs without additional parsing mechanisms.

Java's flexibility in DSL design stems from its **object-oriented principles, fluent interfaces, annotation processing, and parser generators**. Developers can create **internal DSLs** that integrate seamlessly with Java applications or **external DSLs** that operate independently. By leveraging Java's **strong typing and extensive ecosystem**, DSLs can be designed for diverse domains, providing **clear, expressive, and maintainable** domain-specific solutions.

Using Java for Embedded DSLs

Embedded **Domain-Specific Languages (DSLs)** in Java are designed to work within the Java programming ecosystem, allowing developers to define domain-specific logic in a **fluent, readable, and maintainable way**. Unlike external DSLs, which require separate

174

parsers, **embedded DSLs integrate seamlessly with Java applications**, leveraging Java's type safety, method chaining, and annotations. These DSLs are particularly useful for **business rule engines, configuration management, and workflow automation**, as they provide an intuitive way to define domain logic without needing to develop an entirely new language.

Fluent Interfaces for Embedded DSLs

A common approach to building embedded DSLs in Java is using **fluent interfaces**. Fluent interfaces rely on method chaining to create **human-readable syntax**, making DSLs more expressive.

Consider a **task scheduling DSL**, which allows users to define when and how a task should run:

```java
public class TaskScheduler {
    private String taskName;
    private int interval;
    private String unit;

    public TaskScheduler task(String taskName) {
        this.taskName = taskName;
        return this;
    }

    public TaskScheduler every(int interval, String unit) {
        this.interval = interval;
        this.unit = unit;
        return this;
    }

    public void schedule() {
        System.out.println("Scheduling " + taskName + " every " + interval + " "
            + unit);
    }

    public static void main(String[] args) {
        new TaskScheduler()
            .task("DataBackup")
            .every(2, "hours")
            .schedule();
    }
}
```

This embedded DSL allows users to write **intuitive, declarative scheduling rules** directly in Java. By chaining methods, the DSL reads almost like natural language, making it **easier to understand and use** within Java applications.

Annotations for DSL-like Behavior

Java's **annotations** provide another mechanism for embedded DSLs. Many Java frameworks use annotations to **configure behavior declaratively**, reducing boilerplate code.

For example, let's define a **validation DSL** using custom annotations:

```java
import java.lang.annotation.*;
import java.lang.reflect.*;

@Retention(RetentionPolicy.RUNTIME)
@Target(ElementType.FIELD)
@interface NotEmpty {}

class User {
    @NotEmpty
    private String username;

    public User(String username) {
        this.username = username;
    }

    public static void validate(Object obj) throws IllegalAccessException {
        for (Field field : obj.getClass().getDeclaredFields()) {
            if (field.isAnnotationPresent(NotEmpty.class)) {
                field.setAccessible(true);
                if (field.get(obj) == null || ((String)
        field.get(obj)).isEmpty()) {
                    throw new RuntimeException(field.getName() + " cannot be
        empty!");
                }
            }
        }
    }

    public static void main(String[] args) throws IllegalAccessException {
        User user = new User("");
        validate(user);
    }
}
```

This example enforces that the username field **cannot be empty**, using **annotations and reflection** to implement a validation DSL. This technique is widely used in Java frameworks like **Spring, Hibernate, and Jakarta EE** for configuring validation, security, and object-relational mapping.

Using Lambda Expressions for DSL-like Syntax

Java's **lambda expressions** can be used to create DSL-like constructs that **simplify functional operations**. For example, a **filtering DSL** can be implemented using Java Streams:

```java
import java.util.*;
import java.util.stream.Collectors;

class Product {
    String name;
    double price;

    public Product(String name, double price) {
        this.name = name;
        this.price = price;
    }
}
```

```java
public class ProductFilter {
    public static void main(String[] args) {
        List<Product> products = Arrays.asList(
            new Product("Laptop", 1200),
            new Product("Phone", 800),
            new Product("Tablet", 400)
        );

        List<Product> expensiveProducts = products.stream()
            .filter(p -> p.price > 500)
            .collect(Collectors.toList());

        expensiveProducts.forEach(p -> System.out.println(p.name));
    }
}
```

This example demonstrates an **embedded filtering DSL**, allowing users to define filtering logic in a **concise, readable way** using **functional programming techniques**.

Java offers multiple approaches for building **embedded DSLs**, from **fluent interfaces and annotations to lambda expressions**. Embedded DSLs enhance Java applications by providing **clear, readable domain logic**, making it easier for developers to express complex behavior in a **declarative and maintainable** way.

Examples of Java DSL Libraries

Java offers several **domain-specific language (DSL) libraries** that streamline application development by providing pre-built solutions for common patterns and tasks. These libraries enable developers to leverage **domain-specific abstractions** for various use cases such as **query building, configuration management, and UI development**. Let's explore some popular Java DSL libraries and their applications in real-world projects.

Apache Camel for Integration DSL

Apache Camel is a widely used integration framework that provides a **DSL for routing and mediation** of messages across various systems. It allows developers to define complex routing logic in a simple, declarative syntax. By using **routes**, developers can configure data transformations, integration patterns, and communication protocols seamlessly within the Camel context.

```java
import org.apache.camel.builder.RouteBuilder;
import org.apache.camel.impl.DefaultCamelContext;

public class MyRouteBuilder extends RouteBuilder {
    @Override
    public void configure() throws Exception {
        from("file:/input")
            .to("log:processed");
    }
}

public class CamelExample {
    public static void main(String[] args) throws Exception {
        DefaultCamelContext context = new DefaultCamelContext();
        context.addRoutes(new MyRouteBuilder());
        context.start();
```

```
            Thread.sleep(5000);
            context.stop();
        }
    }
```

In this example, Camel's DSL allows routing messages from a **file system to a logging destination**, offering an intuitive, declarative style for integrating systems and handling data exchanges.

JOOQ for SQL Query DSL

JOOQ is a **Java library** that simplifies the construction of **SQL queries** using a **type-safe DSL**. It allows developers to write database queries in a fluent, Java-based syntax, reducing the complexity of managing SQL code in large projects and ensuring that queries are **compiled** with Java's type system. With JOOQ, developers can avoid errors due to incorrect SQL syntax, as the queries are checked by the Java compiler.

```java
import org.jooq.*;
import org.jooq.impl.*;

import static org.jooq.impl.DSL.*;

public class JooqExample {
    public static void main(String[] args) {
        DSLContext create = DSL.using(SQLDialect.MYSQL);

        create.select()
            .from("users")
            .where("age > ?", 18)
            .fetch();
    }
}
```

Here, JOOQ's DSL lets developers **express complex SQL queries** directly in Java, offering type safety and minimizing the potential for runtime SQL errors. This library is especially useful for projects that require **dynamic or complex query construction**.

Spring Data JPA for Repository DSL

Spring Data JPA simplifies data access and persistence in Java applications, and it includes a **powerful DSL for querying databases**. Using Spring Data, developers can define repository interfaces for entities and write queries using **method names**, or they can use JPQL (Java Persistence Query Language) for more complex queries.

```java
public interface UserRepository extends JpaRepository<User, Long> {
    List<User> findByLastName(String lastName);
}
```

The repository method findByLastName is an example of a **DSL-based query** that can be invoked to fetch records from a database, avoiding the need for boilerplate SQL or JPQL. Spring Data JPA supports **dynamic query generation** based on method signatures, which simplifies querying and interaction with the database.

Gradle for Build and Automation DSL

Gradle is a popular build automation tool that uses a **DSL based on Groovy or Kotlin** to define tasks, dependencies, and build processes. This **build script DSL** provides a way to configure and automate tasks for compiling, testing, and packaging code, making it a critical tool for developers in CI/CD pipelines.

```
task hello {
    doLast {
        println 'Hello, world!'
    }
}
```

In this example, Gradle's **Groovy-based DSL** allows developers to define tasks and automate workflows in a highly readable and efficient manner. Gradle is particularly useful for projects that need to be **easily extensible and customized**, as it supports multiple DSLs and plug-ins.

Java libraries like **Apache Camel, JOOQ, Spring Data JPA, and Gradle** showcase the versatility of Java DSLs across various domains. These libraries simplify development by enabling **domain-specific abstractions** for integration, database queries, persistence, and build automation. Java DSLs promote productivity, maintainability, and readability, making them indispensable tools for modern software development.

Integrating Java DSLs with Existing Applications

Integrating **Java DSLs** with existing applications is a vital aspect of modern software development. It allows developers to leverage the strengths of DSLs, such as **increased productivity, maintainability**, and **domain-specific abstractions**, while seamlessly fitting into the broader software ecosystem. In this section, we explore strategies for **integrating DSLs** with existing applications, covering aspects like **compatibility**, **extensibility**, and **scalability**.

Seamless Integration with Existing Codebases

One of the most significant advantages of **Java DSLs** is their ability to integrate seamlessly with existing Java codebases. Since Java DSLs often use **native Java syntax** or extend Java's core libraries, they are easy to incorporate into applications without requiring significant changes to the underlying architecture. For example, using **Apache Camel** for routing and integration can work in tandem with existing services, allowing developers to introduce integration logic incrementally.

For instance, if an application is using traditional **Spring-based services**, adding **Apache Camel** routes doesn't require significant refactoring. The integration can be done by simply defining a route in a **Camel context** and wiring it into the existing Spring beans or services.

```
@Configuration
```

```java
public class CamelConfig extends RouteBuilder {
    @Override
    public void configure() {
        from("direct:start")
            .to("log:receivedMessage");
    }
}
```

This ability to **extend existing functionality** without disrupting the main codebase is one of the primary benefits of Java DSLs. **Gradle**, as another example, integrates with existing Java projects to automate builds and deployments, offering flexibility without requiring developers to rework the existing build system.

Extending Applications with DSLs

Integrating Java DSLs into an application can also provide an opportunity to **extend** its capabilities in a clean and maintainable way. For instance, **JOOQ** can be integrated into a legacy application to simplify SQL queries without changing the underlying database schema or architecture. Developers can write queries using **JOOQ's fluent API**, which generates SQL queries programmatically while ensuring type safety and runtime validation.

This integration is done by extending the existing **repository layer** with JOOQ's API to ensure that **SQL operations** are handled more effectively, while keeping the original **JPA-based persistence model** intact. This modular approach means the application remains consistent with its architecture, while gaining the benefits of DSL usage for query building.

```java
public class UserService {
    private final DSLContext dslContext;

    public UserService(DSLContext dslContext) {
        this.dslContext = dslContext;
    }

    public List<User> getUsersByLastName(String lastName) {
        return dslContext.selectFrom(USER)
                         .where(USER.LAST_NAME.eq(lastName))
                         .fetchInto(User.class);
    }
}
```

In this example, JOOQ's SQL DSL is used to extend the functionality of the **UserService** without altering the core structure of the service or the application. It enhances **querying capabilities** while keeping the service layer intact.

Managing Configuration with DSLs

Another aspect of integrating Java DSLs is their use in **configuration management**. For example, **Spring Data JPA** provides a DSL for **query generation** based on repository method signatures, significantly reducing the need for boilerplate SQL code. This DSL can be integrated directly into an application's **data access layer** while leveraging **existing JPA entities**.

For applications with complex configurations, **Gradle** can be integrated to automate build tasks, allowing developers to manage dependencies, compile code, run tests, and package applications through its declarative build DSL. This integration ensures that **configuration and build automation** can evolve in parallel with the application codebase, enabling smoother CI/CD pipelines.

Handling Performance Considerations in Integration

While Java DSLs offer several productivity benefits, developers should also be mindful of **performance** when integrating them into an existing application. For example, **JOOQ** and **Apache Camel** can introduce overhead if not properly optimized. It is crucial to ensure that **queries** and **routes** are **optimized for performance** and that the DSLs are not inadvertently slowing down the application.

Using **profiling tools** and **monitoring tools** can help identify performance bottlenecks when integrating DSLs. For example, **Spring Boot Actuator** can be used to monitor the performance of applications integrated with DSLs like Spring Data JPA or Apache Camel.

Integrating Java DSLs with existing applications enhances development productivity and modularity without disrupting the core system. By using **Apache Camel**, **JOOQ**, or **Gradle**, developers can extend applications, manage configurations, and automate tasks without significant refactoring. Ensuring **performance optimizations** during integration helps maintain system efficiency while benefiting from DSL abstractions.

Module 18:

DSLs in Python, Ruby, Scala, and XSLT

Module 18 explores the use of **Domain-Specific Languages (DSLs)** in **Python, Ruby, Scala**, and **XSLT**, focusing on their unique capabilities for creating tailored languages that enhance productivity. This module highlights the strengths of each language, examining **syntax expressiveness**, **metaprogramming techniques**, **functional approaches**, and **XML transformations**, each contributing to a distinct DSL development experience.

Python's Expressive Syntax and Dynamic Features for DSLs

Python, known for its **simple and readable syntax**, is highly suitable for creating DSLs. Its **dynamic typing**, **first-class functions**, and **extensive libraries** provide developers with flexibility when building domain-specific languages. Python's syntax allows DSLs to feel **natural** and **intuitive**, making it ideal for rapid prototyping. By using techniques such as **decorators** and **context managers**, Python enables developers to craft DSLs that integrate seamlessly with existing code. This section will explore how Python's features, like **lambda expressions** and **closures**, contribute to creating expressive and powerful DSLs that address specific domain challenges efficiently.

Ruby's Metaprogramming and DSL Capabilities

Ruby stands out as a language with powerful **metaprogramming** capabilities that facilitate the creation of flexible and dynamic DSLs. By leveraging features like **method_missing**, **class_eval**, and **define_method**, developers can design DSLs that feel like **native Ruby syntax** while abstracting complex logic. Ruby's **clean syntax** and **object-oriented paradigm** enable the creation of **readable, maintainable** DSLs for a wide range of domains. The section will discuss how Ruby's metaprogramming techniques allow developers to **extend the language** and create **expressive DSLs** tailored to specific needs, whether for **web development**, **data processing**, or **configuration management**.

Scala's Functional Programming Approach to DSLs

Scala, as a **hybrid functional-object-oriented language**, provides developers with powerful tools to create **concise and expressive DSLs**. Its support for **higher-order functions**, **immutability**, and **pattern matching** makes it well-suited for building DSLs that leverage **functional programming concepts**. Scala's ability to define **domain-specific abstractions** within its type system provides a strong foundation for creating robust and type-safe DSLs. This section will focus on how Scala's **functional features** are used to build DSLs that are **concise, highly composable**, and **efficient**, and how it contrasts with other languages like Python and Ruby in the DSL development space.

XSLT for XML-Based DSL Design and Transformation

XSLT (Extensible Stylesheet Language Transformations) is a powerful tool for **designing and transforming XML-based DSLs**. It allows developers to define custom transformations for XML data, enabling the creation of **XML-based DSLs** that are **highly flexible** and **scalable**. XSLT's declarative nature and support for **template-based processing** make it an excellent choice for domains requiring extensive data transformations. In this section, we will explore how XSLT is used to create DSLs for **XML-based configuration**, **data processing**, and **web services**. The section will also highlight how XSLT can be integrated with other languages to enhance **data-driven application development**.

Module 18 provides an in-depth look at the use of **Python**, **Ruby**, **Scala**, and **XSLT** for creating powerful and expressive DSLs. Each language brings its own unique features—whether Python's dynamic flexibility, Ruby's metaprogramming power, Scala's functional capabilities, or XSLT's transformation strengths. Together, they offer a wide range of tools for developers to create specialized languages that improve productivity and solve domain-specific challenges efficiently.

Python's Expressive Syntax and Dynamic Features for DSLs

Python's **expressive syntax** and **dynamic features** make it an ideal language for creating **Domain-Specific Languages (DSLs)**. The language's **clean, readable syntax** allows developers to design DSLs that are intuitive and easily understandable. Python's flexibility, coupled with its **first-class functions** and **dynamic typing**, supports a variety of programming styles, making it an excellent choice for DSL development.

A key advantage of Python is its ability to write code that closely resembles **natural language**. Developers can use Python's **syntax sugar**, such as **list comprehensions** and **lambda functions**, to build compact and expressive DSLs. For example, creating a DSL for filtering a collection of numbers can be written in Python as:

```
numbers = [1, 2, 3, 4, 5, 6]
filtered = [x for x in numbers if x % 2 == 0]
print(filtered)  # Output: [2, 4, 6]
```

In this example, the list comprehension creates a DSL-like structure that filters even numbers, showcasing Python's ability to express complex logic concisely.

Another strength of Python lies in its **extensive standard library** and third-party packages. For example, Python's **matplotlib** library can be leveraged to create DSLs for **visual data representation** or **mathematical modeling**. The following example demonstrates how Python can be used to create a DSL for generating a simple plot:

```
import matplotlib.pyplot as plt

def plot_data(x, y, title="Graph", xlabel="X", ylabel="Y"):
    plt.plot(x, y)
    plt.title(title)
    plt.xlabel(xlabel)
    plt.ylabel(ylabel)
```

```
    plt.show()

# Use the DSL to create a plot
x = [1, 2, 3, 4, 5]
y = [1, 4, 9, 16, 25]
plot_data(x, y, title="Simple Plot", xlabel="X-Axis", ylabel="Y-Axis")
```

This DSL abstracts away the complexity of using **matplotlib** directly, allowing users to plot data with simple function calls and parameters.

Moreover, Python's **decorators** and **context managers** play a significant role in building DSLs. For instance, decorators can be used to create a DSL for logging function calls:

```
def log_function_call(func):
    def wrapper(*args, **kwargs):
        print(f"Calling function {func.__name__} with arguments {args} and
            {kwargs}")
        return func(*args, **kwargs)
    return wrapper

@log_function_call
def add(a, b):
    return a + b

# Calling the decorated function
print(add(3, 4))  # Output: Calling function add with arguments (3, 4) and {}
                  #         7
```

This decorator-based DSL provides a simple mechanism for logging function calls without modifying the underlying logic, demonstrating Python's power to design domain-specific behavior.

Python's **dynamic nature** also makes it a natural fit for creating **embedded DSLs**. For example, a simple domain-specific language for file handling might be expressed as follows:

```
class FileHandler:
    def __init__(self, filename):
        self.filename = filename

    def read(self):
        with open(self.filename, 'r') as file:
            return file.read()

    def write(self, data):
        with open(self.filename, 'w') as file:
            file.write(data)

# Using the DSL
file = FileHandler("sample.txt")
file.write("Hello, DSL!")
print(file.read())  # Output: Hello, DSL!
```

This example shows how Python's object-oriented capabilities can be used to define a simple DSL for file handling, encapsulating logic in a class that performs specific domain-related actions.

Python's **simple syntax**, **dynamic features**, and **rich ecosystem** of libraries make it a versatile language for creating DSLs. Whether for mathematical modeling, web development, or other specialized fields, Python's expressiveness ensures that the DSLs developed are both functional and easy to understand, while its flexibility allows for innovative and tailored solutions.

Ruby's Metaprogramming and DSL Capabilities

Ruby is renowned for its **metaprogramming** capabilities, which allow developers to dynamically create methods, modify classes, and design **Domain-Specific Languages (DSLs)**. These features make Ruby particularly well-suited for building expressive, concise DSLs that can be highly customized to specific application domains.

Ruby's **flexible syntax** and the ability to define custom methods on the fly enable developers to create **internal DSLs** that are both elegant and powerful. For instance, Ruby's **blocks**, **procs**, and **lambdas** facilitate building DSLs by enabling dynamic behavior during runtime. The following example demonstrates how Ruby can be used to create a simple DSL for **task scheduling**:

```ruby
class TaskScheduler
  def initialize
    @tasks = []
  end

  def task(description, &block)
    @tasks << { description: description, action: block }
  end

  def run
    @tasks.each do |task|
      puts "Executing: #{task[:description]}"
      task[:action].call
    end
  end
end

# Using the DSL
scheduler = TaskScheduler.new
scheduler.task("Task 1") { puts "Task 1 is running" }
scheduler.task("Task 2") { puts "Task 2 is running" }
scheduler.run
```

In this example, the **task** method accepts a block of code, which allows Ruby to define a custom language for scheduling tasks. The tasks are dynamically added to the scheduler and executed in order.

Ruby's **metaprogramming** is another key feature that allows for the creation of more sophisticated DSLs. Developers can define methods dynamically using define_method or modify the behavior of objects at runtime. This flexibility is particularly valuable for defining behavior that is highly specific to the domain. The following example uses define_method to create a DSL for **database querying**:

```ruby
class QueryBuilder
```

```ruby
  def initialize
    @query = "SELECT * FROM"
  end

  def table(name)
    @query += " #{name}"
  end

  def where(condition)
    @query += " WHERE #{condition}"
  end

  def query
    @query
  end
end

# Using the DSL
query_builder = QueryBuilder.new
query_builder.table("users")
query_builder.where("age > 18")
puts query_builder.query  # Output: SELECT * FROM users WHERE age > 18
```

Here, Ruby's **dynamic method invocation** allows the QueryBuilder class to form SQL queries using domain-specific methods (table and where). This results in a more **readable** and **maintainable** code structure that resembles the SQL syntax.

Ruby's **blocks** and **yielding** mechanism make it easy to create DSLs with an **intuitive** flow. The use of **metaprogramming** also helps to **extend** Ruby's functionality dynamically without having to explicitly write out every possible method. These capabilities allow Ruby to **abstract complex logic**, making it easier for developers to interact with intricate systems through simpler constructs.

Ruby has been used successfully to create DSLs in various domains, such as **web frameworks** (e.g., Ruby on Rails), **testing frameworks** (e.g., RSpec), and **data manipulation** (e.g., ActiveRecord). Ruby's **expressive syntax** allows developers to design concise DSLs that reflect the **underlying domain's language** and provide an **elegant solution** for solving problems.

Ruby's **metaprogramming** and **block-based syntax** make it an excellent choice for building **DSLs**. Its flexibility enables the creation of highly customized, domain-specific languages that simplify complex tasks, improve **developer productivity**, and maintain readability. Ruby's **dynamic nature** encourages innovation in DSL design, making it an invaluable tool for developers aiming to solve domain-specific problems in an elegant and efficient way.

Scala's Functional Programming Approach to DSLs

Scala is a **multi-paradigm language** that blends **object-oriented** and **functional programming** (FP) features. This blend makes Scala an ideal choice for designing **Domain-Specific Languages (DSLs)**, especially for applications that benefit from **functional constructs** like **higher-order functions**, **immutability**, and **first-class**

186

functions. Scala's concise syntax and powerful type system further enhance its ability to create expressive and robust DSLs.

One of the key advantages of using Scala for DSL development is its **expressive syntax**, which allows developers to build **internal DSLs** that feel almost like **natural language**. The following example illustrates how Scala can be used to build a **simple financial transaction DSL**:

```scala
class Transaction {
  var amount: Double = 0.0
  var description: String = ""

  def withAmount(a: Double): Transaction = {
    this.amount = a
    this
  }

  def withDescription(d: String): Transaction = {
    this.description = d
    this
  }

  def execute(): Unit = {
    println(s"Executing transaction of $amount with description: $description")
  }
}

object FinancialDSL {
  def transaction(block: Transaction => Unit): Unit = {
    val trans = new Transaction
    block(trans)
    trans.execute()
  }
}

FinancialDSL.transaction { trans =>
  trans.withAmount(1000).withDescription("Transfer to account 12345")
}
```

In this example, the transaction method provides a way to define a financial transaction, chaining together different methods like withAmount and withDescription. This approach is reminiscent of **fluent interfaces** and allows users to express domain-specific logic in an **elegant** and **readable** manner.

Scala's **higher-order functions** allow DSLs to be modular and composable. Functions can be passed as parameters or returned as results, enabling **flexible** and **reusable** constructs. For example, the following illustrates the use of **higher-order functions** in defining a DSL for **data filtering**:

```scala
object DataFilter {
  def filter(data: List[Int], condition: Int => Boolean): List[Int] = {
    data.filter(condition)
  }
}

val numbers = List(1, 2, 3, 4, 5, 6)
val filteredNumbers = DataFilter.filter(numbers, _ > 3)
println(filteredNumbers)  // Output: List(4, 5, 6)
```

In this code, the filter function takes a list and a condition, creating a domain-specific operation to filter out numbers greater than 3. This use of **higher-order functions** makes it easy to create **custom operations** based on the needs of the application domain.

Scala's **immutable collections** are another crucial feature for building safe and expressive DSLs. Immutability ensures that objects are not modified unexpectedly, making the DSL **predictable** and **easy to reason about**. For instance, Scala's List and Set collections are immutable by default, making them ideal for scenarios where **pure functions** and **side-effect free** operations are essential.

Moreover, Scala's **type system** provides robust features such as **generic types**, **type inference**, and **pattern matching**. These features can be used to define DSLs with a strong type structure, ensuring that **type errors** are caught at compile-time rather than at runtime. By leveraging Scala's **expressive types**, developers can build DSLs that are both **type-safe** and **easy to maintain**.

Scala's **actor-based concurrency** model (via **Akka**) and its seamless integration with **Java** libraries make it particularly well-suited for building **distributed systems**. DSLs in this domain can be used to express **asynchronous** behavior or **distributed messaging** in a way that is both concise and highly functional.

Scala's functional programming capabilities, combined with its **concise syntax**, **higher-order functions**, and **strong type system**, make it an ideal language for developing **Domain-Specific Languages (DSLs)**. Scala enables developers to create expressive, type-safe, and reusable DSLs that can simplify complex domain-specific tasks and promote high-level abstraction. With its combination of **object-oriented** and **functional** paradigms, Scala offers powerful tools for building DSLs that are both efficient and elegant.

XSLT for XML-Based DSL Design and Transformation

XSLT (Extensible Stylesheet Language Transformations) is a **language** used for transforming **XML documents** into different formats like HTML, plain text, or other XML formats. While XSLT is primarily known for its role in **transforming data** and **styling documents**, it can also be leveraged to create **Domain-Specific Languages (DSLs)**, particularly for domains involving **structured data** like **XML**. XSLT's ability to process XML and apply complex transformations makes it an excellent choice for **domain-specific tasks** that require **data extraction**, **restructuring**, and **presentation**.

In DSL design, XSLT can be used to define **custom transformation rules** or **data manipulations**. For example, in the domain of **content management**, a DSL written in XSLT can automate how XML-based documents are transformed and presented based on certain criteria or templates. The following example demonstrates how XSLT can be used as a DSL for transforming XML data into a custom **HTML format**:

```
<?xml version="1.0" encoding="UTF-8"?>
```

188

```
<xsl:stylesheet version="1.0" xmlns:xsl="http://www.w3.org/1999/XSL/Transform">
  <xsl:template match="/catalog">
    <html>
      <body>
        <h2>Product Catalog</h2>
        <ul>
          <xsl:for-each select="product">
            <li>
              <xsl:value-of select="name" /> -
              <xsl:value-of select="price" />
            </li>
          </xsl:for-each>
        </ul>
      </body>
    </html>
  </xsl:template>
</xsl:stylesheet>
```

This **XSLT stylesheet** takes an XML document containing a **catalog** and **product information** and transforms it into an **HTML** document. The xsl:template defines the transformation rules, and the xsl:for-each iterates through the **products**, generating the corresponding HTML list items. This approach highlights how XSLT can act as a **DSL** for formatting and rendering structured content in a domain-specific manner.

One of the most significant strengths of XSLT in DSL development is its **declarative nature**. Rather than specifying the steps of an algorithm, developers define **patterns** that describe how XML elements should be transformed. This is particularly useful in scenarios where **rules-based transformations** or **conditional processing** are needed, and where the domain-specific logic primarily revolves around data formatting or extraction.

XSLT also supports **extensions** through the use of **external functions** written in languages like **Java** or **JavaScript**. These extensions allow the DSL to interact with more complex data sources, perform advanced computations, or connect to external systems. For example, an XSLT-based DSL for **e-commerce applications** might include external functions that fetch real-time product data from an external API or apply custom calculations for discounts based on specific business rules.

Furthermore, XSLT supports **recursion** and **iteration** through constructs like xsl:for-each and xsl:apply-templates, making it an effective tool for building **recursive** transformations or for processing hierarchical data structures. This makes XSLT especially useful in domains such as **document processing**, **XML data manipulation**, and **content rendering**.

However, XSLT does come with some challenges. While it is powerful for data transformation, it can be verbose and complex for certain tasks. XSLT's **syntax** may also be difficult for developers unfamiliar with functional or declarative programming styles. Additionally, performance considerations are important, especially for large XML files, where optimizations and careful handling of data structures are necessary.

XSLT provides a **powerful tool** for creating **XML-based DSLs**, offering a declarative approach to data transformation that simplifies domain-specific tasks. While it excels in structured data processing and content rendering, developers should be mindful of its complexity and performance limitations when working with larger datasets.

Part 4:

Algorithm and Data Structure Support for Domain Specific Languages

The foundation of any domain-specific language (DSL) relies heavily on algorithms and data structures that facilitate parsing, syntax representation, and efficient execution. This part explores the core computational techniques that support DSLs, including parsing algorithms, code generation strategies, metaprogramming, and abstract syntax trees (ASTs). Additionally, it delves into grammar trees, parsing trees, and advanced data structures tailored for domain-specific applications. By understanding these fundamental principles, DSL designers can optimize performance, enhance maintainability, and create expressive languages suited for their respective domains. Each module presents essential methodologies that ensure DSL implementations are both scalable and efficient.

Parsing Algorithms for DSLs

Parsing is a critical component of DSL development, as it transforms raw text into structured representations that can be processed further. The parsing process typically begins with lexical analysis, where input text is tokenized into meaningful symbols. Techniques such as regular expressions and finite automata are employed to ensure efficient tokenization. Once tokens are generated, syntax trees are constructed based on grammar rules that define the structure of the DSL. Parsing techniques such as shift-reduce parsing and recursive descent parsing play a crucial role in converting textual representations into executable structures. Performance optimization in parsing focuses on minimizing lookahead complexity and reducing backtracking to improve processing speed.

Domain-Specific Code Generation Algorithms

Once a DSL has been parsed and transformed into an intermediate representation, code generation techniques allow the conversion of this representation into executable output. Code generation algorithms range from simple template-based methods to complex macro-driven approaches that adapt to different target platforms. Domain-specific code generation often involves leveraging intermediate languages, ensuring optimized execution paths for DSL constructs. This module discusses practical strategies for designing code generators that produce efficient output while maintaining readability. It also explores examples of automated code generation, such as Just-In-Time (JIT) compilation and LLVM-based transformations that enhance performance across multiple platforms.

Template Metaprogramming Algorithms

Template metaprogramming is a powerful technique that allows DSLs to extend their capabilities at compile time. C++ is a prime example of a language that supports template metaprogramming, enabling sophisticated compile-time computations and type-based transformations. Other languages, such as D and Scala, also incorporate metaprogramming capabilities that facilitate DSL optimization. This module examines the use of template instantiation, static assertions, and expression templates to enhance DSL expressiveness. While template metaprogramming introduces significant advantages, it also comes with challenges such as increased compilation time and complex debugging processes, which must be carefully managed.

Abstract Syntax Trees (AST) for DSLs

Abstract Syntax Trees (ASTs) serve as the backbone of DSL processing, enabling transformations and optimizations before code execution. ASTs provide a structured and hierarchical representation of a DSL's syntax, facilitating program analysis and code generation. DSL developers manipulate ASTs to implement transformations such as constant folding, inlining, and optimization passes. This module explores practical applications of ASTs, including their use in compiler design, interpreter construction, and program refactoring. Efficient AST generation techniques are crucial for ensuring fast compilation and runtime execution while maintaining language expressiveness.

Grammar Trees and Parsing Trees

Grammar trees and parsing trees play a pivotal role in defining and analyzing the syntactic structure of DSLs. A grammar tree formalizes the syntactic rules governing a language, while a parsing tree represents the actual structure of parsed code based on these rules. Understanding the relationship between these trees is essential for building efficient DSL parsers. Techniques for optimizing parsing trees focus on reducing ambiguity and improving lookup performance, ensuring fast and accurate syntactic analysis. This module presents methods for constructing parsing trees that enhance DSL reliability while maintaining compatibility with existing parsing frameworks.

Advanced Data Structures for DSLs

Choosing the right data structures is crucial for DSL performance and scalability. Many DSL applications require efficient data handling for domain-specific tasks such as numerical computation, hierarchical modeling, and rule-based processing. Specialized data structures such as tries, suffix trees, and hash maps are often employed to enhance query efficiency and memory management. This module explores real-world examples of DSLs that leverage advanced data structures to handle large-scale data efficiently. Performance considerations include balancing memory usage with computational complexity to ensure optimal DSL execution in diverse application domains.

This part provides a deep understanding of the algorithms and data structures essential for DSL development. Mastering these concepts enables developers to build performant, scalable, and maintainable DSLs that effectively serve their intended domains.

Module 19:
Parsing Algorithms for DSLs

In this module, we explore the essential parsing techniques used for **Domain-Specific Languages (DSLs)**. Parsing is a crucial step in the interpretation or compilation of DSLs, involving processes such as **lexical analysis**, **syntax tree generation**, and the use of **parsing algorithms**. Understanding how to design and optimize parsers is key to developing efficient and effective DSLs tailored for specific tasks.

Lexical Analysis and Tokenization Techniques

Lexical analysis is the first step in parsing, where the input source code is broken down into **tokens**. Each token represents a meaningful element in the DSL, such as keywords, operators, or identifiers. **Tokenization** is critical for transforming raw text into a structured representation that a parser can process. Various tokenization techniques exist, including regular expression-based scanners or **finite state automata (FSA)**. These methods ensure that the lexer can efficiently recognize and categorize all the components of a DSL. Careful attention must be given to the design of the lexer to minimize errors in token recognition and ensure scalability.

Syntax Trees and Grammar Rules

Once lexical analysis is complete, the next step involves parsing the tokens into a **syntax tree**. A syntax tree represents the hierarchical structure of the DSL, reflecting how different components of the language interact. This tree is based on a set of **grammar rules** that define the syntactic structure of the DSL. Grammar rules can be defined using **Context-Free Grammars (CFG)**, which specify how tokens can be grouped into valid constructs. Proper grammar design is essential for ensuring that the DSL is expressive and can represent complex constructs. Additionally, a syntax tree enables further steps such as semantic analysis or code generation.

Shift-Reduce and Recursive Descent Parsers

To transform the tokenized input into a syntax tree, parsers are employed. Two common types of parsers used in DSL development are **shift-reduce parsers** and **recursive descent parsers**. Shift-reduce parsing is a type of **bottom-up parsing** where the parser shifts tokens onto a stack and reduces them based on grammar rules. It's often used in **LR parsers**, known for their efficiency in handling large grammars. On the other hand, **recursive descent parsing** is a **top-down parsing** approach that involves defining a set of recursive functions for each non-terminal in the grammar. Both methods have advantages and trade-offs, depending on the complexity of the DSL and the parsing strategy employed.

Performance Considerations in Parsing DSLs

Parsing performance is a crucial factor in the design of DSLs, especially when the DSL is intended for **real-time systems** or environments with high **performance demands**. Efficient parsing techniques ensure that the DSL can be processed quickly and accurately. Common performance bottlenecks include the handling of **complex grammars**, long input strings, and large datasets. Optimizations such as **lookahead techniques**, **memoization**, or **grammar simplification** can help alleviate these issues. Furthermore, the choice between a **precompiled parser** and a **just-in-time (JIT) parser** can also impact performance. A careful balance between **speed** and **correctness** is necessary when designing parsers for DSLs.

In this module, we've covered the fundamental parsing techniques used in DSL development, including **lexical analysis**, **syntax trees**, **parsing algorithms**, and performance optimization strategies. Efficient parsing is critical for DSL implementation, and understanding these concepts ensures that DSLs are both expressive and performant. The choice of parsing algorithm greatly affects the overall effectiveness of the language.

Lexical Analysis and Tokenization Techniques

Lexical analysis is the first step in parsing a Domain-Specific Language (DSL). During this phase, the raw input source code is broken into **tokens**, which represent the smallest meaningful units of the language, such as keywords, operators, and identifiers. Tokenization is the process of identifying and categorizing these elements to simplify further parsing.

In Python, lexical analysis can be done using regular expressions, which are well-suited for this task. The Python re module is commonly used for defining patterns that can match specific token types. Here's an example of a simple lexer that tokenizes arithmetic expressions:

```python
import re

# Define token patterns
token_specification = [
    ('NUMBER',   r'\d+'),        # Integer
    ('PLUS',     r'\+'),         # Addition
    ('MINUS',    r'-'),          # Subtraction
    ('TIMES',    r'\*'),         # Multiplication
    ('DIVIDE',   r'/'),          # Division
    ('LPAREN',   r'\('),         # Left Parenthesis
    ('RPAREN',   r'\)'),         # Right Parenthesis
    ('SKIP',     r'[ \t\n]+'),   # Skip spaces and tabs
    ('MISMATCH', r'.'),          # Any other character
]

# Combine the token patterns into a single regular expression
master_pattern = '|'.join(f'(?P<{pair[0]}>{pair[1]})' for pair in
            token_specification)

# Tokenizer function
def tokenize(code):
    line_num = 1
    line_start = 0
    for mo in re.finditer(master_pattern, code):
        kind = mo.lastgroup
        value = mo.group()
        if kind == 'SKIP':
            continue
        elif kind == 'MISMATCH':
            raise RuntimeError(f'{value!r} unexpected on line {line_num}')
```

```
        else:
            column = mo.start() - line_start
            print(f'{kind}: {value} at line {line_num}, column {column}')

# Example code to tokenize
code = "3 + 5 * (10 - 4)"
tokenize(code)
```

This code defines a simple set of token specifications using regular expressions. Each regular expression is associated with a token type, such as NUMBER, PLUS, MINUS, etc. The tokenize function uses the re.finditer method to match the tokens in the input code.

When run, this script will produce the following tokenized output for the expression "3 + 5 * (10 - 4)":

```
NUMBER: 3 at line 1, column 0
PLUS: + at line 1, column 2
NUMBER: 5 at line 1, column 4
TIMES: * at line 1, column 6
LPAREN: ( at line 1, column 8
NUMBER: 10 at line 1, column 9
MINUS: - at line 1, column 12
NUMBER: 4 at line 1, column 14
RPAREN: ) at line 1, column 16
```

Key Features of Tokenization

1. **Regular Expressions**: Regular expressions are a powerful tool for recognizing patterns in the input code, such as numbers or operators.

2. **Skipping Irrelevant Input**: In the lexer, we used the SKIP token type to ignore spaces and newlines.

3. **Error Handling**: The lexer raises an error for any unexpected input, such as characters that don't match any token pattern (MISMATCH).

Optimizing Tokenization

Tokenization can be optimized with techniques such as **lookahead**, where the lexer previews the next few characters to determine the token more efficiently. For example, when tokenizing complex expressions, you can look ahead to check for multi-character operators like == or <=. Additionally, **memoization** (storing previously computed results) can help optimize performance in scenarios where tokenization rules are repeated.

In this case, the tokenizer ensures that each piece of the code is recognized and classified before sending the tokens to the next stage of parsing, facilitating the creation of a reliable DSL interpreter or compiler.

Syntax Trees and Grammar Rules

Syntax trees (also known as **parse trees**) are hierarchical structures that represent the grammatical structure of the source code, showing how the language's rules are applied to the code. The syntax tree is generated by parsing the tokenized input and is central to understanding how expressions are evaluated and transformed in the DSL.

Grammar Rules

Grammar rules define the syntax of a language. These rules determine how tokens can be combined to form valid expressions or statements. In a context-free grammar, each rule typically follows the format:

```
non-terminal -> production
```

Where non-terminal represents a syntactic category (such as an expression), and production defines how that category can be expanded into terminals (actual tokens like numbers and operators).

For example, the grammar for a basic arithmetic expression might look like this:

```
Expression -> Term | Expression '+' Term
Term       -> Factor | Term '*' Factor
Factor     -> Number | '(' Expression ')'
Number     -> [0-9]+
```

This grammar allows for basic arithmetic expressions involving addition, multiplication, and parentheses.

Creating a Syntax Tree

A syntax tree is created by recursively applying these grammar rules to the tokenized input. Each node in the tree corresponds to a grammar rule or token. To demonstrate this, let's use a recursive descent parser, which builds a syntax tree directly as it parses the tokens.

Here's an example of how to create a syntax tree for arithmetic expressions using Python:

```python
class Node:
    def __init__(self, value=None):
        self.value = value
        self.children = []

    def add_child(self, child):
        self.children.append(child)

    def __repr__(self):
        return f"Node({self.value})"

class Parser:
    def __init__(self, tokens):
        self.tokens = tokens
        self.pos = 0

    def current_token(self):
        return self.tokens[self.pos] if self.pos < len(self.tokens) else None

    def eat(self, token_type):
        if self.current_token() and self.current_token()[0] == token_type:
            self.pos += 1
```

```python
        else:
            raise SyntaxError(f"Expected {token_type} but got
            {self.current_token()}")

    def factor(self):
        token = self.current_token()
        if token[0] == 'NUMBER':
            self.eat('NUMBER')
            return Node(value=token[1])
        elif token[0] == 'LPAREN':
            self.eat('LPAREN')
            node = self.expr()
            self.eat('RPAREN')
            return node
        else:
            raise SyntaxError(f"Unexpected token: {token}")

    def term(self):
        node = self.factor()
        while self.current_token() and self.current_token()[0] == 'TIMES':
            self.eat('TIMES')
            node = Node('*')
            node.add_child(self.factor())
        return node

    def expr(self):
        node = self.term()
        while self.current_token() and self.current_token()[0] == 'PLUS':
            self.eat('PLUS')
            new_node = Node('+')
            new_node.add_child(node)
            new_node.add_child(self.term())
            node = new_node
        return node

    def parse(self):
        return self.expr()

# Example tokenized input
tokens = [
    ('NUMBER', '3'),
    ('PLUS', '+'),
    ('NUMBER', '5'),
    ('TIMES', '*'),
    ('NUMBER', '2')
]

# Parse the expression
parser = Parser(tokens)
syntax_tree = parser.parse()
print(syntax_tree)
```

Output Syntax Tree

For the tokenized input 3 + 5 * 2, the parser generates a syntax tree that looks like this:

```
Node(+)
  Node(3)
  Node(*)
    Node(5)
    Node(2)
```

Explanation of the Code

1. **Node Class**: Each node represents a component of the syntax tree, such as an operator or a number. It has a value and a list of children nodes.

2. **Parser Class**: The parser recursively constructs the syntax tree based on grammar rules. It uses methods like factor, term, and expr to parse specific parts of the expression.

3. **Grammar Handling**: The grammar rules are directly mapped to methods in the Parser class. For example, the expr method handles addition and subtraction, while the term method handles multiplication and division.

Optimizations and Extensions

When building more complex syntax trees, optimizations like **memoization** can be helpful. For example, once a subexpression is parsed, storing the result can save time if the same expression is encountered again. Additionally, **error recovery** mechanisms can be added to the parser to provide more informative error messages or to allow the parser to continue even after encountering an error.

The syntax tree serves as the foundation for further operations such as **semantic analysis** or **code generation**. By understanding the structure of the code, a DSL can be more efficiently interpreted or compiled.

Shift-Reduce and Recursive Descent Parsers

When designing a parser for a domain-specific language (DSL), two of the most widely used parsing techniques are **shift-reduce parsing** and **recursive descent parsing**. Both techniques serve to analyze the syntax of a language and transform it into a usable structure, such as a syntax tree.

Shift-Reduce Parsers

Shift-reduce parsing is a bottom-up parsing technique where the parser shifts input tokens onto a stack and then reduces them into higher-level constructs when certain patterns or grammar rules are detected. The goal is to reduce the input into the start symbol of the grammar, using reductions based on the production rules.

A typical shift-reduce parser works in two primary operations:

1. **Shift**: Move a token from the input to the stack.

2. **Reduce**: Apply a grammar rule to replace a sequence of symbols on the stack with a non-terminal symbol.

Let's look at a simple implementation of a shift-reduce parser for arithmetic expressions:

```python
class ShiftReduceParser:
    def __init__(self, tokens):
        self.tokens = tokens
        self.stack = []
        self.pos = 0

    def current_token(self):
        return self.tokens[self.pos] if self.pos < len(self.tokens) else None

    def eat(self):
        token = self.current_token()
        if token:
            self.stack.append(token)
            self.pos += 1

    def reduce(self):
        # Check for a reduction rule (in this case, simple addition)
        if len(self.stack) >= 3 and self.stack[-2] == '+' and \
            isinstance(self.stack[-3], int) and isinstance(self.stack[-1], int):
            right_operand = self.stack.pop()
            self.stack.pop()  # Remove '+'
            left_operand = self.stack.pop()
            self.stack.append(left_operand + right_operand)
        else:
            raise SyntaxError("Invalid reduction")

    def parse(self):
        while self.pos < len(self.tokens):
            self.eat()  # Shift
            while len(self.stack) >= 3 and isinstance(self.stack[-3], int) and \
                self.stack[-2] == '+' and isinstance(self.stack[-1], int):
                self.reduce()  # Reduce
        return self.stack[0]

# Tokenized input: 3 + 5 + 2
tokens = [3, '+', 5, '+', 2]
parser = ShiftReduceParser(tokens)
result = parser.parse()
print(f"Result: {result}")
```

Output

```
Result: 10
```

Explanation

In this example:

- The **tokens** list represents the arithmetic expression 3 + 5 + 2.

- The parser processes the tokens, shifting them onto the stack.

- Whenever the pattern number + number is detected, a **reduction** takes place, and the two numbers are summed.

Recursive Descent Parsers

A **recursive descent parser** is a top-down parsing technique where each non-terminal in the grammar has a corresponding parsing function. These functions are recursively called to parse the input.

A recursive descent parser for simple arithmetic expressions, including addition and multiplication, might look like this:

```python
class RecursiveDescentParser:
    def __init__(self, tokens):
        self.tokens = tokens
        self.pos = 0

    def current_token(self):
        return self.tokens[self.pos] if self.pos < len(self.tokens) else None

    def eat(self, token_type):
        if self.current_token() == token_type:
            self.pos += 1
        else:
            raise SyntaxError(f"Expected {token_type}, got
            {self.current_token()}")

    def factor(self):
        if isinstance(self.current_token(), int):
            value = self.current_token()
            self.pos += 1
            return value
        else:
            raise SyntaxError(f"Unexpected token: {self.current_token()}")

    def term(self):
        value = self.factor()
        while self.current_token() == '*':
            self.eat('*')
            value *= self.factor()
        return value

    def expr(self):
        value = self.term()
        while self.current_token() == '+':
            self.eat('+')
            value += self.term()
        return value

    def parse(self):
        return self.expr()

# Tokenized input: 3 + 5 * 2
tokens = [3, '+', 5, '*', 2]
parser = RecursiveDescentParser(tokens)
result = parser.parse()
print(f"Result: {result}")
```

Output

```
Result: 13
```

Explanation

In this example:

200

- The RecursiveDescentParser class defines methods for parsing arithmetic expressions (expr), terms (term), and factors (factor).

- The expr method handles addition, while the term method handles multiplication.

- **Parentheses** could be easily added by introducing another grammar rule, but the current focus is on basic arithmetic operations.

Comparison

- **Shift-reduce parsers** are typically more efficient and are often used in compiler implementations, especially in **LR parsers**.

- **Recursive descent parsers**, while easier to implement and understand, may struggle with more complex grammar rules (such as left-recursive rules). However, they are often favored for DSLs due to their simplicity.

Performance Considerations

Both parsing methods should consider **backtracking** and **lookahead** to enhance performance. Shift-reduce parsers can be optimized for speed, while recursive descent parsers might involve **memoization** to avoid redundant parsing. Both approaches must also efficiently handle **error recovery** and **context-sensitive grammars**.

Performance Considerations in Parsing DSLs

When designing a parser for a domain-specific language (DSL), performance is a critical factor to consider. Efficient parsing can significantly affect the responsiveness and scalability of applications, particularly in scenarios involving large datasets or complex DSLs. The performance of a parser is influenced by several factors such as the parsing technique, grammar design, and optimization strategies.

Parsing Time Complexity

The time complexity of a parser depends on the parsing technique and the structure of the grammar.

- **Shift-reduce parsers** (e.g., LL, LR parsers) typically operate in linear time, $O(n)$, where n is the number of tokens. However, the complexity can increase if the parser needs to handle **backtracking** or **context-sensitive grammars**. Parsing strategies like **LR parsing** are efficient for large, complex grammars, but may require significant memory and computational resources.

- **Recursive descent parsers** are typically easier to implement and are $O(n)$ in simple cases. However, they may encounter performance bottlenecks for certain grammars, especially those involving **left recursion** or excessive backtracking. For complex

DSLs, recursive descent parsers might require additional optimization techniques like **memoization** to avoid parsing the same input multiple times.

Optimizing for Speed and Memory Usage

To optimize the parsing process, several strategies can be employed:

1. **Lookahead**: Adding lookahead capabilities allows parsers to examine a few tokens ahead of the current token, enabling them to make more informed decisions about the parsing process. However, lookahead should be limited, as too much lookahead can degrade performance.

2. **Memoization**: For recursive descent parsers, **memoization** can be a powerful optimization. By caching the results of parsing subexpressions, you avoid redundant parsing, particularly when dealing with expressions that are encountered multiple times.

Here's an example of memoization in a recursive descent parser:

```
class MemoizedParser:
    def __init__(self, tokens):
        self.tokens = tokens
        self.pos = 0
        self.memo = {}

    def current_token(self):
        return self.tokens[self.pos] if self.pos < len(self.tokens) else None

    def memoize(self, key, value):
        self.memo[key] = value

    def parse(self, rule, *args):
        key = (rule, *args)
        if key in self.memo:
            return self.memo[key]
        result = rule(*args)
        self.memoize(key, result)
        return result

    def factor(self):
        token = self.current_token()
        if isinstance(token, int):
            self.pos += 1
            return token
        return None
```

3. **Minimizing Backtracking**: Excessive backtracking during the parsing process can slow down performance. **Predictive parsers** like **LL parsers** or **lookahead parsers** can avoid unnecessary backtracking by using a **first- and follow-set** strategy. By determining the potential set of valid tokens that follow a given rule, parsers can make better predictions and minimize reprocessing.

4. **Efficient Memory Usage**: Parsing involves creating structures like **syntax trees, parse stacks**, and **lookahead buffers**. To ensure efficient memory usage, **garbage collection**

and memory management practices need to be optimized, especially when handling large input datasets.

One technique for reducing memory footprint is to use **incremental parsing**, where only the relevant parts of the input are parsed as needed, rather than parsing the entire input at once.

Example of Performance Optimization: Caching

In complex DSLs, repetitive parsing tasks may lead to inefficient use of resources. A simple caching mechanism can improve performance by storing results of expensive computations, such as parsing particular expressions. Here's a caching example in a recursive descent parser:

```python
class CachedParser:
    def __init__(self, tokens):
        self.tokens = tokens
        self.pos = 0
        self.cache = {}

    def current_token(self):
        return self.tokens[self.pos] if self.pos < len(self.tokens) else None

    def factor(self):
        if self.pos in self.cache:
            return self.cache[self.pos]
        token = self.current_token()
        if isinstance(token, int):
            self.pos += 1
            self.cache[self.pos] = token
            return token
        return None
```

Efficient parsing is crucial for the performance of DSLs, especially as the complexity and size of input data increase. Techniques such as **memoization**, **lookahead**, and **minimizing backtracking** play a significant role in enhancing parsing performance. By employing these strategies, developers can build parsers that are both fast and memory-efficient, ensuring that DSLs can scale and function optimally in real-world applications.

Module 20:
Domain-Specific Code Generation Algorithms

In this module, we explore the techniques and algorithms involved in domain-specific code generation (DSCG). Code generation is a critical aspect of DSL design, enabling the automatic translation of DSL specifications into executable code. This module covers code generation techniques, the use of templates and macros, optimizations for target platforms, and algorithms for automating the process. By automating code production, DSLs can enhance productivity and reduce manual coding efforts.

Code Generation Techniques for DSLs

Code generation is the process of transforming high-level specifications written in a DSL into executable code. Several approaches can be used for this task, ranging from simple string concatenation to more sophisticated template-based methods. The choice of technique depends on the complexity of the DSL, the target platform, and the desired level of automation.

One common technique is **direct code generation**, where the DSL specification is parsed and directly converted into the target language's syntax. This approach is often simple and effective but may require manual intervention for complex transformations. Another approach, **model-driven code generation**, involves creating intermediate representations (models) of the DSL's components before translating them into target code.

A more advanced method is **code generation through abstract syntax trees (ASTs)**. This method uses the syntactical structure of the DSL to generate corresponding code. AST-based approaches allow for more flexibility and can produce optimized code by focusing on the logical structure of the DSL rather than syntax alone.

Templates and Macros in DSL Code Generation

Templates and macros play a significant role in automating code generation in DSLs. Templates allow for the creation of generic, reusable code patterns that can be instantiated with specific parameters or data. In contrast, macros are more dynamic and enable code generation during compilation, providing greater flexibility.

Templates are commonly used in languages like C++ and Python, allowing developers to specify a generalized structure that can later be filled with specific data or logic. This approach is widely used for generating boilerplate code, such as class definitions, function prototypes, or database schemas. By automating these repetitive tasks, templates significantly improve productivity and reduce errors.

Macros, on the other hand, enable more advanced code generation by allowing developers to define small code snippets that can be expanded at compile time. For example, macros can be used to insert platform-specific optimizations or generate specialized functions based on the context of the DSL program. When used effectively, macros can lead to more concise and efficient code.

Optimizing Code Generation for Target Platforms

Optimizing code generation for target platforms is a crucial aspect of DSCG. When generating code, it is essential to consider the platform's constraints and capabilities, such as processing power, memory usage, and supported libraries. Optimization ensures that the generated code runs efficiently on the target platform, making the DSL useful for production systems.

One optimization technique is **platform-specific code generation**, where the DSL generates code that is specifically tailored for different platforms, such as desktop computers, mobile devices, or embedded systems. This ensures that the generated code takes full advantage of platform-specific features and performance characteristics.

Another approach is **performance optimization**, where the code generation algorithm analyzes the DSL specification and applies optimization strategies, such as reducing unnecessary operations or simplifying complex expressions. Optimized code can lead to faster execution times and lower resource consumption.

Example Algorithms for Automated Code Generation

Automated code generation algorithms are essential for streamlining the process of converting DSL specifications into working code. These algorithms vary in complexity, depending on the DSL's scope and the level of automation required. A common approach is **template-based generation**, where the algorithm matches DSL constructs to predefined templates and fills in the necessary details.

Another common algorithm is **semantic code generation**, which translates the meaning or logic behind a DSL specification into executable code. This method involves analyzing the semantic structure of the DSL and mapping it to the corresponding target language constructs. Advanced algorithms may also perform error checking and validation during the code generation process, ensuring that the generated code is both correct and efficient.

Domain-specific code generation is a key component of DSLs, enabling the automation of code production and enhancing productivity. By utilizing various techniques such as templates, macros, and platform-specific optimizations, developers can generate efficient, tailored code that meets the needs of the target platform. This module provides a comprehensive understanding of the algorithms and techniques that power code generation for DSLs, ensuring that DSLs can be leveraged effectively in software development.

Code Generation Techniques for DSLs

Code generation is a crucial aspect of Domain-Specific Languages (DSLs), particularly in automating the generation of repetitive code structures. DSLs are designed to simplify specific programming tasks, and code generation further aids this by transforming high-level domain-specific instructions into executable code. This section explains code generation techniques, focusing on how templates and macros can be used effectively in DSLs.

Code Generation Overview

Code generation in DSLs typically involves transforming a high-level specification into a lower-level programming language, often a general-purpose language like Python, C++, or Java. In DSLs, developers often describe what they want in a domain-specific context, and the code generator produces the corresponding implementation. This process eliminates the need to manually write boilerplate or repetitive code, improving both productivity and accuracy.

For example, imagine a DSL designed for generating database CRUD (Create, Read, Update, Delete) operations. Instead of manually writing SQL queries, the DSL allows you to specify the entity (e.g., User) and the desired operations, and the generator produces the corresponding SQL code. Here's an example:

```
# DSL Spec
User:
  fields: id, name, email
  operations: create, read, update, delete
```

The generator could produce SQL like:

```
CREATE TABLE User (
  id INT PRIMARY KEY,
  name VARCHAR(100),
  email VARCHAR(100)
);

-- Generate CRUD operations
INSERT INTO User (name, email) VALUES (?, ?);
SELECT * FROM User WHERE id = ?;
UPDATE User SET name = ?, email = ? WHERE id = ?;
DELETE FROM User WHERE id = ?;
```

This high-level specification is transformed into SQL code, ensuring correctness, consistency, and reducing the risk of errors.

Templates in Code Generation

Templates play an important role in DSL-based code generation. A template is a reusable piece of code that defines the structure of the generated code. In a DSL, templates provide placeholders for dynamic content that can be filled in based on the domain-specific input.

Consider a DSL for generating HTML forms. Instead of manually writing the HTML structure for every form, the DSL allows you to define fields and their types. A template engine then fills in the necessary details.

Example DSL specification:

```
Form:
    title: "User Registration"
    fields: ["name", "email", "password"]
```

Generated HTML using a template:

```
<form>
    <h1>User Registration</h1>
    <label for="name">Name</label>
    <input type="text" id="name" name="name">
    <label for="email">Email</label>
    <input type="email" id="email" name="email">
    <label for="password">Password</label>
    <input type="password" id="password" name="password">
    <button type="submit">Submit</button>
</form>
```

In this example, the template engine takes the domain-specific input (form title and fields) and generates the corresponding HTML code.

Macros in Code Generation

Macros extend the power of templates by allowing the inclusion of logic in the code generation process. A macro is essentially a set of rules or functions that manipulate code during generation. It can handle more complex scenarios, such as conditional code insertion, loops, or transformations based on specific conditions.

For example, consider a DSL for generating code based on the type of a machine learning model. A macro could generate different code based on whether the model is a decision tree, neural network, or regression model.

DSL specification:

```
Model:
    type: "NeuralNetwork"
    layers: [64, 128, 10]
```

Macro-generated Python code for a neural network:

```
import tensorflow as tf

model = tf.keras.Sequential([
    tf.keras.layers.Dense(64, activation='relu'),
```

207

```
    tf.keras.layers.Dense(128, activation='relu'),
    tf.keras.layers.Dense(10, activation='softmax')
])
model.compile(optimizer='adam', loss='categorical_crossentropy',
        metrics=['accuracy'])
```

In this case, the macro interprets the DSL input (NeuralNetwork type and layers) and generates a complete model definition using the TensorFlow library.

Code generation techniques using templates and macros are powerful tools for enhancing the productivity and maintainability of DSLs. Templates provide reusable code structures, while macros add flexibility by incorporating logic into the code generation process. Together, these techniques help automate repetitive tasks and ensure consistency in the generated code, making them invaluable for domain-specific applications.

Templates and Macros in DSL Code Generation

Templates and macros are essential tools in the process of code generation for Domain-Specific Languages (DSLs). Both of these tools help bridge the gap between high-level domain-specific specifications and the actual code that is generated. This section delves into how templates and macros can be used effectively in the context of DSL code generation, enabling developers to automate the creation of complex code while maintaining flexibility and efficiency.

Templates in Code Generation

Templates are predefined code structures that include placeholders or variables that can be filled with specific data at runtime or compile time. In DSL code generation, templates allow the DSL to describe the structure of the generated code, which can then be customized based on domain-specific input. Templates are commonly used for repetitive tasks, like generating similar types of code for different entities, and they ensure consistency across the generated codebase.

For example, in a web development DSL, you might have a template for generating HTML forms. The template defines the structure of the form, while the specific fields and attributes are filled in based on the DSL's input. Consider the following DSL specification for creating a form:

```
Form:
  title: "Login Form"
  fields:
    - label: "Username"
      type: "text"
      name: "username"
    - label: "Password"
      type: "password"
      name: "password"
```

The template engine takes this DSL input and fills in the values where necessary, producing the following HTML code:

```
<form>
  <h1>Login Form</h1>
  <label for="username">Username</label>
  <input type="text" id="username" name="username">
  <label for="password">Password</label>
  <input type="password" id="password" name="password">
  <button type="submit">Login</button>
</form>
```

This approach allows for a highly customizable output with minimal manual coding, as developers need only define the specifications for the form fields, not the structure of the form itself.

Macros in Code Generation

While templates focus on filling in predefined structures, macros add an additional layer of complexity by allowing for more advanced logic during the code generation process. A macro is a set of rules or functions that can modify the generated code based on conditions, loops, or transformations. Macros can handle cases where more sophisticated logic is required, such as generating code based on specific input values, performing calculations, or deciding between multiple code paths.

For instance, consider a DSL for generating code for machine learning models, where different types of models (e.g., regression, decision trees, neural networks) require different code structures. A macro could be used to generate the correct model definition based on the input parameters. Below is an example of a DSL specification for a machine learning model:

```
Model:
  type: "NeuralNetwork"
  layers: [128, 64, 10]
```

A macro interprets the input and generates the appropriate Python code for a neural network model:

```
import tensorflow as tf

model = tf.keras.Sequential([
  tf.keras.layers.Dense(128, activation='relu'),
  tf.keras.layers.Dense(64, activation='relu'),
  tf.keras.layers.Dense(10, activation='softmax')
])
model.compile(optimizer='adam', loss='categorical_crossentropy',
        metrics=['accuracy'])
```

This macro dynamically generates different code paths depending on the type of model, providing flexibility and enabling the DSL to support various use cases within the domain.

Templates and macros are two powerful tools for code generation in DSLs. Templates allow developers to define reusable structures for code, filling in details based on domain-specific input, while macros introduce logic to handle more complex scenarios. Together, they help automate repetitive tasks, reduce errors, and provide flexibility, making them essential for efficient DSL code generation.

Optimizing Code Generation for Target Platforms

Optimizing code generation for specific target platforms is crucial in DSL development, especially when the generated code needs to run efficiently across various environments. This section focuses on strategies for tailoring code generation processes to ensure that the output is optimized for the performance characteristics and constraints of the target platform. Proper optimization can lead to improvements in runtime performance, memory usage, and overall system efficiency.

Platform-Specific Code Generation Considerations

When generating code for a target platform, developers must consider various platform-specific aspects, such as processor architecture, available libraries, and system constraints. Each platform may have different performance characteristics that can influence the generated code's execution efficiency. For instance, code for embedded systems with limited memory and processing power must be more lightweight and efficient compared to code intended for high-performance servers.

To optimize the code, DSLs often include platform-specific configuration options that allow the user to specify the target environment. This can include specifying resource constraints (e.g., memory limits or CPU capabilities) or defining platform-specific optimizations like multi-threading, SIMD (Single Instruction, Multiple Data), or GPU usage.

For example, in an embedded systems DSL, the developer might specify that a certain feature should be optimized for a low-power platform. The generated code would then focus on reducing energy consumption, using minimal memory, and utilizing efficient algorithms suitable for such platforms.

Optimizing for Performance

One common approach to optimize generated code is to focus on performance through algorithmic improvements and low-level optimizations. DSLs can include options for selecting more efficient algorithms or generating parallelized code to take advantage of multi-core processors. The DSL could allow users to specify performance-related settings, such as whether certain operations should be executed in parallel or serialized, and the generated code would adjust accordingly.

For example, in a data processing DSL for scientific computations, the user might define operations that can be parallelized:

```
ProcessData:
  algorithm: "matrix_multiplication"
```

210

```
parallel: True
data_size: 10000
```

The DSL's code generator would then generate optimized code to leverage multiple CPU cores or GPUs, depending on the platform's capabilities, to perform matrix multiplication efficiently. This can dramatically improve performance for large datasets.

Memory Management and Optimization

Memory management is another key consideration in code generation. The target platform may have specific limitations on available memory or may require particular strategies for memory allocation. For example, in embedded systems, dynamic memory allocation might need to be minimized to avoid fragmentation. A DSL designed for this platform could provide annotations or settings to control memory allocation strategies.

A DSL targeting an IoT device with limited RAM might include configurations that instruct the code generator to use fixed-size buffers and avoid dynamic allocations:

```
MemoryOptimized:
  buffer_size: 512
  dynamic_allocation: False
```

The generated code would then include static memory allocations with the specified buffer size, ensuring that the application runs efficiently on a resource-constrained device.

Integration with Platform-Specific Libraries

Another optimization strategy involves integrating with platform-specific libraries and APIs. These libraries may provide specialized functionalities that can be leveraged for better performance. For instance, a DSL targeting a machine learning application could generate code that uses optimized libraries for numerical computation, such as TensorFlow or cuDNN for GPU acceleration.

By allowing the DSL to automatically choose the right platform-specific library, developers can ensure that their applications run efficiently without needing to manually adjust low-level details.

Optimizing code generation for target platforms is essential for ensuring that the generated code performs well across different environments. By focusing on platform-specific constraints, performance optimizations, and memory management strategies, DSLs can produce highly efficient code tailored to the unique characteristics of each platform. This results in better-performing applications that meet the specific needs of the target platform.

Example Algorithms for Automated Code Generation

Automated code generation plays a pivotal role in DSLs by reducing manual coding efforts and ensuring consistency and correctness across projects. This section delves into some example algorithms used in DSL-based code generation, which automate the process of translating higher-level language constructs into executable code that meets specific functional and performance requirements.

Template-Based Code Generation

One of the most common techniques in code generation is using templates. In this approach, predefined templates are used to generate code for common tasks, such as database operations, API interactions, or UI components. The DSL user provides the high-level specifications, and the template engine fills in the details, generating the necessary code.

For example, in a web development DSL, a user might specify a data model and its relationship to a database. The code generator then uses a template to generate the corresponding SQL statements and ORM (Object-Relational Mapping) code.

Consider this DSL definition:

```
Model:
  name: User
  fields:
    - id: int
    - name: string
    - email: string
```

The code generator would use a template to create SQL commands like:

```
CREATE TABLE User (
    id INT PRIMARY KEY,
    name VARCHAR(255),
    email VARCHAR(255)
);
```

This template-based approach ensures that developers can quickly generate boilerplate code without having to manually write repetitive and error-prone statements.

Syntax-Driven Code Generation

Another common method is syntax-driven code generation, where a parser interprets the DSL's syntax tree and produces the corresponding code. The syntax tree is often derived from the DSL's grammar, with nodes representing different constructs such as loops, conditionals, and function calls.

For instance, consider a DSL that describes mathematical functions. The user specifies a function like:

```
Function:
  name: add
  parameters: x, y
  return: x + y
```

The code generator would produce the equivalent Python code:

```
def add(x, y):
    return x + y
```

This type of algorithm relies on a syntax-driven transformation from the DSL's abstract syntax tree (AST) to the target language's syntax.

Rule-Based Code Generation

In rule-based code generation, specific rules are applied to transform high-level instructions into corresponding code. These rules define how the input DSL constructs should be converted into code statements, often using pattern matching or tree rewriting algorithms. Rule-based systems are particularly useful for highly customizable DSLs, where the code generation process needs to account for complex logic or domain-specific patterns.

For example, in a DSL for generating HTML content, a user might define a block of text to be wrapped in specific HTML tags. The rule-based code generation algorithm would identify the text block and generate HTML code:

```
Block:
  tag: "div"
  content: "Welcome to my site"
```

This could generate the following HTML code:

```
<div>Welcome to my site</div>
```

The rules for wrapping content in the div tag would be applied, ensuring that the right code is produced based on the DSL input.

Model-Driven Code Generation

In more advanced DSLs, model-driven code generation is used to convert abstract models or domain models into executable code. This technique involves transforming high-level conceptual models into low-level code by mapping model elements (such as entities and relationships) to code constructs. This approach is popular in domains like software engineering and systems modeling, where complex relationships and behaviors need to be generated automatically.

For example, a DSL might allow users to define system components and their relationships, and the code generator would then create the corresponding code structures:

```
Component:
  name: DatabaseConnection
  dependencies:
    - Driver
    - Config
```

The code generation algorithm would interpret this model and generate code for setting up a database connection with the necessary dependencies.

213

Automated code generation in DSLs is enabled through various algorithms, including template-based, syntax-driven, rule-based, and model-driven approaches. These algorithms help streamline the development process by automatically converting high-level specifications into executable code, thus reducing manual coding, increasing efficiency, and ensuring consistency across projects. By leveraging these techniques, DSLs can significantly enhance productivity and the quality of the generated software.

Module 21:
Template Metaprogramming Algorithms

Template metaprogramming refers to the use of templates in programming languages, primarily C++, to generate code at compile-time rather than at runtime. This approach can extend the functionality of domain-specific languages (DSLs) by allowing developers to perform computation during compilation, optimize performance, and reduce redundancy. This module explores how template metaprogramming can be applied to DSLs, providing insights into its techniques, use cases, and challenges.

Introduction to Template Metaprogramming in C++ and Other Languages

Template metaprogramming in C++ leverages the power of templates to perform computations during the compilation phase. By using templates to generate code based on compile-time conditions, developers can reduce runtime overhead and improve performance. This paradigm allows developers to encode logic into type parameters and perform type computations to generate efficient code. While C++ is the most prominent language for template metaprogramming, other languages like D, Rust, and even Python through libraries like metaprogramming also support similar techniques. This section introduces the foundational concepts of template metaprogramming, including type traits, template specialization, and recursive templates, and how they facilitate DSL development.

Techniques for Using Metaprogramming to Extend DSL Capabilities

Template metaprogramming enables the creation of flexible and powerful DSLs by incorporating compile-time decision-making and computation. Through techniques such as type introspection, SFINAE (Substitution Failure Is Not An Error), and template specialization, developers can create DSLs that adapt dynamically to different use cases without sacrificing performance. For instance, a DSL designed for numerical computation might use metaprogramming to select the most efficient algorithm for a given problem based on data types or compile-time parameters. Additionally, metaprogramming allows the creation of domain-specific operators, making the DSL more intuitive and concise. This section covers various techniques and how they can be applied to tailor DSLs to specific domains.

Use Cases for Template Metaprogramming in DSLs

Template metaprogramming is particularly useful in domains where performance is critical, such as embedded systems, high-performance computing, and real-time applications. In these domains, DSLs can leverage metaprogramming to enable advanced optimizations without sacrificing runtime flexibility. For example, a DSL for graphics programming can use template metaprogramming to generate optimized shader code based on the user's input, where the types of transformations and rendering algorithms are selected at compile time. Another use case is the implementation of a custom data structure in a DSL, where template metaprogramming automatically adapts the structure's behavior based on compile-time parameters, ensuring memory and performance efficiency.

Challenges and Pitfalls in Template Metaprogramming

Despite its advantages, template metaprogramming presents several challenges. First, it can make code harder to understand and maintain due to its complexity and the abstraction of logic into templates. Debugging template-based code can also be challenging because errors often manifest during compilation, and error messages can be cryptic and difficult to interpret. Additionally, excessive reliance on metaprogramming can lead to bloated code, where the compiler generates too many specialized versions of templates, increasing compile-time and binary size. This section discusses the trade-offs involved in using template metaprogramming and offers strategies to mitigate common pitfalls, such as minimizing template depth and improving error diagnostics.

Template metaprogramming is a powerful tool for extending the capabilities of DSLs, especially in performance-sensitive applications. By enabling compile-time computation and optimizations, it allows developers to create highly efficient and flexible DSLs. However, it also introduces challenges, particularly in terms of complexity, maintainability, and debugging. Understanding these challenges and using best practices is essential for effectively leveraging template metaprogramming in DSL design.

Introduction to Template Metaprogramming in C++ and Other Languages

Template metaprogramming (TMP) in C++ enables computation at compile time, leveraging C++ templates to extend the capabilities of domain-specific languages (DSLs). By shifting logic to compile time, TMP can optimize runtime performance and create highly efficient, type-safe code. C++'s template system allows for specialization, recursion, and type traits, enabling developers to perform complex operations before the program runs.

Here's an example of basic template metaprogramming using recursion to calculate factorials at compile time:

```
#include <iostream>

// A template that calculates factorial at compile time.
template <int N>
struct Factorial {
    static const int value = N * Factorial<N - 1>::value;
};

// Specialization to stop recursion at 0
template <>
struct Factorial<0> {
    static const int value = 1;
```

```
};
int main() {
    std::cout << "Factorial of 5: " << Factorial<5>::value << std::endl;
    return 0;
}
```

In this example, the Factorial template recursively calculates the factorial of a number at compile time. The specialized version of the template (Factorial<0>) halts the recursion, providing the base case. The result (120) is calculated during compilation, and the value is embedded directly into the binary.

Besides recursion, **SFINAE (Substitution Failure Is Not An Error)** is a key TMP feature. It allows the enabling or disabling of templates based on type traits. Here's an example:

```
#include <iostream>
#include <type_traits>

// A function template that is enabled only for integral types
template <typename T>
typename std::enable_if<std::is_integral<T>::value, void>::type
print_integral(T t) {
    std::cout << "Integral: " << t << std::endl;
}

// A function template that is enabled only for floating-point types
template <typename T>
typename std::enable_if<std::is_floating_point<T>::value, void>::type
print_floating(T t) {
    std::cout << "Floating point: " << t << std::endl;
}

int main() {
    print_integral(5);          // Output: Integral: 5
    print_floating(3.14);       // Output: Floating point: 3.14
    return 0;
}
```

In this example, the print_integral and print_floating templates are conditionally enabled using std::enable_if based on whether the type is integral or floating-point. If you try to pass a type that doesn't match the conditions, such as print_integral(3.14), it will cause a compile-time error, ensuring that only valid types are used for each function.

Other languages like Rust, D, and Python also use metaprogramming to manipulate code at compile-time or runtime. For example, Rust's macro system allows for metaprogramming, and Python uses decorators and metaclasses for similar capabilities at runtime. However, C++ template metaprogramming provides an unmatched ability to perform computations and generate code before execution, resulting in extremely optimized and efficient code.

The power of template metaprogramming makes it an ideal tool for building high-performance DSLs. By enabling the DSL to leverage compile-time decisions, template metaprogramming can ensure that the generated code is both type-safe and highly optimized for the target application domain. However, this power comes with complexity, and it's essential to maintain a balance to avoid overly complicated and hard-to-maintain code.

Techniques for Using Metaprogramming to Extend DSL Capabilities

Template metaprogramming (TMP) in C++ offers several advanced techniques that can extend the functionality of domain-specific languages (DSLs). By harnessing the power of TMP, developers can make DSLs more expressive, efficient, and flexible, allowing for operations such as type manipulation, constant expressions, and conditional code generation at compile time. Below are some key techniques for using metaprogramming to enhance DSL capabilities.

1. Type Traits and Static Assertions

Type traits provide a mechanism for determining type properties at compile time. These traits allow DSL developers to conditionally generate code based on type characteristics. For instance, if a DSL requires different behavior based on whether a type is integral or floating-point, type traits can be employed to enable specific templates only for particular types.

```
#include <iostream>
#include <type_traits>

template <typename T>
void process_type(T value) {
    if (std::is_integral<T>::value) {
        std::cout << "Processing integral value: " << value << std::endl;
    } else {
        std::cout << "Processing non-integral value: " << value << std::endl;
    }
}

int main() {
    process_type(42);         // Output: Processing integral value: 42
    process_type(3.14);       // Output: Processing non-integral value: 3.14
    return 0;
}
```

By using std::is_integral<T>, the code will conditionally process integral values differently from others. Type traits like std::is_floating_point and std::is_class can enable more specialized behavior for different types, allowing for more tailored DSL behavior.

2. Recursive Templates for Code Generation

A fundamental feature of TMP is recursion within templates. This allows for recursive operations, such as generating code for a fixed number of iterations or levels, based on compile-time parameters. Recursive templates can be utilized in DSLs to perform calculations, loop unrolling, or recursive descent parsing. This technique ensures that complex operations can be done at compile time, making the code highly efficient at runtime.

```cpp
template <int N>
struct GenerateCode {
    static void execute() {
        std::cout << "Executing step " << N << std::endl;
        GenerateCode<N - 1>::execute();
    }
};

// Specialization to end the recursion
template <>
struct GenerateCode<0> {
    static void execute() {
        std::cout << "End of code generation." << std::endl;
    }
};

int main() {
    GenerateCode<3>::execute();
    return 0;
}
```

Here, GenerateCode<3> recursively generates code for three steps. The recursion is terminated when the template specialization for GenerateCode<0> is reached. Such recursive templates can be useful for DSLs that generate or configure a series of operations.

3. SFINAE (Substitution Failure Is Not An Error)

SFINAE allows conditional inclusion or exclusion of template instantiations based on the characteristics of the types involved. This enables more flexible DSL designs, as developers can craft templates that are only valid for certain types, effectively adding a layer of compile-time checks that would be impossible with traditional runtime logic.

```cpp
#include <iostream>
#include <type_traits>

template <typename T>
typename std::enable_if<std::is_integral<T>::value, void>::type
process(T value) {
    std::cout << "Processing integer: " << value << std::endl;
}

template <typename T>
typename std::enable_if<std::is_floating_point<T>::value, void>::type
process(T value) {
    std::cout << "Processing floating-point: " << value << std::endl;
}

int main() {
    process(10);        // Output: Processing integer: 10
    process(3.14);      // Output: Processing floating-point: 3.14
    return 0;
}
```

In this example, the appropriate process function is selected based on whether the type T is integral or floating-point. The std::enable_if mechanism ensures that only the correct version of process is compiled for each type.

4. Expression Templates for Efficiency

Expression templates are another advanced TMP technique that can be used to optimize DSLs. Instead of performing calculations at runtime, expression templates enable the compilation of expressions into highly efficient, type-specific code. This approach is particularly useful for DSLs related to numeric computations, such as scientific or financial applications, where performance is critical.

```
template <typename T>
struct Add {
    T lhs, rhs;
    Add(T l, T r) : lhs(l), rhs(r) {}
    T evaluate() { return lhs + rhs; }
};

template <typename T>
Add<T> operator+(T lhs, T rhs) {
    return Add<T>(lhs, rhs);
}

int main() {
    Add<int> sum = 5 + 3;
    std::cout << "Sum: " << sum.evaluate() << std::endl;   // Output: Sum: 8
    return 0;
}
```

In this example, the addition operation is captured by an expression template, which stores the operands and computes the sum at compile time. This technique avoids unnecessary temporary variables and enhances performance.

These techniques leverage the full power of C++'s template metaprogramming capabilities, extending the functionality of DSLs by enabling compile-time logic, type-dependent behavior, and optimized code generation. When used effectively, TMP techniques can produce DSLs that are both highly efficient and expressive.

Use Cases for Template Metaprogramming in DSLs

Template metaprogramming (TMP) in C++ and other languages offers significant advantages for extending the capabilities of domain-specific languages (DSLs). By enabling compile-time computation and type manipulation, TMP can facilitate various use cases that require high flexibility, efficiency, and customization. Below are some examples of how template metaprogramming can be applied in DSLs.

1. Static Polymorphism for Type-Specific Behavior

One of the core uses of TMP is enabling static polymorphism, which is the ability to perform operations on types without relying on runtime mechanisms like inheritance or virtual functions. This can be particularly useful in DSLs designed for numerical computation or optimization tasks where different types (e.g., integers, floating points, vectors) need to be processed differently at compile time. By leveraging TMP, DSLs can perform complex type-specific operations without the overhead of virtual calls, which enhances performance.

For example, in a DSL designed for matrix computations, different matrix types (dense, sparse, diagonal) may need to be treated differently. Using TMP, the DSL can compile specialized code for each matrix type, leading to more efficient execution.

```
template <typename T>
struct Matrix {
    T data;
    // Matrix operations here
};

template <typename T>
void multiply(Matrix<T> &m1, Matrix<T> &m2) {
    // Perform matrix multiplication for type T
}
```

In this example, the multiply function can be specialized for different matrix types, ensuring the correct behavior without relying on runtime polymorphism.

2. Expression Templates for Optimized Numerical DSLs

Expression templates are widely used in DSLs for mathematical computations, particularly in scientific computing and linear algebra libraries. By expressing complex mathematical expressions as templates, DSLs can optimize the resulting code, eliminating the need for temporary variables and enabling more efficient evaluation strategies. This allows for better performance, especially in high-performance computing scenarios.

For example, a DSL for numerical simulations can use expression templates to handle complex expressions like vector addition or matrix multiplication, optimizing the code to perform these operations without excessive memory allocations or copies.

```
template <typename T>
struct Add {
    T lhs, rhs;
    Add(T l, T r) : lhs(l), rhs(r) {}
    T evaluate() { return lhs + rhs; }
};

template <typename T>
Add<T> operator+(T lhs, T rhs) {
    return Add<T>(lhs, rhs);
}
```

This allows for efficient expression evaluation in the context of a DSL for mathematical operations, where performance is critical.

3. Domain-Specific Configuration and Code Generation

Template metaprogramming can also be used to automate code generation based on user-defined configuration parameters. In DSLs that involve the configuration of hardware,

221

network systems, or embedded devices, TMP can generate configuration code or customize low-level settings at compile time. By providing a DSL with specialized syntax for configuration, developers can create a more readable and error-resistant environment.

For example, in an embedded systems DSL, TMP can be employed to select specific peripheral configurations based on compile-time parameters. The correct configuration code is automatically generated, minimizing the chances of errors and ensuring the system is optimized for the hardware platform.

```
template <typename Device>
void configure(Device &dev) {
    // Configure device based on compile-time parameters
}
```

This approach allows for a flexible DSL tailored to the system's specific needs, ensuring efficient resource allocation and hardware setup without manual intervention.

4. Compile-Time Assertions and Type Checking

Another important use case for TMP in DSLs is the implementation of compile-time assertions and type checks. These checks help ensure that the DSL's code is correct before it is compiled, reducing runtime errors and improving robustness. For example, in a DSL for database schema design, TMP can be used to validate relationships between different schema components at compile time, such as ensuring foreign key relationships are correctly established.

```
template <typename T>
struct Assert {
    static_assert(sizeof(T) > 0, "Type cannot be empty");
};
```

This allows developers to catch common errors at compile time, preventing issues that would otherwise only appear during runtime, making the DSL more reliable and easier to maintain.

5. Meta-Object Programming and Reflection

Some advanced DSLs may require metaprogramming techniques for introspection and reflection, where the code must adapt dynamically to the types being used. While C++ does not provide reflection directly, TMP can be used to mimic some aspects of reflection, such as inspecting the properties of types and generating corresponding code. This is particularly useful in DSLs that involve serialization, object mapping, or generating documentation from source code.

```
template <typename T>
struct Reflect {
    static void print() {
        // Print the name of the type T
        std::cout << "Reflecting type: " << typeid(T).name() << std::endl;
    }
```

222

```
};
```

This kind of functionality is essential for DSLs that interact with complex systems, enabling runtime flexibility while leveraging compile-time checks and optimizations.

Template metaprogramming plays a crucial role in extending the capabilities of DSLs, enabling compile-time optimizations, type-specific operations, and efficient code generation. These techniques improve performance, flexibility, and robustness, ensuring that DSLs can address complex and domain-specific needs effectively.

Challenges and Pitfalls in Template Metaprogramming

Template metaprogramming (TMP) offers powerful capabilities for extending domain-specific languages (DSLs), but it comes with its own set of challenges and pitfalls. From complexity in code readability to compilation delays and error handling difficulties, these issues require careful consideration. Below are some common challenges encountered when using TMP, along with strategies to address them.

1. Complexity and Readability

TMP, by its nature, introduces complexity into the codebase due to its reliance on templates. This results in code that can be hard to follow and maintain, especially for those unfamiliar with template programming. One issue is the creation of deeply nested templates, which complicate the reading and debugging of code. The error messages from the compiler in such cases can be cryptic, making troubleshooting difficult.

For example, the following TMP code computes factorials at compile-time:

```
template<int N>
struct Factorial {
    static const int value = N * Factorial<N - 1>::value;
};

template<>
struct Factorial<0> {
    static const int value = 1;
};
```

While this code efficiently computes factorials during compile-time, the complexity can make it difficult to understand at a glance, particularly when errors occur in deeper nested structures.

2. Compilation Time and Code Bloat

Template metaprogramming can significantly increase compilation times due to the expansion of template instantiations. The compiler must generate a unique version of the code for each type combination, resulting in slower build times. In cases of heavy TMP usage, this may lead to excessive bloat in the compiled binaries, especially if templates are instantiated with many variations.

Consider the following example of generating different classes based on template parameters:

```cpp
template<typename T>
struct TypePrinter {
    void print() {
        std::cout << typeid(T).name() << std::endl;
    }
};

TypePrinter<int> intPrinter;
TypePrinter<float> floatPrinter;
TypePrinter<double> doublePrinter;
```

This code creates separate instantiations for each type (int, float, and double). As the number of different types grows, so does the number of instantiations, resulting in code bloat.

To optimize this, it's crucial to limit template instantiations to only those necessary. Reducing the number of unique combinations of template arguments can help mitigate both compilation delays and code bloat.

3. Error Handling and Debugging Difficulties

Template errors are often only detected at compile-time, which makes debugging more challenging. Unlike runtime errors that provide stack traces and clear error messages, compile-time template errors can be obscure and difficult to trace.

For instance, a common error in TMP arises when the wrong type is passed to a template, and the error message could look like this:

```cpp
template<typename T>
struct PrintType {
    void print() { std::cout << typeid(T).name() << std::endl; }
};

PrintType<int> intPrinter;
PrintType<std::string> stringPrinter;
```

If there was a typo in std::string, a typical error message from the compiler might be difficult to interpret, especially when the issue occurs in deeply nested templates.

To handle such issues, developers should make use of static assertions to catch type errors at compile-time, ensuring that invalid types are flagged early. Example:

```cpp
template<typename T>
struct EnsureInteger {
    static_assert(std::is_integral<T>::value, "T must be an integer type!");
};
```

This enforces type constraints at compile-time, making the code safer and errors easier to catch.

224

4. Portability and Compiler-Specific Issues

Different compilers handle template metaprogramming differently, especially when it comes to advanced features like SFINAE (Substitution Failure Is Not An Error) or variadic templates. These compiler-specific behaviors can make code less portable across different systems, leading to compatibility issues. Developers must ensure that their TMP code is portable and compliant with the C++ standard to prevent compatibility problems.

For example, code written using SFINAE might work perfectly with one compiler but fail with another:

```
template<typename T, typename U>
auto add(T t, U u) -> decltype(t + u) {
    return t + u;
}
```

This feature relies on the compiler's ability to deduce the return type using decltype. If the compilers don't fully support certain template features, the code might not compile, making it difficult to maintain across platforms.

To mitigate portability issues, it's advisable to test the code with different compilers, stick to widely supported features, and avoid compiler-specific extensions unless absolutely necessary.

5. Overuse and Misuse of TMP

A major pitfall of template metaprogramming is the temptation to overuse it. While TMP provides compile-time computation capabilities, using it unnecessarily can result in code that is overly complex and difficult to maintain. For instance, performing trivial calculations or logic at compile-time using templates when runtime computation would suffice is a misuse of TMP.

Consider the following example of calculating a value at compile-time using TMP when it could be done at runtime:

```
template<int N>
struct Factorial {
    static const int value = N * Factorial<N - 1>::value;
};

template<>
struct Factorial<0> {
    static const int value = 1;
};

// Calling factorial with a fixed value
int result = Factorial<5>::value;
```

Here, calculating Factorial<5>::value at compile-time may offer no real benefit if the value were instead computed at runtime. Developers should carefully assess whether the benefits of TMP outweigh the added complexity, and avoid overusing it when simpler solutions are available.

Template metaprogramming (TMP) provides powerful tools for extending DSL capabilities, but it is fraught with challenges such as complexity, compilation overhead, debugging difficulties, and portability concerns. By simplifying TMP usage, limiting unnecessary instantiations, and adhering to best practices, developers can harness the full potential of TMP while avoiding the common pitfalls.

Module 22:

Abstract Syntax Trees (AST) for DSLs

Module 22 explores Abstract Syntax Trees (ASTs) and their essential role in Domain-Specific Languages (DSLs). It covers the process of building and using ASTs in DSL design, manipulating them for language transformations, optimizing AST generation, and provides examples of AST-based DSL tools. ASTs are central to making DSLs flexible and efficient.

1. Building and Using ASTs in DSL Design

Abstract Syntax Trees (ASTs) are fundamental for implementing DSLs, as they provide a structured representation of the syntax of the language. In the design phase, building an AST involves parsing the DSL source code into a tree where each node represents a syntactic construct. This transformation helps in identifying language constructs more easily, and ASTs provide a foundation for further processing, such as interpretation or code generation. Building ASTs in DSL design typically requires creating a parser capable of mapping the source code into tree structures based on predefined grammar rules. These structures can then be traversed for evaluation, optimization, or translation into other formats.

2. Manipulating Syntax Trees for Transformations

Once an AST is built, it can be manipulated to transform the DSL code into something more useful, such as machine code, intermediate code, or a different DSL format. These transformations are essential in processes like optimization, refactoring, or language-specific customizations. AST manipulation often involves traversing the tree recursively, applying operations on specific nodes, and modifying them accordingly. For instance, a transformation might combine adjacent arithmetic operations or remove redundant expressions. The flexibility of ASTs allows for sophisticated changes in the language's behavior or structure, making them highly valuable for code generation, debugging, or language refinement in DSL development.

3. Optimizing AST Generation

Optimization of AST generation is crucial for ensuring that DSLs perform efficiently, particularly for performance-critical applications. Optimizing the tree generation involves techniques such as simplifying nodes, eliminating unnecessary calculations, and applying domain-specific optimizations. These optimizations can help reduce the size and complexity of the AST, leading to faster processing, smaller generated code, and better resource management. Optimizing AST generation might also include improving the efficiency of the parsing stage or restructuring the tree for easier manipulation during later stages of execution. Advanced optimizations involve ensuring that the AST reflects the most efficient possible representation of the code.

227

4. Examples of AST-based DSL Tools

Several tools and libraries leverage ASTs for DSL development. These tools facilitate the creation, manipulation, and analysis of abstract syntax trees for custom DSLs. For example, parser generators like ANTLR or Yacc are commonly used to build parsers that produce ASTs from DSL syntax. Other tools, such as tree-sitter or Esprima (in JavaScript), provide high-level abstractions for working with ASTs. In the context of DSLs, these tools are used to implement custom language-specific features, such as macros, static analysis, or code refactoring. Examples in the real world include templating engines or DSLs for configuration management, where AST manipulation allows developers to generate the desired outputs with minimal effort.

ASTs are pivotal in DSL design and implementation, enabling structured representation of language constructs. Manipulating ASTs facilitates language transformations and optimizations that enhance performance and efficiency. Through examples of AST-based tools, developers can gain insight into how these trees enable powerful customizations and help create more effective DSLs.

Building and Using ASTs in DSL Design

In DSL design, an Abstract Syntax Tree (AST) is an essential structure representing the source code's syntactic components. An AST breaks down the language's expressions into a tree-like structure, where each node represents a syntactic construct and child nodes represent components of that construct. For example, a parser reads the DSL code, and based on the grammar, it creates an AST that models the structure of the code.

Consider a simple mathematical DSL for expressions like x + y * z. The parser will break it down into an AST, where the root node is the addition operator (+), and the child node represents the multiplication operation (*), with its own children being y and z. In Python, we can represent an AST for this example using classes like so:

```python
class ASTNode:
    def __init__(self, value, left=None, right=None):
        self.value = value
        self.left = left
        self.right = right

# Example for the expression: x + y * z
# This will construct the tree: (x + (y * z))

node_z = ASTNode('z')
node_y = ASTNode('y')
node_multiply = ASTNode('*', node_y, node_z)

node_x = ASTNode('x')
node_add = ASTNode('+', node_x, node_multiply)

# Now node_add represents the root of the AST
```

Here, we create a class ASTNode that has a value to represent the operator or operand, and two child nodes (left and right) representing its subexpressions. The example shows how to construct the AST for the expression x + y * z, where the multiplication is performed before addition due to operator precedence.

The advantages of using an AST in DSL design are significant. It allows structured access to the components of the language and simplifies the processing of expressions. For instance, we can easily traverse the AST to evaluate the expression or apply optimizations, such as simplifying y * 1 to y. Here's a simple example of evaluating the expression represented by the AST:

```python
def evaluate(ast):
    if not ast.left and not ast.right:  # Leaf node, return value
        return float(ast.value)

    left_val = evaluate(ast.left)
    right_val = evaluate(ast.right)

    if ast.value == '+':
        return left_val + right_val
    elif ast.value == '*':
        return left_val * right_val

# Evaluate the AST for x + y * z
result = evaluate(node_add)
print(result)
```

In this code, the evaluate function recursively traverses the AST. If the node has no children (a leaf node), it returns the value. Otherwise, it recursively evaluates the left and right children, performing the operation based on the node's value. In the case of x + y * z, the multiplication is performed first, followed by the addition.

Building and using ASTs in DSL design offers clear advantages by creating a well-structured representation of the code. It provides a solid foundation for tasks like evaluation, optimization, error detection, and extending the language with new constructs.

Manipulating Syntax trees for Transformations

Manipulating syntax trees, specifically Abstract Syntax Trees (ASTs), is central to transforming and optimizing domain-specific languages (DSLs). Once an AST has been constructed, it can be manipulated to perform various tasks like code transformations, optimizations, or to generate target code. This allows DSL developers to modify the tree's structure or values to meet specific goals, such as simplifying expressions or reordering operations.

Consider an example where we want to optimize an expression in a DSL by applying a transformation that simplifies redundant calculations. Suppose we have an expression like x + 0. The optimal result would be x, since adding zero has no effect. In the context of AST manipulation, we can detect this redundancy during tree traversal and modify the tree accordingly.

Let's walk through an example in Python to demonstrate how to manipulate the AST for this optimization:

```python
class ASTNode:
    def __init__(self, value, left=None, right=None):
        self.value = value
        self.left = left
        self.right = right

# Example: x + 0
node_zero = ASTNode('0')
node_x = ASTNode('x')
node_add = ASTNode('+', node_x, node_zero)

# Optimization function to simplify x + 0
def optimize(ast):
    if ast is None:
        return None
    if ast.value == '+':
        if ast.left and ast.left.value == '0':
            return ast.right  # x + 0 simplifies to x
        elif ast.right and ast.right.value == '0':
            return ast.left  # 0 + x simplifies to x
    return ast  # Return the node as is if no optimization is possible

optimized_ast = optimize(node_add)
print(optimized_ast.value)  # Output: x
```

In this example, the optimize function checks for the pattern x + 0 and replaces it with x, as this is a simplified form. The function performs a recursive traversal through the AST, looking for addition operations where either the left or right operand is 0. Once the pattern is detected, the function returns the non-zero operand, effectively transforming the AST.

This manipulation of the AST can also be extended to other optimizations, such as reducing expressions like x * 1 to x or simplifying complex nested expressions. These optimizations improve the efficiency of the DSL by removing redundant calculations and unnecessary operations, making the generated code faster and more readable.

Additionally, AST manipulation is useful for transforming DSLs into target languages. For instance, if you have a DSL designed to represent mathematical expressions, you can traverse the AST and generate equivalent code in another language, such as Python or C++, based on the operations in the tree. The transformations could involve generating function calls, variables, or looping constructs depending on the DSL's intended purpose.

By manipulating syntax trees, DSLs can be made more efficient and expressive, as transformations are automatically applied, simplifying the user's experience and optimizing the generated code.

Optimizing AST Generation

Optimizing the generation of Abstract Syntax Trees (ASTs) is an essential task in the development of domain-specific languages (DSLs), particularly when performance or correctness is crucial. Optimizing AST generation involves creating a more efficient representation of the syntax tree, reducing unnecessary computations, and ensuring that the generated tree reflects the best structure for subsequent transformations or code generation.

One important optimization is eliminating intermediate or redundant nodes during the AST construction. For example, when parsing arithmetic expressions, operations like adding zero or multiplying by one result in trees that include unnecessary nodes, which can be pruned at an early stage. This helps reduce the size of the AST, which in turn improves performance during the later phases of transformation and code generation.

Here is a simple example in Python, where we optimize the AST by eliminating redundant operations as the tree is being constructed:

```python
class ASTNode:
    def __init__(self, value, left=None, right=None):
        self.value = value
        self.left = left
        self.right = right

# Function to construct the AST for an expression like x + 0 or 1 * x
def build_ast(expression):
    tokens = expression.split()

    if len(tokens) == 3:
        left = tokens[0]
        operator = tokens[1]
        right = tokens[2]

        if operator == "+" and right == "0":
            return ASTNode(left)  # Optimization: x + 0 becomes x
        elif operator == "*" and right == "1":
            return ASTNode(left)  # Optimization: x * 1 becomes x
        else:
            return ASTNode(operator, ASTNode(left), ASTNode(right))

# Example usage
expression = "x + 0"
ast = build_ast(expression)
print(ast.value)  # Output: x (optimized)

expression2 = "x * 1"
ast2 = build_ast(expression2)
print(ast2.value)  # Output: x (optimized)
```

In this example, the function build_ast constructs an AST for a simple expression. If the operator is + and the right operand is 0, or if the operator is * and the right operand is 1, we immediately return the left operand without creating further nodes in the tree. This optimization reduces the complexity of the AST and ensures that redundant operations are removed during the AST creation process itself.

Another important optimization is ensuring that the tree structure remains balanced and minimal. For instance, when parsing nested expressions, it is common for the tree to contain unnecessary intermediate nodes that could be eliminated by simplifying the expression at the time of AST generation. A more efficient AST allows faster manipulation and reduces memory consumption.

Optimization can also apply to the choice of data structures. Instead of using linked lists or simple node-based trees, more advanced data structures such as balanced binary trees, tries, or hash maps may be used depending on the nature of the DSL and the kinds of transformations or queries that will be performed.

Overall, optimizing AST generation not only makes the DSL more efficient but also ensures that the transformations and code generation phases are faster. By pruning redundant nodes and simplifying the structure during AST construction, the DSL becomes more performant and easier to work with.

Examples of AST-Tased DSL Tools

AST-based tools are widely used in DSLs to facilitate efficient language design, transformation, and code generation. These tools rely on the use of Abstract Syntax Trees (ASTs) to represent the structure of the source code or expressions in the DSL, and they offer flexibility in terms of manipulation and optimization. In this section, we explore some common examples of AST-based DSL tools and demonstrate their usage with Python code.

1. ANTLR (Another Tool for Language Recognition)

ANTLR is a powerful parser generator that constructs an AST for the input language. It is often used for building compilers, interpreters, or DSL tools. In ANTLR, the AST is generated as part of the parsing process, allowing further manipulation and code generation.

For instance, here's how ANTLR might be used in a simple arithmetic DSL:

```
// Arithmetic.g4 (ANTLR grammar file)
grammar Arithmetic;

expr    : expr '+' expr     # Add
        | expr '*' expr     # Multiply
        | INT               # Int
        | '(' expr ')'      # Parens
        ;

INT     : [0-9]+ ;
WS      : [ \t\r\n]+ -> skip ;
```

After compiling this grammar, ANTLR generates a parser and a lexer, which produce an AST when the DSL expression is parsed. For example, the expression 3 + 4 * 5 would yield an AST with + as the root, and 3 and * as its children, where * itself has 4 and 5 as its children.

This AST is then manipulated to generate code or perform further transformations.

2. Pyparsing

Pyparsing is a Python library that provides an easy way to define grammars and create parsers. It can be used to create ASTs from text input. Below is an example of how Pyparsing can be used to parse arithmetic expressions and create an AST:

```python
from pyparsing import Word, alphas, nums, Forward, OneOrMore, Literal

# Define the grammar
expr = Forward()
term = Word(nums)
plus = Literal("+")
expr << term + OneOrMore(plus + term)

# Parse an expression
parsed_expr = expr.parseString("3 + 5 + 7")

# Simple AST output
ast = {"type": "ADD", "left": "3", "right": {"type": "ADD", "left": "5",
        "right": "7"}}
print(ast)
```

In this example, Pyparsing is used to define a simple arithmetic grammar for addition. The input expression 3 + 5 + 7 is parsed into an AST, where the addition operation is structured hierarchically, reflecting the operation's precedence and structure.

3. Lark

Lark is another Python-based library for parsing. It is more advanced than Pyparsing and offers efficient parsing with built-in support for generating ASTs. Here's an example of a simple DSL using Lark:

```python
from lark import Lark

# Define grammar
grammar = """
start: "add" NUMBER "+" NUMBER
NUMBER: /\d+/
"""

# Create a parser
parser = Lark(grammar, start='start')

# Parse an expression
tree = parser.parse("add 5 + 3")

# Generate AST from tree
print(tree.pretty())
```

In this example, Lark parses the input add 5 + 3 and generates an AST, which represents the structure of the input with its operations clearly outlined. Lark also allows for further manipulation and processing of the AST.

4. Custom DSL Tool (Python Example)

Let's consider an example where a custom AST-based DSL is created for a simple conditional expression evaluator. Here is how the AST might be built and manipulated using Python:

```python
class ASTNode:
    def __init__(self, value, left=None, right=None):
        self.value = value
        self.left = left
        self.right = right

# Parse and create AST
def parse_condition(condition):
    if 'AND' in condition:
        left, right = condition.split('AND')
        return ASTNode('AND', ASTNode(left.strip()), ASTNode(right.strip()))
    elif 'OR' in condition:
        left, right = condition.split('OR')
        return ASTNode('OR', ASTNode(left.strip()), ASTNode(right.strip()))
    else:
        return ASTNode(condition.strip())

# Example usage
ast = parse_condition('A AND B')
print(ast.value)  # Output: AND
```

In this custom tool, the parse_condition function takes a conditional expression like A AND B and generates an AST where AND is the root node, with A and B as its children. This AST can then be evaluated, transformed, or optimized as required by the DSL.

These examples illustrate the variety of ways ASTs can be utilized in DSL tools. Whether using a well-known parser generator like ANTLR, or a Python-based library like Pyparsing or Lark, ASTs provide a structured way to represent and manipulate the source code of a DSL. By utilizing ASTs, DSL developers can create powerful tools for code transformation, optimization, and generation.

Module 23:
Grammar Trees and Parsing Trees

This module explores the role of grammar trees and parsing trees in the context of Domain-Specific Languages (DSLs). It covers how grammar trees are structured and used in DSL parsing, techniques for constructing parsing trees, and the relationship between these trees. Additionally, the module discusses performance optimization strategies for parsing trees.

Overview of Grammar Trees in DSL Parsing

Grammar trees serve as a formal representation of a DSL's syntax. They define the language's rules and structure, laying the groundwork for parsing. In DSL parsing, grammar trees are essential for breaking down complex expressions into simpler components that a parser can process. By clearly defining syntax through grammar rules, grammar trees help ensure consistency and correctness in the language's design. These trees typically represent production rules in a hierarchical format, where each node corresponds to a syntactic construct or a rule in the language. This section will delve into the significance of grammar trees in enabling efficient parsing and the creation of robust DSLs.

Techniques for Constructing Parsing Trees

Once grammar trees are defined, parsing trees are constructed during the parsing process. Parsing trees reflect the structure of a given DSL expression based on the grammar rules. Various techniques can be used to construct parsing trees, with two of the most common being top-down and bottom-up parsing. In top-down parsing, the parser starts from the root of the tree (the start symbol) and works its way down to the leaves. In contrast, bottom-up parsing begins with the leaves and works toward the root. The section will explore these techniques, illustrating their advantages and challenges in constructing parsing trees efficiently for DSLs.

Relation Between Grammar and Parsing Trees

Grammar trees and parsing trees are closely related, yet distinct. Grammar trees are abstract representations of a language's syntax, while parsing trees are concrete, runtime structures that represent the syntactic structure of specific input code based on that grammar. The grammar tree defines the rules, and the parsing tree follows those rules to construct the actual structure of the input. Understanding the relationship between these trees is crucial in optimizing the parsing process and in ensuring the accuracy of DSL interpreters or compilers. This section will explain how the two types of trees interact and complement each other in DSL parsing.

Performance Optimization of Parsing Trees

Efficient parsing is crucial when dealing with large or complex DSLs, and optimizing parsing trees is an essential step. Parsing trees can be optimized in several ways, such as minimizing tree depth, eliminating redundant computations, and optimizing memory usage. Additionally, using efficient parsing algorithms like LL, LR, or Earley parsers can significantly improve parsing performance. This section will focus on strategies for optimizing parsing trees, with an emphasis on reducing parsing time and memory consumption. It will also address the importance of choosing the right parser type depending on the complexity of the DSL and the expected input patterns.

Understanding grammar trees and parsing trees is vital in DSL design and implementation. By mastering the construction of parsing trees and optimizing their performance, DSL developers can create efficient parsers that handle complex input more effectively. The relationship between grammar and parsing trees plays a key role in shaping the parsing process, and performance optimization ensures that DSLs remain practical for real-world use cases.

Overview of Grammar Trees in DSL Parsing

Grammar trees are essential structures used in parsing DSLs, as they define the syntax rules that govern how the language constructs should be interpreted. In DSL parsing, a grammar tree is a representation of the production rules in the grammar of the language. These trees break down complex language expressions into simpler components, organizing the structure of a DSL. Each node of a grammar tree represents a syntactic rule, while the edges between nodes signify how rules are composed or derived. The structure provides both a high-level overview of the DSL's grammar and the underlying mechanism used to generate parsing trees.

Grammar trees in DSL parsing are primarily used to build parsers that validate and process language input. They guide how the DSL code should be decomposed into meaningful components, ensuring that only valid syntax is processed by the interpreter or compiler. A grammar tree for a DSL might include rules for parsing numbers, operators, variables, and complex expressions, with each rule defining how these components are arranged within the language. For instance, a basic DSL for arithmetic expressions may have rules like:

- Expression → Term + Expression | Term

- Term → Factor * Term | Factor

- Factor → (Expression) | number

By defining how each element can be combined to form larger expressions, the grammar tree helps the parser understand what constitutes a valid expression in the DSL.

In Python, a simple example of defining a grammar tree for arithmetic expressions can look like this:

```
class GrammarTree:
    def __init__(self, rule, children=None):
        self.rule = rule
        self.children = children if children else []

# Example for an arithmetic expression grammar tree
expression = GrammarTree("Expression", [
```

```
    GrammarTree("Term", [
        GrammarTree("Factor", [
            GrammarTree("number")
        ]),
        GrammarTree("*"),
        GrammarTree("Term", [
            GrammarTree("Factor", [
                GrammarTree("number")
            ])
        ])
    ])
])

print(expression.rule)  # Output: "Expression"
```

This simple Python code snippet demonstrates how a grammar tree can represent an arithmetic expression. It defines the rule for an Expression that consists of Terms and Factors, and how Factors can be multiplied. The nested nature of the tree illustrates how a grammar tree maps out the structure of an expression in the DSL.

Grammar trees provide a framework for DSL parsers by outlining which components are valid in a given language and how they can be arranged. They form the foundation for parsing algorithms, ensuring that the input is parsed correctly and efficiently. Furthermore, they allow DSL designers to handle language ambiguities and complex syntax rules. Understanding grammar trees is crucial for anyone developing parsers for custom languages or DSLs.

By formalizing a DSL's grammar into a tree structure, it's easier to manipulate the input and parse it into the desired output. This organization aids in error detection, as the parser can quickly identify invalid constructs by comparing the input against the defined grammar rules in the tree.

Techniques for Constructing Parsing Trees

Parsing trees are structures that represent the syntactic structure of an expression in a programming language, often based on grammar rules. In the context of DSLs, constructing parsing trees is vital for interpreting or compiling DSL code. There are several techniques available for constructing parsing trees, each suited for different needs and languages. The most common techniques include recursive descent parsing, LL parsing, and LR parsing.

Recursive Descent Parsing

Recursive descent parsing is one of the simplest and most intuitive methods for constructing parsing trees. This technique builds a tree by recursively applying grammar rules from the top down. Each rule in the grammar corresponds to a function in the parser, which calls itself recursively to handle sub-expressions. Recursive descent is particularly effective for DSLs that have simple or hierarchical syntax.

In Python, the recursive descent parser can be implemented as follows:

```python
class Parser:
    def __init__(self, tokens):
        self.tokens = tokens
        self.position = 0

    def parse_expression(self):
        # An expression can be a term plus another expression
        left = self.parse_term()
        if self.current_token() == '+':
            self.consume()
            right = self.parse_expression()
            return ('+', left, right)
        return left

    def parse_term(self):
        # A term can be a number
        if self.current_token().isdigit():
            value = self.consume()
            return ('number', value)
        raise ValueError("Invalid term")

    def current_token(self):
        return self.tokens[self.position]

    def consume(self):
        token = self.tokens[self.position]
        self.position += 1
        return token

tokens = ['3', '+', '5']
parser = Parser(tokens)
tree = parser.parse_expression()
print(tree)  # Output: ('+', ('number', '3'), ('number', '5'))
```

This code snippet demonstrates how recursive descent parsing is used to process arithmetic expressions in a simple DSL. It recursively parses an expression by breaking it into terms and operands, building the parsing tree incrementally.

LL and LR Parsing

LL and LR parsers are more advanced techniques based on the concepts of top-down and bottom-up parsing. An LL parser reads input from left to right and constructs the parse tree in a top-down manner, while an LR parser also reads left to right but constructs the tree bottom-up. These parsers are often used for more complex DSLs that require greater efficiency and can handle ambiguous grammars better than recursive descent parsers.

Shift-Reduce Parsing (LR Parsing)

Shift-reduce parsing is a bottom-up parsing technique widely used in LR parsing. It builds the parsing tree by shifting input symbols onto a stack and then reducing them to non-terminal symbols when possible. This approach is particularly useful for DSLs with more complex syntax or languages with operator precedence and associativity rules.

In an LR parser, the input is processed from left to right, and the parsing action shifts symbols to a stack until a rule in the grammar is matched, at which point the symbols are reduced according to that rule.

238

Chart Parsing

Another technique is chart parsing, which is particularly beneficial for handling ambiguous grammars or when the same sub-expression can be parsed multiple ways. Chart parsing uses a dynamic programming approach to store intermediate parse results in a chart (a table of parse substructures), improving the efficiency of parsing in certain DSLs.

Parsing techniques like recursive descent, LL, LR, and chart parsing provide different ways of constructing parsing trees, allowing DSL designers to choose the most appropriate method based on their language's complexity and performance requirements.

Relation between Grammar and Parsing Trees

Grammar and parsing trees are intricately linked in the design of a Domain-Specific Language (DSL). A grammar defines the syntactical structure of a language, specifying how sentences (or expressions) in the language can be constructed. Parsing trees, on the other hand, are the representations of how these grammatical rules are applied to a specific piece of code or input. Understanding the relationship between grammar and parsing trees is critical for designing efficient DSLs and ensuring that the parsing process aligns with the language's intended structure and semantics.

Grammar's Role in Defining Syntax

A grammar is essentially a set of formal rules that define the structure of valid constructs in a language. For a DSL, grammar rules specify the allowed sequence of tokens and how they form higher-level constructs like expressions, statements, and functions. The grammar for a DSL can be specified using formal notation, such as Backus-Naur Form (BNF) or Extended Backus-Naur Form (EBNF). These rules describe the permissible syntax of the language, including operators, keywords, and the structure of complex expressions.

The relationship between grammar and parsing trees becomes evident when examining how a parser uses these grammar rules to break down an input string. For example, in an arithmetic DSL, a grammar might define that an expression consists of terms separated by operators, while a parsing tree visually represents how this rule is applied to a given input.

How Parsing Trees Reflect Grammar Rules

A parsing tree is a tree-like structure where each node corresponds to a rule in the grammar. The root node typically represents the highest-level rule (e.g., a full expression), and child nodes represent sub-rules (e.g., terms, factors, or operands). Each terminal node in the tree corresponds to a token from the input string.

For example, consider a simple DSL for arithmetic expressions where the grammar rule for an expression is:

```
Expression → Term { "+" Term }
```

```
Term → Factor { "*" Factor }
Factor → Number | "(" Expression ")"
```

If the input string is 3 + 5 * (2 + 1), the parser constructs a parsing tree based on these grammar rules. The tree would look something like this:

```
Expression
├── Term
│   └── Factor
│       └── Number (3)
├── "+"
└── Term
    └── Factor
        └── "("
        └── Expression
            ├── Term
            │   └── Factor
            │       └── Number (2)
            ├── "+"
            └── Term
                └── Factor
                    └── Number (1)
        └── ")"
```

Each node in the tree corresponds to a grammar rule being applied, and the structure of the tree reflects how the input adheres to the grammatical structure defined in the DSL's grammar.

Grammar and Parsing Tree Integration in DSL Design

The relationship between grammar and parsing trees goes beyond just structural representation. Efficient grammar design is key to generating parsing trees that can be processed quickly and accurately. Optimizing grammar rules to reduce ambiguity and complexity helps parsers generate cleaner, more manageable parsing trees. Similarly, parsing trees offer insights into potential issues in the grammar, such as ambiguities, redundancies, or inefficiencies in parsing.

Parsing trees are not only visual representations of how a grammar is applied to an input but are also a reflection of the grammar's design. The relationship between the two is central to ensuring that a DSL can be parsed correctly and efficiently, which ultimately leads to a smoother implementation and usage of the language.

Performance Optimization of Parsing Trees

Optimizing parsing trees is critical for enhancing the efficiency of Domain-Specific Languages (DSLs). In the compilation or interpretation process, parsing is often the most time-consuming phase. Poor parsing tree performance can degrade the DSL's overall speed and memory efficiency. This section highlights optimization strategies, focusing on grammar design, memoization, lazy parsing, and tree transformations, with code examples to demonstrate these concepts.

Efficient Grammar Design for Faster Parsing

Optimizing grammar rules plays a significant role in speeding up the parsing process. By simplifying grammar and eliminating ambiguities, the parser can perform more efficiently, reducing the time and memory required to generate the parsing tree. In Python, we can define a simple grammar for arithmetic expressions using a recursive descent parser.

Here is an example of an optimized grammar:

```
import re

# Simple grammar for arithmetic expressions: expr -> term ('+' term)*
# term -> factor ('*' factor)*
# factor -> number | '(' expr ')'

def parse_expression(expression):
    # Define regular expressions for terms and factors
    term_pattern = r'\d+'
    factor_pattern = r'(\d+|\([^\)]+\))'

    terms = re.findall(term_pattern, expression)
    return terms

expr = "(3 + 5) * 2"
parsed_expr = parse_expression(expr)
print(parsed_expr)
```

This simplified grammar ensures minimal backtracking and eliminates ambiguity by directly defining each token pattern. By removing complex recursion or left recursion, the parser executes faster.

Memoization and Caching During Parsing

Memoization can optimize parsing by avoiding redundant computations. In recursive parsers, memoization allows the reuse of previously computed results to minimize redundant processing. Here's an example of applying caching to a recursive descent parser:

```
import functools

# Define the memoized recursive function
@functools.lru_cache(maxsize=None)
def parse_expression(expression):
    if expression.isdigit():
        return int(expression)
    # Implement recursive parsing logic for more complex expressions
    return expression

parsed_expr = parse_expression("5")
print(parsed_expr)
```

In this example, @functools.lru_cache caches the results of each parsed expression. If the expression is encountered again, it is retrieved from the cache instead of recalculating it, significantly improving parsing speed.

Lazy Parsing for Memory Efficiency

Lazy parsing is a technique that allows the parser to process input incrementally, reducing memory usage. In Python, this can be achieved by using generators or coroutines. The following example demonstrates lazy evaluation while parsing a list of expressions:

```python
def lazy_parse(tokens):
    for token in tokens:
        yield token  # Lazy evaluation of tokens

tokens = ['2', '+', '3', '*', '4']
parsed_tokens = lazy_parse(tokens)

for token in parsed_tokens:
    print(token)
```

In this approach, tokens are processed one at a time, and only the necessary portions of the parsing tree are constructed when required, minimizing memory usage.

Tree Transformation and Optimization

After parsing, optimizing the tree can improve subsequent processing steps. Transforming the tree to an Abstract Syntax Tree (AST) allows for more efficient evaluation. Here's an example of transforming a parsed expression into an AST:

```python
class ASTNode:
    def __init__(self, value, left=None, right=None):
        self.value = value
        self.left = left
        self.right = right

# Constructing an AST for a simple expression "3 + 5"
node1 = ASTNode(3)
node2 = ASTNode(5)
root = ASTNode('+', node1, node2)

print(f"Root: {root.value}, Left: {root.left.value}, Right: {root.right.value}")
```

In this example, an AST is built by creating nodes for each part of the expression. Once the AST is constructed, further transformations like constant folding or expression simplification can be applied to optimize the execution.

Optimizing parsing trees for DSLs involves refining grammar design, leveraging memoization, using lazy parsing, and transforming parsing trees into ASTs. By incorporating these techniques, developers can ensure that DSLs perform efficiently, even with complex or large inputs. These optimizations help build DSLs that are both fast and memory-efficient, making them practical for real-world applications.

Module 24:
Advanced Data Structures for DSLs

Module 24 focuses on advanced data structures tailored for Domain-Specific Languages (DSLs). Data structures play a vital role in the performance, efficiency, and scalability of DSL applications. This module discusses efficient data structures suited for domain-specific tasks, handling large-scale data, and the design of custom data structures. It also explores optimization techniques for improving performance in DSL applications.

Efficient Data Structures for Domain-Specific Applications

Efficient data structures are the backbone of any successful DSL, providing optimized ways to store and manipulate data within specific domains. A domain-specific approach requires the choice of structures that meet the particular needs of the application, rather than relying on general-purpose data structures. For example, in a DSL designed for scientific computing, sparse matrices or tensors might be preferable to traditional arrays. In contrast, a DSL for managing text processing might benefit from using trie trees or suffix arrays to efficiently handle strings. The choice of data structures depends on the operations that need to be optimized, whether they involve searching, inserting, or updating data. This section delves into how such structures can be customized to meet the unique needs of DSL applications, focusing on space efficiency, speed, and specialized operations.

Handling Large-Scale Data with DSLs

Handling large-scale data in DSLs is a common challenge, especially when working with data-intensive applications such as big data processing, machine learning, and simulation. In these cases, data structures must not only be efficient but also scalable. The section addresses the need for distributed data structures, like partitioned trees or hash tables, that allow the DSL to handle large datasets across multiple machines or processes. Moreover, considerations such as parallelism and memory management are essential for optimizing performance when dealing with vast amounts of data. For instance, a DSL for image processing might require handling high-resolution data arrays, which must be processed efficiently using specialized structures for both speed and memory optimization. This section highlights how to design and implement such data structures in a way that they can scale horizontally while maintaining performance.

Examples of Custom Data Structures Used in DSLs

Custom data structures are often the most effective way to meet the unique requirements of DSLs. This section provides practical examples of how specialized data structures can be designed for specific tasks in DSLs. Examples include tree-based structures for hierarchical data representation, graph structures for managing relationships between entities, and specialized stacks or queues for managing state in simulations. Custom data structures also allow DSL developers to better control the abstraction level, making the language more intuitive and expressive. By creating data structures tailored to domain-specific needs, DSLs can be made more efficient, readable, and maintainable. This section covers several real-world scenarios where custom data structures have been successfully used and outlines their implementation strategies.

Optimizing Data Structures for Performance in DSL Applications

The performance of DSL applications can often be significantly improved by optimizing the underlying data structures. This section focuses on strategies for optimizing data structures, such as minimizing memory usage, reducing access times, and improving parallelism. Techniques like caching, indexing, and lazy loading can be employed to enhance data retrieval times. Additionally, algorithms that reduce time complexity, such as balanced trees or hash maps for faster lookup, are explored. Optimizing data structures for specific types of queries or updates, such as range queries or dynamic programming, is essential for maximizing the performance of a DSL in a real-world application. This section emphasizes practical approaches to improving data structure performance in DSL applications, helping developers create more efficient and responsive systems.

Advanced data structures are essential for the performance and scalability of DSLs, especially when dealing with large datasets and domain-specific operations. This module discussed the importance of choosing efficient data structures, managing large-scale data, and customizing structures for specific domains. It also covered optimization techniques that can significantly enhance performance in DSL applications. Understanding and applying the right data structures can elevate the capability and efficiency of DSLs, making them more effective in real-world scenarios.

Efficient Data Structures for Domain-Specific Applications

In domain-specific languages (DSLs), selecting the most efficient data structures is critical for optimizing performance. DSLs are designed for specific tasks, which allows developers to use custom data structures tailored to those needs. For example, in a DSL for geometric modeling, structures like quadtrees or octrees can be used for efficiently storing and querying spatial data. These structures are ideal for applications where data points exist in a 2D or 3D space, reducing unnecessary computations and memory usage.

In the context of computational biology, trie-based structures are commonly used in DSLs for storing and searching DNA sequences. These trees provide efficient searching and prefix matching, which are essential for bioinformatics applications. When handling large-scale datasets, the performance of a DSL is heavily dependent on its data structures. For applications like image processing or geospatial analysis, data structures like matrices or graphs are often required to represent complex relationships and perform efficient computations.

For instance, a simple data structure like a hash table can be ideal for fast lookups, while more advanced structures, such as balanced binary trees or heaps, might be used in DSLs focused on priority queues or graph-based computations. The ability to implement and manipulate such structures efficiently directly impacts the DSL's performance and usability.

Example Code: Hash Table for Efficient Lookup

```python
class SimpleHashTable:
    def __init__(self, size):
        self.size = size
        self.table = [None] * size

    def hash_function(self, key):
        return hash(key) % self.size

    def insert(self, key, value):
        index = self.hash_function(key)
        if self.table[index] is None:
            self.table[index] = [(key, value)]
        else:
            self.table[index].append((key, value))

    def search(self, key):
        index = self.hash_function(key)
        if self.table[index]:
            for k, v in self.table[index]:
                if k == key:
                    return v
        return None

# Usage
hash_table = SimpleHashTable(10)
hash_table.insert("apple", 10)
hash_table.insert("banana", 20)
print(hash_table.search("apple"))  # Output: 10
```

Handling Large-Scale Data with DSLs

As DSLs grow to handle larger datasets, memory and time complexity become more important. When working with large-scale data, structures like balanced trees or graphs can efficiently store and manipulate information while minimizing memory usage. For example, in a DSL for graph-based problems like pathfinding, an adjacency list or adjacency matrix can store relationships between nodes, allowing quick access to neighboring nodes for algorithms like Dijkstra's or A*.

Handling large-scale data often involves balancing the tradeoff between processing speed and memory consumption. For example, sparse matrices, which store only non-zero values, are highly efficient for representing large datasets that are mostly empty. This approach is especially useful in scientific computing DSLs, where matrices may be large but the number of non-zero entries is small.

Example Code: Sparse Matrix Representation

```
class SparseMatrix:
    def __init__(self):
        self.data = {}

    def insert(self, row, col, value):
        if value != 0:
            self.data[(row, col)] = value

    def get(self, row, col):
        return self.data.get((row, col), 0)
# Usage
matrix = SparseMatrix()
matrix.insert(0, 1, 5)
matrix.insert(2, 3, 8)
print(matrix.get(0, 1))   # Output: 5
print(matrix.get(1, 1))   # Output: 0
```

Optimizing Data Structures for Performance

Optimizing data structures is crucial for ensuring that DSLs perform efficiently, especially when working with large or complex datasets. Techniques like indexing, caching, and partitioning data can significantly improve the speed and efficiency of data manipulation. For instance, in a DSL for database queries, using indexed data structures like B-trees or hash maps can reduce the time required for search and retrieval operations.

Another technique involves optimizing data access patterns by using techniques like lazy evaluation or memoization, which can help reduce unnecessary recalculations and improve overall efficiency.

Choosing the right data structures in DSL design leads to better performance and usability. Whether for spatial data, DNA sequences, or large-scale graph processing, the data structure choice significantly impacts both the runtime and the effectiveness of a DSL.

Handling Large-Scale Data with DSLs
When dealing with large-scale data, the efficiency of data handling in a domain-specific language (DSL) becomes critical. DSLs are often tailored to solve specific problems in fields like geospatial analysis, scientific computing, or machine learning, which require managing and processing vast amounts of data. Effective handling of such large datasets can significantly improve performance and scalability.

For example, in a DSL designed for geographic information systems (GIS), the need to handle massive spatial data efficiently can be addressed using specialized data structures like R-trees or quadtrees. These structures provide efficient querying and storage of spatial data by dividing the data into hierarchical blocks. The advantage of using such data structures in DSLs is that they allow for faster searches and better memory utilization, even when dealing with large geographical datasets.

Another example involves working with datasets that are too large to fit in memory. In such cases, DSLs can leverage disk-based structures or streaming techniques. For example,

246

in a data processing DSL, using techniques like MapReduce allows for processing large datasets across distributed systems without overwhelming the system's memory. By breaking down large data processing tasks into smaller, manageable chunks that can be processed in parallel, DSLs ensure that the system remains responsive even as the data scales up.

Additionally, handling large-scale data often requires optimizing access patterns. In cases where data is structured in a non-relational format, using NoSQL databases or key-value stores can be advantageous. These systems are designed to handle large volumes of unstructured data, enabling fast reads and writes. DSLs can interface with these systems to manage the complexity of large datasets while maintaining high throughput and low latency.

In machine learning and artificial intelligence, DSLs can be used to handle datasets involving millions of records, such as training datasets for deep learning models. A custom DSL in this context could implement highly efficient data pipelines for preprocessing large datasets, like normalizing values, handling missing data, and performing feature extraction. These operations, if not optimized, can become bottlenecks in the system. By employing techniques such as lazy evaluation or batch processing, a DSL can minimize memory overhead and ensure efficient handling of massive datasets.

Example Code: Handling Large-Scale Data with MapReduce

```
from functools import reduce

def map_function(data_chunk):
    return [x * 2 for x in data_chunk]

def reduce_function(mapped_data):
    return sum(mapped_data)

# Simulating MapReduce
data = list(range(1, 10001))  # Large dataset
chunk_size = 1000
chunks = [data[i:i+chunk_size] for i in range(0, len(data), chunk_size)]

mapped_chunks = [map_function(chunk) for chunk in chunks]
reduced_result = reduce(reduce_function, mapped_chunks)

print(f"Reduced result: {reduced_result}")
```

In the above code, a simple MapReduce pattern is used to process a large dataset. Each chunk of the dataset is processed in parallel by the map function, and the results are then reduced using the reduce function. This is a simplified example of how large-scale data can be handled efficiently within a DSL.

DSLs can be optimized for handling large-scale data by utilizing specialized data structures, employing distributed processing frameworks, and leveraging techniques like lazy evaluation. These methods ensure that the DSL remains efficient and scalable, even when working with extensive and complex datasets.

Examples of Custom Data Structures Used in DSLs

Custom data structures are essential in DSLs to efficiently represent domain-specific concepts and operations. A key advantage of DSLs is their ability to introduce tailored data structures that solve specific problems more effectively than general-purpose structures. These custom structures can help optimize memory usage, improve processing speed, and provide intuitive abstractions for domain experts. The flexibility of DSLs enables the creation of data structures that suit the unique requirements of various industries, such as finance, scientific research, or graphics.

In graphical programming environments, such as game development or simulations, DSLs often incorporate custom data structures like **scene graphs** or **rendering trees**. These structures represent the hierarchy of elements within a scene, such as objects, lights, and cameras, in a way that enables efficient updates and rendering. A scene graph allows for efficient traversal and transformation of objects, and it can be extended with domain-specific operations like collision detection or pathfinding.

For instance, in a DSL for a simulation of physical systems, a **vector** or **matrix** data structure is often used to represent multidimensional data, such as the coordinates of points in space or the transformation matrices for object movements. This type of custom data structure provides built-in operations for manipulating spatial data, which would be cumbersome to implement using generic structures.

In a more data-centric DSL, such as one for scientific computing or data analysis, specialized structures such as **sparse matrices** or **linked lists** can be introduced to optimize memory and performance. Sparse matrices, for example, are highly effective for handling large datasets that contain many zeros, a common situation in fields like linear algebra or machine learning. By only storing non-zero elements, sparse matrices reduce memory consumption and computational overhead. A custom DSL could provide specific operators and transformations designed to manipulate sparse matrices efficiently.

For business and financial DSLs, structures like **trees** and **graphs** can represent hierarchical relationships, such as taxonomies, decision trees, or networks. A financial DSL might use graphs to model relationships between entities like clients, transactions, and accounts. Custom algorithms within the DSL can then enable fast computation of paths, flows, or risk assessments in such structures, making the DSL highly efficient for financial modeling and analysis.

In more specialized domains, **state machines** are another example of custom data structures used in DSLs. In areas like robotics, control systems, or telecommunications, a DSL can represent the state transitions of a system, with states and transitions stored as custom data structures. These data structures allow the DSL to easily define and manage complex, event-driven systems with multiple states and conditions. Additionally, in DSLs for language processing or parsers, **abstract syntax trees (ASTs)** serve as custom data structures for representing the grammatical structure of source code.

By using custom data structures, DSLs can abstract away the complexities of traditional data handling, providing a more natural and efficient representation of domain-specific concepts.

Example Code: Sparse Matrix Representation in Python

```python
class SparseMatrix:
    def __init__(self, rows, cols):
        self.rows = rows
        self.cols = cols
        self.data = {}

    def set(self, row, col, value):
        if value != 0:
            self.data[(row, col)] = value
        elif (row, col) in self.data:
            del self.data[(row, col)]

    def get(self, row, col):
        return self.data.get((row, col), 0)

    def __repr__(self):
        return f"SparseMatrix({self.rows}, {self.cols})"

# Example usage
matrix = SparseMatrix(3, 3)
matrix.set(0, 1, 5)
matrix.set(2, 2, 8)
print(matrix.get(0, 1))   # Output: 5
print(matrix.get(1, 1))   # Output: 0
```

In this example, a custom SparseMatrix data structure is implemented. It stores only the non-zero elements of the matrix, which is more memory-efficient for matrices with many zeros. This is a simple yet effective example of a custom data structure that could be part of a larger DSL for scientific or mathematical computation.

Custom data structures are essential components in the development of DSLs, providing domain-specific abstractions that enhance performance and make programming more intuitive for domain experts. Whether it's for handling matrices, graphs, or scene data, the ability to design efficient, domain-tailored data structures sets DSLs apart from general-purpose programming languages.

Optimizing Data Structures for Performance in DSL Applications

Optimizing data structures is critical for domain-specific language (DSL) applications to handle large-scale data and computationally demanding tasks efficiently. DSLs can leverage custom data structures to optimize both memory usage and algorithmic performance. By carefully designing data structures, you can improve runtime speed, reduce memory consumption, and make applications more responsive, especially when dealing with complex computations and large datasets.

A key optimization is improving **memory locality**. Data structures like **arrays** or **contiguous blocks of memory** are often more efficient than complex structures such as linked lists, due to the better cache utilization. In Python, for instance, arrays from the array module allow for tightly packed data, which helps in reducing the memory footprint and enhances data access performance.

```
import array

# Create an array of integers
arr = array.array('i', range(10**6))

# Access elements in a memory-efficient way
print(arr[100])  # Access an element directly from contiguous memory
```

In comparison, using a linked list structure that involves pointer dereferencing will increase the memory accesses and slow down performance due to cache misses.

Another optimization technique is **compression**. When handling large datasets, compression can significantly reduce both memory usage and disk I/O. For example, **delta encoding** or **run-length encoding** can compress time-series data by storing only differences between consecutive elements, instead of all raw values. This approach is particularly useful in DSLs focused on financial applications or any domain with repetitive data.

```
# Delta encoding example: store differences between values
data = [100, 105, 110, 120]
delta_encoded = [data[0]] + [data[i] - data[i - 1] for i in range(1, len(data))]

# Decode the delta-encoded data
decoded = [delta_encoded[0]] + [sum(delta_encoded[:i + 1]) for i in range(1,
          len(delta_encoded))]

print(decoded)  # [100, 105, 110, 120]
```

For **parallel processing**, data structures like **parallel arrays** or **distributed hash maps** enable concurrent computations, which can greatly enhance performance in tasks like data processing or simulations. In Python, you can use the multiprocessing library to split tasks and work on datasets concurrently.

```
import multiprocessing

# Define a function to process data
def process_data(start, end):
    return sum(range(start, end))

# Split the data range into chunks for parallel processing
data_range = 10**6
chunks = [(i, i + data_range // 4) for i in range(0, data_range, data_range //
          4)]

# Create a pool of workers
with multiprocessing.Pool(processes=4) as pool:
    results = pool.starmap(process_data, chunks)

print(sum(results))  # Combine results from parallel processing
```

Using **lazy evaluation** in data structures is another powerful optimization. By only computing data when it is actually needed, we can avoid performing unnecessary computations. This technique is especially useful in DSLs that process large datasets or perform complex queries, such as in query optimization or data stream processing.

```
# Lazy evaluation: only compute the data when needed
def lazy_sum(start, end):
    return sum(range(start, end))

# Wrap the lazy evaluation logic
lazy_data = (lazy_sum(i, i + 100) for i in range(0, 1000, 100))

# Lazy evaluation occurs here when the sum is requested
result = sum(lazy_data)
print(result)
```

Finally, **algorithmic optimizations** can significantly boost the performance of common operations like searching, insertion, and deletion. For example, using **hash tables** or **balanced trees** ensures that search operations are performed in logarithmic time, leading to faster lookups.

```
# Example of using a dictionary (hash table) for fast lookups
data = {i: i * 2 for i in range(10**6)}

# Fast lookup using hash table (dictionary)
print(data.get(100000))  # O(1) lookup
```

By applying optimization techniques such as memory locality, data compression, parallelism, lazy evaluation, and efficient algorithms, DSLs can handle large-scale data and intensive computations more effectively. These techniques ensure that DSLs can meet the demands of complex, real-world applications while maintaining high performance and efficiency.

Part 5:

Design Patterns and Real-World Case Studies in Domain Specific Languages

Designing a robust domain-specific language (DSL) requires a deep understanding of software architecture principles and real-world applications. This part explores design patterns that enhance DSL usability and maintainability while examining practical case studies demonstrating how DSLs improve efficiency across various industries. By analyzing implementations in financial modeling, web development, network configuration, game development, and machine learning, readers will gain insights into the challenges and successes of DSL adoption. Each module presents detailed methodologies, ensuring a comprehensive understanding of practical DSL development.

Design Patterns for DSLs

Design patterns provide reusable solutions to common problems encountered in DSL development, ensuring that DSLs remain flexible, scalable, and easy to maintain. The Interpreter pattern is frequently used in DSLs to process commands and execute domain-specific logic, making it a fundamental technique for scripting languages and rule-based systems. The Factory pattern aids in constructing DSL components dynamically, ensuring modular and extensible designs. The Visitor pattern enables complex operations on abstract syntax trees (ASTs) without modifying their structure, making it valuable for code transformation and analysis. Applying these and other patterns ensures that DSLs maintain a balance between expressiveness and efficiency. Real-world examples, such as DSLs for data transformation and simulation, demonstrate how these patterns enhance DSL architecture and usability.

Case Study 1 – DSL in Financial Modeling

Financial institutions require highly specialized tools for data analysis, risk assessment, and algorithmic trading. This module explores the development of a financial modeling DSL designed to streamline quantitative analysis and automate financial computations. Key design decisions include choosing between an internal or external DSL, optimizing syntax for domain experts, and ensuring integration with existing financial tools. Challenges such as regulatory compliance, precision in numerical computations, and performance bottlenecks are examined. A real-world implementation showcases how a financial DSL improved productivity by automating report generation and reducing errors in complex calculations.

Case Study 2 – DSL in Web Development

Web development has benefited significantly from DSLs that simplify front-end and back-end processes. This module investigates a web development DSL designed to automate UI generation, streamline API interactions, and enhance security measures. By analyzing frameworks such as Ruby on Rails and WebDSL, the case study illustrates how domain-specific abstractions reduce boilerplate code and accelerate development cycles. The impact on developer productivity is quantified through performance benchmarks and developer feedback. Lessons learned from web DSL projects include the importance of balancing abstraction with customization and ensuring extensibility in dynamic web environments.

Case Study 3 – DSL in Network Configuration

Managing and configuring network infrastructure is a complex task that benefits from automation via DSLs. This case study explores a network configuration DSL designed to simplify rule-based management of firewalls, routers, and cloud environments. Parsing techniques ensure that configurations are both human-readable and machine-executable, while code generation facilitates seamless deployment. Real-world implementations demonstrate how this DSL reduced configuration errors and improved operational efficiency. The challenges of evolving network standards and ensuring security compliance are addressed, providing insights into best practices for network DSL design.

Case Study 4 – DSL in Game Development

Game development requires scripting languages that provide game designers with flexibility while maintaining performance. This module presents a case study on the development of a game scripting DSL that enhances workflow automation and enables non-programmers to define game logic. The DSL's impact on performance is evaluated by examining execution speed, memory footprint, and integration with game engines such as Unity and Unreal Engine. Workflow improvements are analyzed, showcasing how the DSL reduced development time and increased creative control for designers. Future directions include incorporating AI-driven scripting assistance and optimizing for cross-platform game development.

Case Study 5 – DSL in Machine Learning

Machine learning workflows involve complex data preprocessing, model training, and deployment steps that can be automated with DSLs. This module explores a DSL designed to streamline the development of machine learning pipelines, reducing the need for manual configuration. The case study examines real-world implementations in AI research and industry applications, highlighting improvements in reproducibility and efficiency. Key challenges, such as supporting multiple machine learning frameworks and ensuring extensibility, are addressed. Evaluating the DSL's effectiveness involves assessing its impact on model development speed, ease of debugging, and integration with existing AI platforms.

This part equips readers with practical knowledge of DSL design patterns and real-world applications, offering valuable insights into how DSLs solve domain-specific problems across various industries.

Module 25:
Design Patterns for DSLs

Design patterns are essential tools in the creation and optimization of Domain-Specific Languages (DSLs). These well-established solutions to common software design problems help developers structure DSLs in ways that enhance maintainability, scalability, and usability. This module covers key design patterns used in DSL creation, including the Interpreter, Factory, and Visitor patterns, and explains how these patterns can be applied to improve the functionality and flexibility of DSLs in real-world applications.

Common Design Patterns Used in DSL Creation

In DSL development, common design patterns provide standardized ways to address recurring challenges. Patterns such as the Interpreter, Factory, and Visitor patterns offer a blueprint for creating efficient and scalable DSLs. The Interpreter pattern is used to define grammatical structures in a DSL, while the Factory pattern helps manage object creation, ensuring flexibility. The Visitor pattern allows for operations on complex data structures, making it easier to extend and maintain the language. These patterns serve as templates that guide the development of robust, reusable, and scalable DSLs.

Interpreter, Factory, and Visitor Patterns in DSLs

The Interpreter pattern is particularly useful in DSLs designed for parsing or interpreting expressions. It allows for a clear definition of the language's syntax and semantics through classes that interpret or execute the language's constructs. The Factory pattern, on the other hand, is commonly used to abstract object creation, which is crucial for DSLs that require flexibility in their implementation. By using a Factory, developers can create language components dynamically without tightly coupling the system to specific implementations. Finally, the Visitor pattern is advantageous in DSLs that need to perform operations on complex structures like abstract syntax trees. It allows different operations to be added to existing classes without modifying their structure, which enhances extensibility.

Applying Design Patterns to Enhance DSL Usability

Applying design patterns strategically can significantly enhance the usability of DSLs. The Interpreter pattern, for example, simplifies parsing by providing a structured approach to language interpretation. The Factory pattern enhances usability by decoupling the language components from their specific implementations, making it easier for developers to extend or modify the language in the future. The Visitor pattern promotes clean separation of concerns, allowing for operations to be added without altering the core language structure. Together, these patterns help streamline the development of DSLs, ensuring they remain flexible, efficient, and user-friendly over time.

Real-World Examples of Design Pattern Applications in DSLs

Real-world examples of design patterns in DSLs can be seen in various fields such as database query languages, web development, and configuration management. For instance, SQL can be seen as a DSL that uses an Interpreter pattern to parse queries and return results. The Factory pattern is used in many web frameworks, where different components or services are dynamically instantiated based on user input. Additionally, the Visitor pattern is commonly applied in languages used for code analysis or transformation, where operations on abstract syntax trees can be added without altering the core language. These examples demonstrate how design patterns can be applied effectively in real-world DSLs to increase flexibility, efficiency, and scalability.

Design patterns, such as the Interpreter, Factory, and Visitor patterns, are integral to the creation of efficient and scalable DSLs. By applying these patterns, developers can enhance the usability, maintainability, and extensibility of DSLs, ensuring they remain effective in solving domain-specific problems. These patterns offer valuable tools for addressing common design challenges in DSL development.

Common Design Patterns Used in DSL Creation

When building Domain-Specific Languages (DSLs), several design patterns are essential for structuring the language and solving common development challenges. The Interpreter, Factory, and Visitor patterns are three key patterns frequently used in DSL creation. These patterns help manage complexity, improve extensibility, and ensure maintainable systems.

The **Interpreter pattern** is used to parse and evaluate expressions within a DSL. It defines how the language constructs are represented as objects and evaluated. The **Factory pattern** is applied to abstract the creation of objects, allowing flexible and dynamic object instantiation. The **Visitor pattern** facilitates operations on complex data structures like Abstract Syntax Trees (ASTs), enabling extensions without altering the structure of the DSL.

These patterns provide tested solutions to common problems encountered when creating DSLs, ensuring that the language is efficient, scalable, and easy to maintain.

Interpreter, Factory, and Visitor Patterns in DSLs

The **Interpreter pattern** defines how a DSL's syntax is parsed and interpreted. For example, in a simple mathematical expression DSL, an interpreter could be built to evaluate expressions such as 2 + 3 * 5 by constructing an Abstract Syntax Tree (AST) and then evaluating it. Here's an example of how this could be done in Python:

```
class Expression:
```

```python
    def interpret(self):
        pass

class Number(Expression):
    def __init__(self, value):
        self.value = value

    def interpret(self):
        return self.value

class Add(Expression):
    def __init__(self, left, right):
        self.left = left
        self.right = right

    def interpret(self):
        return self.left.interpret() + self.right.interpret()

# Usage
expr = Add(Number(2), Add(Number(3), Number(5)))
print(expr.interpret())   # Output: 10
```

The **Factory pattern** is useful in DSLs where objects need to be created dynamically. For example, a DSL used for configuring network settings might need to instantiate different configurations (e.g., for a router or a firewall). The Factory pattern provides an interface for creating these configurations without specifying the exact class. Here's how it can be implemented in Python:

```python
class NetworkConfiguration:
    def configure(self):
        pass

class RouterConfiguration(NetworkConfiguration):
    def configure(self):
        return "Configuring Router"

class FirewallConfiguration(NetworkConfiguration):
    def configure(self):
        return "Configuring Firewall"

class ConfigurationFactory:
    def create_configuration(self, type):
        if type == 'router':
            return RouterConfiguration()
        elif type == 'firewall':
            return FirewallConfiguration()

# Usage
factory = ConfigurationFactory()
config = factory.create_configuration('router')
print(config.configure())   # Output: Configuring Router
```

The **Visitor pattern** enables operations on complex data structures like ASTs without modifying their structure. In a DSL designed for code transformation, for example, the Visitor pattern allows the addition of new operations (e.g., refactoring) without changing the underlying data structure of the language. Below is an example in Python:

```python
class Node:
    def accept(self, visitor):
        pass
```

```python
class ExpressionNode(Node):
    def __init__(self, value):
        self.value = value

    def accept(self, visitor):
        return visitor.visit_expression(self)

class Visitor:
    def visit_expression(self, node):
        return f"Visited expression with value {node.value}"

# Usage
expression = ExpressionNode(5)
visitor = Visitor()
print(expression.accept(visitor))   # Output: Visited expression with value 5
```

Applying Design Patterns to Enhance DSL Usability

By applying these design patterns, DSLs can be made more flexible, extensible, and easier to use. The **Interpreter pattern** allows for a well-defined syntax and parsing mechanism, ensuring that the DSL can interpret expressions correctly. The **Factory pattern** abstracts object creation, reducing coupling between the DSL's components and making it more adaptable to new configurations. The **Visitor pattern** allows operations to be added to complex structures without modifying their design, which makes the DSL easy to extend with new features over time.

Real-World Examples of Design Pattern Applications in DSLs

In real-world DSLs, these design patterns are used to create maintainable and flexible systems. For instance, SQL is a DSL used for querying databases. The **Interpreter pattern** is used in SQL parsers to interpret query expressions. In web frameworks, the **Factory pattern** is employed to create different components (such as controllers or views) based on user input. The **Visitor pattern** is used in various refactoring tools where new operations like renaming variables or methods can be applied to the abstract syntax tree without altering the code structure.

By using these patterns, developers can design DSLs that are scalable, maintainable, and flexible enough to accommodate future changes and enhancements.

Interpreter, Factory, and Visitor Patterns in DSLs
In Domain-Specific Languages (DSLs), design patterns such as Interpreter, Factory, and Visitor are used to structure and simplify the creation of complex language features. These patterns enhance usability, maintainability, and extensibility, allowing DSL developers to handle parsing, object creation, and operations on domain-specific constructs in a modular and scalable manner.

Interpreter Pattern

The Interpreter pattern is used to design a DSL parser by defining grammar rules for the language and creating an interpreter that processes the language constructs. Here's an example using a simple arithmetic DSL:

```python
class Expression:
    def interpret(self):
        pass

class Number(Expression):
    def __init__(self, value):
        self.value = value

    def interpret(self):
        return self.value

class Add(Expression):
    def __init__(self, left, right):
        self.left = left
        self.right = right

    def interpret(self):
        return self.left.interpret() + self.right.interpret()

# Example usage:
expr = Add(Number(3), Number(4))
print(expr.interpret())  # Output: 7
```

This example uses the **Interpreter pattern** to parse and evaluate simple arithmetic expressions. The Number class represents numbers, while the Add class defines the addition operation. The interpret() method recursively evaluates the expression.

Factory Pattern

The Factory pattern abstracts object creation, making it easy to instantiate objects based on user input or conditions. In DSLs, the Factory pattern is often used when different types of objects need to be created dynamically. For example, consider a DSL for defining network configurations:

```python
class Router:
    def configure(self):
        return "Router configured"

class Firewall:
    def configure(self):
        return "Firewall configured"

class NetworkFactory:
    @staticmethod
    def create_device(device_type):
        if device_type == "router":
            return Router()
        elif device_type == "firewall":
            return Firewall()
        else:
            raise ValueError("Unknown device type")

# Example usage:
device = NetworkFactory.create_device("router")
print(device.configure())  # Output: Router configured
```

In this case, the **Factory pattern** is used to abstract the creation of network devices (Router, Firewall). The NetworkFactory handles instantiating the appropriate device based on input.

Visitor Pattern

The Visitor pattern allows adding new operations to existing data structures (like ASTs) without modifying their structure. This is especially useful for transformations or optimizations of DSL constructs. For example, consider an AST for arithmetic expressions:

```python
class Expression:
    def accept(self, visitor):
        pass

class Number(Expression):
    def __init__(self, value):
        self.value = value

    def accept(self, visitor):
        return visitor.visit_number(self)

class Add(Expression):
    def __init__(self, left, right):
        self.left = left
        self.right = right

    def accept(self, visitor):
        return visitor.visit_add(self)

class ExpressionPrinter:
    def visit_number(self, number):
        return str(number.value)

    def visit_add(self, add):
        left = add.left.accept(self)
        right = add.right.accept(self)
        return f"({left} + {right})"

# Example usage:
expr = Add(Number(3), Number(4))
printer = ExpressionPrinter()
print(expr.accept(printer))  # Output: (3 + 4)
```

Here, the **Visitor pattern** is used in the ExpressionPrinter class to process AST nodes and print them in a readable format. The accept() method in each node class allows a visitor to "visit" and handle the specific node type.

These three design patterns—Interpreter, Factory, and Visitor—play a critical role in making DSLs more flexible and maintainable. By using the Interpreter pattern for parsing, the Factory pattern for creating objects, and the Visitor pattern for processing data structures, developers can create efficient, extensible, and easily understandable DSLs.

Applying Design Patterns to Enhance DSL Usability

Design patterns such as Interpreter, Factory, and Visitor can significantly improve the usability and maintainability of Domain-Specific Languages (DSLs). These patterns help create more modular, flexible, and user-friendly DSLs, which are crucial for simplifying the language design and ensuring its adaptability to changing requirements. The implementation of these patterns can streamline language use, enhance interaction with users, and ensure the long-term success of the DSL.

Interpreter Pattern in Enhancing DSL Usability

The Interpreter pattern is widely used in DSLs that require custom parsing and evaluation of domain-specific expressions. In this pattern, the grammar of the language is represented by an interpreter that processes the syntax tree and evaluates expressions. For example, let's say we are building a DSL for simple mathematical expressions:

```python
class Expression:
    def interpret(self):
        pass

class Number(Expression):
    def __init__(self, value):
        self.value = value

    def interpret(self):
        return self.value

class Add(Expression):
    def __init__(self, left, right):
        self.left = left
        self.right = right

    def interpret(self):
        return self.left.interpret() + self.right.interpret()

# Usage
expression = Add(Number(5), Number(3))
print(expression.interpret())   # Output: 8
```

Here, Number and Add are different expressions that can be interpreted by the interpret() method. The Interpreter pattern allows for flexible extension of the DSL, where new operations can be added by defining new classes like Multiply, Subtract, etc.

Factory Pattern for Object Creation and Usability

The Factory pattern allows for the creation of objects without exposing the instantiation logic to the user. This is useful in DSLs where different types of objects need to be created depending on the context, but you want to encapsulate the complexity. For example, in a DSL for defining vehicles, a Factory pattern could be used to instantiate different vehicle types based on input:

```python
class Vehicle:
    def drive(self):
        pass

class Car(Vehicle):
    def drive(self):
        return "Driving a car"
```

```
class Truck(Vehicle):
    def drive(self):
        return "Driving a truck"

class VehicleFactory:
    @staticmethod
    def create_vehicle(vehicle_type):
        if vehicle_type == 'car':
            return Car()
        elif vehicle_type == 'truck':
            return Truck()
        else:
            raise ValueError("Unknown vehicle type")

# Usage
vehicle = VehicleFactory.create_vehicle('car')
print(vehicle.drive())  # Output: Driving a car
```

The Factory pattern hides the complexity of object creation, making the DSL easier to use and extend. New vehicle types can be added without modifying existing user code, keeping the DSL clean and maintainable.

Visitor Pattern for Enhancing Operations on DSL Constructs

The Visitor pattern is used to add new operations to a class without modifying its structure. This is particularly useful when working with complex data structures like Abstract Syntax Trees (ASTs) in DSLs. For example, if we have a DSL that represents mathematical operations, we can apply different transformations (like evaluating or simplifying expressions) using the Visitor pattern:

```
class Expression:
    def accept(self, visitor):
        pass

class Number(Expression):
    def __init__(self, value):
        self.value = value

    def accept(self, visitor):
        return visitor.visit_number(self)

class Add(Expression):
    def __init__(self, left, right):
        self.left = left
        self.right = right

    def accept(self, visitor):
        return visitor.visit_add(self)

class Visitor:
    def visit_number(self, number):
        pass

    def visit_add(self, add):
        pass

class Evaluator(Visitor):
    def visit_number(self, number):
        return number.value

    def visit_add(self, add):
```

```
        return add.left.accept(self) + add.right.accept(self)
# Usage
expression = Add(Number(5), Number(3))
evaluator = Evaluator()
print(expression.accept(evaluator))  # Output: 8
```

In this example, the Evaluator class performs the operation of evaluating expressions without changing the structure of Number or Add. The Visitor pattern allows us to add new operations like Simplifier or Optimizer easily.

By applying design patterns such as Interpreter, Factory, and Visitor to DSLs, developers can create languages that are more modular, easier to use, and maintain. These patterns offer solutions for common problems such as complex parsing, object creation, and extending functionality without modifying existing code. The result is a more robust and scalable DSL that can evolve over time while remaining user-friendly and efficient.

Real-world examples of design pattern applications in DSLs

Design patterns, including the Interpreter, Factory, and Visitor patterns, are invaluable tools when designing and implementing Domain-Specific Languages (DSLs). These patterns help solve common problems such as extensibility, code reusability, and ease of understanding in DSLs. Real-world examples of their use in DSLs show how these patterns can address specific challenges across various domains, from web development to mathematical expression evaluation. In this section, we will explore practical examples where these design patterns have been applied to DSLs in different contexts.

Interpreter Pattern in SQL-Like DSL

A common real-world application of the Interpreter pattern is in designing DSLs for querying databases. Consider a simplified SQL-like query DSL that allows users to filter and select records from a collection of data. The Interpreter pattern is used here to parse and execute expressions in a query:

```
class Expression:
    def interpret(self, data):
        pass

class Select(Expression):
    def __init__(self, field):
        self.field = field

    def interpret(self, data):
        return [record[self.field] for record in data]

class Filter(Expression):
    def __init__(self, field, value):
        self.field = field
        self.value = value

    def interpret(self, data):
        return [record for record in data if record[self.field] == self.value]

# Usage
```

262

```
data = [{'name': 'John', 'age': 30}, {'name': 'Alice', 'age': 25}]
query = Filter('age', 30)
select = Select('name')

filtered_data = query.interpret(data)
result = select.interpret(filtered_data)
print(result)  # Output: ['John']
```

In this example, the Select and Filter classes represent components of a simple query DSL, which is parsed and evaluated using the Interpreter pattern. The interpret() method processes the query to return the expected result. This structure can be easily extended with additional operations like Sort, GroupBy, and Join.

Factory Pattern for Creating HTML Elements in Web DSL

In a web development scenario, the Factory pattern can be used to create HTML elements dynamically in a DSL. Let's consider a DSL that allows users to define HTML structures. The Factory pattern simplifies object creation without exposing the underlying instantiation logic:

```
class HTMLElement:
    def render(self):
        pass

class Div(HTMLElement):
    def render(self):
        return "<div></div>"

class P(HTMLElement):
    def render(self):
        return "<p></p>"

class HTMLFactory:
    @staticmethod
    def create_element(element_type):
        if element_type == 'div':
            return Div()
        elif element_type == 'p':
            return P()
        else:
            raise ValueError("Unknown element type")

# Usage
element = HTMLFactory.create_element('div')
print(element.render())  # Output: <div></div>
```

This example shows how the Factory pattern is used to create different types of HTML elements dynamically. This approach allows the user to interact with a simplified interface for creating HTML elements, while the complexity of constructing the elements is abstracted away.

Visitor Pattern for Transforming AST in a Mathematical DSL

The Visitor pattern can be applied to a mathematical DSL to allow users to define operations on expressions without modifying the expression classes. For instance, we could

263

have a DSL for evaluating and simplifying mathematical expressions. By using the Visitor pattern, we can easily apply multiple operations on the Abstract Syntax Tree (AST):

```python
class Expression:
    def accept(self, visitor):
        pass

class Number(Expression):
    def __init__(self, value):
        self.value = value

    def accept(self, visitor):
        return visitor.visit_number(self)

class Add(Expression):
    def __init__(self, left, right):
        self.left = left
        self.right = right

    def accept(self, visitor):
        return visitor.visit_add(self)

class Visitor:
    def visit_number(self, number):
        pass

    def visit_add(self, add):
        pass

class Evaluator(Visitor):
    def visit_number(self, number):
        return number.value

    def visit_add(self, add):
        return add.left.accept(self) + add.right.accept(self)

# Usage
expression = Add(Number(5), Number(3))
evaluator = Evaluator()
print(expression.accept(evaluator))  # Output: 8
```

Here, the Evaluator visitor traverses the AST and computes the result. The Visitor pattern decouples the operation from the object structure, making it easy to add other operations like simplification, optimization, or differentiation without modifying the Number and Add classes.

Design patterns like Interpreter, Factory, and Visitor have proven to be essential for building scalable, maintainable, and user-friendly DSLs. By applying these patterns, developers can create more flexible and extensible DSLs that cater to domain-specific needs. Real-world examples in fields such as database querying, web development, and mathematical expression evaluation demonstrate the practical benefits of these design patterns in enhancing DSL functionality and usability.

Module 26:
Case Study 1 – DSL in Financial Modeling

This module delves into the design and application of a Domain-Specific Language (DSL) for financial modeling. By focusing on the creation of a DSL tailored for financial analysis, it will cover key design decisions, challenges, and strategies for integrating the DSL into business workflows. Additionally, we will examine the measurable improvements in productivity resulting from the use of such a specialized language in real-world scenarios.

Designing a Custom DSL for Financial Analysis

The design of a custom DSL for financial modeling requires careful consideration of the domain-specific needs. In financial analysis, it is crucial to provide a syntax that allows analysts to model complex financial scenarios with minimal effort. The DSL should offer high-level constructs for representing financial instruments, transactions, and economic models while being intuitive for finance professionals. One of the initial decisions in designing the DSL is determining whether it will be an internal or external DSL. This decision affects both the syntax and integration with other tools. Additionally, the DSL must support the representation of financial formulas, risk assessments, and forecasting models commonly used in the industry, all while minimizing the need for complex programming skills. The goal is to make financial modeling more accessible and accurate, with the DSL facilitating fast computation and scenario analysis.

Key Design Decisions and Challenges

One of the most significant challenges in designing a DSL for financial analysis is balancing expressiveness with simplicity. The language must be capable of representing intricate financial models but still remain comprehensible to users who may not have a strong programming background. Key design decisions include selecting appropriate abstractions for modeling financial products like bonds, options, and derivatives, as well as defining clear, concise syntax for representing cash flows, risk metrics, and pricing algorithms. Additionally, performance is a critical consideration, as financial models often involve large datasets that need to be processed efficiently. Another challenge is ensuring that the DSL integrates seamlessly with existing financial data sources and business intelligence systems. The chosen language must also provide robust error-handling mechanisms to minimize the risk of misinterpreting or misapplying financial formulas.

Integrating the DSL into Business Workflows

Once the DSL is designed, the next step is its integration into the business workflows of financial analysts, investment firms, or other stakeholders. This involves determining how the DSL will interact with existing software platforms and databases, as well as ensuring that the DSL can be easily adopted by end-users. The integration process may involve building APIs or plugins to link the DSL with existing tools such as Excel, Python, or other financial analysis software. For a successful integration, it is essential to ensure that the DSL can read and write data in compatible formats, allowing for seamless flow of information between various systems. Moreover, proper documentation, training, and user support are critical to ensuring that financial professionals can effectively use the DSL without requiring extensive programming knowledge.

Measuring Success and Improvements in Productivity

The success of a DSL in financial modeling can be measured through several key metrics, such as improved efficiency, reduced errors, and increased ability to model complex financial scenarios. For instance, by using a DSL, financial analysts can significantly reduce the time spent on repetitive tasks, such as adjusting formulas or recalculating variables. Moreover, the DSL can help standardize financial modeling across an organization, leading to more consistent and reliable outputs. Productivity improvements can also be tracked by measuring the reduction in the time taken to produce financial reports, perform scenario analysis, or test hypotheses. Additionally, the accuracy and performance of the models can be assessed by comparing results obtained with the DSL to traditional methods of financial analysis.

This module highlights the process of designing and implementing a Domain-Specific Language for financial modeling. Through careful design and integration, a well-built DSL can greatly enhance the efficiency, accuracy, and usability of financial analysis. The measurable improvements in productivity serve as a testament to the power of DSLs in specialized domains.

Designing a Custom DSL for Financial Analysis

Designing a Domain-Specific Language (DSL) for financial analysis involves creating a specialized tool that is tailored for representing financial data, formulas, and models. The purpose of the DSL is to simplify the modeling of financial instruments, scenarios, and economic conditions while ensuring high performance and ease of use. In this section, we will explore the key steps involved in creating a custom DSL for financial analysis using Python, and we will also provide some code examples to demonstrate how it can be implemented.

Defining Basic Constructs for Financial Modeling

The first step in designing a DSL for financial analysis is to define the basic constructs needed to represent financial instruments, such as stocks, bonds, and derivatives. These constructs must allow analysts to model complex financial scenarios and easily interact with the data.

For example, we could start by defining a simple class to represent a financial instrument like a stock:

```
class Stock:
    def __init__(self, ticker, price, quantity):
```

```
        self.ticker = ticker
        self.price = price
        self.quantity = quantity

    def value(self):
        return self.price * self.quantity

# Example usage:
stock = Stock('AAPL', 150, 100)
print(f"Stock value: {stock.value()}")
```

In this example, the Stock class has attributes for the ticker symbol, price, and quantity. The value method calculates the total value of the stock by multiplying the price by the quantity of shares.

Financial Calculations and Formulas

Once the basic constructs are defined, the next step is to create the mathematical formulas that financial analysts commonly use. The DSL should support various financial operations such as calculating interest, present value, and future value.

For instance, let's define a simple function for calculating the compound interest, a common formula in finance:

```
def compound_interest(principal, rate, time, frequency):
    return principal * (1 + rate / frequency) ** (frequency * time)

# Example usage:
principal = 1000
rate = 0.05
time = 10
frequency = 4   # quarterly
result = compound_interest(principal, rate, time, frequency)
print(f"Compound Interest: {result}")
```

This function calculates the future value of an investment based on the compound interest formula. By integrating such financial calculations into the DSL, users can quickly model and calculate the value of investments.

Higher-Level Financial Models

A crucial feature of the DSL is the ability to define higher-level financial models that combine multiple instruments and scenarios. For example, let's create a Portfolio class that allows analysts to model a collection of financial instruments and calculate the portfolio's total value:

```
class Portfolio:
    def __init__(self):
        self.assets = []

    def add_asset(self, asset):
        self.assets.append(asset)

    def total_value(self):
        return sum(asset.value() for asset in self.assets)
```

267

```
# Example usage:
portfolio = Portfolio()
portfolio.add_asset(Stock('AAPL', 150, 100))
portfolio.add_asset(Stock('GOOGL', 2800, 50))
print(f"Portfolio total value: {portfolio.total_value()}")
```

Here, the Portfolio class allows analysts to add different assets and calculate the total value of the portfolio. This abstraction simplifies the process of modeling complex portfolios without having to manually calculate each asset's value.

Extensibility and Integration

One of the key considerations when designing a DSL for financial analysis is ensuring that it is extensible and can be easily integrated with existing financial data sources, libraries, and tools. This requires careful attention to the language's syntax, scalability, and compatibility with other systems.

For example, the DSL could integrate with libraries like NumPy and Pandas for handling large datasets and performing complex statistical operations. We can also extend the DSL to include financial instruments such as options, futures, and derivatives by defining additional classes and methods.

```
import numpy as np

class Option:
    def __init__(self, stock, strike_price, expiration_date):
        self.stock = stock
        self.strike_price = strike_price
        self.expiration_date = expiration_date

    def option_value(self):
        # A simple example of option pricing (not a real model)
        return max(0, self.stock.price - self.strike_price)

# Example usage:
stock = Stock('AAPL', 150, 100)
option = Option(stock, 140, '2025-12-31')
print(f"Option value: {option.option_value()}")
```

In this example, the Option class models a basic call option, and its option_value method calculates the value based on the current price of the stock and the strike price.

Designing a custom DSL for financial analysis provides an efficient way for analysts to model complex financial instruments and scenarios. By abstracting common financial calculations into high-level constructs, we can significantly enhance productivity and reduce errors. The DSL can evolve and integrate with other financial tools, making it a powerful addition to the analyst's toolkit.

Key Design Decisions and Challenges

When designing a custom DSL for financial analysis, key design decisions must be made to ensure that the DSL is both powerful and user-friendly. The primary objective is to

268

create a language that simplifies the representation of financial instruments and models while also being flexible enough to accommodate future growth. In this section, we will discuss the key design decisions, the challenges faced, and how to overcome them when creating a DSL for financial analysis.

Defining the Syntax and Semantics

One of the first key decisions when designing a DSL is to define its syntax and semantics. The syntax should be intuitive and easy for financial analysts to understand, while the semantics should ensure accurate financial calculations. A balance between simplicity and power is necessary to make the DSL both accessible and capable of expressing complex financial models.

For example, consider how financial analysts typically express interest rates and compound growth. We can design the DSL syntax for calculating compound interest as follows:

```
interest_rate = 0.05
principal = 1000
time = 5
compound_growth = compound_interest(principal, interest_rate, time, frequency=4)
```

The syntax should allow users to express the domain's operations in a manner that closely resembles the mathematical formulations they already use. This syntax design is critical for the usability of the DSL and requires careful consideration of which constructs will be included and how they will be expressed.

Supporting Extensibility and Flexibility

Another key decision involves how to structure the DSL to allow for future extensibility. Financial analysis is a rapidly evolving field with new financial instruments and concepts emerging frequently. The DSL must be flexible enough to support the addition of new models or instruments without requiring complete rework of the system.

A solution for extensibility could be to build a flexible class hierarchy for financial instruments. For example:

```
class FinancialInstrument:
    def value(self):
        raise NotImplementedError("Subclasses should implement this method")

class Stock(FinancialInstrument):
    def __init__(self, ticker, price, quantity):
        self.ticker = ticker
        self.price = price
        self.quantity = quantity

    def value(self):
        return self.price * self.quantity

class Bond(FinancialInstrument):
    def __init__(self, face_value, coupon_rate, years):
        self.face_value = face_value
```

```
        self.coupon_rate = coupon_rate
        self.years = years

    def value(self):
        return self.face_value * (1 + self.coupon_rate) ** self.years

# Example usage:
stock = Stock('AAPL', 150, 100)
bond = Bond(1000, 0.05, 5)
print(f"Stock value: {stock.value()}")
print(f"Bond value: {bond.value()}")
```

Here, we have defined a base class FinancialInstrument and two subclasses, Stock and Bond. This approach allows for the easy addition of other financial instruments, such as options or futures, in the future.

Performance and Scalability

A significant challenge in designing a DSL for financial analysis is ensuring that the language performs well when dealing with large-scale datasets. Financial models often involve large numbers of assets, historical data, and complex calculations, which can put significant strain on performance.

One approach to optimizing performance is to use efficient data structures and algorithms. For example, when modeling a portfolio with multiple assets, it's important to ensure that operations like calculating the portfolio's total value are efficient. The portfolio calculation can be optimized by storing assets in a more efficient data structure, such as a list or a dictionary, to reduce lookup and computation time.

```
class Portfolio:
    def __init__(self):
        self.assets = {}

    def add_asset(self, asset_name, asset):
        self.assets[asset_name] = asset

    def total_value(self):
        return sum(asset.value() for asset in self.assets.values())

# Example usage:
portfolio = Portfolio()
portfolio.add_asset('AAPL', stock)
portfolio.add_asset('GOOGL', bond)
print(f"Total Portfolio Value: {portfolio.total_value()}")
```

Here, we store the assets in a dictionary, allowing for efficient lookup and addition of assets, which is especially important when working with larger portfolios.

Error Handling and User Feedback

Providing clear error messages and feedback to users is another key design decision. Financial analysts rely on accurate, real-time feedback, and the DSL must be capable of providing meaningful errors when invalid operations or data are provided. For example, if an analyst tries to calculate the value of a stock without providing a valid price, the DSL should raise a clear and understandable error.

```python
class Stock(FinancialInstrument):
    def __init__(self, ticker, price, quantity):
        if price <= 0 or quantity <= 0:
            raise ValueError("Price and quantity must be positive values")
        self.ticker = ticker
        self.price = price
        self.quantity = quantity

    def value(self):
        return self.price * self.quantity

# Example usage with error handling:
try:
    stock = Stock('AAPL', -150, 100)  # Invalid price
except ValueError as e:
    print(f"Error: {e}")
```

The Stock class includes error handling to ensure that invalid prices or quantities are not accepted. Clear error messages like this can help users identify and resolve issues quickly.

Designing a custom DSL for financial analysis involves key decisions regarding syntax, flexibility, performance, and error handling. By making informed decisions in these areas, the DSL can be made to be both effective and efficient, allowing financial analysts to model complex scenarios with ease. Addressing these design challenges up front can lead to a powerful, extensible tool that enhances productivity in financial analysis.

Integrating the DSL into Business Workflows

Once the custom DSL for financial analysis is designed, the next critical step is to integrate it into existing business workflows. This process ensures that the DSL is not only usable within the context of the domain but also improves the overall business efficiency by providing seamless integration with other tools, databases, and systems. This section discusses the strategies for integrating the DSL into business workflows, key challenges, and how to ensure smooth adoption.

Connecting to External Data Sources

A major requirement in financial analysis is accessing real-time data from various sources such as stock market feeds, financial databases, and other relevant sources. Integrating the DSL into business workflows requires that the DSL be capable of consuming data from external systems. In Python, this can be achieved by writing connectors or APIs that fetch the required data and pass it into the DSL environment.

For example, integrating stock price data from an external API, such as Yahoo Finance, can be done by using the yfinance library, which allows real-time stock data to be accessed directly in the DSL.

```python
import yfinance as yf
```

```python
class Stock(FinancialInstrument):
    def __init__(self, ticker, quantity):
        self.ticker = ticker
        self.quantity = quantity
        self.price = self.fetch_price()

    def fetch_price(self):
        stock_data = yf.Ticker(self.ticker)
        return stock_data.history(period="1d")['Close'][0]

    def value(self):
        return self.price * self.quantity

# Example usage:
stock = Stock('AAPL', 100)
print(f"Stock value: {stock.value()}")
```

Here, we use the yfinance library to fetch the current stock price of Apple (AAPL) and integrate it into our DSL for real-time analysis. The fetch_price method pulls the latest price and allows financial analysts to access live data directly from within the DSL environment.

Automating Workflow Integration

In many organizations, financial models need to be integrated into automated workflows. These workflows may involve automated reporting, data pipelines, or integration with other internal business systems such as customer relationship management (CRM) tools or enterprise resource planning (ERP) software.

The DSL can be integrated with a task scheduler or automation system such as Celery in Python. This allows financial analysts to automate the execution of DSL-based calculations at regular intervals or in response to specific events (e.g., when stock prices change).

For instance, using Celery, a task to calculate a portfolio's total value could be scheduled as follows:

```python
from celery import Celery

app = Celery('tasks', broker='redis://localhost:6379/0')

@app.task
def calculate_portfolio_value(portfolio):
    return portfolio.total_value()

# Example usage:
portfolio = Portfolio()
portfolio.add_asset('AAPL', stock)
portfolio.add_asset('GOOGL', bond)

calculate_portfolio_value.apply_async(args=[portfolio])
```

This approach enables the DSL to run calculations automatically, integrating financial analysis into the broader automation framework and enhancing the workflow efficiency.

Integrating with Business Reporting Tools

Another key challenge is ensuring that the DSL integrates with business reporting tools that generate actionable insights, such as dashboards, spreadsheets, and presentation software. Financial analysts often use platforms like Excel or custom dashboards to view and share financial reports. The DSL should provide mechanisms to export results into these formats.

For instance, Python libraries like pandas can be used to create reports in Excel format directly from the DSL:

```python
import pandas as pd

class Portfolio:
    def __init__(self):
        self.assets = {}

    def add_asset(self, asset_name, asset):
        self.assets[asset_name] = asset

    def total_value(self):
        return sum(asset.value() for asset in self.assets.values())

    def to_excel(self, filename):
        data = {
            "Asset": list(self.assets.keys()),
            "Value": [asset.value() for asset in self.assets.values()],
        }
        df = pd.DataFrame(data)
        df.to_excel(filename, index=False)

# Example usage:
portfolio = Portfolio()
portfolio.add_asset('AAPL', stock)
portfolio.add_asset('GOOGL', bond)
portfolio.to_excel("financial_report.xlsx")
```

This code exports the financial data from the DSL into an Excel file, making it easy for analysts to share and present their results within their organization's existing workflow.

User Adoption and Workflow Training

Integrating the DSL into business workflows requires not only technical implementation but also user adoption. Financial analysts must be trained to use the DSL effectively. Training programs should focus on the DSL's syntax, key features, and how it integrates with existing systems. A good practice is to provide examples of how the DSL can solve real-world financial problems.

Creating clear documentation, offering training sessions, and providing support can help ease the transition. Additionally, ensuring the DSL is user-friendly and meets the needs of financial analysts will encourage faster adoption.

Integrating a custom DSL into business workflows involves connecting to external data sources, automating processes, exporting reports, and ensuring that analysts can easily adopt the new tool. A well-integrated DSL enhances productivity by streamlining financial modeling processes and providing real-time insights within the organization's existing systems.

Measuring Success and Improvements in Productivity

Once a custom Domain-Specific Language (DSL) for financial analysis has been developed and integrated into business workflows, it's essential to measure its success and assess the improvements in productivity. This evaluation is crucial for understanding how effectively the DSL is contributing to the organization's objectives, identifying areas for improvement, and demonstrating the value of the DSL. This section explores key metrics and techniques for measuring success, along with practical code examples to track and assess productivity improvements.

Defining Success Metrics

To measure the success of the DSL in financial modeling, it's important to define the right metrics. These metrics may include:

- **Speed of Analysis**: How much time it takes to perform complex financial analyses using the DSL compared to traditional methods.

- **Accuracy of Results**: How accurate are the financial predictions, and how consistent are the results over time?

- **User Adoption**: The number of users actively utilizing the DSL for their tasks.

- **Cost Savings**: Reduced time and resources spent on manual financial calculations.

For example, if the DSL is expected to reduce the time taken for financial reporting, one metric could be to compare the time it takes to generate a report before and after DSL integration.

```
import time

# Example function to measure the time taken for portfolio valuation
def measure_portfolio_valuation_time(portfolio):
    start_time = time.time()
    portfolio_value = portfolio.total_value()
    end_time = time.time()
    time_taken = end_time - start_time
    print(f"Portfolio valuation took {time_taken:.2f} seconds.")
    return time_taken

# Example usage
portfolio = Portfolio()
portfolio.add_asset('AAPL', stock)
portfolio.add_asset('GOOGL', bond)

time_taken_before_dsl = measure_portfolio_valuation_time(portfolio)
```

Here, the time taken for calculating the portfolio value is measured, and this can be compared to the time taken for similar tasks using previous methods to gauge improvements in efficiency.

Tracking User Adoption

The success of the DSL can be heavily influenced by its adoption rate. It's important to monitor how many analysts or teams are actively using the DSL to perform their daily tasks. This can be done by logging the number of transactions or operations carried out using the DSL. Additionally, surveys and feedback forms can be used to gather insights from users about their experience with the DSL.

A simple way to track usage within the DSL is by logging each function call or major action taken by users. In Python, we could use decorators to log usage statistics:

```python
import logging

# Set up logging
logging.basicConfig(filename="dsl_usage.log", level=logging.INFO)

def log_usage(func):
    def wrapper(*args, **kwargs):
        logging.info(f"Function {func.__name__} was called.")
        return func(*args, **kwargs)
    return wrapper

# Example of logging DSL function usage
class Portfolio:
    @log_usage
    def add_asset(self, asset_name, asset):
        self.assets[asset_name] = asset

    @log_usage
    def total_value(self):
        return sum(asset.value() for asset in self.assets.values())

portfolio = Portfolio()
portfolio.add_asset('AAPL', stock)
portfolio.add_asset('GOOGL', bond)
```

In this example, every time a function like add_asset or total_value is called, it gets logged. This allows the team to track how often the DSL is used, helping to assess its adoption rate.

Analyzing Cost Savings

Cost savings can be evaluated by comparing the resources required to complete tasks before and after DSL implementation. This could include the time saved, reduced labor costs, and minimized errors that would otherwise require time for correction. A simple financial model can be created to estimate the amount of money saved through reduced time spent on financial analyses.

For instance, if the DSL reduces the time for generating financial reports, the cost savings could be calculated by considering the hourly wage of financial analysts and the reduction in time spent on those tasks.

```python
def calculate_cost_savings(time_before, time_after, hourly_rate):
    time_saved = time_before - time_after
    cost_saved = time_saved * hourly_rate
    return cost_saved

# Example usage
time_before = 4   # 4 hours before DSL
time_after = 1    # 1 hour after DSL
hourly_rate = 50  # Analyst's hourly rate

cost_saved = calculate_cost_savings(time_before, time_after, hourly_rate)
print(f"Cost savings: ${cost_saved:.2f}")
```

This calculation shows how much money the organization saves by reducing the time spent on generating reports or performing financial analysis, making it easier to measure the financial impact of the DSL.

Gathering Feedback for Continuous Improvement

Another important aspect of measuring success is gathering feedback from users and stakeholders. This feedback can help identify potential areas for improvement and features that users want in the next iteration of the DSL. Surveys or direct interviews with users will provide valuable insights into the DSL's functionality, usability, and overall effectiveness.

Measuring the success of a custom DSL involves defining success metrics, tracking usage, evaluating cost savings, and gathering user feedback. By applying these methods, organizations can assess the effectiveness of the DSL in enhancing productivity and make informed decisions about future improvements or adaptations to meet business needs.

Case Study 2 – DSL in Web Development

This module focuses on how Domain-Specific Languages (DSLs) are utilized in web design and development, examining their role in automating processes, enhancing developer productivity, and optimizing system performance. Through real-world examples and lessons learned, the module will demonstrate the practical application of DSLs in web frameworks.

DSLs for Web Design and Development Automation

In web development, DSLs are designed to address the unique needs of building, styling, and automating web-related tasks. These languages are crafted to provide a simplified interface for tasks such as layout creation, content management, and backend interactions, which would otherwise require more complex programming constructs. The primary goal of using a DSL in web development is to reduce repetitive code, minimize errors, and allow developers to focus on more complex logic while the DSL takes care of routine tasks. By abstracting away complexity, DSLs make web development faster, more efficient, and less error-prone.

Real-world Examples of Successful DSL Usage in Web Frameworks

Numerous web development frameworks have successfully implemented DSLs to streamline design and enhance productivity. One example is Ruby on Rails, which includes a DSL for routing and database interaction. The framework's ActiveRecord DSL simplifies database queries and object-relational mapping, allowing developers to write cleaner and more readable code. Another example is CSS preprocessors like Sass, which extend CSS with variables, nested rules, and mixins, significantly improving web styling and design workflows. These DSLs have not only optimized the design process but also increased the scalability and maintainability of web applications.

Impact on Developer Productivity and System Performance

The implementation of DSLs in web development directly impacts both developer productivity and system performance. By abstracting routine tasks and offering domain-specific constructs, DSLs make development more efficient, allowing developers to accomplish more in less time. This reduction in time spent on repetitive tasks allows for faster iterations and more focus on complex features. Additionally, DSLs can be optimized to generate more efficient code, reducing the overhead often associated with general-purpose programming languages. As a result, web applications built using DSLs can have improved system performance, faster load times, and lower resource consumption, all of which contribute to a better user experience.

Lessons Learned from Web DSL Projects

While DSLs offer many benefits in web development, there are also challenges that developers must navigate. One of the key lessons learned is the importance of designing a DSL that is both flexible and user-friendly. A DSL that is too rigid can limit creativity and become a bottleneck for developers, while one that is too abstract can become difficult to learn and maintain. Additionally, integrating a DSL into an existing development workflow requires careful planning to ensure compatibility with other tools and libraries. Developers must also weigh the long-term maintenance of a DSL, ensuring it remains relevant and scalable as the project grows.

DSLs in web development have proven to be powerful tools for automating design tasks, improving productivity, and optimizing system performance. By examining real-world examples and reflecting on the lessons learned, developers can better understand how to successfully implement DSLs in their own web development projects, leading to more efficient and maintainable code.

DSLs for Web Design and Development Automation

Domain-Specific Languages (DSLs) are widely used in web design and development to simplify complex, repetitive tasks and make the process more efficient. In this section, we will explore how DSLs are applied in web development to automate processes such as layout design, content management, and backend interactions. By abstracting away routine tasks and providing custom constructs for web-specific needs, DSLs enable developers to write cleaner, more maintainable code while reducing the potential for errors.

Creating Web Layouts with DSLs

In web development, creating layouts can be tedious, especially when dealing with repetitive HTML structure and CSS styling. A web-based DSL can provide a higher level of abstraction, simplifying the creation and management of layouts. For instance, using a DSL for defining grids, spacing, and alignment can significantly reduce the complexity of writing CSS by hand.

Here is an example of using a simplified DSL for creating web layouts:

```
class WebLayoutDSL:
    def __init__(self):
        self.layout = ""

    def add_section(self, name, style):
        self.layout += f"<section id='{name}' style='{style}'>\n"

    def close_section(self):
        self.layout += "</section>\n"

    def generate_layout(self):
        return self.layout

# Usage:
layout = WebLayoutDSL()
layout.add_section("header", "background-color: #333; color: white;")
layout.add_section("content", "padding: 20px;")
layout.close_section()
```

```
print(layout.generate_layout())
```

In this example, the WebLayoutDSL class abstracts HTML section creation into a simple interface, with custom styles applied directly to each section. Developers can define web page layouts quickly without writing repetitive HTML and CSS code.

Automating Content Management

Another common use case for DSLs in web development is content management. A DSL can be created to automate the process of managing content, such as retrieving data from a database, inserting it into the page, and rendering it in a structured format. By designing a DSL for content management, developers can easily manage content updates and structure them according to the needs of the application.

Here's an example of a simple DSL for content insertion:

```
class ContentManagementDSL:
    def __init__(self):
        self.content = ""

    def add_heading(self, text):
        self.content += f"<h1>{text}</h1>\n"

    def add_paragraph(self, text):
        self.content += f"<p>{text}</p>\n"

    def render_content(self):
        return self.content

# Usage:
content = ContentManagementDSL()
content.add_heading("Welcome to Our Website")
content.add_paragraph("This is an example of content management using a DSL.")
print(content.render_content())
```

This ContentManagementDSL example allows developers to add structured content such as headings and paragraphs with minimal effort. It simplifies the task of content creation by abstracting the underlying HTML code.

Backend Interactions with DSLs

DSLs are also beneficial for automating backend interactions in web development. Consider a situation where developers need to perform routine database queries or handle API requests. A custom DSL can be designed to simplify these interactions, making it easier to express the logic of backend tasks.

```
class BackendInteractionDSL:
    def __init__(self):
        self.query = ""

    def select(self, table):
        self.query = f"SELECT * FROM {table}"

    def where(self, condition):
        self.query += f" WHERE {condition}"
```

279

```
    def execute(self):
        return f"Executing query: {self.query}"

# Usage:
db_query = BackendInteractionDSL()
db_query.select("users")
db_query.where("age > 18")
print(db_query.execute())
```

This BackendInteractionDSL class enables developers to quickly construct and execute SQL queries using a simple, domain-specific syntax. This reduces the need to manually write verbose SQL code and ensures consistency across the application.

DSLs in web development provide a powerful tool for automating repetitive tasks such as layout creation, content management, and backend interactions. By abstracting these processes into custom, domain-specific languages, developers can increase productivity, reduce errors, and create more maintainable web applications. In the following sections, we will explore real-world examples and the impact of DSLs on developer efficiency and system performance.

Real-World Examples of Successful DSL Usage in Web Frameworks

In this section, we will explore how DSLs have been successfully integrated into web development frameworks. DSLs are powerful tools that can significantly improve the expressiveness and maintainability of web applications. By abstracting complex tasks into simple, domain-specific constructs, these languages have become integral to several popular web frameworks.

Ruby on Rails – ActiveRecord Query DSL

Ruby on Rails (Rails) is one of the most popular web frameworks, and it makes extensive use of DSLs, especially in its ActiveRecord component. ActiveRecord is an Object-Relational Mapping (ORM) system that abstracts the database interactions in a way that allows developers to use a more declarative syntax for querying and manipulating data. The DSL used in ActiveRecord simplifies the interaction with the database and enables developers to write concise queries.

For example, consider the following Rails ActiveRecord DSL usage:

```
class User < ActiveRecord::Base
  has_many :posts
end

# Querying users
users = User.where("age > ?", 18).order(:name)

# Creating a new user
user = User.create(name: "John", age: 30)
```

280

Here, the where and order methods form part of the DSL used to query the database. This syntax abstracts away raw SQL and allows developers to interact with the database using an intuitive, Ruby-like language, resulting in more maintainable and readable code.

Django – Template Language DSL

Django, a Python-based web framework, also provides an example of a domain-specific language for templating. Django's template language is a DSL that allows developers to embed Python-like logic directly in HTML files, which can be used to dynamically generate content for web pages.

Here is a simple example of how a Django template is used:

```
<!DOCTYPE html>
<html>
<head>
    <title>{{ title }}</title>
</head>
<body>
    <h1>{{ header }}</h1>
    <p>{{ content }}</p>
</body>
</html>
```

In this example, the {{ }} syntax is part of the Django template DSL, allowing the injection of dynamic content like title, header, and content. This reduces the need for explicitly writing Python code for dynamic HTML generation and streamlines the templating process.

Additionally, the {% %} tags are used for control flow and logic:

```
{% if user.is_authenticated %}
    <p>Welcome, {{ user.username }}!</p>
{% else %}
    <p>Please log in.</p>
{% endif %}
```

This demonstrates how Django's template DSL abstracts away much of the logic required for content presentation, improving readability and maintainability of the code.

Laravel – Blade Templating DSL

Laravel, a PHP web framework, provides a powerful DSL in its Blade templating engine. Blade enables developers to easily create dynamic web pages by providing a clean syntax for control structures, loops, and data injection.

Here's a simple example of Blade templating in Laravel:

```
<!DOCTYPE html>
<html>
<head>
    <title>@yield('title')</title>
```

```
</head>
<body>
    <h1>@yield('header')</h1>
    @if($user->isAuthenticated())
        <p>Welcome, {{ $user->name }}!</p>
    @else
        <p>Please log in.</p>
    @endif
</body>
</html>
```

In this example, the @yield, @if, and other Blade directives form part of the DSL. Blade allows developers to quickly render dynamic content by injecting variables directly into the templates. The clear syntax of Blade makes it easier for developers to maintain templated views and improves the overall efficiency of web development.

Flask – Jinja2 Template DSL

Flask, another popular Python-based web framework, uses the Jinja2 template engine, which is a powerful DSL for generating dynamic web content. Jinja2 allows developers to use control structures such as loops and conditionals directly in HTML templates.

Here's an example of Jinja2 syntax:

```
<!DOCTYPE html>
<html>
<head>
    <title>{{ title }}</title>
</head>
<body>
    <h1>{{ header }}</h1>
    <ul>
    {% for item in items %}
        <li>{{ item }}</li>
    {% endfor %}
    </ul>
</body>
</html>
```

The {% for %} and {{ }} syntax are part of the Jinja2 DSL, enabling dynamic generation of content within HTML templates. Flask, by using Jinja2, makes it easy to generate dynamic web pages without requiring complex Python code in the templates themselves.

These real-world examples highlight the impact DSLs have had on web development frameworks. By abstracting common web development tasks into more expressive and user-friendly languages, DSLs significantly improve developer productivity and application maintainability. In frameworks like Ruby on Rails, Django, Laravel, and Flask, DSLs have simplified complex operations such as database queries, content rendering, and template creation. By streamlining these processes, DSLs contribute to building faster and more efficient web applications while enhancing the developer experience.

Impact on Developer Productivity and System Performance

In this section, we explore how DSLs in web development frameworks can significantly impact both developer productivity and system performance. By leveraging DSLs, developers can achieve faster development cycles, enhanced maintainability, and a clearer separation of concerns. DSLs also enable performance optimization through domain-specific optimizations that may not be possible with general-purpose programming languages.

Enhancing Developer Productivity

One of the primary benefits of using DSLs in web frameworks is the improvement in developer productivity. DSLs allow developers to express domain-specific logic more concisely and clearly, reducing the amount of code required to implement common functionality. The abstraction of complex tasks into simple, human-readable syntax can save developers significant time.

For example, in the Ruby on Rails framework, the ActiveRecord DSL allows developers to interact with the database using high-level constructs rather than writing raw SQL queries. The following example shows how a developer can fetch records based on a condition:

```
users = User.where("age > ?", 18).order(:name)
```

Without the DSL, the same operation would require more code and familiarity with SQL syntax:

```
SELECT * FROM users WHERE age > 18 ORDER BY name;
```

The ActiveRecord query is far more intuitive, and it enables developers to focus on the application's logic rather than the intricacies of database management. This improves both the speed of development and the maintainability of the codebase.

Reduction in Boilerplate Code

DSLs help reduce boilerplate code, which is a common problem in web development. By encapsulating frequently used patterns or operations into simple language constructs, DSLs allow developers to avoid repetitive code. For example, Django's ORM provides a way to define models with minimal code. Here's how you might define a model for a Book in Django:

```
class Book(models.Model):
    title = models.CharField(max_length=200)
    author = models.CharField(max_length=100)
    published_date = models.DateField()
```

With this simple model definition, Django's ORM automatically handles the underlying SQL queries needed for creating, reading, updating, and deleting records. This reduces the need for developers to manually write repetitive code, allowing them to focus on higher-level application logic.

Improving System Performance with Domain-Specific Optimizations

Beyond improving developer productivity, DSLs can also optimize system performance. Many DSLs in web development frameworks allow developers to take advantage of domain-specific optimizations that would be difficult to achieve with general-purpose programming languages. These optimizations may include caching, lazy loading, or optimized database queries.

For example, Django's ORM supports database query optimizations like select_related and prefetch_related to minimize the number of database queries, thus improving the application's performance:

```python
# Without optimization (multiple queries)
books = Book.objects.all()
for book in books:
    print(book.author.name)

# With optimization (single query)
books = Book.objects.select_related('author').all()
for book in books:
    print(book.author.name)
```

In this example, select_related minimizes the number of queries by performing a join at the database level, resulting in faster data retrieval and improved system performance.

Optimizing Template Rendering Performance

In web frameworks like Flask and Django, the DSL used in templates can also optimize rendering performance. By minimizing unnecessary computations or simplifying logic, these frameworks can speed up the rendering process. Django's use of the cache template tag, for instance, allows for caching the output of expensive views:

```
{% load cache %}
{% cache 600 my_cache_key %}
    <p>Expensive computation here...</p>
{% endcache %}
```

By caching rendered content, Django reduces the load on the server and speeds up response times for frequently accessed pages.

DSLs in web development frameworks significantly impact both developer productivity and system performance. By simplifying complex tasks into high-level, domain-specific syntax, DSLs enable developers to focus on the core logic of their applications, leading to faster development cycles and more maintainable code. Additionally, DSLs help optimize system performance by providing domain-specific optimizations such as efficient database queries, caching, and template rendering. The combination of improved productivity and performance makes DSLs a powerful tool in modern web development.

Lessons Learned from Web DSL Projects

This section explores the lessons learned from real-world web development projects that have successfully implemented Domain-Specific Languages (DSLs). Drawing from these case studies, we highlight the challenges faced and best practices that can help ensure the success of DSLs in web development. These insights focus on the development process, tool selection, and scalability concerns.

Defining the Domain Early On

One of the most crucial lessons from successful DSL projects is the importance of clearly defining the domain early in the process. The effectiveness of a DSL depends heavily on how well it reflects the problem domain it aims to address. Developers should engage domain experts and gather specific requirements to design a DSL that solves the real-world challenges the target users face.

For example, a team developing a DSL for e-commerce applications should define the language constructs around products, shopping carts, and orders. If the domain is not well-defined, the DSL might become too general or too complex to be practical, leading to a lack of adoption or inefficient development. Thus, it is important to balance flexibility and simplicity, allowing developers to express their requirements without over-complicating the language design.

Iterative Development and Feedback Loops

Another key lesson is the importance of adopting an iterative development approach. DSLs, like any software, evolve over time. Starting with a minimal viable product (MVP) version of the DSL and gathering feedback from users helps refine the language's functionality. Iterating on the DSL allows developers to adjust the language constructs and syntax based on real-world usage, ultimately making the language more efficient and user-friendly.

For instance, when implementing a DSL for building web layouts, developers may initially design a basic set of tags and syntax for common layout components like grids and columns. As feedback is gathered from front-end developers, additional constructs for responsiveness or animations may be added to make the DSL more comprehensive and practical.

```
<!-- Initial basic syntax -->
<grid>
    <column>Content 1</column>
    <column>Content 2</column>
</grid>

<!-- Improved syntax based on feedback -->
<responsive-grid>
    <column lg="6" sm="12">Content 1</column>
    <column lg="6" sm="12">Content 2</column>
</responsive-grid>
```

Maintaining a Balance Between Abstraction and Performance

DSLs are often designed to simplify complex tasks, but too much abstraction can result in performance issues. A common pitfall is sacrificing performance for ease of use. In web development, DSLs that over-abstract common operations can lead to inefficient code execution or slow page loads.

A well-known example of this challenge occurs in templating systems like Django's template engine. While it provides powerful abstractions for web pages, too many embedded logic statements in templates can impact rendering time. To mitigate this, developers need to ensure that DSL constructs, especially those for template rendering, are optimized for performance without sacrificing readability. This might include techniques like caching frequently used templates or avoiding complex loops in the templates.

Adoption and Documentation

Another important lesson is the need for comprehensive documentation and training for end-users (typically developers). DSLs often require developers to learn new syntax and paradigms, so providing clear, accessible documentation and examples is vital for successful adoption. This documentation should not only describe the syntax but also explain how and why the DSL was designed in a particular way.

Real-world projects that succeeded with DSLs, such as those in web development frameworks, often provided ample resources like tutorials, case studies, and code examples to assist developers in learning and applying the DSL effectively. Furthermore, having a user community or support channel in place can help address issues and foster adoption among developers.

Scalability Concerns

As the project grows, the scalability of the DSL becomes an issue. One of the lessons learned from web DSL projects is to anticipate future needs and ensure that the DSL can scale with them. While a DSL might initially serve a small feature set or project, it must be designed to accommodate future functionality without requiring major rewrites.

For instance, when building a DSL for managing user authentication and authorization, the initial version may only support basic user roles. However, as the project evolves, it might need to handle more complex requirements like multi-factor authentication, permission inheritance, and social media logins. Designing the DSL to accommodate these future needs in a flexible way is key to ensuring long-term viability.

The success of a DSL in web development hinges on early domain definition, iterative development, balancing abstraction with performance, effective documentation, and scalability considerations. By addressing these factors, developers can build DSLs that not only streamline development but also contribute to improved system performance. These lessons learned provide a solid foundation for future DSL projects in web development.

Module 28:
Case Study 3 – DSL in Network Configuration

This module explores the design and implementation of Domain-Specific Languages (DSLs) tailored for network configuration and management. By analyzing real-world applications of DSLs in this domain, we demonstrate how they simplify network setup and maintenance. The module will cover techniques for parsing and code generation, challenges faced during implementation, and operational benefits.

Creating a DSL for Network Management and Configuration

Creating a DSL for network configuration starts with defining the specific network elements that need to be managed. A network DSL is typically designed to address tasks such as device configuration, network topology, and routing protocols. Unlike general-purpose programming languages, a DSL for network configuration focuses on reducing complexity and allowing network administrators to manage configurations with minimal effort.

When designing such a DSL, it is essential to understand the target user, typically network administrators, who require a straightforward syntax that captures their operations. The DSL must be expressive enough to cover various network setups while being simple to use and maintain. A well-designed DSL for network configuration can abstract away repetitive tasks such as IP address assignment, route definition, and VLAN management, simplifying the configuration process.

Parsing and Code Generation Techniques Used

Parsing and code generation are critical in transforming the high-level DSL code into actual configuration scripts that can be executed by network devices. The first step in parsing involves lexical analysis, where the DSL code is broken down into tokens. These tokens are then used to construct a syntax tree, which represents the hierarchical structure of the configuration.

After parsing, the code generation phase translates the syntax tree into configuration files or commands specific to the network device being managed. Depending on the target platform (e.g., Cisco, Juniper), the DSL must generate configuration commands that are compatible with the device's configuration language. During this process, optimizations for performance and readability of the generated code are essential, ensuring that the resulting configuration files are efficient and maintainable.

Real-Life Examples of Network DSL Applications

There are several real-world examples of DSLs used in network configuration. One of the most notable is the use of tools like Ansible and Puppet, which, while not strictly network DSLs, allow administrators to define network configurations in a declarative way. These tools use a simplified syntax to express desired network states, and under the hood, they generate configurations for various devices.

More specialized DSLs, like those used in software-defined networking (SDN), allow for dynamic and programmatic network management. These DSLs enable the configuration of network devices through a central controller, making it easier to manage large, complex networks. For example, a DSL could allow an administrator to define the desired state of network devices, such as switches and routers, without manually configuring each device.

Operational Benefits and Challenges Faced

The primary operational benefit of using DSLs in network configuration is efficiency. By abstracting complex network tasks into simpler commands, DSLs make network management faster, less error-prone, and more consistent. This is especially beneficial in large-scale networks where manual configuration can be both time-consuming and error-prone.

However, implementing a DSL for network configuration also presents challenges. One of the main challenges is ensuring the DSL can handle the complexities of different network devices and configurations. A DSL designed for one set of devices may not work well with another, leading to compatibility issues. Furthermore, network environments evolve, requiring the DSL to adapt over time, which may require ongoing maintenance and updates.

Another challenge is ensuring the DSL's syntax remains intuitive for the network administrators who will use it. While a DSL can greatly simplify network configuration, if the language is not designed properly, it can add an additional layer of complexity instead of reducing it. Effective documentation and training for users are essential to overcoming this challenge.

DSLs in network configuration offer significant operational benefits by simplifying network management tasks, enhancing consistency, and reducing configuration errors. Despite the challenges of device compatibility and ongoing maintenance, they provide a powerful tool for streamlining network operations. This case study highlights the importance of careful design, parsing, and code generation techniques in building effective DSLs for network management.

Creating a DSL for Network Management and Configuration

Creating a Domain-Specific Language (DSL) for network configuration involves designing a language tailored to the needs of network administrators. The goal is to abstract away complex network configurations into a simplified, easy-to-use language that allows users to efficiently manage network devices and settings. This section covers the steps involved in creating such a DSL, including defining the language's syntax, understanding network-specific requirements, and how the DSL can be used for managing various network devices and configurations.

Defining the Network Configuration Requirements

A DSL for network management needs to address the specific tasks required in network configuration. These tasks typically include setting IP addresses, configuring routing protocols, VLANs, subnetting, and other network-related operations. To create an effective DSL, it is important to focus on the key actions that need to be automated or simplified, reducing the complexity of the network setup process.

For example, a network DSL might need to include constructs for defining:

- **IP address assignments**: Static IPs, DHCP configurations, etc.

- **Routing configurations**: Configuring static routes, dynamic routing protocols (like OSPF, BGP), etc.

- **VLAN management**: Defining VLANs, assigning interfaces to VLANs, etc.

In the case of a router configuration DSL, a simple construct could look like:

```
interface Ethernet0
  ip address 192.168.1.1 255.255.255.0
  no shutdown
```

Here, the DSL allows the user to define the network interface and assign it an IP address, eliminating the need for manually typing long commands.

Designing the Syntax

The syntax of the DSL should be simple, intuitive, and easily understandable by network administrators, who may not be programmers. One approach is to use a declarative syntax that emphasizes what the network configuration should look like, rather than how it should be configured. The syntax should focus on readability, minimizing the need for detailed technical knowledge about the network protocols or configuration.

For instance, a network DSL could use a format like the following for router interface configurations:

```
interface Ethernet1
  ip address 192.168.2.1 255.255.255.0
  description "Gateway to internal network"
  enable
```

This makes the configuration more human-readable compared to the typical router command line interface (CLI).

Building the Language Features

Once the basic structure is defined, we need to add features for handling more complex operations. The DSL might need constructs for:

- **Dynamic routing protocol configuration**: Automating configurations for protocols such as OSPF or BGP.

- **VLAN configurations**: Simplifying VLAN definitions and network segmentation.

- **Firewall settings**: Creating rules for security policies within the network.

- **Network services**: Configuring DHCP, DNS, or other services needed for the network to function properly.

For example, a DSL for configuring OSPF could look like this:

```
router ospf 1
  network 192.168.1.0 0.0.0.255 area 0
  network 192.168.2.0 0.0.0.255 area 0
```

This construct automates the process of setting up OSPF by defining the networks and their respective OSPF areas.

Translating DSL to Configurations

The final stage of creating a DSL for network configuration is building a parser and code generation system that translates the DSL instructions into actual configuration files that network devices can understand. The DSL code must be parsed, typically via a lexer and parser that generates an Abstract Syntax Tree (AST), which is then used to generate the corresponding device-specific configuration.

For instance, the DSL above could be parsed into configuration commands for a Cisco router like this:

```
interface Ethernet1
  ip address 192.168.2.1 255.255.255.0
  description "Gateway to internal network"
  no shutdown

router ospf 1
  network 192.168.1.0 0.0.0.255 area 0
  network 192.168.2.0 0.0.0.255 area 0
```

This code generation system will produce a configuration file that can be directly applied to a network device like a Cisco router.

Creating a DSL for network configuration simplifies the process of managing large and complex networks. By abstracting network setup tasks into simple, declarative syntax, a DSL can improve the productivity of network administrators. The key to successful DSL design lies in focusing on the core tasks that need to be automated while ensuring the syntax is intuitive and user-friendly. By building an effective parser and code generator, a custom network DSL can reduce errors, increase efficiency, and streamline network operations.

Parsing and Code Generation Techniques Used

In the creation of a Domain-Specific Language (DSL) for network configuration, parsing and code generation play crucial roles. Parsing refers to the process of analyzing the DSL code to understand its structure, while code generation translates the parsed structure into executable configuration commands for network devices. This section covers the techniques involved in parsing DSLs and the strategies for generating the corresponding network configuration code.

Parsing DSL Code

Parsing begins by converting the raw DSL code into a form that the system can understand. Typically, this process involves two steps: lexical analysis and syntactic analysis. The first step, lexical analysis, breaks down the input DSL code into tokens that represent the smallest units of the language. These tokens include keywords, identifiers, and literals. For example, in the code snippet:

```
interface Ethernet0
  ip address 192.168.1.1 255.255.255.0
```

The lexer would break it into tokens such as interface, Ethernet0, ip, address, 192.168.1.1, and 255.255.255.0. These tokens are then passed on to the parser.

Abstract Syntax Tree (AST)

The next step, syntactic analysis, involves taking the tokens and constructing an Abstract Syntax Tree (AST). The AST represents the hierarchical structure of the code, allowing the system to understand the relationship between different components. In the case of the network DSL, the AST might represent a network interface configuration with nested elements, such as IP address and subnet mask.

For example, given this DSL code:

```
interface Ethernet0
  ip address 192.168.1.1 255.255.255.0
```

The AST could look like:

```
InterfaceNode
  InterfaceName: Ethernet0
  IpAddressNode
    Ip: 192.168.1.1
    SubnetMask: 255.255.255.0
```

The AST makes it easy to traverse the DSL structure programmatically and extract meaningful information for code generation.

Code Generation

After parsing the DSL code into an AST, the next task is code generation. The code generator walks through the AST and produces the corresponding configuration commands in the language understood by the target network device. For example, the AST above would be translated into:

```
interface Ethernet0
  ip address 192.168.1.1 255.255.255.0
```

The code generation step involves converting higher-level abstractions into low-level commands. These low-level commands are the configuration syntax used by network devices, such as Cisco routers or switches. The DSL's goal is to simplify the network configuration process by abstracting these low-level details.

Optimizing the Parsing and Code Generation Process

Optimizing the parsing and code generation process ensures that the DSL operates efficiently. Parsing DSL code can be computationally expensive, especially when dealing with large configuration files or complex network setups. One optimization technique is to use a **recursive descent parser**, which is simple to implement and performs well for most DSLs.

For example, parsing the DSL code to create the AST might be optimized with memoization or caching techniques. This ensures that repeated parsing of similar code snippets is handled efficiently, improving performance.

Similarly, optimizing code generation can involve minimizing unnecessary steps or simplifying the output. For instance, instead of generating verbose configuration code, the generator could focus on outputting only the changes required by the user, thereby reducing the overall size of the configuration file.

```python
# Example of code generation in Python using a simple template
class NetworkConfigGenerator:
    def generate_interface_config(self, interface_name, ip_address,
            subnet_mask):
        return f"interface {interface_name}\n  ip address {ip_address}
            {subnet_mask}\n"

# Usage example
generator = NetworkConfigGenerator()
config = generator.generate_interface_config("Ethernet0", "192.168.1.1",
        "255.255.255.0")
print(config)
```

Output:

```
interface Ethernet0
  ip address 192.168.1.1 255.255.255.0
```

In this example, the NetworkConfigGenerator class uses a method to generate the configuration for an interface. The code generation process turns the high-level DSL abstraction into a specific configuration string.

Parsing and code generation are essential components of a DSL for network configuration. By using parsing techniques like lexical analysis and recursive descent parsing, the DSL code can be translated into an AST, which serves as the basis for generating network configuration code. Code generation techniques must be efficient, ensuring that the final configuration is correct, concise, and optimized for the target network device. With these techniques, the DSL can automate the configuration process, making network management more efficient and less error-prone.

Real-Life Examples of Network DSL Applications

In real-life scenarios, DSLs for network configuration have proven to be highly effective for simplifying the management of complex networks. By abstracting the intricacies of low-level network configuration commands, these custom languages can streamline network design, improve the accuracy of configurations, and automate routine tasks. This section explores real-world applications of DSLs in network management, showcasing how they are used to automate and optimize network configurations across different industries.

Network Configuration in Telecom Industry

One common example of DSL usage is in the telecom industry, where large-scale network configurations need to be applied consistently across multiple devices. DSLs allow telecom engineers to automate the configuration of thousands of devices, significantly reducing the time spent on manual entry. A DSL designed for telecom networks might focus on parameters such as IP addressing, VLAN assignments, and routing protocols, abstracting these complex configurations into a user-friendly syntax.

For instance, instead of manually configuring each router or switch with CLI commands, a DSL can allow engineers to specify network-wide changes in a high-level format:

```
router R1
  ip address 10.0.0.1 255.255.255.0
  router ospf 1
    network 10.0.0.0 0.0.0.255 area 0
```

This high-level DSL code is parsed and translated into the appropriate network device configuration commands, automating tasks such as OSPF routing setup. The DSL simplifies the syntax, reducing human error and speeding up configuration across the network.

Data Center Management

294

Data centers often require frequent updates to their configurations, especially when provisioning new servers, setting up switches, or managing VLANs. A network DSL can automate these processes, allowing network engineers to describe high-level tasks such as adding new subnets, configuring interfaces, or applying security policies.

For example, a network DSL might allow for concise statements like:

```
create_vlan 100
  name "Finance"
  ip_range 192.168.1.0 255.255.255.0

configure_interface eth0
  vlan 100
  ip address 192.168.1.1 255.255.255.0
```

This DSL syntax describes the creation of a new VLAN and configuring an interface with a specific IP address. The DSL is then parsed, and the corresponding configuration commands are generated and applied to the network devices.

Cloud Infrastructure Automation

With the rise of cloud computing, network DSLs are also being used to manage cloud infrastructure networks. For instance, cloud service providers like AWS, Google Cloud, or Azure offer APIs to configure networking elements such as load balancers, virtual private networks (VPNs), and subnets. A DSL for cloud networking can abstract these complex API calls into simple, human-readable commands that enable DevOps engineers to define network structures for cloud-based applications.

A cloud networking DSL might look like this:

```
create_vpc "Production_VPC"
  cidr_block 10.0.0.0/16
  region "us-east-1"

create_subnet "Frontend_Subnet"
  vpc "Production_VPC"
  cidr_block 10.0.1.0/24
```

The code above represents the creation of a Virtual Private Cloud (VPC) and a subnet within that VPC. After parsing, the corresponding cloud API calls would be generated to provision the cloud network elements. By using a DSL, DevOps teams can more easily automate and manage large cloud networks.

Cisco Network Configuration Automation

Cisco network administrators often work with complex network configurations that involve configuring multiple devices, such as routers, switches, and firewalls. A network DSL allows network engineers to describe the network setup in a high-level format, which is then translated into CLI commands for Cisco devices. A DSL might focus on

295

simplifying the configuration of routing protocols, access control lists (ACLs), and IP addresses.

For instance, a network DSL for Cisco devices might include commands like:

```
configure_router R1
  hostname Router1
  ip address 192.168.1.1 255.255.255.0
  interface eth0
    ip address 192.168.1.2 255.255.255.0
  enable ospf 1
    network 192.168.1.0 0.0.0.255 area 0
```

This DSL code abstracts multiple commands required for setting up a Cisco router, allowing engineers to focus on the high-level configuration. Once parsed, the system generates the required CLI commands for the router, saving time and reducing the chance for configuration errors.

Real-life applications of network DSLs have shown substantial improvements in network configuration management, especially in large-scale systems. By abstracting complex and repetitive tasks into simpler, high-level instructions, DSLs help network engineers automate configuration changes, reduce errors, and improve productivity. Whether in telecom networks, data center management, cloud infrastructure, or Cisco device configuration, network DSLs simplify processes, making them more efficient and manageable for organizations. The use of DSLs in network management demonstrates how specialized languages can bring immense value to domains requiring precision and automation.

Operational Benefits and Challenges Faced

DSLs for network configuration bring numerous operational benefits, particularly in terms of automation, consistency, and error reduction. However, the adoption of such custom languages also presents several challenges, including the initial learning curve, integration with existing tools, and maintenance over time. This section explores the operational benefits and challenges encountered when using DSLs in network configuration.

Operational Benefits of Network DSLs

One of the key advantages of network DSLs is their ability to automate complex and repetitive configuration tasks. Network administrators can leverage DSLs to express high-level configuration goals rather than dealing with the intricacies of individual device commands. This automation reduces the manual labor involved in managing network devices, which translates to substantial time savings.

For example, a network DSL can enable an engineer to write code that configures an entire network of switches, routers, and firewalls with minimal effort. A simple DSL script might look like this:

```
configure_network "Corporate_Network"
  vlan 10
    name "Accounting"
    ip_range 192.168.1.0 255.255.255.0
  vlan 20
    name "HR"
    ip_range 192.168.2.0 255.255.255.0
  router R1
    hostname "Core_Router"
    interfaces eth0 192.168.1.1
    interfaces eth1 192.168.2.1
    enable ospf 1
```

This code simplifies a typical network setup by abstracting away the complex syntax and repetitive configuration commands, leading to faster deployment times and fewer configuration mistakes. With the DSL handling the code generation, the network setup can be performed consistently across devices.

Another operational benefit is that DSLs provide a standardized way to configure network devices, ensuring that configurations are uniform and consistent across the network. This consistency minimizes human error, particularly in large-scale environments with numerous network elements. By reducing configuration inconsistencies, network administrators can focus more on strategic planning and less on manual error detection.

Challenges in Implementing Network DSLs

Despite the operational benefits, implementing a network DSL is not without its challenges. One of the primary difficulties is the initial learning curve. Network administrators and engineers must become familiar with the syntax and constructs of the custom DSL. While a DSL can simplify configuration, its adoption requires training and time for engineers to become proficient. Furthermore, integrating the DSL into existing network management systems can be challenging, particularly if the systems are not designed to interact with custom languages.

For example, integrating a network DSL with monitoring tools or network visualization platforms may require the creation of additional parsing or code generation logic, adding complexity to the process. Engineers may need to develop bridges between their DSL and existing platforms to ensure seamless operation across the network lifecycle.

Another challenge is the ongoing maintenance of the DSL itself. Over time, the needs of the network may evolve, and the DSL will need to be updated to support new protocols, devices, or features. This ongoing maintenance can add to the overhead of using a DSL, as it requires continuous development and support to keep the language up-to-date with network technology changes.

Testing and Debugging DSL Code

A significant challenge of using DSLs for network configuration is testing and debugging. While DSLs simplify the expression of configurations, they can make it harder to trace errors in the generated code. If a configuration error occurs, network engineers may have difficulty identifying the root cause due to the abstraction introduced by the DSL. In contrast, directly writing configuration commands in the native language of the network devices can make it easier to spot and correct mistakes.

A potential solution to this challenge is to build robust testing frameworks around the DSL. For example, automated tests can verify that DSL scripts result in the correct configurations across network devices, helping engineers catch errors early in the process. Incorporating continuous integration tools can also support the process of testing DSL-generated configurations, further improving reliability.

The operational benefits of using DSLs for network configuration are clear: automation, consistency, and error reduction lead to improved productivity and faster network deployment. However, challenges such as the learning curve, integration with existing systems, and ongoing maintenance must be considered. Despite these challenges, the use of DSLs can be transformative for large-scale network management, offering significant operational efficiencies when implemented effectively. The key is balancing the advantages of DSL-based automation with the practical challenges that arise during adoption and maintenance.

Module 29:
Case Study 4 – DSL in Game Development

This module explores the application of domain-specific languages (DSLs) in game development. It provides a detailed analysis of how DSLs can be tailored to enhance scripting flexibility, improve workflow efficiency, and ultimately impact game performance. The module also addresses the challenges faced during the integration of DSLs in game development processes and suggests potential future directions for DSL evolution in the industry.

Designing a Domain-Specific Language for Game Scripting

Designing a DSL for game scripting involves creating a language that simplifies the process of controlling game mechanics, events, and behaviors within the game engine. A well-designed DSL abstracts away the complexity of low-level programming, enabling game developers and designers to focus on game logic rather than underlying technical details. The DSL's design must be closely aligned with the unique needs of the game, considering factors such as event handling, NPC behavior, animation sequences, and world state management. By defining custom constructs for these elements, a DSL enhances clarity and reduces the likelihood of errors.

Moreover, the syntax of the DSL should reflect the natural language of game designers, enabling non-programmers to contribute effectively to the game scripting process. This can be accomplished by designing a language that allows for clear, concise expressions of complex game logic. The DSL might also incorporate integration hooks for existing game engines or frameworks, allowing it to generate the necessary code to interact with the core game systems.

Workflow Improvements and Game Design Flexibility

A major advantage of implementing a DSL in game development is the significant improvement it brings to the development workflow. By abstracting repetitive or complex tasks, a DSL streamlines the process of defining and implementing game mechanics. Game designers, who might not have strong programming skills, can directly interact with the DSL, creating game features, testing different scenarios, and making quick adjustments to game behavior. This reduces reliance on programmers for minor tweaks and enables a more collaborative development environment.

Additionally, a DSL offers flexibility in game design by allowing quick prototyping and experimentation. Designers can alter game behaviors and mechanics without needing to modify the entire game codebase. For example, altering the way NPCs react to player actions or introducing new in-game events can be done by updating the DSL scripts rather than reworking the core code. This modularity makes the game development process more agile and responsive to changes, helping teams experiment with new features and designs with minimal overhead.

Examining the Impact of the DSL on Game Performance

While DSLs in game development provide substantial improvements in workflow and flexibility, they can also have an impact on game performance. The performance of a game can be influenced by the way the DSL scripts are translated into executable code. A well-designed DSL can generate highly optimized code for specific game engines, ensuring that the performance remains high. However, if the DSL is too abstracted or inefficient in terms of resource management, it can lead to performance bottlenecks that hinder the game's responsiveness or frame rate.

To mitigate performance issues, developers must focus on optimizing the DSL interpreter or compiler, ensuring that it generates efficient code. Profiling tools and benchmarking can help identify and resolve performance problems, ensuring that the DSL does not introduce unnecessary overhead. Additionally, the DSL must be integrated carefully with the game engine to avoid conflicts between high-level scripting and low-level engine optimizations.

Challenges and Future Directions in Game Development DSLs

Despite the many benefits of DSLs in game development, challenges remain in their design, integration, and maintenance. One significant challenge is ensuring that the DSL remains flexible enough to accommodate the evolving requirements of the game while maintaining efficiency and scalability. Additionally, game engines are constantly evolving, and DSLs must adapt to these changes without causing disruptions to the game's core systems.

Another challenge is ensuring that game designers can efficiently learn and adopt the DSL. While the goal of a DSL is to simplify development, there may still be a learning curve, particularly for those unfamiliar with programming concepts. Comprehensive documentation, tutorials, and a user-friendly development environment are essential to ease this transition.

Looking toward the future, DSLs in game development could evolve to support more advanced features, such as real-time code generation, interactive debugging tools, or the integration of AI-driven behavior scripting. As game development technologies advance, DSLs will need to adapt to new challenges, such as virtual reality (VR) and augmented reality (AR) games, to provide continued value.

The use of DSLs in game development offers a wide array of benefits, including enhanced workflow, greater design flexibility, and a streamlined development process. However, challenges related to performance optimization, integration, and learning curves must be carefully managed. As game development technologies evolve, DSLs will continue to play a vital role in shaping the future of the industry.

Designing a Domain-Specific Language for Game Scripting

Designing a domain-specific language (DSL) for game scripting involves creating a custom language that allows developers to express game behavior and mechanics in an intuitive, high-level manner. In game development, where game logic can become quite complex, a DSL provides a more natural way of programming game actions, interactions, and events. A DSL for game scripting can significantly reduce the complexity of writing and maintaining game behavior, making the scripting process more efficient and accessible.

Let's consider an example of how we might design a simple DSL for controlling a character's behavior in a game, such as moving and jumping. The DSL needs to be easy to read, understand, and use by non-programmers, such as game designers. The scripting language should abstract the low-level details of game logic and provide high-level constructs for common game actions.

Example: Character Behavior DSL

Imagine a game where a character can walk, jump, or perform various other actions. Below is a basic implementation of how we might design a DSL to handle these actions.

```python
class GameCharacterDSL:
    def __init__(self, name):
        self.name = name
        self.position = 0
        self.is_jumping = False

    def move(self, distance):
        self.position += distance
        print(f"{self.name} moves {distance} units. Current position:
            {self.position}.")

    def jump(self, height):
        if not self.is_jumping:
            self.is_jumping = True
            print(f"{self.name} jumps {height} units high!")
            self.is_jumping = False
        else:
            print(f"{self.name} cannot jump while already in the air.")

# Example of DSL Usage
character = GameCharacterDSL("Hero")

character.move(10)
character.jump(5)
character.move(15)
```

Explanation

In the code above, we've created a simple DSL for controlling a GameCharacter through its move and jump methods. The GameCharacterDSL class allows game designers to use a higher-level, human-readable syntax to describe character actions like moving and jumping. The DSL abstracts the underlying game logic and simplifies the interaction with game mechanics.

For example, character.move(10) tells the character to move 10 units forward, and character.jump(5) makes the character jump to a height of 5 units. The advantage of this

DSL is that it allows game designers, who may not be familiar with low-level programming, to focus on the game logic rather than implementation details.

DSL Syntax

The syntax we've designed for this DSL is both simple and flexible. It uses natural language constructs (move, jump, etc.), which closely reflect the actions game designers are thinking about when creating gameplay. This makes it easier for them to grasp the logic and quickly make changes without needing deep programming knowledge.

However, for the DSL to be effective in a larger game environment, we would also need to extend it with additional features, such as handling animations, interactions with other game objects, or complex logic like pathfinding. This requires careful planning to ensure the DSL remains flexible and scalable, as well as easy to integrate into the existing game engine.

By designing a DSL for game scripting, we are able to abstract away much of the complexity inherent in game development. A well-designed DSL can significantly increase productivity, especially for non-programmers, by enabling them to create, modify, and control game behaviors more intuitively. The next step would be to integrate this DSL into a broader game engine environment for practical use in real-world game projects.

Workflow Improvements and Game Design Flexibility

The introduction of a Domain-Specific Language (DSL) for game scripting provides a transformative impact on game design workflows. Traditional game scripting often involves manipulating low-level code, which can be cumbersome and error-prone, particularly when multiple game designers or non-programmers are involved. A DSL abstracts complex operations, providing a more user-friendly interface for game mechanics. By allowing designers to work at a higher level of abstraction, DSLs improve efficiency, foster creativity, and streamline communication among team members.

One of the key benefits of a DSL in game development is the flexibility it offers in modifying and iterating on game design. With a DSL, designers can quickly tweak game behavior and mechanics without waiting for a developer to write or debug the underlying code. This flexibility is essential for rapid prototyping and iteration, a common requirement in game development.

Let's explore an example that demonstrates how a DSL can enhance workflow flexibility. We will look at how a simple game mechanic, such as a timed event (e.g., a character reaching a certain location), can be expressed and modified within a DSL. This example will show how designers can easily adjust game behavior and test out new ideas without needing a developer to intervene.

Example: Timed Event DSL

In a game, certain actions might need to be triggered after a specific amount of time has passed, such as unlocking a door after a player reaches a certain position. This feature can be abstracted and controlled using a DSL. Below is an implementation of a timed event system in a game scripting DSL:

```python
import time

class GameEventDSL:
    def __init__(self, game_character):
        self.game_character = game_character
        self.events = []

    def add_timed_event(self, event_time, event_action):
        self.events.append({"time": event_time, "action": event_action})

    def execute_events(self):
        start_time = time.time()
        while self.events:
            current_time = time.time() - start_time
            for event in self.events:
                if current_time >= event["time"]:
                    event["action"]()
                    self.events.remove(event)
                    print(f"Event triggered at {current_time:.2f} seconds!")

# Example of DSL Usage
def unlock_door():
    print("The door is now unlocked.")

def on_character_reach_goal():
    print("Character reached the goal!")

character = GameCharacterDSL("Hero")
game_event_dsl = GameEventDSL(character)

# Setting up timed events
game_event_dsl.add_timed_event(2, unlock_door)  # Unlock door after 2 seconds
game_event_dsl.add_timed_event(5, on_character_reach_goal)  # Character reaches
        goal after 5 seconds

# Simulating game loop
game_event_dsl.execute_events()
```

Explanation

In the example, the GameEventDSL class allows game designers to schedule events based on time. The add_timed_event method allows designers to specify an event to trigger after a set amount of time has passed. This is useful for timed game mechanics such as triggering an event when a player crosses a certain point or when a countdown reaches zero.

For example, the DSL user can add events like unlocking a door or triggering a specific character behavior at predetermined times in the game. The system then executes these events based on the passage of time, making it easy for designers to schedule and modify game actions.

With this DSL, the game designer doesn't need to write complex code to handle event timing. Instead, they can focus on describing the event in high-level terms and let the DSL handle the implementation details. This abstraction makes it much easier for non-programmers to engage in game design and reduce errors that might occur when manually coding time-based events.

Benefits for Workflow

The flexibility provided by the DSL streamlines the workflow, making it possible for game designers to rapidly prototype and iterate on gameplay elements. For example, a designer can tweak the timing of events or change the conditions under which certain actions are triggered without requiring any involvement from developers. This rapid iteration is crucial in game design, where testing and adjusting game mechanics on the fly are common.

Moreover, this flexibility also leads to clearer communication within teams. Designers can describe complex game logic in a simplified manner, leading to fewer misunderstandings and faster development cycles.

The ability to quickly and easily define game mechanics using a DSL leads to significant improvements in workflow and flexibility. By abstracting away the complexities of traditional game programming, designers can focus on creative aspects and rapidly prototype features. In turn, this increases productivity, reduces bottlenecks, and enhances the overall development process, enabling quicker iterations and more refined gameplay experiences.

Examining the Impact of the DSL on Game Performance

When developing games, performance is a critical factor that affects the player's experience. A Domain-Specific Language (DSL) can have both positive and negative impacts on performance, depending on how it is implemented. By abstracting away low-level code, DSLs often make game development more accessible and efficient for designers. However, this abstraction can introduce inefficiencies that may compromise the performance of the game, especially in resource-intensive operations. It is important to carefully evaluate the impact of a DSL on performance, especially when it comes to real-time gameplay mechanics.

Impact on Performance

DSLs are designed to make the scripting process easier by abstracting complex logic into simple, high-level constructs. However, this abstraction layer can result in slower execution times compared to manually optimized code. For example, when a DSL is used to define complex game logic, the runtime must parse and interpret the high-level commands, which can introduce overhead. The key challenge is finding the balance between simplifying the development process and maintaining acceptable performance levels.

One area where performance may be affected is in the execution of complex game physics or AI. For example, if a game uses a DSL to define character movements or AI behavior, the DSL might include high-level constructs like "move character towards target" instead of the low-level code that calculates exact physics-based movements. While this approach makes the code simpler to write, it may not be as optimized as using low-level game engines that perform physics calculations directly in C++ or other performant languages.

Example: Optimizing Game Physics DSL

Let's take the case of game physics, where a DSL can be used to specify character movements in a game world. A DSL might provide a simple abstraction like move_towards(target_position), but this can hide the actual physics calculations necessary to ensure smooth and realistic motion. The DSL might interpret this simple command by converting it into several lower-level commands that simulate the physics behind the movement.

Here's an example of a simple DSL that abstracts character movement in a game:

```
class GameCharacter:
    def __init__(self, x, y):
        self.x = x
        self.y = y

    def move_towards(self, target_x, target_y):
        # Simplified movement for the DSL (may introduce inefficiencies)
        self.x += (target_x - self.x) * 0.1
        self.y += (target_y - self.y) * 0.1
        print(f"Character moved to ({self.x}, {self.y})")

# Example usage of the DSL
character = GameCharacter(0, 0)
character.move_towards(10, 10)
```

In this example, the move_towards method updates the character's position incrementally, which is a basic abstraction. However, if the game required more complex physics-based movement, such as handling momentum, gravity, or collisions, the DSL approach would likely need to expand to handle these nuances, introducing more computation. This would not only slow down the performance of individual actions but might also increase memory usage as more resources are needed for parsing and interpreting the DSL commands.

Optimizing the DSL for Performance

To ensure that the DSL doesn't degrade performance, various optimization strategies must be employed. One strategy is to use a Just-In-Time (JIT) compiler or a static code generator to compile DSL code into more optimized lower-level code before execution. This ensures that any overhead introduced by the DSL parsing is minimized, and the resulting game logic is executed as efficiently as possible.

Additionally, in performance-critical sections of the game (such as physics or rendering), it may be necessary to bypass the DSL and write low-level, optimized code directly in the host language (e.g., Python, C++) for those specific operations.

The use of DSLs in game development can have both positive and negative impacts on performance. While DSLs simplify development by abstracting complex logic, they can introduce performance overhead due to the need for parsing and interpreting high-level constructs. However, with proper optimization techniques, such as JIT compilation and selective use of low-level code, these performance issues can be mitigated, allowing developers to maintain a balance between productivity and efficiency.

Challenges and Future Directions in Game Development DSLs

Designing and implementing Domain-Specific Languages (DSLs) for game development presents unique challenges. While DSLs offer significant productivity benefits, such as simplifying game logic and workflows, they also introduce various obstacles that developers must address. These challenges can range from performance concerns to integrating the DSL with existing game engines and ensuring that the DSL scales as the game becomes more complex.

Challenges in Game Development DSLs

One of the key challenges in game development DSLs is ensuring that the DSL remains performant while still abstracting the necessary complexity. As discussed in the previous section, performance can be a major issue when the abstraction layer adds too much overhead, particularly in computation-heavy areas such as physics, AI, or rendering. For example, handling real-time physics or complex animations within a DSL could slow down the gameplay experience if not optimized properly. Game developers must balance the ease of use offered by a DSL with the potential performance drawbacks it may introduce.

Another challenge is integration with existing game engines. Most modern games are built on top of complex game engines such as Unity or Unreal Engine, which use their own scripting languages and frameworks. Integrating a custom DSL into such systems can be difficult, as the DSL needs to interact with the engine's built-in API and manage data across different parts of the system. This requires designing a robust bridge between the DSL and the underlying engine, which could complicate the development process.

Furthermore, scalability is an issue that becomes evident as the game grows. A DSL that works well for a small prototype or simple game may struggle to scale effectively as the game grows in complexity. New game features, additional assets, and expanding game worlds might require significant changes to the DSL to maintain usability and flexibility. Without careful planning, the DSL could become a bottleneck in terms of both performance and development time.

Future Directions

Despite these challenges, DSLs continue to offer a promising direction for game development. One future direction is the integration of DSLs with modern game engines in a way that minimizes overhead. One possibility is the use of Just-In-Time (JIT) compilation, which allows for runtime optimizations that can adapt to the needs of the game. This would help in reducing the overhead of interpreting DSL commands, enabling the high-level abstractions to be compiled into more efficient code for performance-critical tasks.

Another potential future development in game DSLs is the use of machine learning (ML) techniques to optimize game scripting. For example, ML could be used to predict game behaviors or optimize pathfinding algorithms based on previous game data. This integration would allow the DSL to adapt its behavior dynamically, improving both performance and gameplay experience. Additionally, AI-driven tools could help in generating DSL code for various game features, making game development more accessible and less error-prone.

The inclusion of visual elements in DSLs is also an exciting future trend. Graphical DSLs that allow developers to build game logic through intuitive visual interfaces can further reduce development time and improve the accessibility of the game development process. These visual DSLs could integrate directly into game engines and allow designers to work on gameplay mechanics without needing to write complex code manually.

Example: Future of Game DSLs with AI-Driven Development

Imagine a future game DSL that leverages AI to generate optimized code for various gameplay features, such as NPC behavior or terrain generation. For instance, using an AI-powered DSL, a designer could define a high-level command like generate_random_environment() which would result in the DSL generating code for a procedurally generated map, adjusting parameters based on the style of gameplay.

```
# Example of a high-level DSL for terrain generation with AI assistance
class TerrainGenerator:
    def generate_random_environment(self, complexity="medium"):
        if complexity == "low":
            return self.generate_simple_map()
        elif complexity == "high":
            return self.generate_complex_map()
        else:
            return self.generate_balanced_map()

    def generate_simple_map(self):
        return "Simple terrain with few features."

    def generate_complex_map(self):
        return "Complex terrain with multiple biomes and dynamic features."

    def generate_balanced_map(self):
        return "Balanced terrain with variety but manageable complexity."

# AI could help decide the optimal complexity based on previous data
terrain_generator = TerrainGenerator()
terrain = terrain_generator.generate_random_environment(complexity="high")
```

```
print(terrain)
```

In this scenario, the AI could adapt the complexity of the terrain generation based on previous player preferences or actions, optimizing the game world for better player engagement. This type of dynamic and context-sensitive generation is the kind of functionality that future DSLs could offer to improve game development.

The challenges in game development DSLs are significant but not insurmountable. Issues such as performance optimization, engine integration, and scalability require careful consideration and innovative solutions. However, as game development continues to evolve, DSLs have the potential to become even more powerful and efficient, offering new ways to enhance both developer productivity and the player experience. With future advancements in AI, machine learning, and graphical DSLs, the possibilities for the next generation of game development tools are vast and exciting.

Module 30:

Case Study 5 – DSL in Machine Learning

Module 30 explores the application of Domain-Specific Languages (DSLs) in the field of machine learning (ML), particularly focusing on their role in automating machine learning pipelines. This module examines how DSLs can support the development of machine learning models, their successful implementation in AI projects, and their evaluation in real-world scenarios. By discussing case studies and practical applications, this section illustrates the ways DSLs streamline machine learning workflows and improve productivity.

Building a DSL for Machine Learning Pipeline Automation

Creating a DSL for machine learning pipeline automation involves designing a language that simplifies the construction and management of machine learning workflows. These workflows often include steps like data pre-processing, model training, evaluation, and deployment. A DSL can encapsulate these steps in a more declarative and higher-level format, allowing practitioners to express complex pipelines with ease. By abstracting the implementation details, a DSL empowers users to focus on problem-solving and experimentation rather than the intricacies of the underlying framework. This section delves into the design considerations for such a DSL, including how to define the syntax and semantics that facilitate these tasks efficiently.

Supporting the Development of Machine Learning Models with DSLs

Once a DSL is designed, its primary purpose is to facilitate the development of machine learning models. This section covers how DSLs can abstract common tasks in machine learning, such as feature engineering, hyperparameter tuning, and model evaluation. It explores the advantages of using a DSL for these tasks, including the ability to standardize workflows, reduce boilerplate code, and enable reusable components. DSLs can support both traditional machine learning techniques, like regression and classification, as well as newer techniques, such as deep learning. By improving productivity, DSLs help data scientists and machine learning engineers iterate faster and achieve better results.

Case Studies of Successful Implementations in AI

In this section, real-world case studies of DSLs used in AI applications are presented. These case studies highlight the practical benefits of DSLs in machine learning, showcasing how organizations have employed DSLs to streamline their AI projects. For example, some companies have used DSLs to automate feature extraction processes or to manage complex model training pipelines. These case studies also illustrate how DSLs have been integrated with popular machine learning frameworks like TensorFlow, Keras, and Scikit-learn, demonstrating their ability to complement existing technologies. The success stories emphasize how DSLs have led to better scalability, reduced human error, and enhanced collaboration within teams.

Evaluating the DSL's Effectiveness in Real-World Projects

Evaluating the effectiveness of a DSL in real-world machine learning projects involves assessing its impact on various aspects of the workflow, including efficiency, usability, and performance. This section focuses on the challenges of measuring the return on investment (ROI) when using a DSL in machine learning, as well as the key performance indicators (KPIs) to consider. Key factors include the reduction of manual coding, the improvement of automation in data pipelines, and the ease with which models can be deployed. Additionally, the section discusses feedback from end users and the iterative process of refining the DSL based on real-world usage.

This module highlights the growing importance of DSLs in machine learning, particularly in automating workflows and improving productivity. By examining the design and application of DSLs in the context of AI and real-world machine learning projects, it becomes clear that DSLs provide a powerful tool for enhancing collaboration, standardizing processes, and driving faster, more efficient development of machine learning models.

Building a DSL for Machine Learning Pipeline Automation

In this section, we will walk through the process of building a DSL for automating machine learning (ML) pipelines. We'll discuss the steps involved in defining a custom language that simplifies the ML pipeline creation and execution, abstracting away the technical details while making it easier for users to work with complex workflows.

Step 1: Define the DSL Syntax

The first task is to design the syntax of the DSL. The syntax should be intuitive and close to the logical flow of a machine learning pipeline. Let's consider a simple DSL syntax for the steps of a typical ML pipeline, such as data loading, preprocessing, training, and evaluation.

```
pipeline {
    load_data("data.csv")
    preprocess_data(scale=True, normalize=True)
    train_model(model="RandomForest", parameters={"n_estimators": 100})
    evaluate_model()
}
```

In this DSL, pipeline is the entry point, and inside it, we define the sequence of steps involved in the ML process. Each step is a function or operation like load_data, preprocess_data, train_model, and evaluate_model.

Step 2: Implement the DSL Parser

Once we have the syntax defined, we need to implement a parser that can process this DSL code. We'll use Python to implement the parser, leveraging libraries such as pyparsing or ANTLR for parsing. The parser will convert the textual DSL into executable code.

Here's a basic Python parser using pyparsing to handle the syntax we defined earlier:

```python
from pyparsing import Word, alphas, Keyword, Optional, Group, Literal

# Define the basic elements
keyword = Keyword("pipeline") | Keyword("load_data") |
            Keyword("preprocess_data") | Keyword("train_model") |
            Keyword("evaluate_model")
data_argument = Word(alphas + "_.")
parameter_argument = Group(Word(alphas) + "=" + Word(alphas + "1234567890"))

# Define the structure of the DSL
pipeline_expr = Literal("pipeline") + Group(Keyword("{") +
            Group(Keyword("load_data") + data_argument) +
            Optional(Keyword("preprocess_data") + parameter_argument) +
            Optional(Keyword("train_model") + parameter_argument) +
            Optional(Keyword("evaluate_model")) + Keyword("}"))

# Parse the DSL expression
pipeline_code = """pipeline {
    load_data("data.csv")
    preprocess_data(scale=True, normalize=True)
    train_model(model="RandomForest", parameters={"n_estimators": 100})
    evaluate_model()
}"""

result = pipeline_expr.parseString(pipeline_code)
print(result)
```

Step 3: Convert DSL to Python Code

Now that we have parsed the DSL, the next step is to convert it into actual Python code that executes the corresponding machine learning tasks. We will write Python functions that map to each of the DSL commands and then generate code dynamically based on the parsed DSL structure.

Here's how we might implement a simple code generator that takes the parsed DSL and executes the respective steps:

```python
def load_data(file_path):
    # Imagine this loads a CSV into a pandas dataframe
    print(f"Loading data from {file_path}")

def preprocess_data(scale=False, normalize=False):
    # Simple preprocessing logic
    if scale:
        print("Scaling data...")
    if normalize:
        print("Normalizing data...")

def train_model(model_name, parameters):
    # A basic model training placeholder
    print(f"Training {model_name} with parameters {parameters}")

def evaluate_model():
```

```
        # Placeholder for model evaluation
        print("Evaluating model...")

    # Function to convert the parsed DSL into executable steps
    def execute_pipeline(parsed_code):
        for step in parsed_code:
            if step[0] == "load_data":
                load_data(step[1])
            elif step[0] == "preprocess_data":
                preprocess_data(*step[1])
            elif step[0] == "train_model":
                train_model(step[1], step[2])
            elif step[0] == "evaluate_model":
                evaluate_model()

    # Parse the DSL code and execute it
    parsed_code = result[1][0]
    execute_pipeline(parsed_code)
```

Step 4: Execution and Automation

Once the pipeline has been parsed and translated into Python code, the functions load_data, preprocess_data, train_model, and evaluate_model will execute the actual tasks in the ML pipeline. This approach abstracts away the technicalities of interacting with libraries like pandas, scikit-learn, or TensorFlow, providing a simplified interface for users.

For example, when the pipeline is executed, the output might look like this:

```
Loading data from data.csv
Scaling data...
Normalizing data...
Training RandomForest with parameters {'n_estimators': 100}
Evaluating model...
```

By using this DSL, users can easily build, modify, and execute machine learning pipelines without needing to dive deep into the implementation details of each step.

This section demonstrates how to build a custom DSL for automating machine learning pipelines. We've covered the syntax design, parsing process, and conversion to Python code that runs the machine learning workflow. DSLs like this can make complex ML tasks more manageable and provide a high-level abstraction that is more accessible to users.

Supporting the Development of Machine Learning Models with DSLs

In this section, we explore how a custom DSL can support the development of machine learning models by providing high-level abstractions for model creation, training, and evaluation. This approach allows non-expert users to work with machine learning models without needing to write low-level code, streamlining the development process.

Step 1: Designing the DSL for Model Definition

The DSL should provide a simple and intuitive syntax to define machine learning models. Let's consider a basic DSL syntax for defining a model, including specifying its type (e.g., regression or classification), selecting features, and setting hyperparameters. This approach abstracts the model creation process and makes it more accessible.

Here's an example of how the DSL might look:

```
model {
    type: RandomForest
    target: "price"
    features: ["age", "mileage", "brand"]
    hyperparameters: {"n_estimators": 100, "max_depth": 10}
}
```

In this example, the DSL defines a RandomForest model that predicts the target variable price using features such as age, mileage, and brand. The model also includes hyperparameters such as the number of estimators and the maximum depth.

Step 2: Parsing the Model Definition

We now need to parse this DSL syntax into a form that can be translated into Python code. Using the Python pyparsing library, we can create a parser that extracts the model type, target, features, and hyperparameters from the DSL.

Here's a Python code example to parse the model definition:

```
from pyparsing import Word, alphas, Literal, Group, Dict

# Define the components of the model DSL
keyword = Literal("model")
model_type = Keyword("type") + ":" + Word(alphas)
target = Keyword("target") + ":" + Word(alphas)
features = Keyword("features") + ":" + Group(Literal("[") + Word(alphas + " ,")
        + Literal("]"))
hyperparameters = Keyword("hyperparameters") + ":" + Dict(Literal("{") +
        Word(alphas) + ":" + Word(alphas) + Literal("}"))

# Combine components into the model expression
model_expr = keyword + Group(model_type + target + features + hyperparameters)

# Example model DSL code
model_code = """model {
    type: RandomForest
    target: "price"
    features: ["age", "mileage", "brand"]
    hyperparameters: {"n_estimators": 100, "max_depth": 10}
}"""

# Parse the DSL code
parsed_model = model_expr.parseString(model_code)
print(parsed_model)
```

Step 3: Converting the DSL to Python Code

Once we've parsed the DSL, the next task is to translate it into Python code that can be executed. In this case, we need to create a RandomForest model using the scikit-learn library, set its hyperparameters, and prepare it for training.

Here's how to convert the parsed DSL into Python code for model creation:

```python
from sklearn.ensemble import RandomForestRegressor

def build_model(parsed_code):
    # Extract the model type, target, features, and hyperparameters
    model_type = parsed_code[1][0]
    target = parsed_code[1][1]
    features = parsed_code[1][2]
    hyperparameters = parsed_code[1][3]

    # Initialize the model
    if model_type == "RandomForest":
        model = RandomForestRegressor(**hyperparameters)

    # Return the model and feature set
    return model, features, target

# Parse the model code and build the model
model, features, target = build_model(parsed_model)
print(f"Model: {model}")
print(f"Features: {features}")
print(f"Target: {target}")
```

This function initializes a RandomForestRegressor with the specified hyperparameters. The model, feature set, and target variable are returned for further use in training and evaluation.

Step 4: Automating the Model Training Process

Once the model has been created, we can automate the training process by simply adding a few more steps to the DSL. For instance, we can define how the model is trained and evaluated. Here's an extension to the DSL that includes training and evaluation:

```
pipeline {
    model {
        type: RandomForest
        target: "price"
        features: ["age", "mileage", "brand"]
        hyperparameters: {"n_estimators": 100, "max_depth": 10}
    }
    train_model(data="train.csv")
    evaluate_model()
}
```

In this example, the train_model and evaluate_model steps are added to the pipeline, automating the entire workflow from model creation to evaluation.

The code to execute this extended pipeline would involve loading the data, training the model, and evaluating it. Here's a simplified version of the code:

```python
import pandas as pd
from sklearn.model_selection import train_test_split
from sklearn.metrics import mean_squared_error

def train_and_evaluate(model, data_file, target_column):
    # Load data
    data = pd.read_csv(data_file)
```

```
    # Split data into features and target
    X = data[features]
    y = data[target_column]

    # Split into training and testing sets
    X_train, X_test, y_train, y_test = train_test_split(X, y, test_size=0.2,
        random_state=42)

    # Train the model
    model.fit(X_train, y_train)

    # Evaluate the model
    y_pred = model.predict(X_test)
    mse = mean_squared_error(y_test, y_pred)
    print(f"Mean Squared Error: {mse}")

# Use the trained model and evaluate it
train_and_evaluate(model, "train.csv", target)
```

This section demonstrates how a custom DSL can be used to simplify the process of defining and automating machine learning models. By abstracting away the details of model creation, training, and evaluation, the DSL makes it easier for non-experts to work with machine learning models while maintaining the flexibility required for advanced use cases.

Case Studies of Successful Implementations in AI

In this section, we will examine real-world case studies where domain-specific languages (DSLs) were successfully implemented in the field of artificial intelligence (AI). These examples will demonstrate how DSLs can significantly enhance productivity, ease the development of AI systems, and optimize the workflow for machine learning (ML) engineers.

Case Study 1: DSL for Natural Language Processing (NLP)

In the NLP domain, the development of DSLs has helped create intuitive workflows for text preprocessing, feature extraction, model training, and evaluation. A successful example of a DSL in NLP is one designed for simplifying the task of text classification. This DSL abstracts the common machine learning operations like vectorization, feature extraction, and model selection into high-level constructs. The model can be trained using simple, human-readable code such as:

```
pipeline {
    data: "text_data.csv"
    preprocess: "remove_stopwords, tokenize"
    vectorizer: "TF-IDF"
    model {
        type: SVM
        hyperparameters: {"kernel": "linear", "C": 1.0}
    }
    train_model()
    evaluate_model()
}
```

315

In this DSL, the operations are abstracted as high-level commands like remove_stopwords, tokenize, and TF-IDF. This simplifies the workflow for text classification. The pipeline processes data, trains the model, and evaluates it, all within a few lines of code. This DSL significantly speeds up the development time for NLP tasks, as the user does not need to write detailed low-level code for each step.

Case Study 2: DSL for Image Classification

In the domain of computer vision, DSLs have been used to automate the creation and training of deep learning models. One example is a DSL created for image classification tasks using convolutional neural networks (CNNs). This DSL abstracts common operations in image classification, including data augmentation, model building, training, and evaluation.

Here's how the DSL might look for defining a CNN model for image classification:

```
model {
    type: CNN
    layers: [Conv2D(32, kernel_size=(3,3)), MaxPooling2D(pool_size=(2,2))]
    dense: [128, softmax]
    optimizer: Adam
    loss: categorical_crossentropy
}

pipeline {
    data: "image_data.csv"
    preprocess: "resize_images, normalize"
    model: CNN
    train_model()
    evaluate_model()
}
```

This DSL defines a CNN with specific layers such as Conv2D and MaxPooling2D, making it easier for developers to experiment with architectures by changing just a few lines. The model's hyperparameters, such as optimizer and loss function, are also specified in a concise and human-readable way. This allows AI researchers to quickly iterate on different model designs without getting bogged down in the complexities of code.

Case Study 3: DSL for Reinforcement Learning

Reinforcement learning (RL) has many complexities, especially in terms of defining environments, agents, and reward functions. DSLs can simplify these complexities and help developers quickly prototype RL systems. One successful case study is a DSL used to define and train RL agents within a simulated environment, specifically for gaming AI.

Here's a sample of how the DSL might be used to define an RL environment and agent:

```
environment {
    type: GridWorld
    size: (10, 10)
}
```

```
agent {
    type: QLearningAgent
    action_space: ["up", "down", "left", "right"]
    learning_rate: 0.1
    gamma: 0.9
}

pipeline {
    environment: GridWorld
    agent: QLearningAgent
    train_agent(episodes=1000)
    evaluate_agent()
}
```

In this example, the GridWorld environment is defined with a specific size, and the agent uses the Q-learning algorithm. This DSL abstracts the definition of environments and agents, allowing developers to focus on higher-level aspects of their models, such as the environment size, actions, and learning parameters. It also enables rapid experimentation with various environments and agent configurations.

Case Study 4: DSL for Automated Hyperparameter Tuning

One of the challenges in machine learning is the tedious task of tuning hyperparameters to improve model performance. A DSL can automate the process of hyperparameter tuning, thus saving considerable time and effort. In this case, the DSL can be used to define a search space for hyperparameters and then run experiments to optimize the model.

For instance, a DSL used for hyperparameter tuning might look like this:

```
hyperparameters {
    n_estimators: [50, 100, 200]
    max_depth: [5, 10, 15]
}

model {
    type: RandomForest
    hyperparameters: hyperparameters
}

pipeline {
    data: "train_data.csv"
    model: RandomForest
    hyperparameter_tuning()
    evaluate_model()
}
```

This DSL allows specifying a range of hyperparameters for n_estimators and max_depth, and then the DSL automatically runs experiments to evaluate the model with different hyperparameter combinations. The system then evaluates the model's performance based on the defined metrics. This reduces the need for manual tuning and accelerates model optimization.

These case studies demonstrate how DSLs can greatly streamline the development of AI systems. By abstracting complex tasks such as model definition, data preprocessing, and hyperparameter tuning, DSLs help developers focus on high-level design and

317

experimentation. These examples showcase the flexibility, power, and efficiency DSLs bring to the AI development process.

Evaluating the DSL's Effectiveness in Real-World Projects

In this section, we will explore how to evaluate the effectiveness of a domain-specific language (DSL) in real-world machine learning (ML) projects. By analyzing various metrics and feedback from end-users, we can assess how well the DSL meets its objectives and whether it truly enhances productivity, reduces complexity, and supports the goals of machine learning workflows.

Performance Metrics for DSL Effectiveness

The first step in evaluating the effectiveness of a DSL is to define appropriate performance metrics. In the context of machine learning, key metrics include the speed of model development, the ease of model training, the reduction in code complexity, and improvements in reproducibility and maintainability. A DSL should ideally speed up the prototyping phase, allow easy configuration of ML models, and produce consistent results across different environments.

To evaluate these aspects, we can compare the time taken to complete tasks such as feature extraction, model training, and hyperparameter tuning between projects using a DSL and traditional programming approaches. For instance, the following DSL-based pipeline for training a model might be compared to manually coding the steps in Python.

```
pipeline {
    data: "training_data.csv"
    preprocess: "clean_data, normalize"
    model: "LogisticRegression"
    hyperparameters: {"C": 1.0, "solver": "liblinear"}
    train_model()
    evaluate_model()
}
```

In this example, using a DSL allows developers to define a training pipeline in just a few lines, compared to the traditional Python code which would require manually setting up preprocessing, model initialization, and training steps. The speed difference between these two approaches can serve as one key metric.

User Feedback and Usability

Another crucial aspect of evaluating a DSL is user feedback. Since DSLs are tailored for specific domains, they should be intuitive for the target users. Feedback from machine learning practitioners is invaluable in assessing how easy it is for them to adopt the DSL in their workflows. Common questions to consider include: Do users find the DSL syntax intuitive? Does it simplify the machine learning tasks? Are there any common mistakes users make?

To evaluate usability, users could be asked to perform tasks like building and training a model using the DSL and then using traditional Python code. The time spent and errors encountered in each case can be tracked to quantify improvements in productivity. For example, an evaluation task might look like this:

```
pipeline {
    data: "validation_data.csv"
    preprocess: "tokenize, remove_stopwords"
    model: "RandomForest"
    hyperparameters: {"n_estimators": 100, "max_depth": 10}
    evaluate_model()
}
```

This task, done through the DSL, can be compared to the manual implementation of the same operations in Python to determine how much time and effort the DSL saves. If users report high satisfaction and faster completion times, this indicates that the DSL effectively simplifies the ML process.

Maintainability and Flexibility

DSLs are not only designed for speed but also for maintainability. Evaluating how easily the DSL can adapt to new requirements, such as changes in model types or hyperparameters, is essential. A well-designed DSL should allow users to quickly modify and extend their models without requiring a complete rewrite of code. If the DSL supports modular and reusable components, developers can avoid redundancy and improve long-term maintainability.

For instance, a DSL-based pipeline for testing different models might look like this:

```
pipeline {
    data: "train_data.csv"
    preprocess: "clean_data, scale"
    model: "SVM"
    hyperparameters: {"kernel": "linear", "C": 1.0}
    train_model()
    evaluate_model()
}
```

If a user wants to switch from SVM to a decision tree model, it can be done by simply modifying the model field, without needing to rewrite the entire pipeline or change how preprocessing is handled. This flexibility and modularity contribute to the DSL's overall effectiveness.

Scalability and Adaptation to Larger Projects

Finally, evaluating the scalability of the DSL in larger, more complex projects is crucial. As machine learning projects grow in size and scope, it's important that the DSL can handle large datasets, more sophisticated models, and more intricate workflows. A successful DSL should enable users to scale their workflows seamlessly, whether that means working with massive datasets or training complex models with many hyperparameters.

For example, the DSL might include commands for distributing computations across multiple nodes or using GPU acceleration for training large models, like so:

```
pipeline {
    data: "large_train_data.csv"
    preprocess: "normalize, feature_selection"
    model: "NeuralNetwork"
    resources: "GPU"
    hyperparameters: {"layers": [128, 64], "batch_size": 32}
    train_model()
    evaluate_model()
}
```

This support for distributed computing can improve performance when scaling to larger projects, making the DSL effective even in high-demand environments.

Evaluating the effectiveness of a DSL in machine learning projects requires considering various metrics such as speed, user feedback, maintainability, and scalability. The success of a DSL can be measured by how well it simplifies the development process, enhances productivity, and adapts to real-world needs. By comparing DSL-based workflows with traditional programming approaches, we can demonstrate the DSL's value and identify areas for future improvement.

Part 6:

Research Directions in Domain Specific Languages

As the field of domain-specific languages (DSLs) continues to expand, research efforts focus on refining their design, improving tool support, and addressing long-term sustainability challenges. This part explores the emerging trends shaping DSL development, including AI-powered automation, cloud-based DSLs, and cross-domain applications. It examines the future evolution of DSL frameworks, the challenges of maintaining DSLs over time, and the growing role of DSLs in software engineering. Additionally, it highlights ongoing research in parsing, code generation, and industrial adoption, providing a forward-looking perspective on the impact of DSLs on technology.

Emerging Trends in DSL Design

The landscape of DSLs is rapidly evolving with advancements in technology, leading to several notable trends. One significant shift is the rise of visual programming languages, which allow users to define domain-specific behavior using intuitive graphical interfaces rather than text-based syntax. These visual DSLs are particularly beneficial in fields such as robotics, workflow automation, and data science, where users may not have traditional programming expertise. Another emerging trend is the integration of artificial intelligence and machine learning with DSLs, enabling intelligent code generation, optimization, and adaptive behavior based on learned patterns. Cloud-based DSLs are also gaining prominence, offering scalable and distributed execution environments that facilitate real-time collaboration and remote processing. Additionally, cross-domain DSL applications are expanding, bridging traditionally isolated disciplines such as bioinformatics, cybersecurity, and embedded systems through shared DSL methodologies.

Future Directions for DSL Tools and Frameworks

To support the growing complexity of DSL applications, research focuses on improving the tools and frameworks used to develop and maintain DSLs. New development environments are emerging, integrating AI-assisted debugging, automated performance profiling, and real-time collaboration features to enhance productivity. Improvements in DSL performance, such as optimized runtime execution and enhanced memory management, are key areas of focus. The evolution of tools for both embedded and external DSLs aims to strike a balance between ease of use and expressiveness, making DSL adoption more accessible across industries. Open-source DSL frameworks are playing a crucial role in this transformation, encouraging community contributions and fostering innovation in DSL research. These frameworks are expected to drive standardization efforts, allowing developers to build upon existing solutions rather than reinventing core DSL components.

Challenges in DSL Evolution and Maintenance

While DSLs offer significant benefits, their long-term sustainability remains a challenge. As domains evolve, DSLs must adapt to new requirements without breaking existing implementations. Maintaining backward compatibility is particularly difficult, as changes to DSL syntax or semantics may render older scripts or models obsolete. Effective versioning strategies, such as semantic versioning and automated migration tools, are essential for managing DSL evolution. Another challenge is ensuring that DSLs remain usable and well-documented over time, requiring dedicated support and continuous development efforts. Research in long-term DSL sustainability focuses on methods to automate updates, refactor legacy DSLs, and provide compatibility layers that bridge different DSL versions.

The Role of DSLs in Future Software Development

DSLs are expected to play an increasingly central role in modern software development, particularly in agile and DevOps environments where rapid iteration and automation are crucial. By abstracting domain logic into specialized languages, DSLs enable teams to streamline development workflows and reduce the complexity of traditional programming approaches. Collaborative development using DSLs is another promising area, allowing domain experts, software engineers, and data scientists to work together using domain-specific abstractions. As software systems grow more complex, DSLs provide a structured approach to managing modularity, ensuring maintainability, and improving software reliability. The ability of DSLs to enforce domain constraints and reduce the likelihood of errors makes them an indispensable tool in high-assurance software engineering.

Research Directions in Parsing and Code Generation for DSLs

Parsing and code generation remain fundamental aspects of DSL research, with ongoing advancements improving efficiency and flexibility. New parsing algorithms leverage machine learning and statistical analysis to enhance error detection and code completion in DSLs. Additionally, just-in-time (JIT) compilation techniques are being adapted for DSLs, enabling on-the-fly code generation optimized for specific runtime conditions. The development of more efficient abstract syntax tree (AST) representations and intermediate representations (IRs) further contributes to performance improvements. Research into optimizing DSL execution through better parsing techniques aims to reduce computational overhead while maintaining expressiveness. These advancements pave the way for DSLs that are more responsive, adaptable, and capable of handling complex domain requirements.

The Future of Domain-Specific Languages in Industry

The adoption of DSLs across industries continues to grow as organizations recognize their ability to increase productivity and enforce domain-specific best practices. Sectors such as finance, healthcare, manufacturing, and cybersecurity are already leveraging DSLs for automation, regulatory compliance, and system optimization. The future impact of DSLs on software engineering practices will likely include greater emphasis on domain-driven design, increased reliance on AI-generated DSL constructs, and deeper integration with cloud-based infrastructures. As DSLs evolve, they are expected to play a pivotal role in reducing development time, lowering costs, and enhancing software quality. The continued expansion of DSL applications underscores the need for further research into standardization, interoperability, and performance optimization.

This part provides a forward-looking exploration of DSL research, equipping readers with insights into emerging trends, future tools, and industry adoption. Understanding these developments will help developers and researchers stay ahead in the evolving landscape of DSLs.

Module 31:
Emerging Trends in DSL Design

Module 31 delves into the emerging trends shaping the design and development of domain-specific languages (DSLs). It explores the rise of visual programming languages, the integration of AI and machine learning with DSLs, the shift towards cloud-based DSLs, and the increasing use of DSLs across multiple domains. These trends are revolutionizing how DSLs are used to boost productivity in specialized fields, allowing for more intuitive, scalable, and adaptable solutions.

The Rise of Visual Programming Languages

Visual programming languages (VPLs) are gaining popularity as an alternative to traditional text-based DSLs. By representing code and logic through graphical elements, such as icons, diagrams, and flowcharts, VPLs offer a more intuitive and user-friendly interface for developers, especially those without extensive programming backgrounds. This section will explore how VPLs enable users to design and manage complex workflows or processes with minimal coding, making them ideal for applications in areas such as robotics, IoT, and business process automation. With advancements in graphical user interfaces and drag-and-drop functionality, VPLs are evolving into powerful tools for building and automating domain-specific applications.

AI and Machine Learning Integration with DSLs

The integration of AI and machine learning with DSLs is becoming increasingly essential for automating complex decision-making processes and enabling intelligent applications. AI-powered DSLs allow for the creation of more efficient and adaptive models, tailored to the specific needs of the domain they serve. This section will examine how machine learning techniques, such as reinforcement learning and neural networks, can be integrated into DSLs to enhance their functionality. It will also discuss how these integrations enable domain experts to utilize DSLs without requiring deep expertise in AI, making advanced machine learning accessible to a wider audience. The impact of AI and machine learning on DSL development is significant, enabling more sophisticated, predictive, and autonomous applications.

Cloud-based DSLs and Distributed Systems

With the increasing demand for scalability and accessibility, cloud-based DSLs are emerging as a game-changer in distributed system development. Cloud-based DSLs allow developers to design and deploy applications without worrying about underlying infrastructure or hardware limitations. These DSLs facilitate the creation of scalable solutions that leverage cloud computing resources, ensuring high availability and fault tolerance. In this section, we will explore how cloud-based DSLs are designed to integrate seamlessly with distributed systems, enabling developers to focus on their domain-specific tasks while abstracting away complex system management concerns. The shift towards cloud-native DSLs enhances productivity by streamlining development processes and fostering greater collaboration in distributed environments.

Cross-domain DSL Applications

As DSLs evolve, their applicability is expanding beyond individual domains to address challenges across multiple industries. Cross-domain DSLs are designed to integrate various specialized fields, allowing for more comprehensive solutions that bridge gaps between different domains. This section will focus on the potential of cross-domain DSLs to enable collaboration between experts from various industries, facilitating the creation of more integrated and adaptive systems. For example, DSLs used in finance, healthcare, and logistics may share components that allow seamless interaction and data exchange. We will explore how these DSLs can help standardize processes across different sectors, improve interoperability, and create systems that are both flexible and scalable across multiple domains.

The emerging trends in DSL design reflect the ongoing shift towards more intuitive, scalable, and adaptable solutions in specialized fields. Visual programming languages, AI and machine learning integration, cloud-based DSLs, and cross-domain applications are transforming how DSLs are developed and used. As these trends continue to evolve, they promise to expand the capabilities and impact of DSLs across industries, ultimately enhancing productivity and enabling more sophisticated solutions.

The Rise of Visual Programming Languages

Visual programming languages (VPLs) represent a significant departure from traditional text-based DSLs. By enabling users to create applications using visual elements like diagrams, flowcharts, and icons, VPLs make it easier to design, manipulate, and understand complex logic and systems. These languages are particularly useful for non-programmers or domain experts who want to automate workflows or build applications without delving deep into traditional coding. VPLs offer a more intuitive and visual approach, streamlining development processes and allowing more accessibility to a wider audience.

A key advantage of VPLs is the ability to represent logic and control structures visually, which simplifies the overall design of systems. For instance, in applications such as business process modeling, robotics, and Internet of Things (IoT), VPLs help users model tasks using visual blocks that represent different actions or decisions. This enables easier debugging, collaboration, and visualization of the process flow.

Below is an example of a simple VPL concept in Python, where a visual language is used to model a decision-making process based on user input. The following is a rudimentary Python program representing a visual flowchart using the graphviz library:

```python
from graphviz import Digraph

def create_flowchart():
    # Create a flowchart for decision-making
    dot = Digraph(comment='Decision Making')

    # Start node
    dot.node('A', 'Start')

    # Decision node
    dot.node('B', 'Is the input greater than 10?')

    # Outcome nodes
    dot.node('C', 'Yes')
    dot.node('D', 'No')

    # Connecting nodes
    dot.edge('A', 'B')
    dot.edge('B', 'C', label='True')
    dot.edge('B', 'D', label='False')

    # Render the graph to a file
    dot.render('decision_flowchart', format='png', view=True)

# Example to generate the flowchart
create_flowchart()
```

This example demonstrates the power of visual tools to represent decision-making processes. Although simple, this Python code creates a flowchart where nodes represent decisions and outcomes, and edges define the relationships between them. Such visual representations can be very helpful for non-technical users who want to interact with the system without writing code.

In more advanced VPLs, the concepts of variables, loops, conditionals, and actions can be implemented using intuitive drag-and-drop interfaces. Tools such as Node-RED and Blockly further facilitate this type of interaction, enabling users to build applications by simply connecting blocks of pre-built logic.

As the use of visual programming grows, the need for underlying DSLs that can handle complex logic in an accessible way becomes increasingly important. Visual programming offers a more natural way of expressing domain-specific logic, enabling non-programmers to be more directly involved in the software development process.

Visual programming languages are poised to play a major role in domains like IoT development, robotics, and even education, where the learning curve for coding can be a barrier to entry. With advances in AI, machine learning, and user-friendly interfaces, the future of visual programming looks even more promising.

AI and Machine Learning Integration with DSLs

The integration of Artificial Intelligence (AI) and Machine Learning (ML) with Domain-Specific Languages (DSLs) is a rapidly evolving trend in the software development world. By incorporating AI and ML models into DSLs, developers can create more intelligent and adaptive systems, enabling DSLs to handle tasks that were traditionally outside their scope.

This integration can improve the automation, accuracy, and efficiency of DSLs in various domains, including data processing, decision-making, and predictive analytics.

AI and ML-driven DSLs are designed to simplify the process of working with complex models, making it easier for domain experts to use machine learning techniques without needing deep expertise in data science or programming. These DSLs abstract the technical complexity of machine learning algorithms and provide high-level constructs that allow users to focus on the problem at hand rather than the intricacies of model training and optimization.

For example, consider a simple DSL for automating the training and evaluation of a machine learning model. In Python, this can be done using high-level libraries like scikit-learn. Below is an example of how such a DSL could be created, allowing users to define and evaluate machine learning models with minimal code:

```python
from sklearn.datasets import load_iris
from sklearn.model_selection import train_test_split
from sklearn.ensemble import RandomForestClassifier
from sklearn.metrics import accuracy_score

# Define the DSL for model training
class MLDSL:
    def __init__(self, data):
        self.data = data

    def split_data(self, test_size=0.2):
        self.X_train, self.X_test, self.y_train, self.y_test = train_test_split(
            self.data.data, self.data.target, test_size=test_size)
        return self

    def train_model(self, model=RandomForestClassifier()):
        self.model = model.fit(self.X_train, self.y_train)
        return self

    def evaluate_model(self):
        predictions = self.model.predict(self.X_test)
        accuracy = accuracy_score(self.y_test, predictions)
        print(f"Model Accuracy: {accuracy * 100:.2f}%")
        return accuracy

# Example usage of the DSL
data = load_iris()
ml_dsl = MLDSL(data)
ml_dsl.split_data().train_model().evaluate_model()
```

In this example, the MLDSL class provides an abstraction over the process of training and evaluating a machine learning model. The DSL encapsulates the steps of splitting the data, training a model (in this case, a random forest classifier), and evaluating the model's performance. By using this DSL, domain experts can easily interact with machine learning models without needing to write complex code.

By incorporating machine learning capabilities directly into DSLs, users can quickly customize models for specific tasks, such as predicting market trends, classifying customer behavior, or detecting anomalies in large datasets. This trend is especially powerful in fields like finance, healthcare, and marketing, where domain-specific models can be rapidly developed and deployed to gain insights and make informed decisions.

In the future, AI and machine learning will continue to shape the way DSLs evolve, allowing developers to build more intuitive and intelligent systems. The use of AI-powered DSLs can greatly accelerate the development of predictive models, automation workflows, and data-driven applications, creating more opportunities for non-experts to harness the power of machine learning.

Cloud-Based DSLs and Distributed Systems

The rise of cloud computing has significantly impacted the development and deployment of Domain-Specific Languages (DSLs). Cloud-based DSLs enable developers to build, deploy, and manage applications in distributed systems without dealing with the complexities of infrastructure. Cloud providers like AWS, Google Cloud, and Azure offer a wide range of services that can be integrated with DSLs, making it easier to scale applications and manage distributed resources.

Cloud-based DSLs simplify interactions with distributed systems, allowing developers to focus on application logic rather than the underlying infrastructure. These DSLs enable better resource management, automated scaling, and fault tolerance in the cloud. Additionally, they abstract cloud infrastructure complexities and allow developers to build high-performance applications for distributed environments without requiring in-depth knowledge of cloud-specific APIs and configurations.

A good example of a cloud-based DSL is one that helps deploy applications on cloud environments, configure load balancing, and manage distributed databases. Using a DSL in the context of distributed systems allows users to focus on higher-level objectives like service orchestration, resource allocation, and fault recovery, without worrying about the intricacies of cloud infrastructure.

Consider the following example of a DSL written in Python that helps deploy machine learning models to the cloud:

```python
import boto3

class CloudDSL:
    def __init__(self, region_name="us-west-1"):
        self.s3 = boto3.client('s3', region_name=region_name)
        self.ec2 = boto3.client('ec2', region_name=region_name)
        self.sagemaker = boto3.client('sagemaker', region_name=region_name)

    def upload_model_to_s3(self, model_path, bucket_name):
        try:
            self.s3.upload_file(model_path, bucket_name, 'model.tar.gz')
            print(f"Model uploaded to {bucket_name}")
        except Exception as e:
            print(f"Error uploading model: {e}")

    def create_ec2_instance(self, instance_type="t2.micro", ami_id="ami-12345678"):
```

```python
        try:
            response = self.ec2.run_instances(
                ImageId=ami_id,
                InstanceType=instance_type,
                MinCount=1,
                MaxCount=1
            )
            print(f"EC2 instance created with ID:
            {response['Instances'][0]['InstanceId']}")
        except Exception as e:
            print(f"Error creating EC2 instance: {e}")

    def deploy_model_to_sagemaker(self, model_data_url):
        try:
            response = self.sagemaker.create_model(
                ModelName="MyMLModel",
                PrimaryContainer={
                    'Image': 'my_image_uri',
                    'ModelDataUrl': model_data_url
                }
            )
            print(f"Model deployed to SageMaker: {response['ModelArn']}")
        except Exception as e:
            print(f"Error deploying model: {e}")

# Example Usage
cloud_dsl = CloudDSL()
cloud_dsl.upload_model_to_s3("model.tar.gz", "my-model-bucket")
cloud_dsl.create_ec2_instance()
cloud_dsl.deploy_model_to_sagemaker("s3://my-model-bucket/model.tar.gz")
```

In this example, the CloudDSL class abstracts interactions with AWS services like S3, EC2, and SageMaker. The methods provided allow users to upload models to S3, create EC2 instances for compute resources, and deploy the models using SageMaker for machine learning. This DSL simplifies the deployment process by abstracting low-level cloud-specific APIs and providing high-level functionality.

Cloud-based DSLs help accelerate cloud application development by automating and abstracting cloud-related tasks. Developers can easily manage complex cloud-based architectures, whether they're building scalable web services, managing microservices, or deploying machine learning models. With cloud-based DSLs, users can manage distributed systems seamlessly and efficiently, ensuring better scalability, flexibility, and resource management.

In the future, the trend of cloud-based DSLs is expected to grow even further. These DSLs will continue to evolve to support new cloud platforms, services, and distributed architectures, enabling more efficient workflows, automation, and deployment strategies in cloud environments.

Cross-Domain DSL Applications

Cross-domain Domain-Specific Languages (DSLs) have emerged as an innovative solution to bridge various fields and create versatile, high-level abstractions tailored to specific applications across multiple domains. These DSLs are designed to be applicable in more than one field, often used to solve problems that span diverse industries like finance, healthcare, entertainment, and network management. Cross-domain DSLs aim to maximize the reuse of language constructs while maintaining the flexibility to address unique requirements across different sectors.

The key advantage of cross-domain DSLs is their ability to unify disparate domain-specific knowledge into a single language that can be adapted and extended. These DSLs simplify the process of integrating different domains, ensuring that users from different industries can work with the same core language, while benefiting from specialized language constructs suited for their particular field.

One example of cross-domain DSLs is in the integration of machine learning with web development. A DSL could be created to help build web-based applications that involve AI, allowing users to handle both web components and machine learning models in one language. This approach allows developers to create solutions that span both domains without having to switch between multiple languages or frameworks.

Here is an example of a cross-domain DSL in Python for building a web application that integrates a machine learning model for recommendations:

```
# Cross-domain DSL for Web + Machine Learning
from flask import Flask, render_template
import numpy as np
from sklearn.linear_model import LinearRegression

# Sample machine learning model (linear regression)
class RecommendationModel:
    def __init__(self):
        # Training data: x (years of experience), y (salary)
        self.x = np.array([[1], [2], [3], [4], [5]])
        self.y = np.array([50000, 60000, 70000, 80000, 90000])
        self.model = LinearRegression().fit(self.x, self.y)

    def predict(self, years):
        return self.model.predict([[years]])[0]

# Flask web application setup
app = Flask(__name__)
model = RecommendationModel()

@app.route('/')
def home():
    return render_template('index.html')

@app.route('/predict/<int:years>')
def predict_salary(years):
    salary = model.predict(years)
    return f"Predicted salary for {years} years of experience is ${salary:.2f}"

# Running the web server
if __name__ == "__main__":
    app.run(debug=True)
```

In this example, the Python DSL integrates a web framework (Flask) with machine learning functionality (a simple linear regression model). The RecommendationModel class encapsulates the logic of predicting salaries based on years of experience, while the

Flask routes handle user interaction on the web interface. By using a single DSL, developers can seamlessly integrate machine learning models with web applications, avoiding the need to work with separate tools or languages.

Another example of cross-domain DSLs can be seen in healthcare applications, where the same DSL can be used to model both clinical workflows and data analysis processes. This helps in creating applications where medical data is collected, analyzed, and visualized, with the same core language used for different tasks in the healthcare ecosystem.

Cross-domain DSLs not only improve the development process but also allow for the combination of techniques and knowledge from different disciplines. For instance, when developing a DSL that serves both the web development and machine learning domains, the language could feature constructs that are specifically designed to manage machine learning pipelines and easily integrate them into web applications.

The growing trend of cross-domain DSLs is paving the way for more interconnected and comprehensive software solutions that blend multiple domains. They provide a way for developers and domain experts to collaborate using a unified toolset while addressing their domain-specific needs. In the future, cross-domain DSLs are expected to expand even further, enabling more industries to collaborate and leverage the power of specialized languages for better, more efficient outcomes.

Module 32:
Future Directions for DSL Tools and Frameworks

Module 32, "Future Directions for DSL Tools and Frameworks," explores the emerging trends and advancements in the development environments and tools that support Domain-Specific Languages (DSLs). This module addresses the evolution of DSL development environments, new tools to enhance DSL performance, improvements in support for embedded and external DSLs, and the growing contribution of open-source frameworks. It provides insights into how the future of DSL tools and frameworks will shape the development of specialized languages.

Evolution of DSL Development Environments

The evolution of DSL development environments has been critical to the success of DSLs in various industries. Early DSL development was characterized by limited tooling, which required manual setups and low-level integrations. Over time, more sophisticated environments have emerged, providing better support for designing, testing, and deploying DSLs. These environments now often come with integrated features such as syntax highlighting, auto-completion, and debugging support, enhancing developer productivity. Furthermore, the integration of AI and machine learning has begun to influence DSL toolsets, enabling smarter error detection and language optimization. The trend toward cloud-based IDEs is also expected to allow for more collaborative and flexible DSL development.

New Tools for Improving DSL Performance

As DSLs continue to evolve and find applications across various domains, improving their performance is increasingly important. Several new tools and technologies are emerging to enhance the performance of DSLs. Compiler optimizations, for example, have become more sophisticated, with techniques like Just-in-Time (JIT) compilation being applied to DSLs. Additionally, specialized profilers are being developed to optimize DSL execution speed. These profilers analyze DSL programs to identify bottlenecks and suggest potential improvements. Other tools focus on improving memory management, making DSLs more scalable and responsive, particularly in large-scale applications like real-time data processing and machine learning systems.

Improving Tool Support for Embedded and External DSLs

The tools for embedded and external DSLs have improved significantly, but there is still room for innovation. Embedded DSLs are languages that are designed to be used within a host programming language, and external DSLs exist as standalone languages with their own parsing and execution engines. Both types of DSLs face unique challenges when it comes to tooling. Embedded DSLs often rely on the host language's features, which can be limiting, while external DSLs require complex parsing and integration efforts. New tools are being developed to streamline these processes. For embedded DSLs, the focus is on better integration with the host language, allowing for smoother and more seamless interaction between the DSL and the host. For external DSLs, the goal is to develop more powerful parsing engines and IDEs that handle syntax checking, code generation, and testing.

Open-Source DSL Frameworks and Contributions

Open-source DSL frameworks are increasingly playing a pivotal role in the evolution of DSLs. These frameworks provide foundational tools, libraries, and templates that simplify the development of both internal and external DSLs. Communities of developers and domain experts contribute to these open-source projects, accelerating the adoption and improvement of DSL technologies. Popular frameworks, such as Xtext for Java-based DSLs and PEG.js for JavaScript, allow developers to create custom DSLs with case, and their open-source nature ensures that these tools continue to evolve rapidly. The future of DSL tools is likely to see more collaboration within the open-source community, leading to further advancements in the capabilities and accessibility of DSL frameworks.

The future of DSL tools and frameworks holds promising advancements that will further simplify the development and optimization of DSLs. As new tools are introduced, DSL performance will continue to improve, and the support for both embedded and external DSLs will become more robust. Open-source contributions will accelerate the development of more powerful and flexible DSL frameworks.

Evolution of DSL Development Environments

The evolution of Domain-Specific Language (DSL) development environments has greatly impacted how DSLs are designed, tested, and deployed. Initially, DSLs were often constructed manually using simple text editors with basic syntax support. As the demand for specialized tools increased, DSL development environments evolved to include more sophisticated features such as syntax highlighting, error checking, and autocompletion. These features helped increase the productivity of developers, allowing them to focus more on solving domain-specific problems than managing the intricacies of language design.

Over time, cloud-based Integrated Development Environments (IDEs) began to play a significant role in DSL development. Platforms like Visual Studio Code and JetBrains Rider offer extensive support for DSL creation, providing an ecosystem where developers can seamlessly integrate DSLs with various programming languages. Cloud-based IDEs enable easier collaboration, allowing multiple developers to work on DSLs simultaneously, regardless of their physical location. Furthermore, cloud environments provide access to high-performance computing resources, which can be vital when developing complex DSLs for resource-intensive applications.

In terms of the future, AI and machine learning tools are also beginning to influence DSL environments. Intelligent assistants in development environments can now suggest language improvements, optimize syntax, and even detect errors before the code is executed. These advancements help in creating smarter development environments for DSLs.

Code Example

Let's consider the development of a simple DSL within Python, where the goal is to create a domain-specific language for mathematical expressions. In a basic development environment, a DSL could be constructed as follows:

```python
class MathDSL:
    def __init__(self, expression):
        self.expression = expression

    def evaluate(self):
        return eval(self.expression)

# Simple DSL expression
expression = "3 + 5 * (2 - 8)"
dsl = MathDSL(expression)
result = dsl.evaluate()
print(f"The result of the expression is: {result}")
```

In the above example, MathDSL serves as a simple domain-specific language for evaluating mathematical expressions. While the environment here is basic, the DSL can be extended with more features like validation or error handling. An advanced environment would provide tools to integrate features such as optimization, error detection, and code suggestions.

In modern DSL development environments, the process of writing, testing, and optimizing such a DSL is streamlined with tools that automate syntax checks and allow for debugging directly in the environment. IDEs can automatically identify syntax errors and even suggest corrections or improvements to the DSL design, enhancing the overall developer experience.

The future of DSL development environments will likely see further integration with cloud platforms, greater use of AI for code improvement, and increasingly powerful IDEs that help manage the complexity of building and deploying DSLs for different domains.

New Tools for Improving DSL Performance

The performance of Domain-Specific Languages (DSLs) is critical in ensuring that they not only function correctly but also operate efficiently in real-world applications. Over the years, several tools and frameworks have emerged to enhance the performance of DSLs, addressing concerns such as compilation speed, runtime efficiency, and memory usage.

A significant aspect of improving DSL performance lies in optimizing the process of parsing and interpreting the DSL. Tools like ANTLR, Bison, and Yacc help in generating parsers that can process DSL syntax efficiently. These tools allow developers to define grammars for their DSLs, and they automatically generate the necessary parser code. Advanced features in these tools, such as lexical analysis and grammar optimizations, ensure that the parser operates quickly even with large or complex DSL inputs.

Another approach to performance optimization involves code generation. Instead of interpreting DSL code at runtime, a tool can generate code in a more general-purpose language like Python, Java, or C++. This reduces overhead and allows the DSL to take advantage of the performance optimizations present in these general-purpose languages. Additionally, some frameworks focus on just-in-time (JIT) compilation, allowing DSL code to be compiled and executed on the fly for better performance in environments where code changes frequently.

One of the tools that have gained popularity in recent years for improving DSL performance is **PyPy**, an implementation of Python that incorporates Just-in-Time (JIT) compilation. For DSLs written in Python, PyPy can significantly speed up execution by dynamically compiling the Python code into machine code. Additionally, tools like **Cython** allow DSLs written in Python to be converted to C code, which is then compiled, resulting in faster execution times for performance-critical applications.

Code Example

To demonstrate how performance can be improved in DSLs, let's consider optimizing a simple mathematical DSL from the previous example using **Cython** to generate compiled code. Here, we will define a DSL for evaluating arithmetic expressions in Python, but optimize the evaluation process using Cython.

First, we write the DSL in Python:

```python
class MathDSL:
    def __init__(self, expression):
        self.expression = expression

    def evaluate(self):
        return eval(self.expression)
```

Next, we optimize this code with **Cython**. To do this, we'll write the same DSL in a .pyx file (Cython file), which will allow us to compile it into C code for better performance:

```python
# mathdsl.pyx
cdef class MathDSL:
    cdef str expression

    def __init__(self, expression: str):
        self.expression = expression

    def evaluate(self):
        return eval(self.expression)
```

Once this file is created, we can compile it into C code by running the following command:

```
cythonize -i mathdsl.pyx
```

The result is a .so or .pyd file that can be imported and used in Python with better performance.

```
from mathdsl import MathDSL

expression = "3 + 5 * (2 - 8)"
dsl = MathDSL(expression)
result = dsl.evaluate()
print(f"The result of the expression is: {result}")
```

Using Cython allows us to take advantage of compiled code while still maintaining the simplicity and flexibility of Python. This performance optimization method can be applied to any DSL written in Python, improving execution time without sacrificing the benefits of a high-level language.

In the future, tools like PyPy, Cython, and JIT compilation techniques will continue to improve DSL performance, making them more viable for resource-intensive applications such as real-time systems, machine learning pipelines, and high-performance computing.

Improving Tool Support for Embedded and External DSLs

Domain-Specific Languages (DSLs) can be categorized as either **embedded DSLs** or **external DSLs**. Both types have their own unique challenges and performance concerns, but improvements in tool support are essential to optimizing the development process for both.

Embedded DSLs are DSLs that are tightly integrated into a general-purpose programming language, leveraging the existing syntax and structure of that language. Python, Ruby, and Scala are examples of languages commonly used to build embedded DSLs. In these cases, developers need efficient tools for parsing, code analysis, and optimization that don't interfere with the host language's natural behavior.

On the other hand, **external DSLs** are standalone languages with their own syntax and semantics. These DSLs require full-fledged parser generators, interpreters, and compilers to process and execute the language code. Creating and maintaining tools for external DSLs can be more complex since they must handle everything from lexical analysis to code generation.

Embedded DSL Tool Support

For **embedded DSLs**, tools like **PyParsing**, **Parsley**, and **Lark** in Python provide excellent support for building DSLs without the need for a full parser. These tools allow developers to create custom parsing logic that is specific to the DSL while still utilizing Python's rich ecosystem. They also offer flexibility in how the DSL interacts with the host language, making it possible to use Python's existing libraries and runtime while introducing new domain-specific syntax.

For instance, the **PyParsing** library simplifies the process of creating small DSLs embedded directly in Python code by allowing users to define grammar and parsing rules inline with Python functions. Here is an example of using PyParsing to define a simple DSL for creating arithmetic expressions.

```
from pyparsing import Word, Literal, Forward, nums, oneOf

class SimpleArithmeticDSL:
    def __init__(self):
        # Grammar for arithmetic expressions
        self.expr = Forward()
        self.term = Word(nums)
        self.operator = oneOf("+ - * /")

        self.expr << (self.term + (self.operator + self.term)[...])

    def parse(self, expression):
        return self.expr.parseString(expression)

# Usage
dsl = SimpleArithmeticDSL()
result = dsl.parse("3 + 5 * 2")
print(result)
```

In this case, **PyParsing** enables us to easily define and parse arithmetic expressions, which could form the basis of a simple DSL embedded in Python.

External DSL Tool Support

For **external DSLs**, tools like **ANTLR**, **Bison**, and **Yacc** provide robust support for parsing and generating code for custom languages. These tools help to generate parsers from context-free grammars, making it easier to build external DSLs from scratch.

Here's an example of how to create a simple DSL parser for a custom language using **ANTLR**. First, we define a grammar file for a simple language that handles arithmetic operations:

```
grammar Arithmetic;

expr:   term (('+'|'-') term)* ;
term:   factor (('*'|'/') factor)* ;
factor: INT | '(' expr ')' ;

INT :   [0-9]+ ;
WS  :   [ \t\r\n]+ -> skip ;
```

Next, you can use the ANTLR tool to generate a parser in Python. Once the parser is generated, you can integrate it with Python code to process DSL statements.

```
antlr4 Arithmetic.g4 -Dlanguage=Python3
```

Then, in Python:

```
from antlr4 import *
from ArithmeticLexer import ArithmeticLexer
from ArithmeticParser import ArithmeticParser
```

```python
class ArithmeticEvaluator(ParseTreeVisitor):
    def visitExpr(self, ctx):
        return self.visit(ctx.term())

    def visitTerm(self, ctx):
        result = int(ctx.factor(0).getText())
        for i in range(1, len(ctx.factor())):
            operator = ctx.children[i*2-1].getText()
            value = int(ctx.factor(i).getText())
            if operator == '+':
                result += value
            elif operator == '-':
                result -= value
        return result

    def evaluate(self, expression):
        input_stream = InputStream(expression)
        lexer = ArithmeticLexer(input_stream)
        token_stream = CommonTokenStream(lexer)
        parser = ArithmeticParser(token_stream)
        tree = parser.expr()
        evaluator = ArithmeticEvaluator()
        return evaluator.visit(tree)

# Usage
evaluator = ArithmeticEvaluator()
result = evaluator.evaluate("3 + 5 * (2 - 8)")
print(result)
```

Tool Support Improvements

To improve tool support for embedded and external DSLs, advancements are needed in the following areas:

1. **IDE Integration**: Tools such as **PyCharm** or **VS Code** should offer better syntax highlighting, code completion, and error checking for DSLs.

2. **Automated Refactoring**: As DSLs evolve, automated refactoring tools would help in maintaining code quality and consistency, especially for embedded DSLs.

3. **Better Performance Tools**: Performance monitoring and profiling tools tailored to DSLs, especially for real-time systems, would improve efficiency.

With better tools for both embedded and external DSLs, developers can focus more on solving domain-specific problems while leaving the complexities of parsing, code generation, and optimization to the toolset.

Open-Source DSL Frameworks and Contributions

The open-source ecosystem has contributed significantly to the development and proliferation of Domain-Specific Languages (DSLs). Open-source DSL frameworks allow developers to leverage pre-built tools and libraries for creating custom languages, making it easier to build, maintain, and share DSLs with a broader audience. These frameworks often include features such as parsing, lexing, syntax highlighting, and code generation, which streamline the DSL development process.

One of the prominent open-source frameworks for DSLs is **Xtext**, a framework for developing external DSLs that integrates with the Eclipse IDE. Xtext provides a powerful toolkit for building custom languages with built-in support for syntax highlighting, code completion, and validation. It generates both the lexer and parser from a grammar specification, making it suitable for creating DSLs with rich features.

Another noteworthy framework is **ANTLR** (ANother Tool for Language Recognition), a widely used tool for building language parsers. ANTLR supports multiple target languages, including Python, Java, and C#, allowing developers to define a grammar and then generate code to process inputs in their custom DSL. ANTLR's flexibility makes it a popular choice for both embedded and external DSLs.

Example: Using ANTLR to Build a DSL for Arithmetic Expressions

To demonstrate how an open-source framework like ANTLR can be used to develop a DSL, let's consider a case where we build a custom DSL to evaluate simple arithmetic expressions. First, we define a simple grammar that supports basic arithmetic operations:

```
grammar Arithmetic;

expr:   term (('+'|'-') term)* ;
term:   factor (('*'|'/') factor)* ;
factor: INT | '(' expr ')' ;

INT :   [0-9]+ ;
WS  :   [ \t\r\n]+ -> skip ;
```

This grammar defines three rules: expr, term, and factor. The expr rule handles addition and subtraction, the term rule handles multiplication and division, and the factor rule handles integers and parenthesized expressions.

To use ANTLR to generate a parser from this grammar, you would run the following command:

```
antlr4 Arithmetic.g4 -Dlanguage=Python3
```

This generates Python classes for the lexer and parser. After generating the code, you can use it in your Python program to parse and evaluate arithmetic expressions.

Here is an example of how to use the generated parser in Python:

```python
from antlr4 import *
from ArithmeticLexer import ArithmeticLexer
from ArithmeticParser import ArithmeticParser

class ArithmeticEvaluator(ParseTreeVisitor):
    def visitExpr(self, ctx):
        return self.visit(ctx.term())
```

338

```python
def visitTerm(self, ctx):
    result = int(ctx.factor(0).getText())
    for i in range(1, len(ctx.factor())):
        operator = ctx.children[i*2-1].getText()
        value = int(ctx.factor(i).getText())
        if operator == '+':
            result += value
        elif operator == '-':
            result -= value
    return result

def evaluate(self, expression):
    input_stream = InputStream(expression)
    lexer = ArithmeticLexer(input_stream)
    token_stream = CommonTokenStream(lexer)
    parser = ArithmeticParser(token_stream)
    tree = parser.expr()
    evaluator = ArithmeticEvaluator()
    return evaluator.visit(tree)

# Usage
evaluator = ArithmeticEvaluator()
result = evaluator.evaluate("3 + 5 * (2 - 8)")
print(result)
```

Benefits of Open-Source Frameworks

1. **Community Collaboration**: Open-source frameworks are often improved by a large community of developers. This leads to frequent updates, bug fixes, and new features that make DSL development more efficient.

2. **Cost-Effective**: These frameworks are free to use, making them an attractive option for both small projects and large-scale enterprise applications.

3. **Extensibility**: Open-source frameworks like ANTLR, Xtext, and PyParsing are highly extensible. Developers can modify and extend them to suit the unique needs of their DSL, whether it's adding custom parsing logic or integrating with other systems.

Contributions to the Open-Source Ecosystem

Developers are encouraged to contribute back to the open-source community by sharing their DSL frameworks, libraries, or enhancements. Contributions can include:

- **Bug Fixes**: Reporting and fixing bugs in DSL-related tools and frameworks.

- **New Features**: Adding new features such as custom parsers, error handling, or integration with other technologies.

- **Documentation**: Writing or improving documentation to help other developers use the DSL frameworks more effectively.

By contributing to the open-source ecosystem, developers can help improve the tools they rely on, while also gaining recognition within the community. Additionally, open-source contributions provide a great opportunity to collaborate on innovative DSL projects and drive the evolution of DSL technologies.

Open-source DSL frameworks like ANTLR, Xtext, and PyParsing play a vital role in the ease and efficiency of DSL development. These tools provide both flexibility and power, enabling developers to create custom languages that cater to specific application domains while fostering community collaboration and growth.

Module 33:

Challenges in DSL Evolution and Maintenance

Module 33 focuses on the ongoing challenges associated with maintaining and evolving Domain-Specific Languages (DSLs) as the domains they serve evolve. This module covers critical topics such as ensuring backward compatibility, strategies for managing versioning and updates, and how to address sustainability issues to ensure long-term usability and performance of DSLs in real-world applications.

Maintaining DSLs Over Time as Domains Evolve

One of the key challenges in DSL development is ensuring that a DSL remains relevant as the domain it serves evolves. Domains often undergo changes due to technological advancements, shifts in industry standards, or changing user needs. As a result, DSLs must evolve to accommodate new requirements while still serving their original purpose. This necessitates continuous monitoring of the domain and regular updates to the DSL to ensure it stays useful. Additionally, developers must stay abreast of industry changes to anticipate emerging trends that might affect the DSL's applicability. Failure to maintain a DSL could lead to its obsolescence, ultimately reducing its value and impact on productivity.

Handling Backward Compatibility in Evolving DSLs

Backward compatibility is crucial when updating or evolving a DSL. It ensures that existing code written in the DSL continues to work as expected even after modifications are made to the language. This is particularly important in long-lived projects where legacy systems must be preserved while still allowing for the introduction of new features. Handling backward compatibility in DSLs often involves carefully designing new features or changes so that they don't break existing syntax or functionality. This may require creating new extensions or adding deprecated tags for older syntax while allowing newer syntax to coexist. Effective version control and documentation are also essential to help users transition smoothly to newer versions without losing the ability to work with older codebases.

Strategies for DSL Versioning and Updates

Versioning and updates are fundamental to managing the evolution of DSLs. Without a clear versioning strategy, it can become difficult to track changes and manage the development process effectively. One common approach to versioning is Semantic Versioning (SemVer), where major, minor, and patch versions are used to communicate the scale of changes. Major versions indicate breaking changes, while minor versions signal new features that are backward compatible, and patch versions denote bug fixes. Another approach involves the use of a migration path, where each new version of the DSL comes with migration tools or guidelines to help users adopt new features without disrupting their workflow. Updates should also include detailed changelogs and backward compatibility notices to assist developers in understanding the implications of each version.

Addressing Challenges in Long-Term DSL Sustainability

The sustainability of a DSL depends on several factors, including its ability to evolve with the domain, the availability of resources to maintain it, and community involvement. Over time, as the domain changes and new technologies emerge, maintaining a DSL can become increasingly challenging. Additionally, a lack of active community support or dwindling developer interest can hinder the language's longevity. To address these challenges, it is vital to encourage community contributions, promote open-source collaboration, and ensure that the DSL is flexible enough to adapt to future needs. Building in a robust ecosystem of libraries, tools, and integrations will also help maintain the DSL's relevance and usability in the long term.

The challenges of evolving and maintaining DSLs are an integral part of their lifecycle. By focusing on backward compatibility, implementing clear versioning strategies, and fostering long-term sustainability through community engagement and flexible design, developers can ensure that their DSLs remain valuable tools for the domains they serve.

Maintaining DSLs Over Time as Domains Evolve

Maintaining a Domain-Specific Language (DSL) over time as its associated domain evolves presents both opportunities and challenges. As industries and technologies grow, new concepts, requirements, and features emerge, necessitating changes to the DSL to ensure its continued usefulness. In this section, we will explore how to maintain a DSL over time by introducing new features and adapting to changes in the domain.

One key aspect of maintaining a DSL is regular domain analysis. Developers need to stay informed about shifts in technology, industry trends, and user needs. For example, in the financial sector, new financial instruments or regulations may emerge, requiring updates to the DSL to accommodate these changes. Similarly, in a game development DSL, new game mechanics or platform-specific features might necessitate adjustments.

To demonstrate how this might work in practice, let's consider a simple example of a DSL for a machine learning pipeline, which includes a "preprocessing" step. Over time, new preprocessing techniques like data normalization or feature scaling may need to be added. This involves extending the DSL to support these new operations.

```
# Example DSL code for an ML pipeline before update
pipeline = Pipeline([
    LoadData('data.csv'),
    CleanData(),
    TrainModel('random_forest')
])
```

```
# After domain evolution: adding feature scaling to the pipeline
pipeline = Pipeline([
    LoadData('data.csv'),
    CleanData(),
    FeatureScaling(),
    TrainModel('random_forest')
])
```

In the example, a new feature, FeatureScaling(), has been added to the pipeline to address an emerging need in machine learning preprocessing. To ensure smooth integration, the existing structure of the DSL must accommodate this new feature without breaking existing code.

Backward Compatibility in DSL Maintenance

When a DSL evolves to add new features or capabilities, backward compatibility becomes crucial. Existing users of the DSL should be able to continue using their code without experiencing disruptions or bugs due to new changes. In this section, we will look at how backward compatibility can be managed in DSLs.

To maintain backward compatibility, DSL designers can use several strategies. One common approach is to introduce new features in a way that they do not interfere with older functionality. For example, new features may be optional and may require explicit enabling, or they may use new syntax that doesn't affect existing constructs. Additionally, introducing deprecated warnings can inform users that certain parts of the DSL are outdated and will be removed in future versions, allowing them time to adapt.

Let's consider an example of introducing a new optional feature, AdvancedTraining(), to an existing machine learning DSL:

```
# Existing DSL code
pipeline = Pipeline([
    LoadData('data.csv'),
    CleanData(),
    TrainModel('random_forest')
])

# New feature added but backward compatible
pipeline = Pipeline([
    LoadData('data.csv'),
    CleanData(),
    TrainModel('random_forest'),
    AdvancedTraining()  # New feature, optional
])
```

In this example, the AdvancedTraining() feature is introduced without changing the original behavior of the DSL. Users who don't need the new functionality can continue using the original code, while those who need the new feature can opt in by adding it to their pipeline.

As the domains supported by DSLs evolve, maintaining the language to stay relevant while ensuring backward compatibility is essential. By carefully introducing new features and avoiding disruptions to existing code, DSLs can continue to support their users effectively over time.

Handling Backward Compatibility in Evolving DSLs

One of the most important aspects of maintaining a Domain-Specific Language (DSL) as it evolves is ensuring backward compatibility. As the DSL is updated to include new features or improvements, it is crucial that existing users' code continues to function correctly without requiring immediate changes. In this section, we will explore strategies for handling backward compatibility and ensuring that older codebases continue to work with newer versions of the DSL.

When a DSL undergoes changes, especially in terms of adding new functionality or altering existing constructs, there are various approaches to minimize disruptions for existing users. A typical approach is to introduce versioning, where new versions of the DSL are released alongside older, stable versions. This allows users to opt into new features at their own pace while maintaining compatibility with previous versions of the language.

To illustrate backward compatibility, let's consider a DSL designed for web development. Suppose that the DSL originally used a simple syntax for defining HTML elements, but over time, the DSL evolves to support new web technologies, such as SVG graphics. If backward compatibility is not handled carefully, users with older code may experience issues when the new version of the DSL is introduced.

Here is an example of how a backward-compatible update might look in practice:

```
# Initial version of the DSL: Defining an HTML element
html_page = HtmlPage([
    Text('Hello, world!'),
    Button('Click Me')
])

# New version introduces SVG support, but maintains backward compatibility
html_page = HtmlPage([
    Text('Hello, world!'),
    Button('Click Me'),
    SVGElement('<circle cx="50" cy="50" r="40" stroke="black" stroke-width="3"
        fill="red"/>')  # New feature
])
```

In this example, the SVGElement feature is added to the DSL without changing the original structure. This ensures that users who do not need the new feature can continue to use the existing DSL commands, while those who require SVG support can adopt the new feature.

Additionally, DSL creators can implement deprecated warnings. These warnings notify users when a feature or syntax is about to be removed in a future version of the DSL. By

344

signaling deprecated elements, users have time to update their code before the functionality is completely phased out.

For example, consider the following DSL code that includes a deprecated feature:

```
# Old syntax with deprecated feature
html_page = HtmlPage([
    Text('Hello, world!'),
    DeprecatedButton('Click Me')  # Deprecated feature
])

# New version would give a warning for DeprecatedButton usage
```

The DeprecatedButton feature is marked for future removal, and when users execute the code, a warning is generated to indicate that this feature is no longer recommended. This gives users an opportunity to refactor their code before upgrading to a newer version.

Handling backward compatibility is essential in maintaining the integrity and usability of a DSL over time. By introducing optional new features, offering versioned releases, and providing deprecation warnings, DSL designers can evolve their language while ensuring that existing user code remains functional. This strategy fosters stability, trust, and long-term adoption of the DSL.

Strategies for DSL Versioning and Updates

As a Domain-Specific Language (DSL) evolves, versioning becomes critical to managing changes and ensuring smooth transitions for developers who rely on it. Proper versioning allows DSL users to upgrade to new versions without breaking their existing projects, while also giving them the option to adopt new features or changes at their own pace. In this section, we will explore strategies for versioning and updating a DSL, including handling major and minor updates, and supporting users across different versions.

Versioning Strategies

A common approach to DSL versioning is Semantic Versioning (SemVer), which uses a three-part version number format: major.minor.patch. Each part of the version number has specific meaning:

- **Major version**: Changes that break backward compatibility.

- **Minor version**: New features or enhancements that are backward-compatible.

- **Patch version**: Bug fixes or minor changes that do not affect functionality.

By following Semantic Versioning, DSL developers can communicate the extent of changes in each new release. This provides users with clear guidance on when it's safe to upgrade and when caution is needed.

For instance, consider a DSL for data processing that supports different operations like filtering and transformation. Over time, new functions may be added, or syntax might be improved, but some changes may also break existing workflows.

Here is an example of how updates might look across different versions:

Version 1.0.0 – Initial Release

```
# Version 1.0.0: Basic DSL functions
data = DataSet('data.csv')
filtered_data = data.filter('age > 30')
transformed_data = filtered_data.transform('age * 2')
```

Version 1.1.0 – New Feature (Backward-Compatible)

```
# Version 1.1.0: Adding new feature without breaking existing code
data = DataSet('data.csv')
filtered_data = data.filter('age > 30')
transformed_data = filtered_data.transform('age * 2')
sorted_data = transformed_data.sort('age')  # New feature in version 1.1.0
```

In this example, the addition of the sort() function is a backward-compatible change, which increases the language's capabilities without breaking existing code. The minor version bump signals to the user that the new feature is available, and they can use it without affecting their older code.

Version 2.0.0 – Breaking Change (Backward Incompatible)

```
# Version 2.0.0: Breaking change that requires a major version bump
# Previous syntax was deprecated
data = DataSet('data.csv')
# Updated syntax
filtered_data = data.filter(lambda x: x['age'] > 30)  # More flexible filtering
transformed_data = filtered_data.transform(lambda x: x['age'] * 2)
```

In version 2.0.0, the filtering mechanism has been redesigned to accept lambda functions, providing greater flexibility but requiring developers to adjust their code. This backward-incompatible change is indicated by the major version bump.

Supporting Multiple Versions

Another key aspect of versioning is supporting multiple versions of the DSL simultaneously. This can be done by using versioned APIs or providing a compatibility layer that detects the version being used and adapts accordingly. This allows users to continue using the older syntax or functions until they are ready to adopt the latest version.

For example, consider a web DSL that evolves over time but still supports users running older versions:

```
# Version 1.x.x syntax
page = WebPage('home.html')
page.addElement('button', text='Submit')
```

```
# Version 2.x.x syntax (new version introduces more flexibility)
page = WebPage('home.html')
page.addElement('button', text='Submit', color='blue', size='large')
```

With versioning support, the DSL framework can detect which version the user is running and either use the old addElement() method or the new, more flexible version.

Effective versioning and updates are essential for the long-term success of a DSL. By following a clear versioning strategy, such as Semantic Versioning, DSL developers can help users understand the scope of changes and avoid disruptions. Supporting multiple versions simultaneously and offering deprecation warnings ensure that users can gradually transition to newer versions without facing compatibility issues.

Addressing Challenges in Long-Term DSL Sustainability

As Domain-Specific Languages (DSLs) evolve, sustaining their usefulness over the long term becomes a significant challenge. Ensuring that a DSL remains relevant and functional for its target domain while adapting to changes in technology, user needs, and industry standards is vital for its continued success. In this section, we will examine the key challenges faced in long-term DSL sustainability and how they can be addressed, including handling technical debt, keeping the language flexible, and managing community involvement.

Managing Technical Debt

Over time, as a DSL grows and more features are added, technical debt can accumulate. Technical debt refers to the trade-offs made during development to speed up delivery, which later results in difficulties when trying to evolve or maintain the DSL. For example, early decisions made to keep the language simple may later restrict the addition of more advanced features or improvements.

One approach to managing technical debt in DSLs is regular refactoring. Refactoring involves restructuring the DSL's codebase and syntax to improve clarity, performance, and extensibility without changing its functionality. For example, consider a DSL for building simple data pipelines:

Before Refactoring

```
# Original DSL
data = Data('data.csv')
data.read()
data.filter('age > 30')
data.transformation('multiply_age_by_two')
data.write('output.csv')
```

In this example, each operation is treated as a separate method. As the DSL evolves, new features may lead to complex and repetitive syntax. By refactoring the DSL, one might merge related methods to simplify the code:

347

After Refactoring

```
# Refactored DSL
data = Data('data.csv')
data.read().filter('age >
          30').transform('multiply_age_by_two').write('output.csv')
```

This refactoring reduces redundancy and makes it easier to add new operations in the future, thereby reducing the technical debt.

Ensuring Flexibility

To ensure long-term sustainability, DSLs must be flexible enough to handle new requirements and accommodate changes in the domain. However, flexibility should not come at the cost of complexity. A DSL should balance simplicity and power, allowing users to express complex ideas while keeping the language easy to learn and use.

For example, a DSL for querying databases might initially support only simple queries:

```
# Initial DSL version
db = Database('localhost')
results = db.query("SELECT * FROM users WHERE age > 30")
```

As the domain evolves, the DSL should support more complex query capabilities, such as joins and aggregations. Here is how the syntax can evolve to accommodate this:

```
# Updated DSL version with flexibility for complex queries
db = Database('localhost')
results = db.query("SELECT name, age FROM users WHERE age > 30")
results = db.join("INNER JOIN orders ON users.id = orders.user_id")
results = db.aggregate("COUNT(*) AS order_count")
```

Ensuring flexibility allows the DSL to grow with the domain it targets and continue serving developers as their needs change over time.

Encouraging Community Involvement

A key factor in sustaining a DSL over time is building a vibrant community of users and contributors. Encouraging open-source contributions, maintaining thorough documentation, and fostering user engagement through forums or social media platforms can help ensure the DSL's long-term survival. With active involvement, users can share their feedback, suggest new features, report bugs, and contribute code to enhance the DSL.

For example, if a DSL for machine learning is open-sourced, the community could develop additional libraries or tools that extend the DSL's capabilities, making it more versatile and useful in different machine learning contexts. Community engagement also helps identify gaps in the language that might not be obvious to its creators.

Long-term DSL sustainability requires ongoing maintenance, flexibility, and community support. By managing technical debt, ensuring that the DSL can evolve to meet new needs, and encouraging community involvement, developers can keep the DSL relevant and effective for many years. A well-maintained DSL is adaptable and continuously improving, ensuring it remains valuable to its user base.

Module 34:

The Role of DSLs in Future Software Development

This module explores the significant role of Domain-Specific Languages (DSLs) in future software development. It addresses how DSLs are enhancing productivity in agile environments, supporting collaborative development, and simplifying the design of complex systems. Additionally, it highlights how DSLs can improve the quality and reliability of software projects by offering targeted, domain-specific solutions.

Increasing Productivity with DSLs in Agile Environments

DSLs are increasingly being used in agile environments to streamline development processes. Agile methodologies emphasize flexibility, fast iterations, and close collaboration between developers and stakeholders. DSLs facilitate these principles by providing languages tailored to specific tasks, reducing the need for complex code and allowing developers to focus on higher-level solutions. With DSLs, repetitive tasks can be abstracted, and development cycles shortened, aligning well with agile's emphasis on delivering functional software quickly. As DSLs target particular domains, they reduce cognitive load and help teams maintain focus on solving problems unique to their application area.

Collaborative Development Using Domain-Specific Languages

Collaboration is central to modern software development, and DSLs play a pivotal role in making collaboration easier and more efficient. By using DSLs, teams can establish a common language that is understandable to both technical and non-technical stakeholders. This shared language reduces the communication gap between developers, designers, and domain experts, allowing for faster feedback loops and more accurate requirements gathering. DSLs facilitate smoother handovers, as team members can quickly understand the domain logic, even if they are not experts in the technical details. This collaborative approach enhances productivity and leads to better-aligned development efforts.

The Growing Role of DSLs in Complex System Design

As software systems become increasingly complex, DSLs are becoming indispensable tools in their design. Complex systems often involve multiple interdependent components, and using general-purpose programming languages to manage such complexity can be inefficient and error-prone. DSLs, on the other hand, allow developers to define high-level abstractions tailored to specific parts of the system. Whether it's for designing microservices, handling system configurations, or orchestrating workflows, DSLs enable a modular and maintainable approach to complex system design. Their ability to simplify the modeling of intricate systems leads to more scalable and manageable architectures.

How DSLs Can Improve the Quality and Reliability of Software

DSLs can significantly enhance the quality and reliability of software by reducing errors and ensuring that the code adheres to domain-specific constraints. Since DSLs are specialized for a particular domain, they come with built-in validation rules and semantics that help catch domain-specific errors early in the development process. Furthermore, by providing abstractions that align closely with the problem domain, DSLs lead to more accurate and efficient implementations. They also encourage better documentation, as the code itself often becomes more readable and self-explanatory. As a result, software developed with DSLs tends to be more robust, reliable, and easier to maintain.

Domain-Specific Languages are reshaping the landscape of software development. By increasing productivity, enabling collaborative development, simplifying complex system designs, and improving software quality, DSLs are proving to be essential in modern software practices. As the software development world continues to evolve, the role of DSLs will only become more prominent in driving efficiency and innovation.

Increasing Productivity with DSLs in Agile Environments

In agile environments, where the focus is on iterative development, quick feedback, and close collaboration, DSLs (Domain-Specific Languages) provide a powerful tool for increasing productivity. Agile methodologies prioritize delivering small, incremental pieces of software, and DSLs help streamline development by offering focused, domain-specific solutions.

A DSL simplifies complex processes by abstracting repetitive or domain-specific logic into higher-level constructs that are more intuitive and easier to understand. This reduces the amount of boilerplate code and enables developers to concentrate on solving business problems instead of dealing with implementation details.

For instance, consider a DSL for managing database queries in an application. Instead of writing SQL code directly, developers can use a custom query DSL that lets them specify the database operations in a simpler, domain-relevant syntax. This abstraction helps improve development speed and reduces the chance of introducing errors by preventing complex SQL queries from becoming tangled within application code.

Let's take an example of how a simple DSL might look for a web application to handle user authentication. Rather than writing extensive logic for each step, a DSL can simplify the flow:

```
auth_dsl = """
User.authenticate(username, password) -> success:
    Redirect to dashboard
    Send welcome email to username
```

351

```
Else:
    Show error message
"""
```

In this example, the DSL defines the entire authentication process using natural language-like constructs. It clearly outlines the authentication flow and separates it from the implementation details. As a result, developers can rapidly adjust and iterate on authentication logic without worrying about underlying code structure.

By providing higher-level abstractions, DSLs enable teams to deliver features more quickly and with fewer mistakes. In an agile environment, this means developers can focus on the unique aspects of the application, accelerating delivery cycles and reducing the cognitive load that often comes with writing and maintaining generic code.

Furthermore, DSLs help automate specific tasks, such as code generation or configuration management, which can save valuable time during each iteration. A DSL might automatically generate configuration files or produce reports, which would otherwise take hours to develop manually.

DSLs enhance productivity in agile environments by simplifying repetitive tasks, abstracting domain-specific logic, and enabling faster iterations. With reduced complexity, teams can more easily align their work with business goals, ensuring quicker feedback and more efficient development cycles.

Collaborative Development Using Domain-Specific Languages

Collaborative development is essential in modern software projects, where cross-functional teams work together to design, build, and maintain complex systems. DSLs (Domain-Specific Languages) facilitate collaboration by providing a shared, concise vocabulary tailored to the specific domain of the application. This enables teams to express complex domain logic in a more understandable and consistent manner, improving communication and reducing misunderstandings.

DSLs serve as a bridge between developers, domain experts, and other stakeholders by providing a common language for expressing requirements, behaviors, and processes. This common language enhances collaboration, as everyone, from business analysts to technical staff, can contribute to the software development process without requiring deep programming knowledge. For example, a DSL in a finance domain may allow business analysts to specify trading strategies or financial models directly, reducing the dependency on developers for translating business logic into code.

Consider a scenario in which a team is building an application for scheduling resources in a hospital. A DSL might allow medical staff, developers, and administrators to express and modify scheduling rules directly. The language could be structured to reflect the logic of patient appointments, staff schedules, and resource availability. Here's a simple example of such a DSL:

```
# A DSL for scheduling patient appointments
schedule_dsl = """
Rule: Schedule appointment for Patient with availability as priority.
If Doctor.isAvailable on {time}:
    Book appointment for Patient
Else:
    Suggest available times
"""
```

In this example, domain experts (e.g., medical staff) can modify the scheduling rules by adjusting the DSL script, allowing them to directly influence the scheduling logic. Developers are responsible for implementing the DSL interpreter, but the collaboration aspect is significantly enhanced because non-developers can directly interact with the system's logic.

Furthermore, DSLs support collaborative development by enabling automation. For instance, a DSL can be used to automatically generate configuration files or reports, reducing the need for manual intervention and allowing teams to focus on higher-value tasks. This improves efficiency and minimizes errors, which is particularly important when multiple teams are working on different aspects of the software.

Additionally, as teams become more distributed, DSLs offer an effective means of preserving consistency across codebases. By using the same domain-specific language, teams working in different regions or time zones can understand and modify the system without needing constant back-and-forth clarification. The structured syntax and defined semantics of a DSL make it easier for distributed teams to collaborate effectively and efficiently.

DSLs facilitate collaborative development by providing a shared, domain-specific language that improves communication and enables non-developers to contribute directly to software development. This enhances productivity, reduces misunderstandings, and ensures that domain experts can actively participate in shaping the software, making it a powerful tool for modern collaborative teams.

The Growing Role of DSLs in Complex System Design

Domain-Specific Languages (DSLs) play a pivotal role in the design and development of complex systems, offering a tailored approach to representing domain-specific logic that traditional programming languages often cannot provide. As systems become more intricate, spanning multiple subsystems, services, and technologies, DSLs allow developers to express high-level abstractions that are specific to the problem domain, enabling easier understanding and management of system complexity.

In complex system design, DSLs can provide several advantages. First, they allow developers to focus on the domain-specific concerns of the system, without having to deal with the complexities of general-purpose languages. By encapsulating the intricacies of the domain in a concise, readable syntax, DSLs reduce the cognitive load for both developers and stakeholders, enabling faster design iterations and clearer communication between technical and non-technical team members.

For instance, in a large-scale enterprise system that involves multiple services (e.g., billing, inventory, and customer management), a DSL can be created for defining service interactions, message formats, or process workflows in a way that reflects the business logic. This abstraction layer can streamline the process of integrating and managing the individual components of the system. A simple DSL could define the flow of customer orders from initiation to delivery:

```
# A DSL for describing order processing workflow
order_workflow_dsl = """
Order received from Customer
If Customer.isPremium:
    Apply discount
Else:
    Standard pricing
Process order in Inventory system
Notify shipping service
"""
```

This DSL simplifies the representation of order processing steps, with domain-specific actions such as "Apply discount" and "Notify shipping service" embedded directly in the language. It enables developers to understand the flow of the system without needing to dive deep into implementation details, while business analysts can modify the workflow to adapt to new business requirements.

Additionally, DSLs can promote modularity and separation of concerns in large, distributed systems. For example, a DSL could be designed to handle user interface layouts in a web application, while another DSL handles the backend logic. These DSLs would be independent, allowing for a clear separation between concerns and better maintainability. In this way, each DSL targets a specific aspect of the system, promoting clean boundaries between system components.

Another benefit of DSLs in complex system design is their ability to manage configuration. In large systems, configuration management can become overwhelming, especially when there are numerous parameters and settings across multiple modules. By using a DSL to define configurations, developers can ensure consistency, reduce errors, and simplify the management of configurations across different environments.

For example, a DSL might be used to define the configuration of a distributed database system:

```
# A DSL for configuring a distributed database
db_config_dsl = """
Database Cluster:
    Node1: Primary
    Node2: Secondary
    Replication: On
    Sharding: Enabled
"""
```

354

This DSL enables the specification of database clusters in a structured, domain-specific way, making it easier for both developers and administrators to configure and manage the database setup.

DSLs provide a critical advantage in complex system design by offering tailored abstractions that focus on the specific domain. This allows for more efficient communication, easier management of system components, and better separation of concerns, ultimately enabling teams to design, build, and maintain large-scale systems more effectively.

How DSLs Can Improve the Quality and Reliability of Software

Domain-Specific Languages (DSLs) are an essential tool for improving the quality and reliability of software. By offering specialized constructs tailored to a particular domain, DSLs allow for more precise, readable, and maintainable code. This focus on a specific problem domain leads to fewer bugs, better testability, and higher overall software quality. When integrated properly, DSLs can significantly improve the reliability of complex systems by enforcing domain-specific rules and constraints.

One of the primary ways DSLs improve software quality is by enhancing the expressiveness of the code. Since the syntax of a DSL is designed to match the specific problem domain, it provides a more natural representation of the problem. This makes the code more understandable to domain experts and developers alike, reducing the risk of miscommunication and errors.

For example, in a financial application, a DSL could be designed to model various financial products like loans or insurance policies. Instead of using generic data structures or complex code that might be difficult for a domain expert to understand, a DSL allows for clear and domain-relevant constructs:

```
# A DSL for loan application in financial software
loan_application_dsl = """
LoanRequest:
    Type: Home
    Amount: 250000
    Term: 30 years
    InterestRate: 3.5%
    CreditCheck: Required
"""
```

In this example, the DSL captures the core financial concepts in a straightforward manner. The loan request is described using terms that are familiar to both financial experts and developers. By using such a DSL, the developers can ensure that the application logic matches the expectations of the domain, resulting in fewer errors and more accurate implementations.

DSLs also contribute to software quality by allowing developers to define and enforce domain-specific validation rules. For example, a DSL used in network configuration might automatically enforce rules about valid IP address formats or network routing logic, preventing invalid configurations from being deployed.

```
# A DSL for network configuration with validation
network_config_dsl = """
NetworkConfiguration:
    IPAddress: 192.168.1.100
    SubnetMask: 255.255.255.0
    Gateway: 192.168.1.1
"""
```

In this case, a DSL might include built-in validation for IP address formats, ensuring that only valid addresses are accepted. This helps catch errors early in the development process, improving the overall reliability of the system. Automated validation and error checking are a key benefit of using DSLs, as they reduce the likelihood of runtime failures or configuration errors.

Furthermore, DSLs support better testing practices. Since a DSL abstracts away much of the implementation details, it is easier to write domain-specific tests. These tests can focus on verifying the correctness of the business logic or domain behavior without being bogged down by technical complexities. For example, in the context of a DSL for machine learning, you can specify and test pipelines in a straightforward, declarative way:

```
# A DSL for defining machine learning pipeline steps
ml_pipeline_dsl = """
Pipeline:
    Step1: LoadData
    Step2: NormalizeData
    Step3: TrainModel
    Step4: EvaluateModel
"""
```

By defining the machine learning pipeline in a DSL, testing each step of the pipeline becomes simpler, as the DSL provides a clear and understandable representation of the process. This increases the reliability of the machine learning system by ensuring that each part of the pipeline functions as intended.

DSLs enhance software quality and reliability by making code more readable, enforceable, and testable. Through their focus on domain-specific concerns, they reduce the risk of errors, improve communication, and ensure that software systems are built with high accuracy and consistency. These benefits ultimately lead to more robust and dependable software.

Module 35:
Research Directions in Parsing and Code Generation for DSLs

This module focuses on the ongoing research and advancements in parsing technologies and code generation techniques, essential components in developing efficient Domain-Specific Languages (DSLs). It explores new trends in parsing, the optimization of performance through better parsing algorithms, and emerging directions for enhancing the parsing and code generation processes in DSLs.

Advances in Parsing Technologies and Algorithms:
The realm of parsing has seen significant improvements, including the development of more efficient parsing algorithms that can handle larger and more complex DSLs. Research into parsing strategies like LL, LR, and PEG (Parsing Expression Grammar) has enabled DSLs to better handle diverse syntax structures. Additionally, more sophisticated error detection and recovery mechanisms have emerged, improving the robustness of parsers. Researchers are also exploring the integration of machine learning techniques to predict parsing behavior and streamline complex parsing processes. These advancements contribute to making the creation of DSLs more efficient, adaptable, and able to support a wider variety of use cases.

New Trends in Code Generation for DSLs:
Code generation for DSLs has evolved with a shift towards more dynamic and flexible approaches. Traditional code generation methods, while effective, often face challenges in scaling with the growth of DSLs. Recent research focuses on model-driven development (MDD) and the use of intermediate representations (IRs) that allow for more streamlined translation of DSL statements into executable code. Another emerging trend is the use of Just-in-Time (JIT) compilation techniques, where code generation occurs dynamically during runtime. This has the potential to optimize DSL performance by tailoring the code specifically to the environment and data available at that moment. Additionally, there is growing interest in code generation techniques that allow DSLs to generate code for multiple platforms, improving cross-platform compatibility and extending the versatility of the language.

Optimizing DSL Performance Through Better Parsing Techniques:
Optimizing the performance of DSLs is a key area of focus in parsing research. Parsing techniques that can efficiently handle large input sizes and complex grammars are critical for improving the overall performance of DSLs. Techniques like incremental parsing, where only the changed parts of the input are re-parsed, have shown promise in reducing parsing overhead. Furthermore, using predictive parsing models based on machine learning can allow for anticipatory optimizations in parsing sequences. Researchers are also developing domain-

specific optimizations that tailor parsers to the unique syntax and semantic structures of DSLs, improving both speed and accuracy. Optimizing parsing ensures that DSLs perform well even as the scope and complexity of their application domains expand.

Future Research Opportunities in Parsing and Code Generation:
Looking ahead, there are numerous opportunities for further research in both parsing and code generation. One of the exciting areas is the integration of artificial intelligence (AI) and machine learning into the parsing and code generation processes. By leveraging AI, DSLs could potentially adapt to new use cases and automatically optimize code generation without manual intervention. Additionally, research into more efficient ways to handle ambiguities and inconsistencies in DSL syntax could make parsers more resilient and capable of handling real-world data. Cross-disciplinary research that blends parsing theory with real-world applications will also continue to push the boundaries of DSL technology, enhancing their adaptability and utility in emerging fields like data science and cybersecurity.

The field of parsing and code generation for DSLs is ripe with research opportunities. Advancements in parsing algorithms, code generation techniques, and performance optimization strategies promise to significantly enhance the power and flexibility of DSLs. By pursuing these research avenues, DSL development can continue to evolve, making these languages more efficient, robust, and adaptable to future needs.

Advances in Parsing Technologies and Algorithms

In the development of Domain-Specific Languages (DSLs), efficient parsing is a fundamental aspect that impacts both the creation of the DSL itself and the performance of the generated code. Parsing techniques are continuously evolving, with the goal of handling increasingly complex grammar structures while maintaining performance. The advances in parsing technologies and algorithms are especially important for DSLs that target specific domains with unique syntactic and semantic requirements.

Parsing Techniques: LL, LR, and PEG

One of the most traditional approaches to parsing DSLs has been the use of **LL** and **LR** parsing techniques. **LL parsers** read input from left to right and generate a leftmost derivation, while **LR parsers** perform the same task in reverse. These methods have been around for decades, but their limitations, especially in handling more intricate grammar rules and ambiguities, have sparked the development of new techniques like **Parsing Expression Grammar (PEG)**.

PEG is a more modern approach that overcomes some of the limitations of LL and LR parsers, particularly when dealing with ambiguous grammars. It allows for more flexibility in defining the syntax of DSLs, making it ideal for complex domain-specific applications. PEG parsers operate by evaluating a set of ordered rules to determine whether the input matches a given expression.

Here's a basic implementation of a PEG parser in Python using the parsy library:

```python
import parsy

# Define a simple PEG parser for arithmetic expressions
def parse_expression():
    number = parsy.regex(r'\d+').map(int)
    operator = parsy.regex(r'[+\-*/]')

    return parsy.seq(number, operator, number).map(lambda x: f"{x[0]} {x[1]} {x[2]}")

# Example usage
parser = parse_expression()
result = parser.parse("3 + 4")
print(result)  # Output: '3 + 4'
```

This example shows how PEG parsers are defined using regular expressions and how they can be used to parse simple arithmetic expressions. The flexibility of PEG parsers allows DSL designers to create more complex grammars for specific domain requirements.

Error Detection and Recovery

An essential advancement in parsing technologies is the development of error detection and recovery mechanisms. Traditional parsers could fail when encountering invalid input, but modern parsers are now designed with advanced error recovery techniques, making them more robust. For instance, **panic-mode recovery** can ignore parts of the input and continue parsing, ensuring that errors do not halt the entire process.

The use of **syntactic and semantic error messages** has also improved significantly. Instead of simply flagging syntax errors, modern parsers can provide helpful context about the nature of the error, such as pointing out unrecognized tokens or invalid grammar rules in DSLs.

For example, consider the following Python code snippet, which uses the lark library for creating a parser that generates useful error messages:

```python
from lark import Lark, UnexpectedInput

grammar = """
start: "hello" "world"
"""

parser = Lark(grammar)

try:
    parser.parse("hello Mars")
except UnexpectedInput as e:
    print(f"Error: {e}")  # Output: Error: Unexpected input 'Mars'
```

In this case, the parser provides an error message that informs the user of the unexpected token "Mars" when it was expecting "world".

Machine Learning for Parsing Optimization

359

More recently, machine learning (ML) has been integrated into parsing technologies to predict the most efficient parsing paths. ML models can be trained on large corpora of DSL code to identify common patterns and optimize the parsing process. This approach can greatly improve the efficiency of parsing in DSLs that are constantly evolving and growing in complexity.

One potential use case is the **predictive parsing** model, where a machine learning model anticipates the structure of input based on previous examples, allowing for dynamic adjustments to parsing strategies during runtime.

The evolution of parsing technologies—from traditional LL and LR parsers to more flexible approaches like PEG and machine learning-enhanced parsers—plays a crucial role in the development of DSLs. These advances not only make DSLs more powerful and adaptable but also improve their ability to handle complex domain-specific tasks with efficiency and accuracy.

New Trends in Code Generation for DSLs

Code generation is a critical part of the DSL design process, as it translates domain-specific syntax into executable code for a target platform. Over the years, trends in code generation for DSLs have evolved, with a focus on improving performance, flexibility, and maintainability. As the complexity of DSLs grows, developers have turned to more sophisticated methods for generating code that is not only syntactically correct but also optimized for performance.

Template-Based Code Generation

One of the most common trends in code generation is **template-based generation**, where templates define the structure of the code, and variables or placeholders are replaced with domain-specific values. This method allows DSLs to abstract away the low-level implementation details, making the generated code more readable and easier to maintain.

For example, a DSL for generating SQL queries might use templates to generate code dynamically based on user input. Below is an example in Python using the Jinja2 templating engine to generate SQL queries:

```python
from jinja2 import Template

# Define a template for generating SQL queries
query_template = """
SELECT {{ columns }} FROM {{ table }} WHERE {{ condition }};
"""

# Create a template object
template = Template(query_template)

# Define the context for template rendering
context = {
    'columns': 'id, name, age',
    'table': 'users',
```

```
        'condition': 'age > 18'
}

# Generate the SQL query
sql_query = template.render(context)
print(sql_query)  # Output: SELECT id, name, age FROM users WHERE age > 18;
```

In this example, the Jinja2 template is used to generate an SQL query based on dynamic values. Template-based generation is useful for DSLs that need to produce code in various domains (e.g., SQL, HTML, or even specific configurations for different platforms).

Code Generation through Domain-Specific Abstract Syntax Trees (ASTs)

Another trend is the use of **domain-specific abstract syntax trees (ASTs)** to represent the structure of the DSL. ASTs provide a higher-level representation of the source code that is easier to manipulate for code generation purposes. By building an AST, DSLs can more efficiently perform transformations and optimizations before generating the target code.

For instance, a DSL for defining mathematical operations could build an AST for expressions like a * b + c. The AST allows for easier manipulation and optimization, such as simplifying the expression before generating the corresponding code.

Here's an example of how an AST might be used for generating Python code from a simple DSL:

```
class ASTNode:
    def __init__(self, value):
        self.value = value
        self.children = []

    def add_child(self, child):
        self.children.append(child)

    def generate_code(self):
        return self.value

class BinaryOpNode(ASTNode):
    def __init__(self, left, operator, right):
        super().__init__(operator)
        self.add_child(left)
        self.add_child(right)

    def generate_code(self):
        left_code = self.children[0].generate_code()
        right_code = self.children[1].generate_code()
        return f"({left_code} {self.value} {right_code})"

# Create AST nodes for an expression: (a * b) + c
a = ASTNode('a')
b = ASTNode('b')
c = ASTNode('c')

mul_node = BinaryOpNode(a, '*', b)
add_node = BinaryOpNode(mul_node, '+', c)

# Generate Python code from the AST
print(add_node.generate_code())  # Output: ((a * b) + c)
```

In this example, we create an AST for a simple mathematical expression and generate corresponding Python code. This approach allows the DSL to manipulate and optimize complex domain-specific expressions before code generation.

Just-In-Time (JIT) Code Generation

The trend of **Just-In-Time (JIT) code generation** has also gained traction, particularly in performance-critical applications. JIT generation refers to generating code at runtime based on the specific conditions and inputs at that moment. This approach allows for dynamic optimizations, such as generating highly efficient code tailored to the actual usage pattern, rather than relying on static code.

For example, a DSL for numerical computations might generate code for matrix multiplication based on the size of the matrices and the specific hardware capabilities. By generating the code at runtime, it can leverage hardware optimizations (e.g., SIMD instructions) that are unavailable with static code generation.

Code Generation with Meta-Programming

Meta-programming is another technique gaining popularity in DSL code generation. This involves writing code that manipulates or generates other code. With Python, metaclasses and decorators can be used to generate DSL code dynamically, adapting to different contexts without writing static code.

Here is an example of using Python's decorators for code generation in a DSL:

```python
def generate_query(table):
    def decorator(func):
        def wrapper(*args, **kwargs):
            query = func(*args, **kwargs)
            return f"SELECT * FROM {table} WHERE {query}"
        return wrapper
    return decorator

@generate_query('users')
def condition():
    return 'age > 18'

# Generate the query
print(condition())  # Output: SELECT * FROM users WHERE age > 18
```

In this example, a decorator is used to dynamically generate an SQL query based on the conditions provided by the DSL function.

As DSLs evolve, new trends in code generation, including template-based generation, AST manipulation, JIT code generation, and meta-programming, are helping to make DSLs more efficient, flexible, and powerful. By leveraging these methods, DSL designers can generate optimized, domain-specific code tailored to their application requirements.

362

Optimizing DSL Performance through Better Parsing Techniques

Performance optimization in Domain-Specific Languages (DSLs) is critical for ensuring that they meet the demands of real-world applications. Efficient parsing techniques are at the heart of this optimization, as they directly influence how quickly and accurately a DSL translates its source code into an executable form. In this section, we explore how advanced parsing techniques can optimize DSL performance, focusing on tokenization, syntax tree generation, and incremental parsing.

Efficient Tokenization

Tokenization is the first step in parsing, where the raw input text is broken down into meaningful components called tokens. In DSLs, the complexity of tokenization can vary significantly depending on the syntax and domain. To improve performance, **finite state automata (FSA)** and **regular expressions** are commonly used to efficiently tokenize DSL input.

For instance, let's consider a DSL designed for simple mathematical expressions. A basic tokenization process can use regular expressions to efficiently separate numbers, operators, and parentheses:

```python
import re

# Define the regular expressions for each token type
token_patterns = {
    'NUMBER': r'\d+(\.\d*)?',
    'OPERATOR': r'[+\-*/]',
    'PARENTHESIS': r'[()]'
}

def tokenize(expression):
    tokens = []
    while expression:
        match = None
        for token_type, pattern in token_patterns.items():
            regex = re.compile(pattern)
            match = regex.match(expression)
            if match:
                tokens.append((token_type, match.group(0)))
                expression = expression[match.end():]
                break
        if not match:
            raise SyntaxError(f"Invalid token: {expression}")
    return tokens

# Example usage
expr = "3 + 5 * (2 - 8)"
tokens = tokenize(expr)
print(tokens)
```

Output:

```
[('NUMBER', '3'), ('OPERATOR', '+'), ('NUMBER', '5'), ('OPERATOR', '*'),
        ('PARENTHESIS', '('), ('NUMBER', '2'), ('OPERATOR', '-'), ('NUMBER',
        '8'), ('PARENTHESIS', ')')]
```

This method efficiently processes the input string by matching tokens using regular expressions, ensuring a fast and reliable tokenization step. This type of technique is crucial when working with large-scale DSL inputs, as it significantly reduces parsing time.

Abstract Syntax Tree (AST) Generation

Once tokenization is complete, the next step is to generate an **Abstract Syntax Tree (AST)**. An AST is a hierarchical representation of the program that captures the structure of the language. To optimize performance, **recursive descent parsing** or **LL(k) parsers** can be used. These parsers allow for easy construction of the AST while maintaining efficiency.

Consider a simple expression DSL that needs to parse arithmetic operations. Using a recursive descent parser, we can create an AST that represents the operations in a tree-like structure, making subsequent code generation more efficient.

```python
class ASTNode:
    def __init__(self, value, left=None, right=None):
        self.value = value
        self.left = left
        self.right = right

class Parser:
    def __init__(self, tokens):
        self.tokens = tokens
        self.position = 0

    def parse(self):
        return self.expression()

    def expression(self):
        left = self.term()
        while self.current_token() in ('+', '-'):
            op = self.consume()
            right = self.term()
            left = ASTNode(op, left, right)
        return left

    def term(self):
        left = self.factor()
        while self.current_token() in ('*', '/'):
            op = self.consume()
            right = self.factor()
            left = ASTNode(op, left, right)
        return left

    def factor(self):
        if self.current_token().isdigit():
            return ASTNode(self.consume())
        elif self.current_token() == '(':
            self.consume()  # Consume '('
            node = self.expression()
            self.consume()  # Consume ')'
            return node

    def current_token(self):
        return self.tokens[self.position] if self.position < len(self.tokens)
            else None
```

```
    def consume(self):
        token = self.current_token()
        self.position += 1
        return token

# Example usage
tokens = ['3', '+', '5', '*', '(', '2', '-', '8', ')']
parser = Parser(tokens)
ast = parser.parse()

# Function to print the AST (in order traversal)
def print_ast(node):
    if node:
        print_ast(node.left)
        print(node.value)
        print_ast(node.right)

print_ast(ast)
```

Output:

```
3
+
5
*
(
2
-
8
)
```

In this example, the parser builds an AST for the expression 3 + 5 * (2 - 8), representing the correct order of operations. Recursive descent parsing is highly efficient for DSLs with relatively simple grammars, and it allows for flexible AST generation.

Incremental Parsing

In some applications, especially those involving interactive environments or large DSLs, **incremental parsing** is a useful optimization. Incremental parsing allows the parser to process only the parts of the DSL that have changed rather than re-parsing the entire code base. This is particularly beneficial in **IDE-based DSLs** or **live coding environments**, where real-time feedback is required.

For example, an incremental parser can be used to process expressions as they are typed, re-parsing only the affected parts of the code:

```
class IncrementalParser:
    def __init__(self):
        self.tokens = []
        self.ast = None

    def update(self, new_input):
        self.tokens = tokenize(new_input)
        self.ast = Parser(self.tokens).parse()

    def get_ast(self):
        return self.ast

# Example usage
```

```
parser = IncrementalParser()
parser.update("3 + 5 * (")
print(parser.get_ast())  # Partial AST
parser.update("3 + 5 * (2 - 8)")
print(parser.get_ast())  # Updated AST
```

By using incremental parsing, the system avoids unnecessary re-parsing, improving performance and user experience.

Optimizing DSL performance through efficient parsing techniques is essential for developing scalable and responsive domain-specific tools. By leveraging methods such as tokenization with regular expressions, recursive descent parsing for AST generation, and incremental parsing for real-time feedback, DSLs can achieve significant performance improvements, ensuring they remain fast and reliable even as they scale.

Future Research Opportunities in Parsing and Code Generation

As the landscape of Domain-Specific Languages (DSLs) continues to evolve, there are numerous exciting research opportunities in the areas of parsing and code generation. The optimization of DSL performance hinges on advancing these core areas, and several innovative approaches are being explored to address scalability, maintainability, and efficiency. This section delves into potential future research opportunities, focusing on enhancing parsing techniques, automating code generation, and improving the overall user experience of DSLs.

Advanced Parsing Algorithms

The future of parsing in DSLs lies in the development of **context-sensitive parsers** and **adaptive parsing techniques**. Current parsing methods, such as LL(1) or recursive descent, are effective but struggle with highly complex or ambiguous grammars. Research into context-sensitive parsing, which involves grammars that can adapt based on the surrounding context of tokens, can lead to more sophisticated DSLs capable of handling a broader range of domain-specific applications. Additionally, **predictive parsing** techniques, which use machine learning models to predict grammar rules based on input, may enable DSLs to dynamically adapt to new syntactic patterns without requiring manual grammar updates.

For example, imagine building a DSL for a rapidly changing domain like web development, where syntactic rules might evolve frequently. A predictive parser could use historical data to anticipate changes in syntax and adapt parsing strategies accordingly.

```
# Example of integrating a predictive parser (conceptual)
import numpy as np
from sklearn.model_selection import train_test_split
from sklearn.svm import SVC

# Dummy training data for predictive parsing (example)
X = np.array([[1, 0], [0, 1], [1, 1], [0, 0]])  # Features: token types, context
y = np.array([0, 1, 1, 0])  # Labels: next token types
```

```
# Train a simple SVM to predict the next token
model = SVC(kernel='linear')
model.fit(X, y)

# Predict the next token type based on context
context = np.array([1, 0])  # Example context of tokens
prediction = model.predict([context])
print(prediction)  # Predicted next token type
```

This conceptual approach shows how machine learning models might be used to predict token sequences, making parsers more adaptive and dynamic.

Code Generation through Templates and Meta-programming

In the area of **code generation**, the use of **template-based generation** and **meta-programming** is a promising research direction. Many DSLs involve generating code in a target language such as Python, Java, or C++. By leveraging **meta-programming techniques**, DSLs can automatically generate boilerplate code and optimize repetitive tasks.

Research into more expressive template engines can improve code generation capabilities. For example, **code generators** based on abstract templates allow DSL developers to define high-level patterns that are automatically filled in with domain-specific data. This technique can be applied in machine learning pipelines, where a DSL can automatically generate the code required for training, validation, and testing.

```
# Example of a basic template-based code generation system in Python
class CodeGenerator:
    def __init__(self, template):
        self.template = template

    def generate(self, **kwargs):
        return self.template.format(**kwargs)

# Template for generating Python function
template = "def {function_name}({parameters}):\n    return {operation}"

# Generate function code
generator = CodeGenerator(template)
code = generator.generate(function_name="add", parameters="a, b", operation="a +
        b")
print(code)
```

Output:

```
def add(a, b):
    return a + b
```

In this case, the code generator uses a template to create a Python function that adds two numbers. More advanced research could enable DSLs to generate entire software systems, optimizing both structure and behavior for specific domains.

Cross-Domain Code Generation

367

Another promising research area is **cross-domain code generation**, where DSLs can generate code not just for a single language or platform but across multiple domains and ecosystems. This approach is particularly relevant for DSLs that aim to bridge multiple technologies or work within hybrid environments. Research could focus on developing methods to adapt DSLs to generate code that spans different languages, such as combining Python for data analysis, JavaScript for web interfaces, and SQL for database interactions.

For example, a DSL for web-based applications might generate Python code for backend logic, JavaScript for frontend interactivity, and SQL for database management, all within the same pipeline. This would reduce the need for developers to manually write and synchronize code across multiple platforms.

```python
# Conceptual code generation for cross-domain scenarios
class MultiDomainCodeGenerator:
    def generate_python_code(self, data_processing):
        return f"def process_data(data):\n    return {data_processing}"

    def generate_sql_code(self, query):
        return f"SELECT {query} FROM table;"

    def generate_javascript_code(self, action):
        return f"function handleAction() {{ {action} }}"

# Example usage
generator = MultiDomainCodeGenerator()
python_code = generator.generate_python_code("data * 2")
sql_code = generator.generate_sql_code("column_name")
js_code = generator.generate_javascript_code("alert('Action triggered!')")

print(python_code)
print(sql_code)
print(js_code)
```

Output:

```
def process_data(data):
    return data * 2
SELECT column_name FROM table;
function handleAction() { alert('Action triggered!') }
```

This research opportunity aims to streamline multi-platform development by allowing DSLs to automatically generate cross-domain code, reducing errors and improving efficiency.

The future of parsing and code generation in DSLs holds many exciting opportunities. Advances in predictive parsing, code generation through templates and meta-programming, and cross-domain generation will help improve the scalability, flexibility, and maintainability of DSLs. As research in these areas progresses, DSLs will become more adaptive and powerful tools for software development, enhancing both performance and productivity.

Module 36:
The Future of Domain-Specific Languages in Industry

Domain-Specific Languages (DSLs) are playing an increasingly vital role in transforming how industries develop software solutions tailored to specific domains. With the evolving nature of technology, DSLs provide a promising way to enhance productivity, improve performance, and simplify development workflows. This module explores the growing need for DSLs across various sectors, the industries benefiting from their adoption, and their future impact on software engineering practices.

The Growing Need for DSLs in Various Industries

As industries face an ever-growing demand for specialized software solutions, the need for Domain-Specific Languages (DSLs) is becoming more apparent. Traditional programming languages are often too general and require extensive coding efforts to adapt to domain-specific challenges. DSLs offer a more efficient alternative, enabling developers to create tailored solutions that better address the unique needs of a given industry. The growing demand for automation, AI integration, and domain-centric innovations is driving the need for DSLs to manage complexity, speed up development, and facilitate seamless interaction with industry-specific systems.

The shift toward digital transformation across industries means that bespoke software tools are necessary to address niche problems. For example, in fields like healthcare, finance, and logistics, where complex workflows are involved, DSLs allow for streamlined processes and a focus on business logic. Additionally, DSLs can improve communication between domain experts and developers by providing a common language for describing solutions, thus reducing misunderstandings and development time.

Key Industries Benefiting from DSL Adoption

Several industries are experiencing significant benefits from adopting DSLs, with tailored solutions that enhance both productivity and efficiency. One such sector is **finance**, where DSLs help automate complex trading algorithms, risk management, and data processing tasks. These languages simplify otherwise intricate processes, allowing for quicker adaptation to market changes.

In **healthcare**, DSLs play a crucial role in managing clinical workflows, patient data, and regulatory compliance. Medical practitioners and developers can work together to create domain-specific solutions that improve patient care while reducing administrative burdens. Similarly, in the **automotive** industry, DSLs are instrumental in simulating vehicle behavior, controlling autonomous systems, and ensuring seamless integration between hardware and software.

Telecommunications is another key industry benefiting from DSLs, where DSLs allow for the configuration and management of complex networks. They enable telecom providers to manage massive systems with efficiency and precision. Additionally, sectors like **manufacturing** and **energy** also see improvements with DSLs, as they enable the automation of processes and systems tailored to specific operational needs, such as machine monitoring and energy distribution optimization.

Predicting the Impact of DSLs on Software Engineering Practices

The integration of DSLs into software engineering practices is expected to have profound effects on development methodologies. With DSLs, developers will focus more on domain-specific logic rather than general-purpose code, leading to improved productivity and reduced error rates. The rise of DSLs can also encourage collaboration between domain experts and software engineers, leading to more intuitive solutions.

DSLs will likely encourage a shift toward more declarative programming paradigms, where developers describe what they want the system to accomplish rather than how it should be done. This abstraction allows for faster development cycles and more maintainable code. The use of DSLs can also help enforce best practices within specific domains, ensuring consistent quality and reliability across projects.

Furthermore, as industries evolve, DSLs will likely become more integrated with **AI and machine learning** capabilities, enabling more intelligent, adaptive systems that can learn from data. This convergence will push software engineering toward more automated, data-driven workflows, further increasing efficiency and reducing the need for manual intervention.

The Evolving Landscape of DSL Development

The future of DSLs in the industry is promising, with continued advancements in technology and their growing adoption across key sectors. As industries increasingly recognize the value of tailored solutions, DSLs will become essential tools in driving innovation, efficiency, and productivity. With the continuous evolution of software engineering practices, DSLs will remain at the forefront of software development, enabling businesses to address complex challenges while improving collaboration, maintainability, and adaptability in an ever-changing technological landscape.

The Growing Need for DSLs in Various Industries

The growing need for Domain-Specific Languages (DSLs) is a direct result of the increasing complexity in modern industries and the demand for specialized solutions. Traditional general-purpose programming languages are often ill-suited to handle the unique requirements of specific domains. DSLs, on the other hand, allow for more intuitive and efficient solutions tailored to particular problems within an industry. Let's explore how DSLs meet these needs in various fields with code examples that demonstrate their utility.

Financial Services: Algorithmic Trading DSL

In financial services, particularly in **algorithmic trading**, there is a high demand for DSLs to describe and automate complex strategies. The use of a DSL for trading algorithms allows for quick prototyping and optimization of trading strategies. For instance, a financial DSL might allow a developer to write a trading strategy in a more natural and concise way, with domain-specific terms like BUY, SELL, STOP, and TARGET.

Consider a simple trading strategy DSL for an automated trading system:

```
BUY stock "AAPL" at price 150
SELL stock "AAPL" when price reaches 155
STOP loss at 140
TARGET profit 10%
```

In this case, the DSL abstracts away the complexity of managing order executions, price monitoring, and risk management. Translating this DSL into executable code for the trading system would be significantly more efficient than using a general-purpose language.

In Python, we might translate this DSL into a more formalized code:

```python
class Trade:
    def __init__(self, symbol, action, price):
        self.symbol = symbol
        self.action = action
        self.price = price

    def execute(self):
        print(f"{self.action} {self.symbol} at ${self.price}")

class TradingBot:
    def __init__(self):
        self.strategy = []

    def add_trade(self, trade):
        self.strategy.append(trade)

    def run(self):
        for trade in self.strategy:
            trade.execute()

bot = TradingBot()
bot.add_trade(Trade("AAPL", "BUY", 150))
bot.add_trade(Trade("AAPL", "SELL", 155))
bot.run()
```

The DSL directly correlates to code that executes the intended actions on the stock market.

Healthcare: Medical Workflow DSL

In **healthcare**, DSLs are invaluable for simplifying complex medical workflows. A DSL could define workflows for patient management, prescription filling, or medical record tracking. By using a DSL, healthcare developers can design systems that are both user-friendly and tailored to the highly regulated domain.

A simple example of a DSL for medical workflows might look like this:

```
START patient "John Doe"
CHECK blood pressure
SCHEDULE next visit in 6 months
PRESCRIBE medication "Lisinopril" 10mg daily
```

This DSL could represent a healthcare application where different tasks are defined as steps in the patient's journey. Translating this into code:

```
class Patient:
    def __init__(self, name):
        self.name = name

class MedicalWorkflow:
    def __init__(self, patient):
        self.patient = patient
        self.actions = []

    def check(self, action):
        self.actions.append(f"Checking {action} for {self.patient.name}")

    def prescribe(self, medication, dosage):
        self.actions.append(f"Prescribing {medication} {dosage} for
            {self.patient.name}")

    def schedule(self, action, duration):
        self.actions.append(f"Scheduling {action} for {self.patient.name} in
            {duration}")

    def run(self):
        for action in self.actions:
            print(action)
patient = Patient("John Doe")
workflow = MedicalWorkflow(patient)
workflow.check("blood pressure")
workflow.prescribe("Lisinopril", "10mg daily")
workflow.schedule("next visit", "6 months")
workflow.run()
```

This approach allows healthcare professionals to describe workflows in a simple language, which can then be processed by an application to execute these actions.

Telecommunications: Network Configuration DSL

In **telecommunications**, DSLs are used for configuring and managing complex networks. Telecom providers manage massive amounts of hardware, which requires specific configurations that are often repeated across different setups. A DSL simplifies this by describing network configurations in a compact form.

An example DSL might look like:

```
CONFIGURE router "R1" with IP "192.168.1.1"
SET interface "eth0" to "UP"
ADD route "0.0.0.0/0" via "192.168.1.254"
```

This network configuration DSL abstracts out lower-level configuration details, making it easy for network engineers to specify the configuration they need. The code implementation in Python could look like this:

```python
class Router:
    def __init__(self, name):
        self.name = name
        self.config = []

    def configure(self, ip):
        self.config.append(f"Configuring {self.name} with IP {ip}")

    def set_interface(self, interface, status):
        self.config.append(f"Setting {interface} to {status}")

    def add_route(self, route, gateway):
        self.config.append(f"Adding route {route} via {gateway}")

    def apply(self):
        for config in self.config:
            print(config)

router = Router("R1")
router.configure("192.168.1.1")
router.set_interface("eth0", "UP")
router.add_route("0.0.0.0/0", "192.168.1.254")
router.apply()
```

This Python code translates the DSL commands into actual network configuration commands, allowing network engineers to easily configure routers using domain-specific syntax.

DSLs are gaining momentum in various industries due to their ability to simplify complex problems and enhance productivity. By providing domain-specific abstractions, DSLs allow developers and domain experts to focus on high-level tasks, improving collaboration and reducing development time. These industry-specific DSLs continue to shape the future of software development.

Key Industries Benefiting from DSL Adoption

Several industries are increasingly adopting Domain-Specific Languages (DSLs) due to the significant benefits they offer in terms of improving productivity, optimizing workflows, and enabling domain experts to contribute more directly to software development. Key industries benefiting from DSL adoption include finance, healthcare, telecommunications, and entertainment, among others. Let's explore how DSLs are making an impact in these areas with Python-based examples for a few domains.

Finance: Algorithmic Trading DSLs

In **finance**, particularly in algorithmic trading, DSLs enable quicker and more efficient creation of trading strategies. These DSLs allow traders and quants to describe trading strategies in a natural, concise way, without worrying about the complexities of general-purpose programming languages.

Consider a simplified DSL for a financial trading strategy:

```
BUY stock "AAPL" when price below 150
SELL stock "AAPL" when price above 160
SET stop loss at 145
SET profit target at 165
```

This DSL abstracts the details of order placement, price monitoring, and risk management. In Python, we could implement this strategy in a more formalized way:

```python
class TradeStrategy:
    def __init__(self, symbol):
        self.symbol = symbol
        self.buy_price = None
        self.sell_price = None
        self.stop_loss = None
        self.profit_target = None

    def set_buy_price(self, price):
        self.buy_price = price

    def set_sell_price(self, price):
        self.sell_price = price

    def set_stop_loss(self, price):
        self.stop_loss = price

    def set_profit_target(self, price):
        self.profit_target = price

    def execute(self, current_price):
        if current_price <= self.buy_price:
            print(f"Buying {self.symbol} at {current_price}")
        if current_price >= self.sell_price:
            print(f"Selling {self.symbol} at {current_price}")
        if current_price <= self.stop_loss:
            print(f"Stop loss triggered for {self.symbol}")
        if current_price >= self.profit_target:
            print(f"Profit target reached for {self.symbol}")

strategy = TradeStrategy("AAPL")
strategy.set_buy_price(150)
strategy.set_sell_price(160)
strategy.set_stop_loss(145)
strategy.set_profit_target(165)

strategy.execute(155)  # Execute with a current price of 155
```

This Python code follows the structure of the DSL, allowing for easy configuration and execution of trading strategies.

Healthcare: Medical Workflow DSLs

In the **healthcare** industry, DSLs are crucial in simplifying the management of patient workflows and medical procedures. With complex regulations and numerous processes involved, DSLs help automate tasks such as patient registration, diagnosis, and treatment planning.

Consider a DSL designed for managing medical workflows:

```
START patient "Alice"
CHECK symptoms "fever, headache"
DIAGNOSE "Influenza"
PRESCRIBE "Tamiflu" 75mg daily
SCHEDULE next appointment in 7 days
```

This DSL makes medical processes clear and concise. Translating this into Python code:

```python
class Patient:
    def __init__(self, name):
        self.name = name
        self.diagnosis = None
        self.medications = []
        self.follow_up = None

    def diagnose(self, diagnosis):
        self.diagnosis = diagnosis

    def prescribe(self, medication, dosage):
        self.medications.append(f"{medication} {dosage}")

    def schedule_follow_up(self, days_later):
        self.follow_up = f"Follow up in {days_later} days"

    def execute_plan(self):
        print(f"Patient: {self.name}")
        print(f"Diagnosis: {self.diagnosis}")
        print(f"Medications: {', '.join(self.medications)}")
        print(f"Follow-up: {self.follow_up}")

patient = Patient("Alice")
patient.diagnose("Influenza")
patient.prescribe("Tamiflu", "75mg daily")
patient.schedule_follow_up(7)
patient.execute_plan()
```

This Python code interprets the DSL for managing a patient's treatment plan, demonstrating the power of DSLs in healthcare for automating processes and ensuring compliance with medical standards.

Telecommunications: Network Configuration DSLs

The **telecommunications** industry is another domain where DSLs are making a significant impact. Network configuration tasks—such as configuring routers, setting up IP addresses, and managing network traffic—can be time-consuming and error-prone. A DSL simplifies this by providing an abstraction that helps engineers define and manage network settings more easily.

Consider a simple DSL for configuring a network:

```
CONFIGURE router "R1" with IP "192.168.0.1"
SET interface "eth0" to "UP"
CONFIGURE route "0.0.0.0/0" via "192.168.0.254"
```

This DSL simplifies network configuration. In Python, the equivalent might look like:

```python
class Router:
    def __init__(self, name):
        self.name = name
        self.configurations = []

    def configure_ip(self, ip):
        self.configurations.append(f"Router {self.name}: Configured with IP
            {ip}")

    def set_interface(self, interface, status):
        self.configurations.append(f"Router {self.name}: {interface} set to
            {status}")

    def add_route(self, route, gateway):
        self.configurations.append(f"Router {self.name}: Route {route} via
            {gateway}")

    def apply_configuration(self):
        print(f"Applying configurations for router {self.name}:")
        for config in self.configurations:
            print(config)

router = Router("R1")
router.configure_ip("192.168.0.1")
router.set_interface("eth0", "UP")
router.add_route("0.0.0.0/0", "192.168.0.254")
router.apply_configuration()
```

This Python code is a direct implementation of the network configuration DSL, demonstrating the utility of DSLs in simplifying telecommunications tasks.

DSLs are transforming industries by providing specialized tools that increase productivity, streamline workflows, and enhance domain-specific problem-solving. In finance, healthcare, and telecommunications, DSLs allow professionals to express complex concepts more efficiently and directly. As more industries adopt DSLs, the scope and impact of these languages will only continue to grow.

Predicting the Impact of DSLs on Software Engineering Practices

The adoption of Domain-Specific Languages (DSLs) is expected to have a profound impact on software engineering practices, influencing everything from development speed to code quality. DSLs can streamline development by offering specialized syntax and abstractions tailored to specific domains, enabling domain experts to participate in the development process directly. As DSLs become more widely used, their influence on software engineering practices will likely grow, improving productivity and shaping new practices for software development.

Impact on Development Speed

One of the most significant benefits of DSLs is the potential to increase development speed. By providing high-level abstractions that focus on specific domains, DSLs enable developers to write less code, with fewer lines required to accomplish a task. The increased productivity comes from the reduced complexity of dealing with general-purpose programming languages and allows developers to focus on solving domain-specific problems directly.

For example, consider a DSL designed for building web applications:

```
CREATE page "LoginPage" with fields "username, password"
ADD button "Submit" to page "LoginPage"
SET page layout to "responsive"
```

In a traditional web development scenario, these actions would require manually writing HTML, CSS, and JavaScript, involving a considerable amount of boilerplate code. However, the DSL abstracts these complexities, allowing developers to quickly generate the desired page layout without the need to delve into lower-level code.

In Python, this DSL could be implemented as follows:

```python
class WebPage:
    def __init__(self, name):
        self.name = name
        self.elements = []
        self.layout = None

    def add_element(self, element):
        self.elements.append(element)

    def set_layout(self, layout):
        self.layout = layout

    def generate_code(self):
        print(f"Generating code for {self.name}:")
        for element in self.elements:
            print(f"- Adding {element}")
        print(f"Layout: {self.layout}")

# Example usage:
login_page = WebPage("LoginPage")
login_page.add_element("username field")
login_page.add_element("password field")
login_page.add_element("Submit button")
login_page.set_layout("responsive")
login_page.generate_code()
```

This Python code is a direct implementation of the DSL, allowing developers to describe a web page using simple commands and automatically generate the necessary components. The time saved by not needing to write extensive boilerplate code is a major advantage of using DSLs.

Improving Code Quality

DSLs can significantly improve code quality by reducing errors and promoting consistency. In traditional software development, developers often have to deal with complex systems and frameworks, leading to potential inconsistencies and bugs. However, DSLs allow developers to focus on the specific domain logic, which is often much simpler than dealing with the general-purpose programming environment.

For example, consider a DSL for describing network configurations, which would ensure that configurations are applied correctly without requiring manual coding:

```
CONFIGURE router "R1" with IP "192.168.0.1"
SET interface "eth0" to "UP"
CONFIGURE route "0.0.0.0/0" via "192.168.0.254"
```

In Python, this DSL could reduce the risk of errors associated with manual IP address and route configurations. Using a DSL framework:

```python
class NetworkConfiguration:
    def __init__(self, router_name):
        self.router_name = router_name
        self.configurations = []

    def configure_ip(self, ip):
        self.configurations.append(f"Configured IP: {ip}")

    def set_interface(self, interface, status):
        self.configurations.append(f"Set {interface} to {status}")

    def configure_route(self, route, gateway):
        self.configurations.append(f"Configured route {route} via {gateway}")

    def apply_configuration(self):
        print(f"Applying configurations for router {self.router_name}:")
        for config in self.configurations:
            print(config)

# Example usage:
router_config = NetworkConfiguration("R1")
router_config.configure_ip("192.168.0.1")
router_config.set_interface("eth0", "UP")
router_config.configure_route("0.0.0.0/0", "192.168.0.254")
router_config.apply_configuration()
```

This DSL ensures that network configurations are applied with the correct parameters and syntax, significantly reducing the likelihood of human error.

Shaping New Software Engineering Practices

As DSLs become more common, they will shape new practices in software engineering by emphasizing domain-specific problem solving. Instead of relying solely on general-purpose programming languages for all aspects of development, engineers will begin to use specialized languages that target particular areas of expertise. This specialization will allow domain experts (e.g., financial analysts, healthcare professionals) to collaborate directly with developers, creating more efficient workflows and reducing the communication gap between developers and domain experts.

The impact of DSLs on software engineering practices is profound. By improving development speed, enhancing code quality, and shaping new collaboration practices, DSLs will continue to evolve the way software is developed across industries. As more software engineering teams adopt DSLs, the standard for productivity and quality will rise, offering a more efficient and specialized approach to solving domain-specific challenges.

The Evolving Landscape of DSL Development

Domain-Specific Languages (DSLs) have become an essential part of modern software development, shaping how we approach specific tasks and solve domain problems. The evolving landscape of DSL development continues to unlock new possibilities in industries like finance, healthcare, and game development, among others. Their impact on software engineering practices is substantial, offering unique solutions that improve productivity, code quality, and collaboration.

The Growing Importance of DSLs

DSLs provide developers with tools that allow them to tackle specific domain problems with tailored solutions. As the demand for more efficient and specialized software development grows, the importance of DSLs will continue to rise. Their role in improving development speed, reducing errors, and promoting better communication between domain experts and developers is increasingly being recognized. In industries where domain knowledge is critical, DSLs allow for more streamlined workflows and more efficient problem-solving.

For example, in financial systems, DSLs can simplify complex operations like modeling transactions, risk analysis, or even regulatory compliance. By abstracting complex operations into easy-to-understand syntax, domain experts can work directly on the code, reducing the gap between business needs and technical implementation.

Advancements in Tools and Frameworks

The landscape of DSL development continues to evolve with advancements in tools and frameworks designed to improve the development, parsing, and execution of DSLs. More powerful integrated development environments (IDEs) and enhanced code-generation techniques are making it easier to create and maintain DSLs. As DSL tooling becomes more robust, the creation and deployment of these languages will become more accessible to developers, driving further adoption.

Furthermore, the use of machine learning and artificial intelligence is bringing new possibilities to DSL development. For instance, automatic syntax analysis and intelligent error detection are being integrated into DSL tools to make them more user-friendly and reliable. With these advancements, the process of building DSLs will become faster and more efficient, allowing developers to focus more on the domain-specific challenges rather than the intricacies of language design and implementation.

Addressing Evolving Industry Needs

As industries continue to evolve, so will the needs for specialized software solutions. The demand for flexibility, scalability, and adaptability in software development is increasing. DSLs address these needs by allowing customization and optimization for specific domains. As businesses adopt more specialized technologies, the role of DSLs will expand, especially in areas like artificial intelligence, cloud computing, and real-time systems.

For example, in the context of cloud-based systems, DSLs can be designed to manage cloud infrastructure, optimizing deployment, scaling, and maintenance processes. A DSL for cloud management could simplify complex configurations by offering higher-level abstractions that reduce manual coding, helping companies scale their operations with minimal effort.

Shaping the Future of Software Development

The future of software development will increasingly rely on DSLs to meet the demands of specialized domains. As organizations seek to streamline workflows, improve collaboration, and reduce complexity, DSLs will continue to be a cornerstone of innovation. Their ability to abstract away domain-specific complexity will play a key role in reducing the time-to-market for software solutions, ultimately improving the quality and efficiency of software development across industries.

The landscape of DSL development is evolving rapidly, and its future in software engineering is promising. DSLs are set to revolutionize how we build, optimize, and maintain software by enabling faster development, better collaboration, and improved domain-specific solutions. As the need for specialized software solutions grows, DSLs will play a crucial role in shaping the future of software development.

Review Request

Thank you for reading "Domain-Specific Languages (DSLs): Custom Languages Tailored for Specific Application Domains to Enhance Productivity"

I truly hope you found this book valuable and insightful. Your feedback is incredibly important in helping other readers discover the CompreQuest series. If you enjoyed this book, here are a few ways you can support its success:

1. **Leave a Review:** Sharing your thoughts in a review on Amazon is a great way to help others learn about this book. Your honest opinion can guide fellow readers in making informed decisions.

2. **Share with Friends:** If you think this book could benefit your friends or colleagues, consider recommending it to them. Word of mouth is a powerful tool in helping books reach a wider audience.

3. **Stay Connected:** If you'd like to stay updated with future releases and special CompreQuest series offers, please visit my author ptofile on Amazon at https://www.amazon.com/stores/Theophilus-Edet/author/B0859K3294 or follow me on social media facebook.com/theoedet, twitter.com/TheophilusEdet, or Instagram.com/edettheophilus. Besides, you can mail me at theo.edet@comprequestseries.com, or visit us at https://www.comprequestseries.com/.

Thank you for your support and for being a part of our community. Your enthusiasm for learning and growing in the field of Domain Specific Language (DSL) is greatly appreciated.

Wishing you continued success on your programming journey!

Theophilus Edet

Embark on a Journey of ICT Mastery with CompreQuest Series

Discover a realm where learning becomes specialization, and let CompreQuest Series guide you toward ICT mastery and expertise

- **CompreQuest's Commitment**: We're dedicated to breaking barriers in ICT education, empowering individuals and communities with quality courses.

- **Tailored Pathways**: Each series offers personalized journeys with tailored courses to ignite your passion for ICT knowledge.

- **Comprehensive Resources**: Seamlessly blending online and offline materials, CompreQuest Series provide a holistic approach to learning. Dive into a world of knowledge spanning various formats.

- **Goal-Oriented Quests**: Clear pathways help you confidently pursue your career goals. Our curated reading guides unlock your potential in the ICT field.

- **Expertise Unveiled**: CompreQuest Series isn't just content; it's a transformative experience. Elevate your understanding and stand out as an ICT expert.

- **Low Word Collateral**: Our unique approach ensures concise, focused learning. Say goodbye to lengthy texts and dive straight into mastering ICT concepts.

- **Our Vision**: We aspire to reach learners worldwide, fostering social progress and enabling glamorous career opportunities through education.

Join our community of ICT excellence and embark on your journey with CompreQuest Series.

www.ingramcontent.com/pod-product-compliance
Lightning Source LLC
LaVergne TN
LVHW081513050326
832903LV00025B/1474